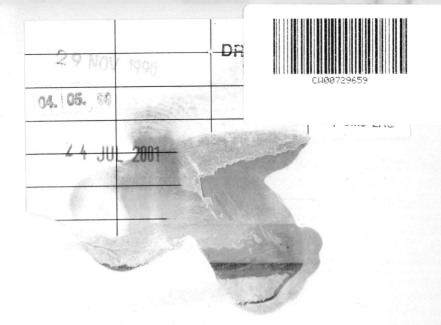

WHAT ARE LITTLE GIRLS MADE OF?

A Comedy

PETER COKE

SAMUEL FRENCH

FRENCH

LONDON

NEW YORK   TORONTO   SYDNEY   HOLLYWOOD

ISBN 0 573 11483 8

CHARACTERS

Adrian Eagle
Ricky
Rear-Admiral Henry Lane, C.V.O., D.S.O., D.S.C.
Isabel Merryweather
Mrs Barry
An Old Man
Lady Colestar (Madeleine)
Very Hesketh-Palmer
Jenny
Gloria

The action takes place in "Alimony", an Antique Shop, part of a large Georgian house on the outskirts of London

ACT I   Late afternoon

ACT II   Late afternoon, about a year later

Time—the present

ACT I

"Alimony": an antique shop, part of a large Georgian house on the outskirts of London. Late afternoon

The hall of the house has been turned into a showroom. It is filled with an assortment of interesting mixed antiques. Although rather a muddle, the result is colourful and charming. Two long windows on to the street are arranged as "shop windows". The front door, between them, has a collection of Chinese bells which tinkle loudly when people enter or leave the shop. The wide, winding, white-painted staircase leading upstairs has an elaborate rope hooked across it with a printed hanging notice saying "Private. No admittance." Someone has scrawled underneath "That means YOU. Please." A door leads to a small room now used as an Office. Another into the rest of the ground floor. Before the play starts there is the prolonged wailing of an infuriated baby

When the Curtain rises the noise is heard issuing from a bundle wedged with cushions into a corner of the sofa. The crying increases

Adrian Eagle hurries in from the Office. He carries a tray of tea. He is a gentle, nervous lad of about twenty

Adrian (*putting down the tray and hurrying to the bundle*) Shh! For God's sake shh! If the Admiral hears you he'll make me walk the plank. And you too, probably. (*The threat has no effect*) Oh, do be a good little boy. Or girl, I forgot to ask. Not that it matters if only you'll be quiet. (*Pleading*) Baby, shut up; please! Is there something wrong? I'm not going to change your nappy if that's what it is. I mean I would, but I . . .

The telephone rings. The baby stops crying. Adrian looks amazed, and goes to answer it

Hullo? Alimony Limited . . . No, madam, not how to get it; a place to spend it in. . . . Not at all; good-bye. (*He replaces the receiver*)

The shop door opens, and Ricky comes in. He is tough and good-looking, aged about twenty-five

Adrian rushes and stands guiltily screening the baby

Ricky Mind if I have a look round?
Adrian No, please do.

Ricky walks round looking at the pictures

Are you interested in anything special?

Ricky Well, yerknow, pictures mostly. Buy them for my old man. He's got a place hires them out, yerknow, to film and telly studios.

Adrian How interesting.

Ricky Bloody boring really. But, yerknow, have to do something in my spare time, don't I?

Adrian You don't do it full time?

Ricky What?

Adrian Help your father.

Ricky (*after a moment*) Don't you recognize me?

Adrian I'm sorry; should I?

Ricky (*shortly*) No. Makes a nice change really, yerknow. These are all the pictures you've got?

Adrian I'm afraid at the moment, yes.

Ricky Nothing sort of quite right. (*Glancing in the cases*) But, yerknow, you've got some nice stuff here. Real class. I'll call in again.

Adrian (*moving to the open door*) Yes, please do. And I'm sorry about not recognizing you if you're somebody who should be.

Ricky Don't give it a thought. (*Nodding at the baby*) Looks almost real, yerknow.

Adrian What?

Ricky The doll.

Adrian Actually it's a baby.

Ricky pokes it. It shrieks

Ricky (*leaping back*) Christ! So it is. Sorry—Daddy . . .

Ricky goes out

Adrian No, no, it's not mine, it's . . .

But Ricky has gone. Adrian hurries to the baby

There, there, he can't have hurt you as much as that.

It continues screaming

What is it: the indignity? Or wind? That's probably more like it. Do you feel all blown up? What do they usually do? Turn you upside down? Let's have a go. (*He gingerly picks up the bundle, and reverses it. Silence*) Bingo! But you can't stay like that: the blood'll all run into your feet. Head.

He turns it up the right way, and the wailing re-starts. He reverses it again. The crying stops. He then, very cautiously, turns it up the right way. It starts crying again

You're a bloody menace—oh, sorry, you're a menace. I can't go on treating you like a sort of human egg-timer all the afternoon. (*Noticing the tea-tray*) Would something to eat stop you? Have you got any teeth? I suppose not. Wait a minute. (*He dips his finger in to the milk-jug, then puts it into the baby's mouth*)

Silence

Ah, that was it. Good. But you must've got it all off by now: leave go. Baby, leave go: I'm not your mother! (*Getting his finger away*) Mummy'll be here any moment—she said five, and it's long after—and then you can have as much as you like.

Henry's voice is heard from the top of the stairs

Henry (*Off*) Isabel!

Adrian (*to the baby in a horrified whisper*) The Admiral! We're sunk. I daren't let him find you here. (*He dithers about anxiously with the baby*) I suppose you'd suffocate in a cupboard. We'll have to risk the Office. Only how to keep you quiet? (*He suddenly picks up a cushion-cover, dips the corner into the milk, and shoves it into the baby's mouth*) There, suck that. And for God's sake don't wail.

Adrian hurries into the Office with the baby. Rear-Admiral Henry Lane comes down the stairs reading—through half-moon spectacles—from account books held in either hand. He is a distinguished-looking man with beautiful silver hair, whose gruffness and irritability do not mask his immense charm

Henry These figures don't even begin to make sense. Listen: last week: Wages and insurance, twenty-one pounds. Taxis and carriage, seventeen pounds. Stationery, four twenty. Repairs and framing, twenty-six fifty. How in the name of Heaven can all that add up to your total: fourteen twenty-five? (*Looking up*) Where the hell are you? *Donner und!* Where the hell's anybody? Where's that damn boy? (*Shouting*) Eagle!

Adrian hurries out of the Office

Adrian Yes, sir?

Henry Why the hell's everyone abandoned ship?

Adrian I was—just attending to something in the Office, sir.

Henry What?

Adrian (*awkwardly*) Well—a lady came in to try to sell a Derby tea-set, and, I was really attending to—part of that.

Henry Sometimes I wonder about you, Eagle. When was the Battle of Trafalgar?

Adrian I'm—not quite sure, sir.

Henry (*shaking his head disapprovingly*) At least you must know the answer as to the whereabouts of my daughter?

Adrian Uum—out, sir.

Henry Decrepit as I am, that I can see. Where?

Adrian Er, shopping, I think, sir.

Henry Shopping? (*Suspiciously*) Do you mean you've let her go off to an auction sale again?

Adrian I'm only the employee, Admiral.

Henry Well, you won't be employed much longer if you're not careful. I told you to warn me if she showed any signs of sneaking off to another sale.

Adrian She said it was the sack if I did.

Henry Well, remember in future, she's far too cowardly to axe you, but I'm not. (*More kindly*) It's not out of bloody-mindedness that I try to control her, my boy. It's to stop the whole ship foundering.

Adrian But we sell a lot, sir.

Henry Oh, yes, if it wasn't for Isabel's hare-brained schemes we'd have a flourishing business.

Adrian (*looking round*) And we have a wonderful stock, sir.

Henry Too wonderful: that's just it. If she takes a hundred pounds, she goes out and buys a hundred and twenty. Not that the article's necessarily worth a hundred and twenty. But she's decided not to let the rival bidder get it owing to him resembling a man who once assaulted her grandmother on the Promenade at Nice.

Adrian (*laughing*) How funny!

Henry (*acidly*) Do you find it funny that at other times she lets someone snap up a bargain because she likes the way his hair grows or his nostrils curve?

Adrian It is rather amusing.

Henry Amusing foot and me elbow! How long have you been here?

Adrian Three weeks and two days, sir.

Henry Well, Mr Eagle, let me inform you that unless you help control Isabel's foolhardiness and rash spending, boost sales—(*emphasizing*)—and see that any such sales are put down correctly for a change, with their stock number and price—legibly—you will not be employed for another three weeks and two days. (*Going upstairs*) With which happy thought I leave you. (*Going upstairs*) To resume my efforts to get the books a little more shipshape. (*Stopping*) By the way, I kept being interrupted. Has Isabel secretly acquired another animal?

Adrian Animal, sir?

Henry Don't try a music-hall act with me. I heard repeated sort of yowling.

Adrian (*involuntarily*) Oh, my God!

Henry What is it? Nothing as ordinary as a cat or dog, I'm sure.

Adrian I didn't mean she's got a pet, sir.

Henry Then why appeal to the Deity?

Adrian It was just an exclamation—at the thought of you being disturbed.

Henry Actually I'm not sure I'm right in forbidding a pet. If she had another outlet it might keep her away from the sales. See if you can't interest her in something, Eagle. Preferably not a dog which I'd have to walk. Any suggestions?

Adrian Stamps? I collect them.

Henry Her geography's even vaguer than her arithmetic. Something less demanding: wine-making, spiritualism, something like that; I leave it to you. (*He again starts to go up the stairs*)

Adrian (*looking out of the window*) Wait a minute, Admiral, I think that's her now—getting out of a taxi.

Henry (*descending again*) Has she got anything terrible with her?

Adrian Empty-handed as far as I can see.

Henry Thank God.

The door bursts open, the bells rings, and Isabel Merryweather comes in. She is a charming, vague, pretty woman of about forty

Isabel You'll never guess what I've bought!

Henry *Donner und!*

Isabel And before either of you shriek it'll never sell I know it will, and even if it doesn't I don't care because I love it. Is that tea?

Adrian Cold, I'm afraid.

Isabel Be a darling, and put the kettle on.

Adrian goes into the Office with the teapot

I desperately need a cup. If one can have a hangover in the afternoon that's what I've got.

Henry How?

Isabel Your fault, really, darling. I was taken short, and rushed into the Piccadilly ladies . . .

Henry What the hell have I got to do with the Piccadilly ladies?

Isabel Nothing; I hope. But on the way out, who do you think I ran into?

Henry If I want to play guessing games I'll go on the television.

Isabel Jenny.

Henry Jenny who?

Isabel Jenny, your god-daughter, of course—what other Jennies do we know? She was even more fashionable than usual: hair like seaweed, and clothes from Oxfam Reject.

Henry And to think her mother always had her frocks from Chanel and Molyneux.

Isabel Well, her daughter's got a vest and knickers from Marks and Spencer's. She had nothing on underneath as far as I could see, so I whipped her off to Oxford Street, and made her put them on then and there. She complained all the way through lunch.

Henry Is that why you took to the bottle?

Adrian enters

Isabel Well, Jenny'd heard of an exciting new American cocktail: methylated spirits and orange juice.

Adrian What!

Isabel Well, that's what it tasted like. And I didn't want to seem old-hat, so when she had another I had another. And I suddenly realized why it's called "On the Floor".

Henry I hope at least it stopped you getting to the sale.

Isabel No, it didn't. I don't remember actually going there. But I woke up there.

Henry Pray God, too late?

Isabel No; just in time to hear the auctioneer—a lovely man with blazing blue eyes—announcing the Lot I wanted; Number two-four-four. So away I bid, and was delighted to get if for far less than I expected. The trouble was it wasn't what I expected.

Henry Oh my God.

Adrian What was it?

Isabel Well, I hadn't heard him quite right. He hadn't said two-four-four—he'd said two-two-four.

Henry (*ominously*) So?

Isabel So instead of getting a lovely Lalique vase with a frieze of mermaids tumbling in the spray, I got an ostrich.

Adrian An ostrich!

Isabel Such a pretty chap. His tail a little moth-eaten, but he has the sweetest expression.

Henry (*stamping up the stairs*) I'm leaving before I use a sweet expression.

Isabel Oh, I'd rather hoped you'd go and collect him for me.

Henry stamps off at the top of the stairs

I didn't really, of course. I got into conversation with a most charming young man—he had the sweetest little mole—(*pointing on herself*)—just here . . .

Adrian Is he going to deliver it?

Isabel Right. If he gets here. I'm a little worried about the police; he's only got a motor-cycle. Any excitements while I was out?

Adrian I had lots of people in; but mostly just picker-uppers.

Isabel And putter-downers in the wrong place, I know. Maddening.

Adrian But I did manage to sell the dessert service.

Isabel (*going to it*) Not this sick-green one?

Adrian Yes.

Isabel I only bought it because the poor man had had such a shattering time with his wife and his dog running away the same week. You're a genius.

Adrian Actually I feel rather guilty. I think she was a bit smashed.

Isabel Then we must pay the cheque in quickly before she sobers up. (*She starts to collect up the plates*) If you'd like to start packing it—(*she breaks off, listening*) What's that?

Adrian (*transfixed*) What?

Isabel That noise.

Adrian Could it be the kettle?

Adrian rushes off into the Office

Isabel looks surprised, but goes to a mirror and arranges her hair. She again hears something, and pauses, listening. Certain it comes from the Office she moves towards the door

Adrian comes out with the teapot. He is humming. She watches him in amazement

Isabel Why are you humming? I've never heard you hum before.
Adrian I just—felt like it.
Isabel Why?
Adrian I thought it was appropriate: "Tea for Two": you and me.

As the baby's cry is heard clearly he bursts into louder humming. Under Isabel's stare, it dies out. They both listen

(*feebly*) Shall I pour the tea?
Isabel No, you'll tell me what that noise is.

The cries stop

Adrian I don't hear anything.
Isabel I don't now, but I did quite clearly. What was it?
Adrian (*miserably*) Uum . . .
Isabel It must be awful to be as truthful as you: you suffer so much. Well?
Adrian A baby.
Isabel Your baby?
Adrian (*horrified*) No, no! Nothing to do with me. Really it isn't. I hadn't even seen the woman before, let alone—I mean I have absolutely no connection with her, or it.
Isabel Then why's it here?
Adrian It got left. (*In a rush*) I did my best not to have it left—honestly I did—I knew you'd lose your cool—I mean that you wouldn't approve, and that it'd make trouble. And it has. I've had the most awful time: it's kept yelling and . . . (*He breaks off suddenly, listening*) Why's it quiet suddenly? Hope it hasn't fallen on the floor or something . . .

Adrian rushes off into the Office

Isabel hurriedly pours herself a cup of tea, and sips it nervously

Adrian returns with the silent baby

(*anxiously*) I hope it's all right. It looks funnier.
Isabel (*unsympathetically*) Well, it's your baby, you'd better do something about it. What sort of "funny"?
Adrian Sort of—swelled up.
Isabel What! (*She rushes to look at it*) Dear Heaven! Quick, give it to me. (*She seizes and examines it*) Its mouth's stuffed full. (*She scoops with her finger*) Quickly, pass me something small.
Adrian What?
Isabel I don't know; something I can scoop with. Anything. One of those lace-bobbins.

Adrian hands her an ivory lace-bobbin, and she operates

It's all right, it's all right. No, stay still. I won't be a moment. There!

She hooks out something, and the baby starts yelling

(*Rocking it in her arms*) There, there, there, it's all over. No need to make that noise. Everything's all right. Did the nasty man try to choke you? Well, you're quite safe now, there, there ...

The baby's cries die down to silence

(*To Adrian*) What on earth had it got hold of?
Adrian (*examining the bobbin*) It's a sort of lump of stuff. Lord! It's one of the bobble things off the cover I gave it to suck.
Isabel My best eighteenth-century brocade!
Adrian Sorry.
Isabel It'll probably have some extraordinary effect on it.
Adrian Oh, I hope not.
Isabel I meant in the future. (*To the baby*) Your whole outlook may be influenced by being given such an early taste of antiques ...

The bells ring, and Miss Very Hesketh-Palmer comes in. She is of indeterminate age, well but flamboyantly dressed, with a manner that ranges from cosy sweetness to commanding authority

Very Excuse! One may look?
Isabel One certainly may.
Very Though shame abandon such a burgeoning day, eh?
Isabel It is lovely.
Very Sort of day when wish I were bird. The bliss of swooping and soaring in clear azurine skies. Even if branches do break on landing. Sympathize?
Isabel Oh, yes. Though I've never really aimed higher than being a butterfly.
Very (*hugging her arm*) Affinity—affinity! Used to have glorious nightmares after asparagus. Stood on rail dress-circle Drury Lane. Then sailed over amazed stalls. Glorious! Always Drury Lane. No, falsehood. Last time, Albert Hall. But moron threw ice-cream. Clogged wingfeathers. Flew with limp; nearly landed on Conductor. End of nightmares. Vexatious. Never been airborne since. Glub down beds of asparagus, but instead of flight, collywobbles.
Adrian Perhaps you should try lobster and cheese sauce.
Very (*delightedly*) Shall, shall! Inspirational. Am glad I came. Name: Hesketh-Palmer.
Isabel Mrs, Miss, or titled?
Very Miss. By choice. Not locked dully in marriage cupboard. Ready any time to be plucked off shelf.
Isabel I see. How can we help you, Miss Hesketh-Palmer?
Very Awful mouthful, eh? Call me Very.
Isabel I beg your pardon?
Very Very. Baptismal Christian name.
Isabel Short for Verity?

Very Short for nothing. That's it: Very. My father VERY disappointed I wasn't a boy.

Isabel How—original.

Very Are you?

Isabel No, rather ordinary: Isabel.

Very Could be worse. Son?

Adrian Oh, Mrs Merryweather's not my mother! I just work here. Adrian.

Very Knew an Adrian in Derbyshire. Bonkers. Wouldn't take his trousers off. Solution: studs down the sides. Then: plonk—plonk—plonk. Hope not like him.

Adrian (*looking at his trousers*) I don't think so.

Very Kinder, we trust. Waited till Nurse out of room; put handle of poker in fire; took it out; then called Nurse to poke fire. Not nice.

Isabel Not nice at all.

Very Got his dues. Fell overboard. (*Suddenly looking dartingly skywards*) See stars and small electric eels?

Isabel I can't say I do.

Very (*to Adrian*) You?

Adrian No.

Very (*plucking at her waist*) Knew I shouldn't have bought it. Far better stomach-sag than stars, eh? Agony anyhow. Back when released . . .

Very hurries off

Adrian Released from what?

Isabel I don't know. Some sort of stays or something, I suppose. We certainly do get them! What an afternoon!

Adrian I'm awfully sorry about the baby, but I hadn't any choice. The mother suddenly had raging toothache. We rang the dentist, and before I knew where I was she'd gone, but—the baby hadn't.

Isabel Do we know the poor thing?

Adrian I'd never seen her before.

Isabel What's her name?

Adrian (*miserably*) I didn't actually get it.

Isabel She must have said on the phone to the dentist?

Adrian Yes, I suppose she must. But she dumped the baby in my arms, and as I'd never actually held one before I was busy trying not to let it squiggle away.

Isabel It's all rather exciting and mystifying. (*Rocking the baby*) It's a dear little baby.

Adrian Only with you.

Isabel Yes, I always had a way with babies. Even the screamiest used to settle down with me. I think they sensed I adored any sort of baby. Of course I always longed for one of my own.

Adrian Wouldn't your husband agree?

Isabel He certainly didn't like babies. Just after we married one was sick into his bowler on the tube. But he was perfectly willing for us to have one. They—just didn't arrive.

Adrian Why not?

Isabel Your mother and father should be fined for parental neglect. I've told you about sex—I'm not now going to start on obstetrics. I'll just say we tried—Heaven knows we tried—and enjoyed every moment of it. But the Lord, in his wisdom, decided I wasn't a populator.

Adrian What a shame.

Isabel Yes, a terrible shame. (*Watching the baby with infinite tenderness*) There's something so miraculous about babies. They're so helpless; so dependent—need so much from one. (*Suddenly looking up*) But I'd have been a frightful mother.

Adrian I'm sure you wouldn't.

Isabel I knew absolutely nothing about anything when I married. I'd've been one of those who lets her child cram itself with ice-cream, and then slaps it for being sick.

Adrian I don't believe it.

Isabel True. Oh, not now. Now I'd be a superlative mum. (*With sudden dawning excitement*) Though I wonder! I wonder if it's too late?

Adrian (*horrified*) I thought you couldn't.

Isabel I don't mean actually to give birth. But—(*looking at the bundle she carries*)—if a baby were to arrive—out of the blue so to speak . . .

Adrian (*aghast*) But that baby's not out of the blue! It's got a perfectly good mother.

Isabel Called?

Adrian I've told you; I don't know.

Isabel Exactly. What perfectly good mother leaves her baby in an unknown shop, and doesn't even give her name and address?

Adrian She had a terrible toothache.

Isabel She could still have groaned out "I'm Mrs Smith of Two Holly Drive, and the baby's Belinda", couldn't she?

Adrian She may have told me, and I didn't take it in.

Isabel You know perfectly well she didn't. And why? (*Triumphantly*) Because she's abandoned this baby!

Adrian Oh, I'm sure she hasn't.

Isabel Why?

Adrian She—she didn't look the sort of woman who'd adandon her baby.

Isabel Absurd: they don't look anything special. Of course, she's abandoned this baby.

Adrian In an antique shop!

Isabel It's no more peculiar than on a doorstep, or in a phone kiosk. She's probably had her eye on us for some time—saw we did good business so could afford a child—and said to herself "That's the ideal place to abandon my baby". (*Hugging the baby*) Except that you're not abandoned any more, are you, my darling? You're my baby now, and it's going to be wonderful for both of us.

Adrian No, no, Mrs Merryweather! You mustn't get carried away like this. It's not your baby. I know its mother'll come back.

Isabel (*happily*) And I know she won't.

Adrian But even if she doesn't you can't sort of—hang on to it. We must dial nine-nine-nine.

Isabel (*strongly*) We must do nothing of the sort! Get on to the police, and the poor little mite would be bound up in red tape, thrown from court room to court room, and charity institution to charity institution, and end up so maladjusted she'd only be fit to become a traffic warden. No, no, no; the woman chose us, and as I'm perfectly willing to be chosen, we'll get on with it without telling anyone.

Adrian You can't possibly!

Isabel (*to the baby*) Uncle Adrian's an old fusspot, isn't he, baby? Though we can't go on calling you "baby". We must think of a name. How exciting. Now what?

Adrian Don't ask me, please!

The door opens, and an Old Man, in old-fashioned clothes and hat, comes in

Isabel Good evening.

The Old Man does not answer, but proceeds to hasten round the shop peering very closely, through thick spectacles, at anything which takes his interest

Can I help you at all?

He does not appear to hear. Isabel shrugs, and motions Adrian to help watch

Is there anything you're specially interested in?

He does not reply. They follow him round. He suddenly turns to Isabel, and puts his hand in his pocket. She steps back in alarm. But he produces a paper bag

Old Man Sweet?

Isabel (*taking one*) Oh, thank you so much.

The Old Man examines Adrian; then offers him the bag

Old Man You?

Adrian Thank you. (*He puts his hand in the bag, but brings it out empty*) There aren't any, actually.

Old Man What! (*He looks*) Damn. Back shortly.

The Old Man hurries out

Isabel The stars were right when they said "a disturbed day". They might have added "with disturbed people". (*To the baby*) I hope you weren't born under Pisces, baby? Oh! We shall never know. How is he going to know what sign to look at for advice?

Adrian I really don't think we need bother about that, Mrs Merryweather. If he . . .

Isabel Or is it a "she"? (*She ascertains*) Yes! How lovely. I shall call her Lucinda. No, then she'd be called Cindy, which sounds pantomimy. What about a lovely old name like Victoria?

Adrian Mrs Merryweather, I see the most horrid consequences . . .

Isabel Then stop seeing them, and think of names.

Adrian I can think of one: Admiral Henry Lane.

Isabel Oh, my God, yes, what's father going to say? Oh, I'll get round him. He loves anything female; we must make her look lovely, and then just produce her. (*Getting busy*) The first thing is to give her a bath. I don't remember ever bathing a real baby. How thrilling. You'd better help.

Adrian I haven't any idea how.

Isabel I think the hand-basin in the bathroom'll be big enough. Go and make sure Henry's safely in his study, and then——

Adrian (*interrupting*) I can't be a part of this, Mrs Merryweather, I really can't. I'm still certain the mother's going to come back.

Isabel Oh, do stop being so silly. Of course she's not coming back.

Adrian (*frozen*) I know you're always right, Mrs Merryweather, but here she is . . .

Isabel turns in alarm as the shop-door opens, and Mrs Barry comes in. She is an untidy woman, who, at the moment, has great difficulty in speak-in clearly

Mrs Barry (*taking the baby from Isabel*) Are you all right, Boo Boo?

Isabel I beg your pardon?

Mrs Barry I've been so worried about Boo Boo. I'm only talking like this as I've had a terrible time at the dentist. My face is still all frozen.

Isabel I feel a bit frozen, too.

Mrs Barry I'm sorry to have left her so long. I thought he'd pull it out, and that'd be the end of it. But he wanted to save it, and—oh, Boo Boo, Mummy has had a time!

Isabel Boo Boo's had quite a time, too. Now look, sit down, Mrs er . . .

Mrs Barry Barry.

Isabel I beg your pardon?

Mrs Barry Barry.

Isabel Oh, Barry, what a nice name. Sit down, Mrs Barry, and—(*gesturing to Adrian*)—have a nice cup of comforting tea—(*she sits her on the sofa*) and—(*getting it*)—an aspirin. I always keep a bottle in the shop because it's astonishing the number of clients who have headaches— even before hearing the prices. Of course, not nearly as many as those who ask to use "the toilet". It always makes me furious. I can't really think why—except that it puts one in such a low category. I mean, they'd never dream of going into a jeweller's or a chocolate shop, and ask to use the "toilet", would they? (*Hastily*) Not that you can't, after your ordeal.

Mrs Barry No, thank you.

Isabel Sure? Because I want you to feel quite relaxed and at ease.

Mrs Barry Quite sure, thank you.

Isabel Good. Feeling a little better?

Mrs Barry The tea's very nice.

Isabel (*sitting beside her*) I'm glad. Because—I'm wondering if you and I mightn't come to some sort of arrangement.

Adrian (*anxiously*) Mrs Merryweather, I think I ought to ...

Isabel (*severely*) Occupy yourself with cleaning that table, yes. I can see from here: there's dust an inch thick. (*Turning again to Mrs Barry*) Do you feel well enough for a little talk, Mrs Barry?

Mrs Barry Still a bit muzzy. But I know you'd be fair. It'd all have to be very secret though. My husband's terribly against it.

Isabel (*astonished*) You've thought about it before?

Mrs Barry Oh, yes. We've had terrible rows actually. But as I say to him, what with rising prices and his wretched Union always making him strike, we've got to make a sacrifice or two, even if it's something really loved.

Isabel What a sensible, broad-minded, attitude.

Mrs Barry But it's not Albert's. So I'm afraid payment would have to be in cash.

Isabel I'm perfectly willing.

Mrs Barry That way Albert mightn't find out.

Adrian Mrs Merryweather ...

Isabel (*fiercely*) Shh! (*To Mrs Barry*) Surely Albert would notice?

Mrs Barry I don't think so.

Isabel He must be remarkably unobservant.

Mrs Barry Not really. You see: we have others.

Isabel Oh, good. How many?

Mrs Barry I'm not quite sure.

Isabel You must be!

Mrs Barry You see, some of them are put away.

Isabel How awful for you; I am sorry. But this one's quite all right?

Mrs Barry Oh, yes. And I really wouldn't feel too guilty as it came to me through a friend.

Isabel (*amazed*) You mean it isn't your husband's?

Adrian pushes a small article so that it falls on the floor

(*fiercely*) Pick it up.

Mrs Barry And there's more than a bit of jealousy as it's far nicer than his.

Isabel He's got one that isn't yours?

Mrs Barry Two, actually. Before we were married, of course. One I never saw. Albert doesn't like to talk about it. I think it had an accident which was really his fault. The other I must say I don't like at all.

Isabel I don't wonder.

Mrs Barry It's a very wishy-washy colour. You know: looks as if it came out of the oven before it was ready.

Isabel My dear, you have been unfortunate. But let's get back to my one. Have you any sort of figure in mind?

Mrs Barry Well, something pretty substantial. I can't think one very often comes on the market.

Isabel Neither can I. I realize how lucky I am you brought it here.

Mrs Barry Well, to be honest, I have shown it to one other person. But I got the impression she'd stick it in a cupboard and forget it, so I said "no".

Isabel I should think so.

Mrs Barry I want to know it's going to a nice home. Silly, really, I should probably get a far better price if I sent it to a sale.

Isabel Really!

Mrs Barry Oh, yes. But I shan't. I'm told they're very likely to damage it.

Isabel I shouldn't be at all surprised.

Mrs Barry My friend sent hers, and they dropped it!

Isabel No!

Mrs Barry Yes! And what was worse they never confessed. Just wrote and said it hadn't sold, and when she went to collect it there were all the pieces roughly glued together.

Isabel rises slowly

Isabel Mrs Barry—I know you've had a drug injection, and I've been on American cocktails . . .

Adrian I've been trying to tell you, Mrs Merryweather, Mrs Barry came in about selling her Derby tea-set.

Isabel considers how to re-orientate for a moment

Isabel Her Derby tea-set. Exactly. (*Explaining a little too elaborately*) Of course that's what she came in about. (*To Mrs Barry*) I just like to know the background of my transactions. What I was leading up to—(*fiercely*) —before my assistant stopped dusting—was that as we've both had an unsettling day, it might be unwise to conclude a sale prematurely. Therefore, why don't you take Baa Baa home——

Mrs Barry Boo Boo.

Isabel —Boo Boo home, and come again tomorrow, with a sample cup and saucer.

Mrs Barry (*getting up*) It's a good idea; Boo Boo should be potted and bedded. (*Shoving the bundle at Isabel*) Say good-bye to the nice, kind lady, Boo Boo. (*Shoving it at Adrian*) And to the nice, kind gentleman.

Adrian Good-bye.

Mrs Barry I'll pop in when I'm normal again, 'bye—

Mrs Barry goes out

Isabel There's only one thing for a moment like this, Adrian. A large gin. (*Starting up the stairs*) I'll bring you one, too. No, come and fetch it; I'd better stay and pretend to understand the books with father. If not he'll insist on doing them when I want to watch the football match on telly.

Adrian (*stopping as he is about to follow her*) There's a woman dithering as if she might come in.

Isabel Probably only a wretched "pricer", wanting to find out what her own things are worth. Cope, and then come . . .

Isabel goes off at the top of the stairs. The bells ring, and Lady Colestar comes in. She is in her thirties, extremely smart, and almost embarrassingly enthusiastic

Lady Colestar I've fought the temptation of coming in, but your fascinating collection beckons too strongly.

Adrian I'm glad.

Lady Colestar (*coming in*) Oh, my dear! Even more of a treasure-house than it seemed from outside. It really is quite overwhelming. Where do you find all these lovely things?

Adrian Mrs Merryweather, the owner, works very hard.

Lady Colestar My dear, she must slave. She's brilliant. I'd like everything. I really don't know where to start. (*Picking up a solitaire set*) Oh, my dear, would you believe it: a solitaire set! I haven't seen one of those since I was a little girl in pigtails. I always used to be brought it by my grandmother when I was ill in bed. How much is it?

Adrian Forty pounds.

Lady Colestar Forty pounds! My dear, it's absurd.

Adrian The old marbles are almost unobtainable.

Lady Colestar Well, it's so nostalgic I really must think of having it. Put it on one side.

Adrian does so, and taking up a receipt-book, writes it down

What's that amusing little box in that case?

Adrian Would you like to see it?

Lady Colestar If it's not the most terrible bore.

Adrian I'll get the key. (*He does so from a drawer*) We have to lock everything up as we have so many thefts. (*He opens the case and shows her the box*)

Lady Colestar People really are too dreadful. (*Taking the box*) Oh, that really is most attractive. What is it?

Adrian A papier-mâché snuff-box.

Lady Colestar It's too divine. Ruinous?

Adrian Eight pounds.

Lady Colestar (*nodding*) Ruinous. But put it with the other.

Adrian Thank you. (*Excitedly he writes it down*)

Lady Colestar (*pointing*) What's that odd little object?

Adrian (*handing the object to her*) A Victorian gentleman's cigarette-holder.

Lady Colestar (*examining it*) In the shape of a woman's leg! My dear, how amusing. She's even got a garter! It's divinely naughty. I know someone who'd fall about at it. (*Looking*) The label can't say fifteen pounds!

Adrian That includes V.A.T.

Lady Colestar But fifteen pounds!

Adrian It's meerschaum, and very unusual.

Lady Colestar Robbery. But rather a lovely way to be robbed: add it to the others. Oh! Don't tell me that's a vinaigrette?

Adrian A little bright-cut George the Third one.

Lady Colestar It's mignon! I don't care what the price is: I'm not even going to ask; put it on the pile. Now—(*Looking around the shop*) let's see what else. I haven't been in such an exciting shop for years. It's exhilarating. Oh, that framed fan! How simply too beautiful.

Adrian It's got something rather nice on its lid which is stuck on the back.

Lady Colestar Tell me, quickly.

Adrian In old-fashioned writing there's "For Fanny. In the hope that it will cool her ardour for a most unsuitable gentleman."

Lady Colestar Oh, my dear, how touching. Poor little Fanny! It almost makes one weep for her. Can't you see the whole picture: that terrible mother in black and jet presenting it to her quivering daughter. I've simply got to have it; take it down.

Adrian adds it to the pile, and excitedly writes in the invoice book

Adrian As there's so much I think I'd better call Mrs Merryweather. (*Calling upstairs*) Mrs Merryweather!

Lady Colestar No, no, don't dream of disturbing her on my account. She deserves the cup of tea I'm sure she's having. Finding such treasures as these must drain every drop of her energy . . .

Isabel comes down the stairs

Adrian Oh, Mrs Merryweather, er . . .

Lady Colestar Lady Colestar.

Adrian (*impressed*) Lady Colestar was interested in so much I thought you ought to meet her.

Lady Colestar I congratulate you, Mrs Merryweather; you're a brilliant woman.

Isabel I am glad I came down.

Lady Colestar Never did I think to find again a shop displaying such taste, discrimination, and—at the risk of seeming effusive—I must add: sheer delight.

Isabel You're really too kind.

Adrian Her Ladyship's had these put aside.

Isabel Some of the very nicest things.

Lady Colestar The only difficulty is not to take the lot. (*She suddenly stops dead in her tracks, and for a moment is speechless*) Yes. (*She then moves towards the door*) But I really must rush. Thank you so very much.

Adrian But these things . . .

Lady Colestar I'll look at them again on my next visit. I left my poodle at the Dog Parlour next door, and they'll have finished clipping him hours ago. I simply daren't stay. But it's been a joy, and I can't thank you both enough. Good-bye.

Lady Colestar goes out

Isabel And people say how lovely it must be to run a shop!

Adrian Shall I go and find her car and puncture her tyres?

Isabel Adrian! I've never before heard you suggest anything wicked.

Adrian Well, it was going to be such a wonderful sale.

Isabel Never mind—her cheque would probably have bounced. Help me put everything away again before somebody nips them. It's just one of those afternoons; no sales, odd customers, and—(*sighing deeply*)—babies snatched from one's very arms.

Adrian I hoped you'd forgotten that.

Isabel I can't. I know it was stupid being carried away at the thought of it. And I really knew there wasn't a chance. But it would have been so wonderful.

Adrian It really wasn't a very nice baby when you looked at it closely.

Isabel It's no use trying to comfort me.

Adrian What about a kitten?

Isabel (*sharply*) What about it?

Adrian Mightn't it be an idea as—sort of company?

Isabel Father calculated out last cat broke over eighty-six pounds' worth of stock in its nine years.

Adrian A parrot! Couldn't do any damage. And he'd talk.

Isabel And make a mess. No, it's baby or nothing, and as I can't see a way of . . . (*She breaks off*)

Very enters

Very (*smiling expansively*) Two inches more all round, but, oh, the bliss of bulging! (*Angrily*) Was not "delighted and amazed" as per advertisement. Was compressed and agonized. Shall demand back my four pounds plus P and P. Plus my P and P. (*To Adrian*) Think I'll get it?

Adrian Oh, I expect so.

Very And I. Can always threaten. Won't want picture of me in belt in *Daily Mirror*. Not like model in illustration. At all! But back to purpose of visit. Espionage!

Isabel How exciting! But how, exactly?

Very Self: spy.

Isabel For our side or—the others?

Very Price spying.

Isabel My God! You're not from the Customs and Excise!

Very Customs and Excise! (*She spits*) Unladylike, but consentaneous.

Isabel I'm not sure what it means, but it isn't bad enough for them.

Very No, no, comparing prices. (*Picking up a small box, and looking at the label*) Five pounds. Getable?

Isabel Well, four-fifty, anyhow.

Very Refuse recognize decimals. (*Picking up a cribbage board*) Cribbage board; twelve pounds. Average?

Isabel This happens to be a very well inlaid one, so it's a bit expensive.

Very picks up another article, but as she is about to look at the price, she turns her head away, and bangs it down

Very No; not fair.

Isabel What isn't?

Very (*tapping herself*) Rival.

Isabel Rival what?

Very Dealer. Opening emporium down street.

Adrian The one they've just painted mauve and yellow?

Very The same.

Isabel We wondered what it was going to be.

Very Angry?

Isabel No, delighted. The more the merrier. Your customers will come on to us, and ours to you.

Very Generous.

Adrian What's it going to be called?

Very "Fakes."

Isabel Isn't that slightly asking for trouble?

Very Avoiding. No-one can say not warned.

Isabel Where was your shop before?

Very Wasn't.

Adrian You've never had a shop before?

Very (*shaking her head*) Know nothing.

Isabel But you must have had some experience?

Very Worked for crook in Streatham six months. Called his wife what she was: got the sack. Not before breaking whole table of glass—(*demonstrating*)—with bag. Very satisfactory. Meant only cornflakes for month, but her hysterics worth it.

Isabel Is someone backing you now, then?

Very (*nodding*) Hitler.

Isabel I beg your pardon?

Very Hitler. (*She puts a finger as a moustache, and raises the other hand*)

Isabel darts a look at Adrian

Adrian Adolf Hitler?

Very The same.

Isabel How exactly?

Very We shall park?

Isabel Yes, of course, I'm so sorry. (*Motioning her to the sofa*) Adrian and I were just thinking of having a little gin. Will you join us?

Very Never touched gin since friend Violet Oxberry drank whole bottle and fell down dead.

Adrian Dead drunk?

Very Dead to be buried.

Isabel Well—better than pneumonia, I suppose?

Very Possible. (*Opening her handbag*) Always carry own tipple. Izarra. Known?

Isabel I can't say I do.

Very (*producing yellow- and green-filled bottles and small glasses*) Nectar. Made by herbs and monks in the Alps. Live on it. You will?

Isabel I will, thank you.

Very (*pouring*) One strong, one not so strong. Never remember which. So mix.

Henry comes down the stairs carrying papers

Henry If you could remember five and seven make twelve and not eleven . . . (*He breaks off as he sees Very*) Oh. Sorry . . .

Isabel No, don't go; it's not a customer. The owner of the new antique shop down the road: Miss Hesketh-Palmer. (*To Very*) My father: Admiral Lane.

Very Love sailors. What a beauty! Welcome aboard, Admiral, welcome aboard.

Henry (*tetchily*) No, no. If it's my ship it's I who should welcome you aboard.

Isabel (*placatingly*) Well, don't let's have an argument.

Very Yes, let's. Love a good altercation.

Isabel Father's naval vocabulary is not "good".

Very Splendid. Need new filthy swear-words. (*To Henry*) Say some.

Henry I do not swear in front of ladies. Except my daughter.

Very Courteous as well as handsome. What luck! Drink to our better acquaintance.

Isabel (*to Henry*) A liqueur made in the Alps.

Henry Try anything once.

Very That's the spirit. (*To Adrian*) You will?

Adrian Well, just a very small one.

Very No smalls. My father: if you're going to have a drink have a good one.

Henry (*approvingly*) Sounds a very sensible man.

Very But foolhardy. Kicked to death by ostriches in Transvaal. (*Lifting her glass*) Down the hatch.

Very swallows hers at a gulp. The others, surprised at its strength, sip slowly

The other half?

Isabel and Adrian shake their heads

I shall.

Henry (*holding out his glass*) Can't let you alone.

Very (*delightedly*) Sounds dreamy. Perhaps true when know each other better, eh?

Very gives Henry an enormous wink. He winks back. Isabel and Adrian look amazed

Shall we have a song?

Isabel (*hastily*) Not just at the moment. Tell us how Hitler's responsible for your shop.

Very Have.

Isabel You didn't actually.

Very Ah, that's it. Memory gone. Buzz-bomb. (*She imitates a buzz-bomb, the cut-out, the explosion*) Me in the grocer's. Buried in raisins. Had to be dug out. Never able to face Christmas Pudding since.

Adrian How awful!

Very Beetled home, raisins still in hair. No home. Hitler'd called there, too.

Isabel How terrible for you.

Very Terrible living with sister ever since. Habits laughed at, Izarra frowned on.

Henry Ridiculous.

Very But escape this year. In attic oil-painting rescued from Hitler by wheelbarrow. Not mine; fell through ceiling flat above. Taken to keep rain off wheelbarrow. Now Sotheby's: twenty thousand.

Isabel You got twenty thousand pounds?

Very (*shaking her head*) Got nothing. So interested visits Sotheby's, spent all, other sales. Hence shop.

Henry Isn't it a bit risky?

Very No worse off if lose all.

Henry A brave way of looking at it. But how are you going to know how to run it? Who's going to keep your books?

Very No books.

Henry (*appalled*) No books!

Very Time wasting.

Isabel I do so agree.

Henry You have to keep books.

Very Why?

Henry Because you'll land in the jug if you don't.

Very Wouldn't be the first time.

Adrian You've been in prison before?

Very (*nodding happily*) Indecent exposure.

Henry Good God!

Very Wasn't, of course. Merely showing chit in Trafalgar Square no bra long before Women's Lib. Freedom, hooey: because of good bosoms. Want to see?

Isabel (*hastily*) I don't think just at the moment.

Very Probably wise. (*Sadly*) Hot-water bottles best covered.

Henry To get back to the books. Would you like me to draw you up a simple system?

Very (*beaming at him*) As kind as good-looking. Praises.

Henry (*moving to stairs*) I've got a new account book in my study. I'll jot down the headings, and be back in a jiffy.

Henry goes off at the top of the stairs

Very A stunner.

Isabel Little do you know what you're letting yourself in for, Very. He's accounts mad.

Very On occasion madman better than no man. Where's yours?

Isabel You mean my husband?

Very Not about. Gone off, or gone up?

Isabel Off actually. With an Italian Contessa. Three years ago.

Very Congratulations or commiserations?

Isabel Oh, I'm delighted. She has a lovely villa on Lake Como. I go and stay, and he's charming to me and bloody to her. And then, of course, I got all the lovely lolly to run—(*gesturing around the shop*)—"Alimony".

Very Approved. Highly. But babies?

Isabel None.

Very Fortunate. Diarrhoea and rickets.

Isabel You're as bad as father; that's all finished. Nowadays they're hardly any trouble at all.

Very Phooey! Sister's grandchildren ghastly. Nursery: Chamber of Horrors. Go in armed.

Isabel It must be the parents!

Very (*nodding*) Teetotal M.P.s.

Isabel Perhaps they'd like me to look after one?

Very Better werewolves.

Isabel (*eagerly*) I'm sure I should be able to tame them. Do ask.

Very You want so badly?

Isabel (*nodding*) Suddenly again. An overwhelming want. You see, I had a baby in my arms this afternoon. It filled me with such extraordinary happiness, and content. I could give one so much. I long to.

Very (*taking her hand, and speaking surprisingly gently*) My dear—I longed. Deeply, too. Before raisins. (*Sighing*) Unfulfilment stultifying. Every way. Bad. Inhibiting. Tormenting. (*Suddenly matter-of-factly*) We must get you a baby. But not from sister's snake-pit.

Isabel It's very easy to say.

Very Easy to accomplish. Spare babies everywhere.

Isabel Yes, I suppose there must be when you think of the number that're born every minute.

Very Enough money adoption?

Isabel Adoption? Oh, I could manage it. (*Excitedly*) What an idea! Yes, why shouldn't I adopt a baby?

Adrian Wouldn't it get in the way of the shop a bit?

Isabel Damn the shop! You'll just have to work twice as hard. (*To Very*) You're a marvel!

Very Decision. Boy or girl?

Isabel Of course! I could choose. Wonderful. But how difficult. Which do you think?

Very Slugs and snails and puppy-dog tails, any day.

Isabel Which do you think, Adrian?

Adrian Don't ask me; I'd rather not be embroiled!

Isabel Nonsense, you must be embroiled as much as possible: marvellous experience for when you have one of your own. (*To Very*) Yes, I think a boy. Oh, I don't know. Father'd insist on him going in the Navy, and he'd be up the rigging all the time.

Adrian Will he altogether welcome either?

Isabel If it comes young enough. He was terribly against a wolf-hound I wanted once. But it arrived an adorable little puppy, and he never noticed how enormous it got.

Very Decision. Home grown or cosmopolitan?

Isabel You mean I could have a little coloured boy?

Very Friend Amanda had Chinese. Great success. Became dentist. Drilling a dream.

Isabel Or what about a dear little Indian boy?

Very Can hear Temple bells ringing . . .

They pause and listen, as, indeed, a muffled ringing can be heard

Adrian What is it?

Very Oh! Not Temple bells. Alarm clock. (*She takes the ringing clock from her handbag*) Warning me—the dear.

Isabel Of what?

Very Ah. That's the puzzle. Solved by other friend. Diary. (*She takes it from her bag and peers at it*) What's the time?

Adrian Five-thirty. Tuesday.

Very Five-thirty, Tuesday. "Blow up Archbishop." That's wrong. Done that.

Adrian Blown up the Archbishop?

Very (*nodding*) Searing letter in red biro. Won't do that again.

Isabel What?

Very Not answer first letter. But that last Tuesday. (*Turning the pages*) Ah. Half-past five: Hang Charles the First. (*Getting up*) Yes, must rush. But as soon as he's up: back to import babies . . .

Very rushes out

Isabel (*feeling her forehead*) I somehow think Izarra's not my drink.

Adrian Nor mine.

Isabel If we're not careful she'll have us rowing children from Calcutta.

Adrian I'm glad—I thought you were for it.

Isabel I am—for one child, properly arranged.

Adrian From—abroad?

Isabel I'm not sure about that. Let's see what's available. How d'you think we find out who deals in babies?

The street door opens. Lady Colestar hovers in the doorway

Lady Colestar Do I dare come in?

Isabel Haven't they finished clipping the poodle?

Lady Colestar (*coming in*) Oh, my dear, you'd be absolutely right to bar the way with a flaming scimitar. It was disgraceful of me wasting your time earlier on. But I was going to buy all those gorgeous things, I really was. I felt so terrible about it when I got home that I leapt in the car again, and here I am to apologize.

Isabel There was no need to do that.

Lady Colestar But your poor young man was so sweet and helpful. (*To Adrian*) Do forgive me.

Adrian Oh, yes, your Ladyship.

Isabel What was it made you change your mind—the prices?

Lady Colestar Oh, no! I always make a fuss, of course, for the fun of seeing whether I'll get a little reduction. But I think your prices are most reasonable.

Isabel For that statement alone all is forgiven.

Lady Colestar Oh, thank you. What happened was: I suddenly had a vision of my husband. With a whip.

Isabel My dear!

Lady Colestar Oh, a metaphorical one. You see—it's dreadful—but I'm a "compulsive buyer". I simply go mad at the sight of lovely things. Our house—really quite large—is crammed to the attics with treasures. John even built me a three-roomed extension: that's overflowing, too.

Isabel You must have enormous fun.

Lady Colestar Oh, I do! I adore it. But John says that I must stop. That he earns a great deal of money, but there are other things to spend it on than antiques that we can't even house, let alone see.

Isabel Perhaps you'd like to sell some to me?

Lady Colestar I should only come and buy them back again. John tricked me into seeing a psychiatrist. But of course he just said it was compensation.

Isabel For what?

Lady Colestar Well, you see, it's devastating: we haven't any children——

Isabel (*interrupting her by going and almost embracing her*) My dear, I am glad you came back! Come and sit down and tell me all about it.

Adrian Shall I go?

Isabel No, no, you'll be able to remember any bits I forget. (*To Lady Colestar*) Unless you mind?

Lady Colestar Good gracious, no. What's one more after I've bared my soul—and very often my body—to specialists and quacks all over the world?

Isabel None was any good?

Lady Colestar Witch doctors couldn't have done less. For John or me.

Isabel Oh, I do sympathize. (*Tentatively*) Have you—have you ever thought of adopting?

Lady Colestar My dear, we're on every list that's still open.

Isabel You mean it's difficult?

Lady Colestar Difficult? Impossible.

Isabel It can't be!

Lady Colestar I should know: we've tried for three years.

Isabel But how awful! I thought they let anyone have one who was—vaguely respectable.

Lady Colestar My dear, they're not there to let anyone have. There's an appalling shortage of babies.

Adrian I've always understood there were hundreds waiting for homes.

Lady Colestar Not now we're in the Permissive Age. Abortion, and the Pill, means there just isn't a supply of spare ones as there used to be.

Isabel I suppose they must've cut down the number, but surely . . .

Lady Colestar Then all the unmarried mothers; there's no shame about it now. A congenial social climate encourages them to bring up their own babies.

Isabel (*woefully*) Yes, I've seen them brandishing them on the front pages of the *Daily Express*.

Lady Colestar John and I have quite shamelessly even tried large bribes . . .

Adrian Nothing?

Lady Colestar Insults.

Isabel But that's here. What about coloured babies?

Lady Colestar Almost as hopeless.

Isabel No!

Lady Colestar A few years ago no-one would look at them. Now it's become "fashionable" to have a coloured child: the conscience of the world, etcetera, etcetera. Most agencies have closed their lists for either sort for at least a year.

Isabel How terribly depressing.

Lady Colestar (*jumping up*) What'll be even more depressing is if I'm caught by those damn traffic women again.

Isabel Oh, no, don't go. I'm sure we might help each other somehow.

Lady Colestar (*opening the door*) My dear, I'm on the double lines, and I've been nicked twice this month already. But I'll come in again, I promise; and buy something. (*Coming back into the shop*) In fact, I really must take that gorgeous fan now, and that . . .

Isabel (*ushering her out*) No! Think of your husband brandishing his whip . . .

Very enters and hears the last remark

Very Husband beats you?

Lady Colestar No, no, he doesn't.

Very Pity. Knew brigadier beat wife. Concocted devilish revenge. Could have told you.

Lady Colestar That's most kind, but—another time. (*To Isabel*) See you very soon.

Lady Colestar skirts warily round Very, and goes out

Very (*to Adrian*) Am against whips. But hairbrushes another thing, eh? When you marry . . . Oh, thought! Mrs Lane. Admiral's wife. Endless sleep?

Isabel For about five years.

Very (*with an approving upward nod*) Rest happily, dear lady. (*To Adrian*) Back to hairbrush. Back of hairbrush. Humane, but satisfactory noise.

Adrian I see. Uum, did you hang the King all right?

Very On wall, facing shop door. Heavy frame probably pull down partition, but present effect staggering. Gave idea. Know daughter of old Nurse King of Siam's children. What say to Siamese baby?

Isabel It's no good.

Very What's no good?

Isabel That customer—far more suitable than I am—has tried every colour and creed. And there's not the remotest chance of adoption.

Very For sure?

Isabel Very sure.

Very Scotch and soda! (*Brightening up*) But despair unknown to Hesketh-Palmer. What's needed: more Izarra. (*She prepares her drink*)

Isabel Not for me, thank you.

Adrian Nor me.

Very Me, yes. (*She gulps a large one*) Now. Stir, stir, brain. (*After a moment*) Blank. But Izarra creeping up. Other ways of getting babies? Babies. Babies. Babies. Unwanted babies? (*Suddenly*) Alleluia! Foreign girls! Rushing over to end all on Health Scheme.

Adrian But they come to get rid of their babies.

Isabel (*excitedly*) You mean we might get one of them to change her mind?

Very (*shaking her finger and speaking clearly to imagined foreigner*) You, silly girl. Not good get rid bambino. Understand? Not good. Pope very angry. Nursing Home very nasty. Possible mice. Understand? (*Imitating mice*) Dirt. Hurry. Sordid. Dangerous. Perhaps mortuary.

Isabel Frighten her like that, she'll lose it on the spot.

Very (*addressing the girl*) No need fright. We very nice. You come us; have bambino very secret, every comfort.

Isabel Upstairs here! We've got masses of spare bedrooms.

Very (*to the girl*) We give lovely bedroom upstairs.

Isabel I'll get new curtains . . .

Very (*to the girl*) New pretty curtains. (*To Isabel*) Warm?

Isabel (*to the girl*) Beautifully warm. Central heating, and a blower.

Very (*to the girl*) Breakfast in bed . . .

Isabel Flowers everywhere . . .

Very Gentle visits, art galleries, Zoo . . .

Isabel T.V. in your room . . .

Very (*to Isabel*) Colour?

Isabel (*to the girl*) Yes, we'll hire you a colour-set—

Very (*to the girl*) All care and comfort till last moment. Then you leave last moment here, and go happily home.

Adrian (*who has watched them in complete amazement*) But you haven't even contacted the girl yet.

Very Peanuts.

Isabel Yes, it shouldn't be difficult to hear of one.

Adrian They're not going to advertise they're coming over for that reason.

Isabel Of course not! But—their friends, and—people in the village'll know.

Very That's it!

Adrian What is?
Very You are.
Adrian What?
Very (*to Isabel*) You can spare him few days?
Isabel To find the girl?
Very (*nodding*) Week in France. Week in Italy. Mornings in cafés, nights in bars.
Adrian I couldn't possibly!
Isabel Of course you could. We'll give you a special fund for handing out drinks. You'll soon hear of someone.
Adrian I shan't, Mrs Merryweather! And even if I did I wouldn't understand! I don't speak a word of anything foreign.
Isabel Oh, you are useless.
Adrian (*hopefully*) So you'll drop the whole idea?
Very No, we won't. We'll approach from other angle. Airports!

Henry comes downstairs with books and papers

Henry Sorry to have been a bit long . . .
Very But a moment, Admiral, but a moment.
Henry I've drawn up a very simple scheme: just eleven columns . . .
Very So—few?
Isabel Darling, we're trying to decide something important—
Henry Nothing's more important than properly kept books. (*To Very*) Now— (*handing her books*) This is for your daily accounts—
Very Ah, yes.
Henry Normal columns: Date; Time; Stock number; Reference, if any; Description of Article; Price Obtained; Price Paid; Profit; V.A.T. owed; Remarks; Miscellaneous.
Very Beautifully simple. Very clever.
Henry Thank you. (*Handing Very another book*) This one you may find a little more complicated . . .
Isabel I'll say.
Henry Your weekly accounts. (*With a disapproving look at Isabel*) To be made up regularly. Every Saturday night.
Very Of course. Idea! Charming office over shop. Come tomorrow—sundown—large whisky—cigar optional—explain without interruption.
Henry Not a bad suggestion.
Very Another. Do me honour of opening shop.
Henry Have you lost the keys?
Very Ceremonial opening. Ribbon across entrance. Cut by you.
Henry With my old sword!
Very Marvellous!
Henry It may have a touch of rust. When would you require me?
Very Tomorrow.
Henry (*trotting upstairs*) I'll get to work on it right away.
Very On deck, noon?
Henry Aye. Aye.

Henry touches his forehead in salute and goes off

Isabel How do you manage it?

Very Learnt early. No figure, no beauty: so guile. Unsuspected: never fails. But back to baby. Where were we?

Adrian At the airports.

Very That's it. That's where to catch a breeder. Tired, strange, bewildered: easy.

Adrian But how are you going to know the—reluctant mothers from the ordinary passengers?

Very A point.

Isabel Well, they're female—

Very —young—

Isabel —pregnant. There can't be many like that every planeload.

Very (*to Adrian*) You go up to them . . .

Adrian No, no, I don't!

Very Ask if taxi wanted.

Isabel Brilliant.

Adrian But do I look like a taxi-driver?

Very More like than . . . (*She points to Isabel and herself*)

Adrian I can't drive, anyhow.

Very Scotch and soda. Have to go next idea.

The alarm clock in her bag goes off again. She takes it out, and consults her diary

Five-thirty: "Stanley Baldwin." (*Puzzled*) Stanley Baldwin?

Isabel Seems unlikely.

Very Plumber! Just like him. Concentrate on finding girl. Back when gurgling stops.

Very dashes out

Isabel She's a woman right after my own heart. We are lucky.

Adrian (*doubtfully*) She's certainly—full of ideas. Whether they're very practical . . .

Isabel Who wants to be practical?

Adrian Well, I don't mind it, actually. In fact—at the risk of being interfering, Mrs Merryweather . . .

Isabel You interfere as much as you like; what is it?

Adrian I do feel you should think quite a lot more before—embarking on this baby scheme.

Isabel What is there to think about?

Adrian Well, it's all been so sudden. I mean, one weighs up all the pros and cons, and makes preparations, even before buying a budgerigar.

Isabel You are an extraordinary boy. Never mind, you'll change after you've been with us a few months.

Adrian I suppose I shall have to. Or go mad.

The bells ring, and Jenny comes in. She is very pretty, but looks as Isabel described her

Isabel Good afternoon . . . (*Breaking off*) Jenny! My dear, what a lovely surprise. Haven't taken your knickers off, I hope?

Jenny Nor my vest.

Isabel (*to Adrian*) This is Jenny, father's god-daughter. Adrian, who's come to help us in the shop.

Jenny and Adrian exchange greetings

Adrian (*collecting plates*) I'll go and pack up the dessert service, shall I?

Isabel Oh, would you?

Adrian goes out with the plates

Such a tactful boy.

Jenny I've been fussed about you all the afternoon, so as soon as we closed I thought I must come and see if you're O.K.

Isabel Why shouldn't I be?

Jenny Well, you were very odd at lunch. Kept telling me about an Italian who chased you on a bicycle.

Isabel Oh Lord! I didn't tell you what happened when he caught me?

Jenny In full detail.

Isabel Oh my God! I am sorry.

Jenny I enjoyed every moment of it. It was the people at the other end of the restaurant who got a bit up-tight.

Isabel (*after having covered her mouth with her hand in horror*) I swear I'll never ever drink again in a public place.

Jenny I shan't either; I've had a terrible afternoon.

Isabel Oh, you poor dear. Head or stomach?

Jenny Conscience.

Isabel Don't be silly, darling—getting high at lunch once in a while . . .

Jenny I wasn't. In fact it made my brain very clear. That was the trouble; I started thinking about what I do.

Isabel You do very well. Chelsea Public Library wouldn't be the same without you.

Jenny It would, you know. But it's not that I don't like being there. Or would mind if I wasn't there. That's just it. I'm aesthetically numb.

Isabel Sounds horrible. What does it mean?

Jenny (*after a moment*) I don't appreciate anything enough. Feel deeply enough about anything. Just—slush through life. Don't do much harm, but don't do much good either.

Isabel I've seen you be wonderfully patient with all those old fools looking for sex on the shelves.

Jenny Is that enough?

Isabel What else is there?

Jenny That's what I want to find out; and is the other reason for coming. Do you think I could get Henry to lend me about five hundred pounds?

Isabel If anyone could it'd be you. But he committed half his pension to buy this house, and though the shop takes masses of money, the Inland Revenue and the bloody V.A.T. seem to take it all away again. Why do you want it?

Jenny To go and watch elephants.

Isabel (*after a moment*) Is it a pop group?

Jenny No, no. The animals.

Isabel Oh. Where?

Jenny In East Africa.

Isabel Oh. Why?

Jenny Because I want to think it all out, and I read a fascinating book about elephants. They're wise and primeval, and—alone with them—I think I might come up with an answer.

Isabel considers this for a moment

Isabel Well, darling, if you really feel like that, you must go and join some elephants.

Jenny (*laughing, and flinging her arms round Isabel*) I knew you were crazy enough to understand.

Very enters

Very Ah, found one. Very quick. Clever.

Isabel This is Jenny. Miss Hesketh-Palmer.

Jenny Hullo.

Very (*walking round her*) Hips narrow. But should be all right.

Isabel No, no . . .

Very (*interrupting*) Yes, yes: modern science copes. Doesn't look very far gone. Is she certain?

Isabel No, no, she's not here for that.

Very Doesn't matter, she'll do. Very well, I'd say.

Jenny Do for what?

Isabel But she isn't going to have one, even.

Very No reason she shouldn't, is there?

Jenny Have one what?

Very Takes more time than other way, but more satisfactory.

Jenny Look, I don't want to be rude, but what the hell are you both talking about?

Isabel It's a little misunderstanding, darling. Very—Miss Hesketh-Palmer—is trying to find me a baby to adopt . . .

Very Every avenue explored, every avenue blocked. So you make one for her, eh?

Isabel She's just off to Africa for a year.

Very Ideal. Three months good age to hand over.

Jenny (*amused*) I see. I'm to have a baby and give it to you?

Isabel You mean you'd consider it?

Very Of course. Very nice girl.

Isabel She is a nice girl. (*To Jenny*) You know it is an idea, darling. Having a baby would certainly be something accomplished. Something good. (*In a rush*) You'd have none of those unending nappies, and know it was coming to a wonderful home and education and upbringing and almost too much love and I'll swindle the books somehow so you can have a lovely free year with as many elephants as you can find.

Jenny (*amused*) What about a father?

Isabel Oh, yes.

Very Must know someone who'd do it.

Jenny Sorry, I don't. I've never liked sex that much.

Very Always men hanging about ready.

Isabel You wouldn't mind, just once, quickly, would you?

Jenny You mean what's ten minutes compared with a year in Africa?

Very What sense.

Jenny I haven't even to listen to you. (*Hugging Isabel*) You're even crazier and wickeder than I thought. (*To Very*) And I'm not sure the same doesn't go for you.

Very Do hope. Sane and good so boring.

Jenny goes to the stairs

Jenny I'm going to see if Henry'll save me from a fate worse than death.

Isabel And if he won't?

Jenny We'll see.

Jenny laughs at them, and goes off upstairs

Very Hopeful?

Isabel Well, father's nicely overdrawn and owes income tax.

Very Good, good. But didn't like that "not keen on sex".

Isabel When you come to think of it, it is rather a lot to ask.

Very Phooey. Had friend sang Mimi in *Bohème* same night.

Isabel Same night as—which?

Very Having baby, of course. Other she'd manage between acts.

Isabel Jenny's always been odd. (*Doubtfully*) I think she might do it.

Very If not nine months wasted. Must have second string.

Isabel It was only by complete chance we found this string.

Very Ah! But thoughts then only revolving round ready-made babies. Quite another kettle specially manufactured.

Isabel That's true.

Very Know any possible breeders?

Isabel Don't think I do.

Very Customers?

Isabel I've never really discussed it with any of them.

Very Must. Somehow. (*She walks about the shop. Suddenly she seizes up a coral and silver rattle. Waving it*) Alleluia!

Isabel What?

Very Special display. (*Picking up articles*) Children's things. Rattle. Christening mug. Doll . . .

Isabel Yes! Then it'd be easy to bring up the subject with anyone who's enthusiastic.

Very (*looking at the price on the doll*) Enthusiasm soon dampened by price.

Isabel Then we must reduce things a bit. (*With a cry*) A sale! That's it. Masses of bargains. Sure way to get the women in. We'll start this very moment. (*Calling*) Adrian! I've got some lovely Victorian baby clothes if only we had something to model them on . . .

Very suddenly lets out a cry.

Very (*beating her head*) Fool, Hesketh-Palmer, fool!

Isabel Why?

Very Model. Gloria. Most possible. Wait . . .

Very dashes out as Adrian comes in

Adrian Yes, Mrs Merryweather?

Isabel Write a large notice saying "Sale".

Adrian Won't a sale rather let down the tone?

Isabel Damn the tone. Start clearing the window. It'll be a double blessing: there're masses of horrible mistakes I've been longing to get rid of. That ghastly lamp, for instance, that the owner swore was early Ming, and turned out to be late Peter Jones. (*Writing on a label*) I shall reduce it to a pound.

Adrian But you paid fifteen!

Isabel Yes, I'll murder that cheating woman if she comes in again. (*Looking round*) Where's her "perfect" Paisley shawl with all the moth holes?

Very hurries in, then turns to speak in the direction of the street

Very Come along, dear, come along. (*To Isabel*) Impossible hasten her. (*In a ringing whisper*) Disguises subject (*To the door*) At last . . .

Gloria strolls in. She is a largely built, very beautiful, languid girl, dressed and made up in the last-minute fashion. She speaks with a drawl

(*presenting her*) Gloria. Friend coming "Fakes" first week to attract customers.

Isabel Hullo. I'm sure you'll do that.

Gloria Darling!

Very (*picking up a necklace, with a large wink to Isabel*) This: necklace thought might interest.

Gloria (*taking it*) Yes. Pretty. Have you a mirror?

Isabel Hold that one, Adrian.

Adrian picks up a large hand-mirror and holds it while Gloria examines herself, to Adrian's embarrassment. Behind her back Very elaborately raises her eyebrows in question. Isabel nods eagerly

Gloria Yes, I think it's me. But whereabouts on me is it me? (*She tries it in her hair, loops it round her wrist, and poses with it at her waist. To Adrian*) What do you think?

Adrian It's fifteen pounds.

Isabel (*quickly*) Which is very cheap when you consider the workmanship. If you examine the way the little stones are set . . .

Gloria Don't bother with the sales talk, darling. If I like it I shall buy it even if the stones are glued on.

Isabel (*slightly taken aback*) How nice to meet someone with a mind of their own.

Gloria I should know what suits me: it's my living.

Very Gloria—famous model.

Isabel Oh, how interesting. What sort of modelling?

Gloria Any sort I can get, darling.

Very Mostly nude.

Isabel Topless?

Gloria Come out from under your antimacassar, darling.

Very F.F.N.s.

Adrian F.F.N.s?

Gloria You can come out from under your tea-cosy, too.

Very Full Frontal Nudes.

Isabel How exciting.

Gloria It isn't, darling. God knows I'm no prude, but the things they ask you to do.

Very Every position, every place.

Gloria It's true, darlings. I've been nude in the bath. Nude up a tree. Nude on the counter of Selfridge's Food Hall . . .

Very New Zealand lamb.

Isabel It's intriguing. Just the sort of thing I'd like to have done when I was young.

Gloria You wouldn't, darling. Try lying in a field of cows on a summer day. The gnats. My bum looked like a pepper-pot.

Adrian clears his throat

The trouble is I'm getting beyond it.

Very Phooey. You're lovely.

Gloria Yes, I am. (*To Isabel*) But between you and me and the B.B.C., I ache so much. I can't hold all these positions they want. You've no idea. Last week they had me hanging from a hook in a butcher's shop.

Very (*to Isabel*) Imagine when let down: blood and sawdust between toes.

Isabel Uugh.

Gloria I could hardly stand the next day. Then one old pouf had me coming out of a refrigerator. I didn't mind my tits being bright blue—

Adrian's coughing nearly chokes him.

—but the agony in my legs and shoulders during the night. That's why I'm trying more and more jobs like old H.P.'s given me.

Very Less of adjective, dear.

Gloria If ever I get my pad nicely furnished . . .

Very (*interrupting*) She has nice flat in—(*emphasizing*)—Shepherd Market.

Isabel (*realizing*) Has she!

Gloria (*wrinkling her nose*) But the furniture's grotty—bad for trade—I mean, for when friends come in. And I must have central heating. When that's all fixed I shall probably give up F.F.N.s. Just do weeks like at "Fakes". (*To Isabel*) Would you ever want me?

Isabel Well, not really: I have Adrian.

Gloria's eyes open at the comparison

Very She needs money: very extravagant.

Gloria Only on stock-in-trade—clothes, hair, massage, week-ends in those awful health-places . . .

Very Loves eating.

Isabel Oh, I do sympathize. Chocolates?

Gloria Suet puddings.

Very (*meaningly*) Do anything for them.

Isabel (*catching on*) Oh! Sit down, Gloria, dear. I think we're going to be great friends.

Very Izarra for everyone. (*She pours out*)

Adrian (*hastily*) It's just on closing time. I'll go and get ready.

Adrian bolts out

Very (*impatiently*) Well! Go on.

Isabel (*to Gloria, awkwardly*) Puddings and chocolates have gone up so terribly in price, haven't they?

Gloria Ghastly, darling. You'd never guess what they charged me for jam roly-poly in the Strand last week.

Isabel Furniture's exorbitant, too.

Gloria H.P.'s certainly is.

Isabel So is mine, I'm afraid. But er—do you like it?

Gloria (*looking round approvingly*) It's all right.

Very Bush-beating maddening. Come to point.

Isabel Gloria—have you ever thought of children?

Gloria Only of how to prevent them.

Isabel Suppose I completely refurnished your flat—with the nicest things in the shop—installed central heating, and paid your living costs for a year—including all the puddings you could eat . . .

Gloria Heaven!

Isabel Would you consider not preventing one?

Gloria looks puzzled

Very (*tapping her knee*) Have baby, and hand over.

Gloria Oh.

Gloria considers the proposition, practically expressionless. They watch her anxiously

(*At long last*) Do you supply the man, or do I?

Isabel Oh, I think I do. I'd like to sort of—find out a bit about him first, and that might be awkward if he was one of your—friends.

Very (*to Gloria*) Favourable?

Gloria I'd be worried about my figure. I'd be sunk if my boobs dropped.

Isabel They wouldn't! With proper ante-natal exercises you should be an even better shape than now.

Gloria Something. (*Looking at her watch, and getting up*) I'm doing tooth-paste at six . . .

Very Give you time to chew over.

Isabel I shall be most anxious; you'll let me know soon?

Very Opening "Fakes" twelve tomorrow. (*To Gloria*) Answer then, eh?

Gloria O.K. (*Going to the door*) Nice to have met you.

Isabel Oh, the necklace. Do have it—as a sort of token of good will.

Gloria I'll have it, but I'll pay for it.

Isabel No, no, just take it.

Gloria I'd sooner pay, thanks. (*Opening her bag*) Fifteen, wasn't it?

Isabel The trade price: thirteen, to you.

Gloria (*giving her notes*) I'm not in your trade any more than you're in mine, darling. Thanks a lot. Bye-bye . . .

Gloria goes out

Very She'll do it.

Isabel D'you really think so?

Very Sure. Know something, Can put pressure.

Isabel (*worried*) I don't think it really matters about her—profession.

Very Scotch and soda, no! Some of the best characters in history; mothers who were—models.

Isabel Yes, and she's so beautiful it should be a marvellous baby. Oh!

Very What?

Isabel What about the father?

Very Mere bagatelle.

Isabel Yes, but a bagatelle that's got to be found. I don't really know how we're going to set about it . . .

But at this moment the street door opens and the Old Man hurries in, and scuttles round peering at everything as he did before

Isabel and Very watch him. Then Very follows round behind him, bending to examine his features. He suddenly turns and they almost collide. He pushes a paper bag at her

Old Man Liquorice all-sorts this time. Like 'em?

Very Love 'em. (*She takes one*)

The Old Man makes a further rapid inspection, and then holds the bag out to Isabel

Old Man You?
Isabel Thank you. (*She takes one*)

The Old Man pockets the bag, and goes to the door

Old Man Will be in again.

   The Old Man goes out

Very (*looking after him*) Don't think so. Do you?
Isabel As a bagatelle?
Very Yes.
Isabel (*firmly*) No.
Very Pity. But no despair. He'll turn up.

   Adrian comes in in his coat

Isabel and Very gaze at him hopefully

Adrian I'm just off, Mrs Merryweather. Anything I can do before I go?
Isabel Well, not before you go . . .
Very When you come back.
Adrian What?
Isabel Well, I have wonderful news, Adrian. You know how badly I wanted a baby?
Adrian Yes.
Isabel Well, I think I'm going to get one.
Very Maybe two.
Adrian (*enthusiastically*) Oh, I am glad.
Isabel The only thing we've got to do is to find a father.

Adrian's enthusiasm changes to horror

Adrian No, Mrs Merryweather!
Isabel Just think about it.
Adrian No, Mrs Merryweather.
Very Very lovely girl.
Adrian I don't care! I couldn't, I really couldn't. I'd do a lot for you, Mrs Merryweather, but that, no. (*Backing out of the front door*) No, I won't. I won't. I really won't . . .

   Adrian disappears

Very Pathetic.
Isabel No, he's a dear. Just very shy.
Very I'll work on him.
Isabel (*hastily*) No, I don't think you'd better. He's awfully good in the shop: I don't want him to leave, or have a nervous breakdown.
Very Then who next?

Henry appears in full naval uniform at the top of the stairs

Henry What about it?

Isabel (*horrified*) No, Father, I don't think so.

Henry Bit tight, certainly. But I thought if I was doing it at all, I might as well do it in style.

Very Admirable, Admiral? Let's see closer.

Henry No, no, I'm only holding the trousers. The buttons'll have to be moved. Just wanted the general effect judged.

Very Spectacular!

Henry Good. I'll see if I can unearth the rest.

Henry goes off

Isabel I don't suppose there's anything actually against it in the prayer-book, but no.

Very Know what you mean. Bit long in tooth anyhow.

Isabel So what?

Very Three tries, no hit. Worrying.

Isabel There must be someone. Who else do we know? The Vicar? If reports are true it wouldn't be the first time.

Very Don't want churchy voice.

Isabel That's true.

Very Window-cleaner very strong.

Isabel Yes, but if he didn't like the idea he might refuse to clean our windows any more. I think someone unconnected with us might be better.

Very How to find?

Isabel Yes, we can't very well put a card in the window.

Very Alleluia!

Isabel What?

Very *The Times*. Agony column.

Isabel (*rushing to get it*) Of course!

Very Always men advertising for strange jobs.

Isabel (*looking in the newspaper*) Not today, I'm afraid. Wait a moment. Yes, I'm not sure this isn't the very thing. "Single man, very fit" . . .

Very Ideal!

Isabel "Wide experience, seeks interesting and different work."

Very What more interesting and different?

Isabel Oh!

Very What?

Isabel "Anything legal considered."

Very Scotch and soda!

Isabel It could hardly be considered legal, I suppose?

Very Soppy fool.

Isabel (*still looking*) And no others.

Very Must be.

Isabel There aren't.

Very Not today. Other days.

Isabel But we may wait for months before a suitable one advertises.

Very Then why wait? We advertise!

Isabel Yes, of course we could. Brilliant.

Very (*going to the telephone*) Strike while iron hot. Number?

Isabel (*reading from the paper*) Seven-four-two three-double-six-nine. Extension eight-eight.

Very (*dialling*) Very expensive. Must be brief.

Isabel Well, you should be good at that.

Very Life too short for useless words. (*Into the telephone*) Advertisement for "Required" column. (*Covering the receiver*) Sounds half-witted. (*Into the telephone*) Yes. Ready? "Personable, intelligent, strong, agile young man wanted—for profitable, enjoyable task". . . . Correct. No! Wait a mo', wait a mo'!

Isabel What is it? What is it?

Very Says don't waste money—will come round himself immediately . . .

CURTAIN

ACT II

The same. Late afternoon, about a year later

The shop looks completely different, and much less crowded. A lot of the former stock has gone—though the stuffed ostrich is there—and been replaced by new articles including several pieces of antique children's furniture: a high-chair, an oak cradle, a rocking-horse, one or two dolls, etc.

Henry is sitting with two clipboards of papers. Isabel is unpacking a carton of newspaper-wrapped Staffordshire figures, and placing them on a table to appraise them

Henry (*impatiently*) Do stop darting about, woman, and pay attention.

Isabel I must decide how much to pay for this Staffordshire before the owner comes back.

Henry But little Gloria may be here any moment. We must ensure my Nursery List is complete.

Isabel You've been drawing it up for three months: it must be complete. Anyhow, Very's not taking delivery of little Gloria for at least another half-hour.

Henry Well, if there's something missing in an emergency don't blame me.

Isabel We've got everything she could possibly ever want. Oh, except cod-liver oil. Add that.

Henry Oh, not cod-liver oil! I remember it from when I was a boy: the whole place'll stink like a fish-factory.

Isabel Four pounds for this hideous girl with sheep. Or is it a dog? A stupid-looking animal, anyhow; put three.

Henry Well, make up your mind, make up your mind.

Isabel Three-fifty. And there won't be any stink because it'll be in capsules. For God's sake forget all those ridiculous ideas of when you were a boy. Little Gloria's a space-age baby, and we're going to bring her up in a space-age way.

Henry There's no "we" about it. I agreed because it'll keep you too busy to go to sales, but I'm not having anything whatsoever to do with her.

Isabel Yes, I know, dear. Put down a new warm pair of slippers for yourself.

Henry Why?

Isabel I don't want you catching cold when you paddle out to attend to her in the night.

Henry Now, look here, Isabel . . .

Very rushes in with a sheet of paper

Very Quick! Quick! Been phoning. Yours *caput*.

Henry Not again? (*He picks up the receiver and listens*) Yes, the blasted thing's dead.

Very Quick. Quick. Japanese dealer in shop. Bought masses. Glasses so thick doesn't see properly, thank God. (*Thrusting the paper at him*) Add up. I can't.

Henry I don't wonder. What are all these five shillingses and sixpences?

Very Proper, decent, understandable, coinage.

Henry Oh, well, perhaps Japanese won't notice. (*He starts adding up*)

Very Hurry; may decamp without paying.

Isabel You haven't left him alone in the shop?

Very Had to.

Isabel But where's your new assistant?

Very Gone. Would loll.

Isabel Would what?

Very (*demonstrating*) Loll. Stuck hat-pin in his bottom. Never seen since.

Isabel But that's the third this month.

Very Fourth. (*Showing on fingers*) Chewer. Pincher. Smeller. Loller. Maybe fifth lucky. (*To Henry*) Ready?

Henry (*fiercely*) Shh!

Very (*to Isabel in her penetrating whisper*) Anything you want unload Tokyo?

Isabel Masses. He wouldn't be interested in—(*nodding towards the ostrich*)—Minnie, I suppose?

Very That neck. Difficult packing.

Isabel And the legs, I suppose. I'm afraid she'll be buried with me.

Henry There you are. Two hundred and eleven pounds.

Very Alleluia! (*To Henry*) Gratitude. (*She goes to the door*)

Henry You're sure Gloria's going to bring the baby to you at four?

Very Or my name's not Violet, Patience, Very Hesketh-Palmer.

Very hurries out

Henry I still think it'd have been wiser to have had the baby brought straight here.

Isabel No, no, Very's right. If Gloria cried, I'd have cried—the baby would've been awash. This way it'll be easier for all of us.

Henry If there's not some appalling muddle, which I'll bet my bottom dollar there will be.

Isabel She's not nearly as scatty as she likes to appear. Look at the success she's made of "Fakes".

Henry God knows how.

Isabel (*fervently*) And I only hope He forgets when she gets to the gates.

Henry (*suspiciously*) What d'you mean?

Isabel Nothing. (*Unwrapping another figure*) What a lovely man; wish I'd known him. Must be worth fifteen with such a glorious chin. Why aren't you reading out your list?

Henry Because you damn well don't give me a chance.

Isabel You'd got as far as the sleeping-bag.

Henry (*reading from the list*) "Wool bootees."

Isabel Yes, four pairs.

Henry "Matinée jacket." What the hell's that?

Isabel Never mind; we've got it. (*Unwrapping*) Four pounds for this damp-looking female.

Henry "Bucket for soiled nappies." Oh, my God! Don't expect me to touch it.

Isabel I shan't let you touch little Gloria if you're not careful.

Henry I'm not going to.

Isabel Yes, you are; you're going to help me bath her tonight.

Henry I am not!

Isabel Please, dear. It'll be a bit of an ordeal the first time. You did say you'd help originally.

Henry When it was Robin, Jenny's baby. She's sort of related; it would have been different.

Isabel Well, you have to admit it was just as well we had Gloria's to fall back on. I know Jenny says the Nairobi specialist promises she'll be fit to travel in six months, but she may write that just to cheer us up.

Henry I warned her elephants were dangerous.

Isabel Any animal's dangerous when it's doing that. (*Holding another figure*) This has its head stuck on! Talk about dealers being dishonest, the public are far worse. He swore they were all perfect. Three pounds. No fifty pee off for trying to deceive me: two-fifty.

Adrian comes in from the street door with a small parcel, and something he hides behind his back

Adrian Has little Gloria arrived?

Isabel No, ages yet.

Henry Got it?

Adrian (*giving him the parcel*) Yes.

Isabel I thought you were supposed to be delivering pictures.

Henry I asked him to buy something I read about at the same time.

Isabel What?

Henry If you must know it's a Tinkle Block.

Isabel A what?

Henry (*unwrapping it*) Want to see for myself. (*He produces the toy*) Ah, yes. Splendid. Here. (*He rolls it towards Adrian*)

Adrian Nice noise. (*He rolls it back to Henry*)

Henry Rolls well. And beautifully smooth to touch. (*He rolls it back to Adrian*)

Adrian Pretty colours. (*He rolls it back to Henry*)

Henry No sharp edges if put in the mouth.

Isabel Which of you is it for?

Henry It's an educational toy to counter-balance all your ridiculous lambs and rabbits.

Adrian (*embarrassedly producing a bunch of flowers*) These are a few flowers I brought for the occasion.

Isabel Oh, that is kind. Isn't that a nice thought, Father?

Henry Isn't she a bit young to appreciate them?

Isabel They're for me, you booby. It's sweet of you, Adrian. Thank you. Oh, the hot-water bottle for her cot. (*She picks it up*) Watch, both of you; I want to show you how to fill it.

Henry I was filling hot-water bottles before you were born.

Isabel The wrong way. Now, look. (*Demonstrating*) First put it down flat on the table—as there isn't one free we'll have to do it on the floor. (*Getting down*) Push it down with the flat of your hand to get out the air . . .

Henry As effective against your tummy, and far less trouble.

Isabel One is the method followed by hospital nurses, the other by fools who get burnt. (*Demonstrating*) Then fill almost full—from a jug, not the kettle . . .

There is a tremendous kicking at the front door

Henry What the hell's that?

Isabel (*going to the door*) The Customs and Excise men! Hide the Stock Book.

Adrian looks out

Adrian It's all right. (*He opens the door*)

Very marches in carrying a well-wrapped baby, and a basket of shawls and toys, etc.

Very (*singing*) "She was one of the early birds
        And I was one of the worms."

Isabel (*breathlessly*) You've got her?

Very (*presenting the bundle*) Gloria in all her glory.

They crowd round

Isabel She's sweet!

Henry Ugly little brute.

Isabel How can you? She's beautiful.

Adrian Rather small.

Isabel You were small at three months.

Very Eyes like a little houri.

Isabel Can I hold her?

Very She's your little houri. (*She passes her to Isabel*)

Isabel I'm going to cry.

Henry Oh, my God!

The baby starts screaming

Isabel Now look what you've done.

Henry Fine pair of lungs.

Very Probably future opera star. Marvellous. See her already: alone in spotlight, knee deep in roses and lilies of the valley. Italian lessons necessary.

Isabel I don't think we need book them just yet.

Very Had friend: know wonderful tips. Two teaspoons of mustard before main aria.

Henry The only tip we want is how to stop her yelling.

Isabel It's a lovely yell.

They all stand watching her scream

Adrian You don't think she's got a pin stuck in her somewhere?

Isabel You're as old-fashioned as Father; no-one uses pins nowadays.

They again watch her

Henry (*suddenly*) Nappy rash!

Very What?

Henry That's why she's crying—nappy rash.

Isabel (*having glanced at him strangely*) I shouldn't think so. But I'll powder her well after her bath tonight.

Henry Dry her properly, and it's not necessary. And if she's not dry it can clog in the folds of her skin and cause torture.

Isabel I wondered what those books were you kept smuggling in; thought they were pornography. (*Rocking the baby*) There, there, no need to worry, pet; we have a child-expert with us.

Very Probably first tooth. Good sign. Napoleon born with two.

Henry Her gums must be massaged with teething jelly.

Isabel (*suddenly dumping the baby into his arms*) You get on with it, then.

Henry (*aghast*) Don't be absurd, Isabel. I can't . . .

The baby suddenly becomes silent

(*Delightedly*) She likes being with me. Don't you, little Gloria? She's a dear little baby. Pretty as a rose. (*Raising her in his arms*) Hup we go . . .

Isabel (*seizing her*) No, we don't; you'll make her sick. (*Going to the stairs*) I'm going to put her in her cot before she gets too excited.

Henry See that it lies north–south—prevents premature puberty.

Isabel You can come and watch, Adrian.

Adrian (*doubtfully*) Oh, can I? (*But he follows her up the stairs*)

Isabel She must get used to you from the beginning because she's going to see a lot of you.

Adrian (*unhappily*) Oh—good . . .

Henry I shouldn't give her anything at first except perhaps a little boiled drinking-water.

Isabel (*eyes wide open*) Thank you.

Very Sweet dreams, little houri.

Isabel, the baby, and Adrian go off at the top of the stairs

Henry Doesn't "houri" mean what I think it means?

Very You sailors! Also "nymph of Persian paradise".

Henry You do come out with the most extraordinary knowledge.

Very How kind. But bootless trifles. Far rather be master of facts like you.

Henry I merely assimilated what the sea taught me.

Very Far more, far more. Look at quickness of baby lore. Marvellous.

Henry Thank you.

Very Much admire men who don't sink back. Keep abreast. Keep figure.

(*She sits on the sofa*)

Henry Very kind. Talking of figures, you've never brought your books for me to check.

Very Can't weigh more than twelve stone.

Henry Just over eleven-and-a-half, actually.

Very No stomach at all.

Henry Because I've done regular exercises since I was a midshipman.

Very Such strength of mind.

Henry Oh, nothing elaborate. Just contracting and expanding the appropriate tummy muscles.

Very Show.

Henry Well—it's just . . . (*He demonstrates*)

Very Marvellous.

Henry Simple; that's the point. Can be done while waiting for the bus.

Very Such economy.

Henry Which brings us back to your books.

Very (*patting the sofa for him to sit beside her*) Another snippet of knowledge.

Henry sits

Love silver hair.

Henry That's very kind. It has kept rather well.

Very Can hardly refrain stroking.

Henry (*a little warily*) So what about me coming along and casting an eye over your ledgers?

Very So authoritative.

Henry Shall I do that?

Very Welcome any hour, day—(*emphasizing*)—or night, Henry.

Henry suddenly fully realizes what is happening. But as he is about to get up, she plonks her bag in his lap, and starts taking out the bottles

Izarra. That's what's needed.

Henry In the afternoon?

Very (*pouring out*) Not set times for drink—or love.

Henry To return to the subject of your accounts . . .

Very (*lifting her glass*) Here's to sea-blue eyes.

Henry (*falling into the trap*) Green, actually.

Very Never! (*With a little beckoning wave*) Closer inspection.

Henry Oh, well, if you see them as blue . . .

Very No, no, exactitude necessary. (*Leaning towards him*) Open wide . . .

As Henry draws back in alarm he is saved by the telephone ringing

Henry May be important. (*He leaps up and goes to the telephone*)

Very (*furiously*) Bloody invention.

Henry (*into the receiver*) Admiral Lane. . . . What? You'll have to speak louder. . . . Not as loud as that. And slower. . . . Don't know what you're talking about. (*Calling*) Isabel! Phone. (*To Very*) Some foreign idiot. A lot of mumbo-jumbo about fakes.

Very (*leaping up*) Scotch and soda! Japanese?

Henry Could easily be.

Very (*snatching the telephone*) Mr Fung? . . . It's self: Hesketh-Palmer. Delayed by slight accident. Return imminent.

Isabel hurries down the stairs

Isabel I thought the phone was out of order?

Henry Evidently the fools have seen to it. (*Fervently*) Thank God!

Very (*into the receiver*) Scotch and soda! Coming. (*Putting down the telephone*) Forgot. Left Japan packing. Now shop full, phone ringing, chaos reigning . . .

Very rushes out

Henry Never leave me alone with that woman again.

Isabel (*amused*) Do you mean she . . . ?

Henry Yes. Haven't been so scared since I was torpedoed.

Isabel How very funny.

Henry Wasn't funny at all. She nearly scuttled me. And I never even saw the attack coming.

Isabel I have—for months.

Henry You might have warned me.

Isabel I thought you were old enough to look after yourself.

Henry It was so unexpected. Before tea . . .

Isabel I wish I could have seen!

Henry You laugh any more, and I shan't help you with your baby. How is she?

Isabel Marvellous. I am lucky, Father. I'm thrilled with her.

Henry Let's go and have a look, shall we?

They start up the stairs

Isabel I do hope she won't take against Adrian. He will insist on singing "Rockabye Baby", very off-key . . .

Very rushes in

Very Sound the alarm! Adversity! Mr Fung half-demented. Three-quarter incoherent.

Isabel Do you want me to come and help?

Very No, no; it's you need help.

Henry What d'you mean?

Very Jenny's on way.

Henry Jenny!

Isabel Jenny's in Kenya.

Very No, Cromwell Road.

Isabel What are you talking about?

Very Your phone bonkers, so she rang "Fakes". I Gloria—delivery; Mr Fung inadequate answer-service.

Henry And she told him she was on her way?

Very Fung thinks. Suddenly better. Sudden cancelled passage. So sudden: whoosh!

Isabel But if she was at the air-terminal she may be here any moment!

Very With baby!

Henry My God!

Very Now two babies.

Isabel I can't have two babies!

Very Calm, calm. Easily fixed.

Isabel It's not easily fixed! We never told Jenny about there being another one. (*Rushing round collecting the shawl and toys*) She mustn't know: she'd be furious.

Very (*moving to the door*) Daren't leave Fung; and woman in mink. Stall, stall . . .

Henry No, no, we must draw up a plan now; we can't have the place crawling with babies.

Very Alleluia! Lady Colestar.

Isabel Madeleine, of course! She'd be only too willing to take one.

Very Deal temporarily. Self back when Japan and Mink dispatched. Alleluia! Disaster averted; blessings earned . . .

Very rushes out

Henry It's all very well her alleluiaing. Say Lady Colestar doesn't like the look of it?

Isabel She's so desperate she'd accept a little gorilla. Anyhow if she didn't, I know at least half-a-dozen others who'd snatch at the opportunity. Since we've sold more children's things you've no idea how many women have confided that . . .

Henry (*interrupting impatiently*) Never mind women's confidences now. It still means we shall have two babies till it's all fixed up.

Isabel There's really no reason why we shouldn't keep them both for a day or two; there's plenty of everything.

Henry No, you don't! I know you—you'd end up by wanting both of them. I'll put up with one's messing and yelling. Two, no.

Isabel It'd be awfully selfish, anyhow, with Madeleine almost ill with longing. It'll be lovely surprising her!

Henry With which one?

Isabel Well—Jenny's, I suppose.

Henry It doesn't seem right to give away my own god-daughter's.

Isabel But we've accepted little Gloria: I love her.
Henry Damn difficult.

The street door opens, and a Girl appears

Isabel (*sotto voce*) Damn, I'll get rid of her. (*To the Girl*) I'm afraid we're just about to close, but can I help you?
Girl You can—mostly by recognizing me.
Henry There is something familiar . . .
Isabel Jenny!

It is. She is completely changed, having cut her hair, and being plainly and smartly dressed

Henry *Donner und!* So it is. What have you done to yourself?
Jenny What you've always wanted—become nice and ordinary.
Henry Good God!
Isabel Come in, darling. But where's the baby?
Jenny (*awkwardly, as she is throughout the scene*) I'll tell you about him in a moment. Let me look at you first. (*Kissing them*) You both look smashing.
Henry Where's your hair?
Isabel Made into one of those awful fly-whisks, I suppose?
Jenny It was too hot . . .
Isabel I think it suits you. You look lovely. Have you quite recovered?
Jenny I'm fine.
Henry Your letters were very vague. What exactly happened?
Jenny Oh, don't let's talk about it. It's all happily over.
Isabel You've been very naughty altogether. Never sent any photos of little Robin.
Jenny We lived in the wild.
Henry (*suspiciously*) We?
Jenny Yes. That's partly what I've come to tell you.
Isabel What?
Jenny Prepare for a surprise. I'm married.
Isabel Darling, how wonderful! When?
Jenny Just last week.
Henry (*anxiously*) White?
Jenny Very.
Henry Thank God!
Isabel Someone you met out there?
Jenny No, here. You've met him too, actually.
Henry We have?
Jenny Bill.
Isabel Not Bill of *The Times*?
Jenny Yes.
Isabel How marvellous! He was a charming man—beautiful lobes to his ears.

Henry Damn his lobes. Who is he?

Isabel The father of the baby, darling.

Henry Oh! *The Times* newspaper.

Jenny He was at a complete dead end then, so on the spur of the moment travelled out to Kenya with me. We naturally saw lots of each other, and —it happened.

Henry What?

Isabel You're worse than Adrian. They fell for each other.

Henry Oh.

Jenny He got into "tea", and now they've transferred him to a super office job in Edinburgh. So of course I came back too, and thought the first thing I'd do is clear things up with you.

Isabel It's wonderful news.

Jenny It's not.

Isabel Why?

Jenny Oh, dear, you're not going to like this, and I feel awful about it, and wish I hadn't, but it seemed a solution at the time . . .

Henry Stop babbling, girl. What are you trying to say?

Jenny (*to Isabel*) I'm terribly sorry, but—I've never had a baby.

Isabel Never had one!

Jenny I lost it. (*In a rush*) And between worry at your disappointment, and fear you might make me start another, I thought it best to pretend I'd had one, and then keep away till you'd got over the idea.

Isabel All invention?

Henry What a deceitful thing to do.

Jenny (*to Isabel*) Are you terribly disappointed?

Isabel (*righteously*) Of course I'm disappointed. Deeply disappointed. And hurt. You know how I wanted one.

Jenny I do—I feel awful.

Adrian starts to come down the stairs, carrying a tray with a mug

Adrian She's a little restless, Mrs Merryweather, so I thought I'd heat some milk.

Isabel (*nervously*) Oh, good. (*To Jenny*) Adrian's very sweetly given us—a kitten . . .

Adrian drops the mug off the tray

Adrian Oh, I'm so sorry . . .

The baby starts to cry loudly, off

Jenny That doesn't sound like a kitten.

Isabel (*feebly*) No, it doesn't very, does it?

Jenny It's a baby.

Isabel Er, it does sound like that.

Jenny You're not going to say Adrian gave you that?

Isabel (*crossly*) Of course not.

Jenny Then what's it doing up there?

Isabel (*to Henry*) Help, father.

Henry (*to Adrian, fiercely*) What was the date of the Battle of Trafalgar?

The baby cries louder

Isabel There's no reason why I shouldn't have a baby up there, is there?

Jenny D'you mean you've got a baby already?

Isabel Well, in a sort of way, yes. Sit down and I'll explain.

Jenny You've had a baby all the time?

Isabel No, no, no. Not all the time; it's only just come. I do wish you'd sit down.

Jenny (*excitedly*) I'm not going to sit down.

Isabel I'm terribly sorry, darling.

Jenny I'm not. It's marvellous. You've no idea how marvellous. (*Flinging her arms round them in turn*) I love you, I love you, I love you . . .

Jenny runs out of the shop

Isabel Some sort of African fever, do you think?

Henry Relief at being let off the hook, I'd guess.

Adrian I'm awfully sorry if it was something I did, Mrs Merryweather.

Isabel It wasn't, Adrian. It's all turned out rather well really. (*Sadly*) Except for poor Madeleine.

Henry What she's never heard of she can't grieve over.

Isabel That's true. (*Listening*) There's certainly someone grieving; I'd better go and do something about it.

Adrian Shall I heat the milk?

Isabel (*going up the stairs*) Let me see first.

Henry (*following her*) Probably been given the wrong diet. We must carefully balance the protective foods, the body-building foods, and the energy-giving foods.

Isabel (*going up the stairs*) Must we?

Henry Lots of wholemeal bread, and liver. That'll give her energy, and see her bowels work properly.

Henry and Isabel go off

Adrian sees his flowers, and picking them up starts to unwrap them

The door opens and Mrs Barry comes in carrying a baby. She looks much the same as in Act I, but seems uneasy

Mrs Barry Good afternoon. May I look round?

Adrian Yes, of course. Oh, it's Mrs Barry, isn't it?

Mrs Barry How clever. I'm afraid I've hardly been in since I sold Mrs Merryweather that Derby tea-set. I was always afraid it might stare guiltily at me.

Adrian Someone bought it only the other day, as it happens.

Mrs Barry Oh, good.

Adrian Can I show you anything?

Mrs Barry No, no, just browsing.

Adrian The baby looks very well.

Mrs Barry Thank you.

Adrian Not grown very much really though?

Mrs Barry (*crossly*) He's a very good size for three months.

Adrian Three months? Oh, it isn't Boo-Boo?

Mrs Barry Of course not. It's her little brother, Cyril.

Adrian Oh, I see.

Mrs Barry Actually—I do hope you don't mind—I did want to browse—but I also wondered if I could—(*lowering her voice*)—use the toilet.

Adrian (*embarrassed*) Oh. Well, uum—Mrs Merryweather doesn't—I mean, are you really . . .?

Mrs Barry Yes, I am. I've been out shopping all day.

Adrian Oh Lord. Well, as you're a sort of customer—I suppose it's all right, just once. (*Opening the back door*) It's the first door on the left.

Mrs Barry Thank you so much. (*She dumps the baby into Adrian's arms*) I won't be a moment.

Adrian No, no—Mrs Barry . . . !

But Mrs Barry has gone out of the door

Adrian walks about gingerly with the baby. It starts to whimper

Now, none of that, Cyril. I'm not at all in the mood to cope. Look—flowers. (*He waves them in front of Cyril*) Pretty flowers. (*Cyril starts to wail*) Little pest. (*He sees the bottle of Izarra, dips the corner of his handkerchief in it, and puts it into the baby's mouth. Immediately there is silence*) Enjoy it, because I don't suppose you'll ever get it again.

Mrs Barry comes back

Adrian whips the handkerchief out of the baby's mouth

Mrs Barry I've just remembered; I've left my bag in the butcher's. I won't be a moment.

Adrian No! Mrs Barry . . . (*He stretches out the bundle to her*)

But Mrs Barry goes out

The baby starts to wail again

All right; I don't care if you become a lush—would you like the green one for a change? (*He again dips the handkerchief, and puts it in the baby's mouth. Silence*) Which is the nicest? (*He pretends to listen*) Really? Well, I don't know that I can accept the judgement of one so young. I'll have to see for myself. (*He pours himself out a glass*) I've never drunk before evening in my life. But much longer with this outfit, Cyril, and I should think I'll be having it for breakfast. (*He swallows it at a gulp*) And to think a year ago I thought it strong. Have another dip to keep me company.

Very bursts in

Very Fulmination at "Fakes". (*Seeing the baby*) Oh, it's arrived. Good. Have rung Madeleine Colestar. Hysterical with joy. But on way. Can you add?

Adrian What?

Very Japanese figures. Fung fallen for me. Bought a whole lot more. Joy great, but sums staggering. Rush and compute. I'll take baby. (*She takes the baby from him*)

Adrian Well, I'd much rather, actually. She won't be long.

Very No, should be here any moment.

Adrian (*puzzled*) You'll explain to her?

Very Clearly. (*Waving him out*) Off to the Orient. Off to the Orient.

Adrian goes out of the shop

(*Rocking the baby*) Well, Robin Redbreast. Hope your life is as exciting as mine. What's dirty rag? Oh, ka-ka. (*She takes out Adrian's handkerchief, and gingerly drops it into the waste-paper basket*)

The baby wails

Not pretty noise, Robin. What is it? Achy-packeys? I know. Herbs from the Alps. Cures all. (*She pours out a glass of Izarra, dips her finger in it, and puts it in the baby's mouth. Silence*) Beats Mum's milk, eh? Now Auntie for her achy-packeys. (*She swallows her drink and starts to pour another*)

Lady Colestar hurries in

Lady Colestar It can't be true—it can't be true!

Very Then I'm a Dutchman in wooden clogs. (*Giving her the baby*) Sex, male. Name Robin. Dampness temporary.

Lady Colestar (*breathlessly*) I can't believe it.

Very As substantial as self. And is that something.

Lady Colestar He's gorgeous. I'm going to faint.

Very Give back then.

Lady Colestar No, I shan't put him down for hours. (*Examining him*) He's angelic. Look at that sweet little nose. A bit red. Are you cold, my precious? Mummy'll give you her fur. (*She slips off her fur wrap, and, putting it round him, sits nursing him on her lap*) Is that better, Robin, baby? (*To Very*) How can I ever thank you?

Very Not me, Isabel, Jenny. (*Looking round*) Where, one knows not.

Lady Colestar He's marvellous. I shall give a celebration party that'll put Buckingham Palace in the shade.

Very Rapture. Shall wear Mandarin's robe. Or perhaps fish-tail train, plumes in hair ... (*She is interrupted by the return of Mrs Barry*)

Mrs Barry enters

Mrs Barry Sorry to have been . . . (*She breaks off*) Oh!

Very We can help you?

Mrs Barry Well, I've come to collect my baby.

Very Wrong shop. No babies. But excellent stock. (*Waving round the shop*) Browse, browse. (*To Lady Colestar*) Isabel overloaded nursery rubbish. Am sure loan very——

Mrs Barry (*interrupting*) You don't understand: I've come for Cyril.

Very Cyril who?

Mrs Barry Cyril Barry.

Very Unheard of.

Mrs Barry (*getting excited*) My boy. I left him here.

Very No, no—somewhere else.

Mrs Barry I tell you it was here. Where's the boy?

Very What boy?

Mrs Barry (*getting hysterical*) The boy who was here.

Very You've boys on the brain. (*Trying to usher her to the door*) Suggest go home. Do some gardening.

Mrs Barry (*avoiding her*) I'm not going home without my boy. I know it was here. (*Looking round distractedly*) I remember the things. The toilet's there.

Very Well, use it, then go home.

Mrs Barry (*wailing*) I don't want it, I want my boy. It's like some terrible dream. (*Wandering round*) But I'm sure it was this shop. I remember the ostrich. I remember . . . (*She suddenly sees the baby on Lady Colestar's lap where it is almost hidden in fur*) What's that?

Very Belongs to customer. Now. (*Firmly*) Farewell.

Mrs Barry No, I demand to see what she's got there.

Very Demand refused. Hop off!

Mrs Barry I insist. I insist on seeing!

Lady Colestar I really don't mind if she's so keen. (*Lifting up the bundle*) There you are—my baby Robin.

Mrs Barry Your baby Robin! It's my baby Cyril. (*She seizes him and hugs him to her*) Cyril, Cyrily, my baby, my baby . . .

Very Return baby at once.

Lady Colestar (*to Mrs Barry*) You're making a mistake, my dear; that's my baby.

Mrs Barry I know my baby! You're both mad.

Very Who's mad immaterial. Baby Robin. Not Cyril. (*Taking it and giving it to Madeleine*) Belongs Colestar.

Mrs Barry (*again snatching Cyril back*) He does not! He's mine! It's a plot; it's a plot. I'm going.

Very (*standing in her way*) With baby, not.

Lady Colestar Sit down, dear, and let's talk it over calmly.

Mrs Barry I will not sit down. It's a nightmare.

Very Then wake, realize mistake; hand back baby.

Mrs Barry I can't bear it! Help! (*Rapping on the window*) Help, help! Police!

Isabel and Henry hurry down the stairs

Henry What the hell's happening?

Mrs Barry (*rushing to Isabel*) It's me, Mrs Barry, Mrs Merryweather. Thank God. Thank God. These two creatures are trying to steal my baby.

Isabel Oh, I'm sure not.

Very Demented woman trying to take Lady Colestar's baby.

Isabel What baby?

Very Scotch and soda! Don't you start. Jenny's baby.

Isabel Jenny hasn't got a baby.

Very (*sinking into a chair*) Treat for shock—treat for shock.

Mrs Barry I know it's my baby, I know it!

Henry (*trying to calm her*) Well, know it quieter, woman.

Mrs Barry Same shawl. (*Showing Isabel*) Hole Albert burnt with cigarette.

Isabel Yes, yes, I'm sure it's your baby. It's all just some little mistake. Now I suggest you take Boo-Boo home . . .

Mrs Barry (*wailing*) It's not Boo-Boo, it's Cyril.

Isabel Well, take whichever it is home, and I'll come round later and explain.

Mrs Barry (*hurrying to the door*) No, don't come near. You're all mad. Should be closed down. Yes, that's it. Shall tell police to close you down . . .

Mrs Barry goes out

Very Empty threat. Know Albert. Fiddles goods from factory. Won't allow her contact police.

Henry Well, I suppose that's something.

Isabel What on earth have you been doing?

Lady Colestar (*in a daze*) My baby? Where's my baby?

Very (*to Isabel*) Found baby here. You said Jenny bringing baby . . .

Isabel But she didn't.

Henry She hasn't got a baby.

Very Certain?

Isabel Quite certain.

The door opens, and Jenny comes in happily carrying a bundle

Jenny Look! A surprise. My baby!

Very (*rising*) Shall return "Fakes". Japanese confusion nothing compared Bedlam here.

Isabel No, don't desert me!

Henry You told us you didn't have a baby.

Jenny Yes, I'm awfully sorry, darlings. Actually I did have one, but . . .

Jenny is interrupted by Very taking the baby from her

Very All's well ends well. There. (*She puts it into Lady Colestar's arms*)

Jenny No! (*She takes it back again*) I want to keep it; that's just the point.

Lady Colestar (*rising*) I think I'm about to become deranged . . .

Very (*genuinely distressed*) Dear lady, dear lady, even self speechless with dismay.

Lady Colestar I must lie flat.

Isabel Yes, of course. (*Leading her to the stairs*) Come up to my bedroom, you poor thing.

Very Atonement or hari-kari.

Lady Colestar In silence, in the dark.

Isabel I'll draw the curtains, and I've some lovely old-fashioned smelling salts—

Isabel and Lady Colestar go off upstairs

Very (*beating her breast*) Brute. Brute. Punishment and penance. No fudge for six weeks.

Jenny I'm so sorry if I'm the cause of all this. I thought you'd like to see my baby.

Henry It's the shock of seeing something that doesn't exist.

Jenny I only said it didn't because the elephants changed me. Or I suppose it was Bill, really. When the baby arrived everything was suddenly solved. I knew it was what I'd really always looked for. (*Looking at the baby*) He's such a super baby—I couldn't have handed him over. So I thought it best to pretend he hadn't arrived.

Very Shows ingenuity.

Jenny Then when I heard you'd already got one I thought it was safe to produce mine.

Henry With Isabel about it's never wise to assume anything. When Miss Hesketh-Palmer's about, too, it's fatal.

Very Where's a Christian name?

Henry I've—never been much for Christian names.

Very Lessons must commence.

Jenny I'll leave you. I want to see your baby, anyhow.

Henry (*hastily*) She didn't mean it literally.

Jenny (*starting up the stairs*) All the same I'll go up if I may.

Henry (*hastily following*) I'll show you . . .

Jenny exits up the stairs

Very The telephone won't always ring, Henry.

Henry (*after a scared glance at her*) The nursery's a bit difficult to find . . .

Very Second, apt, baptismal name: Patience!

Henry scuttles off after Jenny

Very goes to the telephone and dials

"Fakes"? Adrian? . . . Me. How goes? Tonight? Certainly not! Nor any other night. (*Hastily*) But don't say that: he might reduce buying. . . . Then say singing *Lucia di Lammermoor* at Covent Garden.

Isabel comes down the stairs

Ring when coast clear. (*She puts down the telephone*) Pressing dinner invitation from Fung.

Isabel Are you going?

Very What? Lose honour for raw fish and lychees? (*She shakes her head vigorously*) Besides: ghastly conscience Madeleine. (*She sits on the sofa*)

Isabel Yes, she's terribly upset, poor dear.

Very Must make restitution.

Isabel But how can we?

Very Baby essential.

Isabel Jenny'll never give up hers.

Very Alternative—(*glancing upstairs*)—little houri in Nursery.

Isabel (*strongly*) And she's staying in Nursery! I'm so upset for Madeleine I'll do anything for her, but she's not having little Gloria.

Very Adamant?

Isabel Adamant. (*She sits in the armchair*)

Very Then next novation.

Isabel I really haven't any ideas left.

Very Phooey! Self; bottomless well.

Isabel (*crossly*) Then let down your bucket. (*She ponders*)

Very rocks from side to side in concentration

Isabel Anything?

Very Preliminary seethings.

Isabel I wish you'd have them without rocking about; you make me feel giddy.

Very Must get juices flowing.

They go on thinking

Alleluia!

Isabel What?

Very Supermarkets.

Isabel What about them?

Very Always babies left outside.

Isabel (*horrified*) But they belong to people.

Very One bomb, all gone.

Isabel What's a bomb got to do with it?

Very Hitler'd take all; we only take one.

Isabel It's got nothing to do with Hitler.

Very (*darkly*) Ah, you didn't know him.

Isabel Neither did you.

Very But will when I meet him. (*With relish*) Then, Adolf, then!

Isabel (*faintly*) Don't you think . . .

Very (*interrupting*) Every night in bath—between soaping foot, and other foot—refine torture. Best part of day.

Isabel Well, let's leave all that till bath time. We'll also leave the babies outside supermarkets. They've got mothers and fathers who own and need them.

Very (*cheerfully*) Alleluia! Solution! Child ill-treated by parents.

Isabel Eh?

Very Act of Mercy. Remove. Give to Madeleine.

Isabel You couldn't possibly!

Very Phooey! Put on uniform, march in, say "Department of Health and Social Security", march out with baby. Or alternative watertight scheme.

Isabel Oh, I'm sure you could! I mean you mustn't.

Very Why? Cruel parents punished, baby saved, Madeleine overjoyed.

Isabel But they may love their baby really.

Very Then why ill-treat it? Argument flawless; prepare for planning.

Isabel I'm sure it's not flawless. And I won't prepare.

Very If scared, safe job only; chauffeur of get-away vehicle.

Isabel There won't be any get-away vehicle, and I won't be its chauffeur! I won't be anything. And you're not to, either.

Very Too late. Full steam up.

Isabel Well, I'll let some out. If you won't promise to drop the whole thing I shall tell Father about your books.

Very You wouldn't!

Isabel See how much further you'd get with him when he knows you haven't made them up for at least six weeks.

Very (*after a moment's consideration*) Soon remedied. Shall have a little fire.

Isabel It won't burn other things. I shall tell him if you insist.

Very Elucidate.

Isabel Such as how you got a very beautiful Chelsea plate for almost nothing at a sale because at the viewing you drew cracks on it in pencil.

Very (*with dignity*) Fabrication put about by Antique Dealers Society as excuse for non-membership.

Isabel Then what about that chess-set you got for a song? Because the Red Queen was missing, And where was she? In your handbag.

Very (*shaking her head*) A fortuitous misapprehension.

Isabel You just might bamboozle him into believing that, I suppose. But all your plausibility won't get round that little incident of "receiving stolen property".

Very (*her face falling*) Never knew you knew.

Isabel He brought it here first. I didn't dare.

Very ponders for a moment

Very Weapons unfair, but defeat overwhelming. No act of mercy.

Isabel Thank you. No ill-will either, I hope?

Very (*tapping Isabel's cheek*) Delighted find unexpected steel behind satin. (*Her face falling again*) But Madeleine?

Isabel It's awful. What are we going to do?

The shop door opens, and the Old Man comes in

As usual he takes no notice of them, but shuffles round peering closely. Nearing Very he offers the paper bag.

Old Man Glamorous today. Fondants.
Very Lovely. Two possible?
Old Man (*crossly*) No.

He continues his inspection and comes to an abrupt stop before the ostrich

Nice.
Isabel Isn't he? Even better without the dust.
Old Man How much?
Isabel (*amazed*) You mean price-wise? (*She rises*)
Old Man Of course.
Isabel Uum—sixteen pounds.
Old Man (*rapidly peeling notes off a roll*) I'll send my old woman to fetch it. (*Offering Isabel his bag*) Fondant?
Isabel Yes, I need it; thanks.
Old Man 'Bye for now.

The Old Man goes out, leaving the door ajar

Isabel It's a miracle! (*She sits again*) I've wanted to get rid of that more than anything we've ever had in the shop.
Very An omen! Want enough: Jericho falls. Get to work.
Isabel How?
Very (*pouring out*) Blessed herbs, plus concentration. (*Demonstrating*) Sip, and—(*swallowing*)—focus. Sip and focus.
Isabel On what?
Very Babies for Madeleine, of course.
Isabel (*nodding*) Sip, and focus.
Very Shorter sips, longer focusing.

They sip, and pause with their eyes closed

Gloria comes in with a parcel. She stares at them

Gloria Is it Yoga?
Very I hear a voice.
Gloria Of course you do, it's me.
Very Gloria! Welcome!
Isabel (*panicking*) No! You're not welcome. At least you are, of course, but it's no good. I mean if you'd phoned I'd have told you. Little Gloria's not here. Father's taken her to the seaside; in the north of Scotland.
Gloria Odd. (*Shrugging*) But I suppose if he wanted to . . .
Isabel You don't mind?
Gloria Not in the least, darling.
Isabel Oh, what a relief. I thought you'd changed your mind.

Gloria No. I just found in all the fuss I hadn't brought her favourite golly . . .

Very Coals to Newcastle.

Isabel But most kind of you to hump it. I hope you don't miss her too much?

Gloria Not at all. I'm sure it's awful, but just as there are blacks and whites so there are maternal and un-maternal. I find I'm, strongly, the last.

Isabel (*hugging her*) I love you more than ever.

Very Apologies hectic take-over earlier. Siege of Tokyo responsible.

Gloria Suited me, darling. Though I've masses to tell you.

Very (*hopefully*) Lurid?

Gloria Not very.

Very Curses. (*Patting the sofa*) Spill. We'll suck what juice we may.

Isabel You look wonderful.

Gloria Don't I? You were quite right about my figure. (*Turning to show it off*) Better than ever. (*She sits*)

Very (*in a whisper to Isabel*) Sip and focus.

Isabel Oh, yes!

Very Gloria. (*Meaningly*) Why not better still?

Gloria (*with narrowed eyes*) No, darlings.

Isabel You know what she means?

Gloria A sister for little Gloria?

Isabel Not for us. For a most deserving case with a wonderful home.

Gloria It'll have to stay empty. I'm not going through all that again.

Very Confinement; shelling peas.

Gloria Not the conceiving. That man!

Very Anxiety earn fee inhibiting.

Gloria It was no excuse for every boring detail of his school sex, his University sex, his Paris sex, and his no sex since. I could hardly keep awake.

Isabel They were so difficult to find—we had to use him.

Very Self thought strangely fascinating.

Gloria You only saw him with his clothes on, darling. But it wasn't that part I'm really complaining about. It was those awful last weeks. Talk about a Juggernaut . . .

Isabel (*looking around the shop*) We've one or two very nice new pieces.

Gloria Even with a friend breaking two tables last week I'm still over-crowded.

Very A sun-drenched sojourn in Jamaica?

Gloria Absolutely impossible, darling.

Isabel Why?

Gloria Well, first with my new figure I'm on tops as a model again. I hardly have time to change my eyelashes.

Very Self tried once; they fell into a sandwich.

Gloria And second, I've met the most drooly man. I mustn't even think of him in front of you.

Very (*eagerly*) Disclose particulars immediately.

Gloria Yesterday I had to go to an interview—about an F.F.N. on Concorde. Should be good: me nude and Concorde empty.

Isabel All seats will sell overnight.

Gloria Darling! Well, off I went, and there behind the desk was this palpitating throb.

Very (*holding her heart*) Sympathetic thumpings.

Gloria You'd both love him. He knows lots about antiques—he raved about my bedroom furnishings when he woke this morning.

Isabel Gratifying. I hope you gave him one of our cards.

Gloria But you see it means I couldn't possibly leave London.

Very Point taken. Ecstatically your part, gloomily our part. (*Excitedly*) But Alleluia!

Isabel Why?

Very Gloom pierced by Hesketh-Palmer flash. (*To Gloria*) A substitute.

Gloria For what?

Very Motherhood. Your girl-friends, Shepherd Market. Possible?

Gloria (*thinking*) Well, I suppose it wouldn't be impossible. Business is very quiet once the Motor Show's over.

Isabel You might find someone?

Gloria When I think of it, I'm certain—on the right conditions.

Isabel We could let her have a lovely room here—

Very —central heating and blower—

Isabel —flowers and breakfast in bed . . .

Gloria She'd need a lot more than that, darlings.

Lady Colestar comes downstairs

Lady Colestar I do apologize for being so silly. I feel slightly better; I'll totter home.

Isabel (*rising and going to her*) Oh, Madeleine, I was so sorry. But never mind—wonderful, wonderful news.

Lady Colestar I don't think I can stand any more wonderful news.

Very All arranged. Definite baby within the year.

Lady Colestar We'll talk about it some other time.

Very Understand hesitation. But this one copper-bottom guarantee. Certain delivery, or leap from Waterloo Bridge.

Isabel You don't just have our words. This lady promises, too.

Lady Colestar (*to Gloria*) You think there's a real chance?

Gloria As I was saying to them, if the terms are right.

Lady Colestar Oh, they would be right. If you can manage it, you can have anything.

Very (*quickly*) Reasonable. But finance unwise. Hidden award preferable.

Isabel An antique! Some lovely piece that'll go up and up in value.

Lady Colestar One of mine!

Isabel But you love them.

Lady Colestar Nothing compared to a baby. I shall need the rooms for nurseries anyhow. There'll have to be a great turn-out; you could have anything you liked.

Isabel No, no.

Very (*quickly*) Yes, yes.

Isabel Well, we'll see.

Lady Colestar Yes, there's lots of time. I still feel as if I'd had a major operation. (*Going to the door*) I rushed out leaving the dogs unwalked, and my husband up a ladder. I'll ring and arrange a quiet undisturbed discussion. But I'm thrilled. Thank you all so much.

Lady Colestar goes out

Gloria That was a bit jumping the gun, wasn't it?

Very Ensures your urgent action.

Gloria I must say it won't be so difficult if she'll exchange something really valuable. (*Thinking*) Florence'd jump at it.

Isabel She must be discreet.

Gloria Not Flo then. What about Carmen? Or better, Edna. No, Stella; she's a dear. None of them as beautiful as me, of course.

Very If Rubens unobtainable, copy must suffice.

Gloria Darling! Tell you what; I'll make a list, and then you can both come and I'll have them all round for drinks.

Isabel I suppose we really ought to have a man's opinion.

Very (*firmly*) Not Henry. Competition unfair.

Isabel They'd eat Adrian.

Gloria (*rising*) Well, that's your problem, darlings. (*Going to the door*) I'm meeting my drool again tonight: I must go and relax in readiness.

Isabel Do you think he'd help us pick?

Gloria Over my nude, dead body, darlings! 'Bye . . .

Gloria goes out

Very Splendid afternoon's work.

Isabel Yes, but for some reason I feel a little loose-taily.

Very Naturally necessary tie up minor . . . (*Breaking off*) Minor? Scotch and soda!

Isabel What?

Very What are little girls made of? Not only of the mother, alas.

Isabel Oh, my God, yes. A father.

Very Transient, but critical.

Isabel Do you think we should advertise again?

Very Fifteen pounds; three applicants, one queer?

Isabel I never imagined it'd be so difficult.

Very Blame bloody permissiveness.

Isabel What avenue didn't we explore before?

Very (*thinking*) Men. Where? The City. Clubs. Sauna Baths. Conveniences . . .

Isabel All so difficult to penetrate. I think individuals would be better. Who do we know?

Very Mr Fung would. But . . . (*She shakes her head vigorously*)

Isabel (*suddenly*) Bill! Of course. (*She dashes to the stairs and calls*) Jenny!

Very What Bill? Which Bill?

Isabel The one from *The Times*. Jenny's Bill. He's over.

Very Over what?

Isabel Here. To go into tea. It's terribly lucky.

Jenny appears at the top of the stairs

Jenny I'm just teaching Henry how to change nappies.

Isabel Only a moment, darling. Do you think Bill would oblige again?

Jenny How?

Isabel As a father.

Jenny Well, give us time.

Isabel No, I meant with someone else.

Jenny (*furiously*) Certainly not! I've never heard anything so disgusting in all my life.

Jenny goes off

Very Modern youth! When not permissive, prudes.

Isabel It's most ungrateful.

Very (*thoughtfully again*) Men. Where? (*Her attention is suddenly rivited*) One looking in window now.

Isabel If all the lookers came in and bought I'd be a millionaire.

Very Hitch up skirt. (*She goes to the window*)

Isabel Don't be absurd.

Very Could be one of the ones likes older women.

Isabel We want him as a father, not for me.

Very We want him, full-stop. (*She waves gaily*)

Isabel No, no, Very . . .

Very If no good himself may know someone— (*She makes beckoning motions*)

Isabel We can't possibly just ask him!

Very (*stopping her gestures*) No, we can't; little idiot's beetling off like bat out of hell.

Isabel Don't wonder with you behaving like a demented "Madam". In any case it's not a subject one can broach with a man one's never even seen before.

Very Wrapped in enough camouflage anything can be broached. In Rome when had audience with Pope . . . what about this one?

Isabel What one?

Very Dresden tea-pot examiner.

Isabel (*looking through the window*) Oh, yes. Rather dishy. Gorgeous Adam's apple.

Very More important: lusty.

Isabel I've seen him before somewhere.

Very Good. (*She waves vigorously*)

Isabel That doesn't mean I know him!

Very You can say you made a mistake.

Isabel You can. It's your mistake. And I hope you feel inventive—he looks tough.

Very Easy . . .

Ricky comes in

(*accusingly*) Where are my sheets?

Ricky Your sheets?

Very Sheets, Mr Arbuthnot, your laundry lost.

Ricky I'm not Mr Arbuthnot, lady, and I don't know what you're talking about, yerknow.

Very Not Mr Arbuthnot? (*Peering at him*) Truth. Far too good-looking. Apologies, apologies, multiple apologies.

Isabel My friend's rather—short-sighted.

Ricky It's O.K. I was coming in anyway, yerknow. I wanted to see if you had any new pictures.

Isabel Do look, please.

Ricky goes round the shop looking

Very (*in her idea of sotto voce*) Have affected entry; take advantage.

Isabel Let's not jump the gun and frighten—the stag. (*To Ricky*) Anything you like?

Ricky Yerknow I don't think there is really. Though while I'm here I've got to give my bird something; can I look at those boxes?

Isabel Yes, of course; I'll unlock the case. Excuse me a moment, Very.

Very Willingly. Opportunity reverse blood. (*She sits in the chair at the bureau putting her feet high above her head against it*)

Isabel unlocks the case

Isabel (*to Ricky*) Any particular one?

Ricky What about that green chappie?

Isabel (*giving it to him*) Isn't it pretty? Imitation malachite: five pounds.

Very (*to her feet*) She'll let him escape.

Ricky What about that china job?

Isabel Ah, my prize piece. Not china, enamel. A very rare Battersea scent-bottle. A little bust of Flora Macdonald.

Very (*getting to her feet*) Bet you a nail-cut knows more about former than latter.

Isabel (*after a worried glance at her*) It opens at the neck here, under her plaid scarf.

Ricky Say that's cute, yerknow. How much?

Isabel A bit expensive. Over a hundred.

Ricky *Pounds?*

Very About as much brain as a football. (*She suddenly sits bolt upright, and cranes to look at him intently. Then returns to her original position*)

Ricky (*putting it back*) Bit out of my price-bracket, yerknow.

Very Should try Woolworths.

Isabel (*moving near Very*) Stop muttering.

Very Then "broach".

Ricky (*having picked up a skewer*) What's this?

Isabel A meat-skewer. We sell them for opening letters now.

Very (*muttering again*) Never mind what you sell; tell him what we want to buy.

Ricky drops the skewer

Ricky Oh, sorry.

He and Isabel collide as they stoop to pick it up

Oh, yerknow I am sorry. Have I hurt you?

Isabel A little winded, that's all.

Ricky Here, sit down. (*Going and fetching a small chair*)

Isabel No, I'm quite all right, really.

Ricky Sure?

Isabel Yes.

Ricky Oh, good. Because, yerknow, I hadn't realized, yerknow, how late it was. I've got an important—meeting. (*Going to the door*) I'll come, yerknow, and look when I've more time.

Very leaps up, and stands between him and the door

Very You'll stay now.

Ricky Eh?

Very Said you'll stay. (*Emphasizing*) Mr Ricky Hands.

Ricky You know me?

Isabel Ricky Hands! Of course! You used to play football on the telly.

Ricky (*acidly*) I still play, lady.

Very Never watched since you missed open goal I could have filled with my left foot.

Ricky I had a sudden muscular spasm. Anyhow I haven't time to talk football now, yerknow. Excuse me . . .

Very (*standing firm*) No, I won't.

Ricky Lady, have sense; I've got to the goal, yerknow, when eleven trained men tried to stop me.

Very But never one untrained women. (*She suddenly turns the key in the lock, and, showing it to Ricky, puts it down the front of her dress*) And challenge even full-back to get it from there.

Isabel Very dear, I don't think . . .

Very (*interrupting*) Now—(*holding out her hand*)—give back, Ricky Hands.

Ricky Give back what?

Very Flora Macdonald.

Ricky I don't know what you're talking about.

Very Flora Macdonald, the scent-bottle you stole.

Ricky Here, don't you start accusing me, lady.

Very Start and finish. (*Again holding out her hand*) Come on.

Ricky I tell you I haven't got it.

Isabel (*having checked*) He must have—it's gone.

Ricky You probably put it some other place, yerknow.

Very No, you put it. In your left-hand pocket.

Ricky Now have some sense, lady . . .

Very Don't need it. Saw you.

Ricky Oh, you did, did you? Well, yerknow, if you're so sure, why don't you get on to the coppers? There's your phone, pick it up, and get on to them.

Isabel Shall I?

Very No. He knows ridiculous law. Futile rule; must wait till thief "outside" shop before taking action.

Ricky Then for Chris' sake open up, let's go outside, and take action.

Very No wonder you're not at the top any more if so under-estimate intelligence of opposition.

Ricky O.K. So what? Are you going to search me?

Very considers for a moment

Very No.

Ricky What, then?

Very Nothing, then.

Ricky We can't just stand here, yerknow.

Very No, let's sit. (*She sits on a small chair near the door*)

Ricky And do what for Chris' sake?

Very Wait till you return Flora.

Ricky You're going to have a bloody long wait, then.

Very And you—yerknow!

Ricky considers this

Ricky I can't wait. Yerknow I've got a special training session at five.

Very Though you need it, I think you're going to miss it.

Ricky again considers

Ricky Oh, all right, then; there's your bloody bottle. (*He throws it into a chair*) I only put it in my pocket—yerknow—while I made sure there was nothing better to buy. I was always going to pay, yerknow.

Isabel (*sweetly*) You still can: a hundred and twenty-five pounds.

Ricky You've a hope, darling. Come on, get that door open.

Very draws up the chair, and sits staring up at him

    What are you doing?

Very Pondering atonement.

Isabel (*excitedly*) Of course!

Isabel moves to Ricky, and walks slowly round him, examining him from head to foot

Ricky Here, what is this?

Very We're appraising. (*To Isabel*) What think?

Isabel Rather suitable.

Very Except character.

Isabel Not necessarily inheritable.

Very Perhaps can overlook if rest exemplary. (*To Ricky*) Show teeth.

Ricky Show you my teeth?

Isabel All your own?

Ricky Of course they're my own. (*Baring them*) There.

Very Passable. Height?

Isabel What's that got to do with it?

Very Don't want to match giant with pygmy: endless difficulties. (*To Ricky*) About five-eleven?

Ricky And a half. But what the hell's going on?

Very Any serious diseases? Mental or physical?

Ricky Look, I'd hardly be a top footballer if I had, would I?

Isabel Hair. As a family do you lose it early or keep it late?

Ricky (*exasperated*) I don't know.

Very (*severely*) Then think.

Isabel Do your father and grandfather still have to go to the barber's?

Ricky Well, of course they go to the barber's off and on, yerknow.

Isabel Good.

Very Family record of fertility?

Ricky Eh?

Very Do they produce offspring as often as they go to the barber's?

Ricky Here, yerknow I don't like all this. What is it?

Very Answer question.

Isabel How many brothers and sisters?

Ricky Scotty, George, Gary, Leo, Ken. Mary, Joan, Anne, Dulcie. And one or two yerknow that never made it.

Very Promising. (*To Isabel*) Want to see him stripped?

Isabel Well, I wouldn't mind actually.

Ricky I should co-co. Here, stop this, and let me out.

Very (*to Isabel*) Legs good on telly. Take the rest as proportional?

Isabel (*disappointedly*) Oh, all right.

Very (*to Ricky*) You'll do.

Ricky Thanks a lot, I'm sure. And what do I do exactly?

Very (*after a moment*) We want a baby.

Ricky (*aghast*) No, no! That, no!

Isabel You won't make us a baby?

Ricky No, I bloody well won't.

Isabel Why not?

Ricky We don't have to go into all that, yerknow. I'm just not going to, that's all.

Very (*severely*) Either baby, or your Manager informed of theft.

Ricky He'd never believe you.

Isabel In the papers you've been in so much trouble lately I think he might.

Very You want us to get him here now, and see?

Ricky (*after a moment*) No. I can't afford even rumour— (*After a moment*) But—yerknow—(*desperately*)—I can't, I really can't.

Very Can't? You mean all that hugging and kissing after a goal tells own story?

Ricky No, no! I could, of course I bloody could! It's just that—yerknow, oh, well, I suppose once, now, wouldn't do much harm. (*Gloomily*) Which of you is it?

Very Flattery appreciated.

Isabel Neither of us. She'll be very pretty and attractive.

Ricky (*alarmed*) It's not today?

Very No. Have to arrange. In about ten days.

Ricky (*desperately*) Then I can't, possibly! You don't understand. I don't even do it with my own bird. I'm in the strictest training yerknow, to prove I'm good enough to transfer to a top team again. Say you wanted me to, yerknow—perform the night before a trial game?

Very Wouldn't make any difference.

Ricky Of course it makes a difference! Yerknow, saps your energy.

Very Old wives' tale.

Ricky It's not! That goal—yerknow the one you talked about earlier. That wasn't no muscular spasm; that was Marlene.

Isabel Marlene.

Ricky My bird. She went on and on the night before the match that I don't love her, and yerknow all that crap. In the end got me to prove I did. Twice. Result—I couldn't have scored if the posts'd been fifty yards apart.

Very Imagination.

Ricky Maybe. But, yerknow, that's the way it works with me. We're all different, yerknow. Jimmy—yerknow the goalie shares the same digs with me—he can be at it all night, and he plays all the better. But, yerknow, with me . . .

Very (*interrupting*) Jimmy? Is he the ginger-headed one?

Ricky Yah.

Very (*to Isabel*) Gorgeous to have a red-headed baby.

Isabel Lovely—especially if it's a girl.

Very (*to Ricky*) Do you think Jimmy might stand in for you?

Ricky If the bird's young and pretty your only trouble'd be to stop him.

Very You could arrange?

Ricky (*eagerly*) Sure! And the other bloke who shares with us, yerknow, the right-winger, he'd be only too willing, too. Yerknow I can get you half the team if you want 'em.

Isabel How marvellous!

Very Alleluia! (*Shaking his hand*) Ricky Hands, Flora Macdonald is forgotten.

Ricky You'll keep mum, and I can scarper?

Very If Jimmy's sent round for discussion tomorrow.

Ricky He will be, cross my heart.

Very (*warningly*) We can always come down to the ground remember.

(*She opens the door*)

Ricky Dear God—not that!

Isabel Not if you keep your side of the bargain.

Ricky It's a cinch. Not that I'm sure really you shouldn't come down yerknow. With you as Managers we'd be in the Cup Final . . .

Ricky goes out

Very (*almost dancing around the shop*) Bliss and Beatitude. Bliss and Beatitude! Haven't been so happy since day Maharajah proposed.

Isabel It means a baby practically in Madeleine's arms.

Very Far more, far more!

Isabel What?

Very Exhilaration and excitement overwhelms.

Isabel (*also excited*) You mean all those gorgeous footballers! Yes, yes, marvellous!

Very We spread the joy.

Isabel What I've always dreamt of, without knowing how.

Very Houseful of gurgling.

Isabel Constant cries of happiness.

Very Year after year—

Isabel —more and more—

Henry comes down the stairs

Henry Here, have you two been on the Izarra?

Very Something even more intoxicating.

Isabel It's wonderful, Father. Everything's solved. We're going to have a life of complete bliss.

Henry *Donner und!* How?

Isabel Well, you know about the scores of women like Madeleine and myself longing for unobtainable babies . . . ?

Very Adoption impossible . . . ?

Isabel Frustration unbearable . . . ?

Henry Yes, Yes. So what?

Very Five spare bedrooms upstairs—

Isabel —a supply of Mother-Donors—

Very —a football team of Father-Donors—

Isabel —seekers come with antiques, and leave with babies—

Very —antique sales pay Donors—

Isabel —and Doctors—

Very —resident Nurse—

Isabel —flowers and delicacies—

Very —maternity gowns—

Isabel —baby clothes . . .

Henry Pipe down, pipe down! The authorities won't begin to allow it.

Very Authorities phooey.

Isabel They'll never know.

Very Shops: perfect "fronts".

Isabel We'll start tomorrow.

Very (*holding up her hand*) Suggest slight postponement.

Isabel But why?

Very Once commenced: pandemonium. Time needed settle personal affairs. Also Preparation and Planning. Eh, Admiral?

Henry Surprisingly sensible.

Very (*turning the open notice to closed, and locking the door*) Early, but—(*casting the fly with the lightest touch*)—books more important. (*She goes to the bureau*)

Henry Books?

Very (*flicking the files tantalizingly*) Ledgers. (*Picking up a clipboard, pencil and sharpener*) Appointment sheets. Addresses. Bookings—(*Sliding a clipboard in front of Henry*) All hand to Battle Stations. Sharpen pencil . . .

Henry sharpens his pencil enthusiastically and sits on the sofa ready to write (*To Isabel*) Little houri crying.

Isabel listens to the silence

Isabel I don't hear . . . (*Breaking off as she understands*) Yes, I do. I'll go and see what she wants—

Smiling, Isabel goes off upstairs

Very (*going round quietly, switching off the main lights*) Jot down: Column, Male Donors. Column, Baby Seekers. Column, Date interviewed. Column Appointment. Column, Conception. Column, Date of Birth. Column, Sex. Column, Collection. (*She ends up near the telephone, which she silently nips off the receiver*) Endless enthralling columns. So now, Henry dear—lets—put—our—heads—together . . .

Very stealthily approaches Henry with blazing eyes

Adrian (*off*) Miss Hesketh-Palmer, Miss Hesketh-Palmer . . .

Adrian hurries in carrying a large cardboard box

Very (*furiously*) Go away; exit, exit!

Adrian I can't exit—the most terrible thing's happened.

Very What, what?

Adrian A lady came into your shop and left these . . .

He takes two identical bundles from the box. As they start wailing loudly—

the CURTAIN *falls*

FURNITURE AND PROPERTY LIST

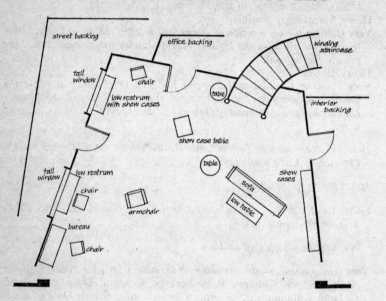

ACT I

On stage: Sofa. *On it:* brocade-covered cushions, bundle containing "baby"
Small armchair
3 upright chairs
2 occasional tables
1 low table
1 show-case table
Bureau. *On top:* telephone, lamp, receipt-book, pens and pencils,
copy of *The Times*
Antiques of all kinds in available spaces and on floor. *Specific objects
include:* green dessert service, ivory lace-bobbins, solitaire set,
papier mâché snuff-box, carved cigarette-holder, vinaigrette, framed
fan, cribbage board, coral rattle, christening mug, doll, pseudo
Ming lamp, hand-mirror, necklace

On walls: pictures (for sale)—also stacked on floor

Across stairs: ornate rope with notice tied to it

On main door: OPEN/CLOSED notice, collection of Chinese bells
Carpet
Stair-carpet
Window curtains

Off stage: Tray with teapot, milk jug, sugar bowl, 3 cups, 3 saucers, 3 spoons
(Adrian)
Account books **(Henry)**
Empty paper bag **(Old Man)**
Business papers **(Henry)**
Paper bag with liquorice all-sorts **(Old Man)**

Personal: **Old Man:** thick spectacles
Very: large handbag containing several yellow-and-green-filled bottles
and small glasses, small alarm-clock, diary
Gloria: wristwatch, handbag with pound notes

ACT II

Strike: Most of former antique stock
All used glasses, cups, etc.

Set: Antiques, including stuffed ostrich, child's high chair, rocking-horse,
dolls, oak cradle, green malachite box, enamel scent-bottle in form
of bust of Flora Macdonald, meat-skewer·
3 clipboards, pencil and sharpener on bureau
Files on bureau
Carton of wrapped Staffordshire figures on sofa
Hot-water bottle on sofa

Off stage: Sheet of paper **(Very)**
Tinkle block (wrapped) **(Adrian)**
Bunch of flowers **(Adrian)**
"Baby", basket of shawls and toys **(Very)**
Tray and empty mug **(Adrian)**
"Baby" **(Mrs Barry)**
"Baby" **(Jenny)**
Paper bag with fondants **(Old Man)**
Roll of notes **(Old Man)**
Parcel containing gollywog **(Gloria)**
Large cardboard box with 2 "babies" **(Adrian)**

Personal: **Adrian:** handkerchief

LIGHTING PLOT

Property fittings required: ornate pendant, wall brackets, desk lamp
Interior. A hall/showroom. The same scene throughout

ACT I   Late afternoon

To open: General effect of early evening light

No cues

ACT II   Late afternoon

To open: All practicals on. Dusk outside windows

Cue 1   As CURTAIN rises   (Page 38)
             Start slow fade of daylight

Cue 2   **Very** switches off main lights   (Page 67)
             Snap off (1) pendant, (2) desk lamp as she reaches them

EFFECTS PLOT

ACT I

Cue 1   Before and as CURTAIN rises   (Page 1)
Baby cries

Cue 2   **Adrian:** "I would, but I . . ."   (Page 1)
Telephone rings

Cue 3   **Ricky** pokes baby   (Page 2)
Loud cry

Cue 4   **Adrian** "reverses" baby several times   (Page 2)
Wailing ceases, each time, then restarts

Cue 5   **Adrian** puts finger in baby's mouth   (Page 3)
Wailing ceases

Cue 6   **Adrian:** ". . . you and me."   (Page 7)
Baby cry becomes audible from off stage

Cue 7   **Isabel:** ". . . what that noise is."   (Page 7)
Cry ceases

Cue 8   **Isabel** puts bobbin in baby's mouth   (Page 8)
Baby cries, then dies down

Cue 9   **Very:** ". . . Temple bells ringing."   (Page 22)
Muffled alarm clock rings

Cue 10   **Very:** ". . . go next idea."   (Page 27)
Alarm clock rings

ACT II

Cue 11   **Henry:** "Oh, my God!"   (Page 41)
Baby screams

Cue 12   **Henry:** ". . . absurd, Isabel. I can't."   (Page 42)
Baby stops

Cue 13   **Henry:** "Open wide . . ."   (Page 42)
Telephone rings

Cue 14	**Adrian:** "Oh, I'm so sorry ... "	(Page 47)
	Baby cries loudly, off stage	
Cue 15	**Henry:** ". . . Battle of Trafalgar?"	(Page 48)
	Baby cries louder	
Cue 16	After **Henry** and **Isabel** exit	(Page 48)
	Crying stops	
Cue 17	After **Mrs Barry** exits	(Page 49)
	On stage baby whimpers—continues until drink is put in its mouth	
Cue 18	**Mrs Barry** exits	(Page 49)
	Repeat cue 17	
Cue 19	**Very:** "Oh, ka-ka."	(Page 50)
	Repeat cue 17	
Cue 20	**Adrian** takes babies from box	(Page 67)
	2 on-stage babies wail—continue until CURTAIN	

A large range of sound effects on record and cassette is available from Samuel French Ltd.

MADE AND PRINTED IN GREAT BRITAIN BY
LATIMER TREND & COMPANY LTD PLYMOUTH
MADE IN ENGLAND

Tara Pammi can't remember a ... when she wasn't lost in a book— ... romance, which was much more exciting than a mathematics textbook at school. Years later, Tara's wild imagination and love for the written word revealed what she really wanted to do. Now she pairs alpha males who think they know everything with strong women who knock that theory *and* them off their feet!

When **Emmy Grayson** came across her mother's copy of *A Rose in Winter* by Kathleen E. Woodiwiss she sneaked it into her room and promptly fell in love with romance. Over twenty years later, Mills & Boon Modern made her dream come true by offering her a contract for her first book. When she isn't writing, she's chasing her kids, attempting to garden, or carving out a little time on her front porch with her own romance hero.

BILLION-DOLLAR WIVES

TARA PAMMI

EMMY GRAYSON

MILLS & BOON

First published in Great Britain 2025
by Mills & Boon, an imprint of HarperCollins*Publishers* Ltd,
1 London Bridge Street, London, SE1 9GF

www.harpercollins.co.uk

HarperCollins*Publishers*, Macken House, 39/40 Mayor Street Upper, Dublin 1, D01 C9W8, Ireland

Billion-Dollar Wives © 2025 Harlequin Enterprises ULC

Her Twin Secret © 2025 Tara Pammi

Still the Greek's Wife © 2025 Emmy Grayson

ISBN: 978-0-263-34456-1

03/25

HER TWIN SECRET

TARA PAMMI

MILLS & BOON

CHAPTER ONE

THE LAST THING Adriano Cavalieri—chairman of Bancaria Cavalieri, one of the most prestigious privately owned banks in Italy—wanted to face when he returned home to Milan after four weeks of touring Southeast Asia on a rigorous schedule was the undeniable proof of his wife's infidelity.

In the form of scandalous, tacky photographs that belonged on a filthy tabloid, no less.

He had acquired said wife, who had been a waitress/exotic dancer in Vegas nine months ago, in a once-in-a-lifetime, uncharacteristic impulse that mocked him now. A wife who was a mere twenty-two to his thirty-four—a cliché if he had ever known one.

The media outlets were still writing about his choice, after all these months. Fed and fueled by the fact that he had kept her out of the public eye.

Neither had Adriano stopped wondering the reason behind his own actions.

It wasn't as if Nyra was exceptionally beautiful to have turned his head when other beautiful women hadn't.

Her face, Adriano remembered from the first moment, had possessed a feral alley cat look with chiseled cheekbones, a sharp nose and a wide mouth. A face that was popular on the catwalk from the few shows he'd attended for Fashion Week in Milan.

Although hers was no doubt a result of missing several meals over a few years. A nondescript black cocktail dress had hung on her bony shoulders, making her look like a scarecrow whose stuffing had fallen out.

The only lushness to her was her wide mouth and those brown eyes—ordinary in every way—except for the depth with which they sparkled when she smiled.

And she had turned that smile on him, at the end of the first round of the game. Like an amplified sunbeam, it had cracked the frost around his uninterested, unmoving heart.

Even now, if he closed his eyes, he could remember how she'd bent over him, her hands caught between his on the table, her thick curls a curtain hiding them from the world itself and said, "Please, act like you've already bought me for this week, Mr. Cavalieri."

One moment of their gazes colliding, one whispered entreaty, one soft graze of her cheek against his jaw, and he'd lost himself utterly.

And now, as he stared at the scandalous photos on his desk, that lush mouth open, her head thrown back in ecstasy with some man, he wondered if that moment had been orchestrated too.

He closed his eyes, wishing he'd never laid eyes on those photos. Which, in itself, was a strange thing, because he'd never shied away from truth.

It was a reminder of how well Bruno, his head of security and his best friend of nearly three decades, knew him that he'd first told Adriano on his flight back that he had "bad stuff involving Nyra" but to let him investigate a little more.

While even Adriano himself didn't understand his relationship with his wife, it seemed Bruno, and even his childhood nanny, Maria—one of the very few people he trusted wholeheartedly in his life—approved of it. Maria, going as far as to say he smiled now, instead of baring his teeth at everyone in his sphere.

Given that Nyra had been up to something shady for the past month, he had braced himself for something bad as soon as he had gone on this trip.

After all, she'd sold her wedding ring and, according to Adriano's mother, several valuable keepsakes from the family villa here in Lake Como, things her parents valued because this duke or that king had gifted it to some old, fat, privileged ancestor of his.

He'd initially laughed at his mother's claim—at his father's utterly hypocritical horror that he'd brought a common thief into their family. Such a stain on their reputation, the pair had declared, after splashing their own scandalous affairs for all of society to see for three decades.

Only to learn later, on Bruno's investigation into the missing heirlooms, that the claim had been truthful.

Then her trips to London, which he had only discovered because he'd seen her walk into a seedy part of the city while he'd whizzed away in a chauffeured car in the middle of a meeting.

When he'd asked her about it, she had laughed and claimed he must have been mistaken. Because she'd been cooped up in the apartment, struggling with her latest painting.

Later, with one word to Bruno about her whereabouts, he'd learned that she'd indeed been in London twice in one month.

Still, he had waited for her to come to him.

Then other things had started disappearing, like his platinum cuff links and the diamond bracelet his mother had bought Nyra that she hadn't liked one bit. Little things he wouldn't have noticed unless he was keeping an eye out.

To think, he'd even tried to justify it as an undiagnosed case of kleptomania. But she was not a magpie who stored all the things she stole, nor could he see any change in her clothes or her spending habits.

Even after becoming his wife, she'd always dressed in loose, dowdy clothes that she made from his discarded shirts and sweaters, like some hippie artist.

Much to his mother's, and sometimes his, dismay.

In nine months, she had shown no interest in designer clothes, or expensive jewelry, or leaning into the role of a society wife. She'd never even joined him for a dinner with guests from his circle.

All she wanted, she'd admitted to him after one of their marathon sex sessions in the little apartment by Navigli Lake District, where she preferred to stay, was to paint, read, while away time in cafés looking for inspiration when he was absent and to spend time with him when he was present.

It was so intoxicating to be one of the things she wanted in her simple life that Adriano had defied his mother's incessant demands that his wife needed to take part in his life.

They had even slid into a strange sort of domestic

bliss, his life with Nyra thoroughly compartmentalized from his work and society and even family. If his business associates and the world in general carped on about Adriano Cavalieri's wife being absent from grand dinners and charity galas, he hadn't given a damn.

A part of him had reveled in keeping her to himself.

And when that moment arose outside of that cozy apartment, outside of touching her, when he thought it a madness, when he needed at least the illusion of control over his life, he told himself that she was an expensive hobby he had acquired in a fit of acting out.

After all, he'd spent the first thirty-five years of his life, dutifully fixing the family bank and growing its fortunes, holding together the car crash of his parents' marriage and taking care of a slew of illegitimate half-brothers and half-sisters his parents had spread around like bees spread pollen.

Stealing away from his own life to the one he shared with Nyra—long nights of sex, soft moments of silence and surrender, being alone together while she painted and he worked—had become his reward. His escape. *His...haven.*

He had expected them to get bored with each other, their passion to wither and die, their near-secret relationship to lose its charm, sooner or later. Then he would give her a nice settlement, make sure she was looked after for the rest of her life, before quietly divorcing her.

But he hadn't expected this...betrayal that seemed to cut through him as mercilessly as a knife sliced through butter. Rending him into so many pieces. His limbs shook, his extremities felt cold. And yet everything felt extraneous to the hard thumping of his heart in his chest.

The why of it was a vicious echo in his head.

Why had she done it?

Why hadn't she simply asked him for money? Was all the passion they'd shared nothing but an act? Or was it that she'd found a new man and hadn't wanted to let go of the security Adriano had provided just yet?

So many lies…and now he couldn't distinguish what had been real and what had been pretense. Everything felt tainted, the past and the present.

His gaze drifted to the photos over and over again, like some ghoulish spectator drawn to a disastrous train wreck.

Cristo, he'd never had a taste for masochism, and yet looking at those pics of her half naked and writhing in another man's arms made bile crawl up his throat.

And Adriano realized how deep she'd sneaked under his skin, how hard this betrayal of hers had struck him. How he might never recover from it.

A pained growl escaped his lips and it might as well have been a wretched scream for a man who rarely let himself feel things. And he buried his face in his hands, trying and failing to fight the sense of losing something precious.

Nyra Shah Cavalieri gazed down the length of the heavy mahogany sixteen-seat dining table at Adriano Cavalieri, her husband of nine months. But he didn't look at her. Not once, in two hours of this unending dinner.

With a sigh, she looked out the floor-to-ceiling glass windows toward the sweeping vistas of Lake Como. Lush green hillsides dotted with elegant villas and charming villages greeted her but did nothing to cheer her up. The setting sun painted the sky with vivid splashes of pinks and oranges. But even the artist in her couldn't appreciate the magnificent view.

The villa had always felt more like a prison than a home to her. Especially since anytime she stayed here, it was because Adriano was traveling and she found herself the recipient of a variety of taunts and surprising trash talk, for all the sophistication they claimed, from his parents and his younger siblings Fabiola and Federico.

Gold digger was a common one along with *witch*, and when Nigella, his mother, got really upset, Nyra had even heard *slut* sometimes.

She let it slide off her like water over a rock. Sometimes, she even wondered what Nigella's, and this privileged family's, reaction would be if they truly found out her background. If they knew what a taint she could bring on the mighty Cavalieri name.

Although it was anticipating Adriano's reaction anytime she considered telling the truth that worried her the most. The idea of seeing contempt—even disgust, in his gray-green eyes when he set them on her—made her stomach clench tight.

Her husband was an intensely private man and nine months later, Nyra still didn't know why he'd married her. Not that she had ever probed him about it. Gift horses and all that.

When he wasn't there, when his touch didn't anchor her to this reality, like the last four weeks, this life he'd given her felt like a particularly colorful daydream. Maybe Nigella's name-calling didn't bother her because Nyra felt like she was all those things in his world. An impostor who could be found out at any moment. She'd even tried to tell Nigella in a roundabout way that her position as the Cavalieri matriarch was not threatened.

She much preferred the cozy apartment near Lake Navigli. Not that she had ownership there either. She had followed Adriano with nothing but the hotel uniform she'd been wearing. All she had was her art supplies, gifted by him. But still, that space—with its huge four-poster king bed and the sunroom where she painted, and the small balcony with its view of the busy lakefront with all its charming cafés and sparkling Italian water, was theirs.

They'd stamped every inch of it with their lovemaking and their comfortable silences and their whispers and laughter long into the night.

And now, all of that was going to change. Irrevocably.

A tremor started in her legs and traveled up her spine, and the glass of water in her hand rattled on the table. Both excitement and dread filled her.

For months, she'd floated along on a different plane with him and this was a thud of reality. And it had made her realize how much she wanted to build this life with him, how bright and wonderful the future could be for them and their…growing family.

Family…the word moved through her like a giant gong. This was a new chance, a real start at something she'd never even dreamed she might have.

Though, how was she supposed to convey this huge news to him if he wouldn't even look at her? Why did she get the sense that something was terribly wrong?

He'd gone up those winding stairs as soon as he'd stepped inside, barely sparing her a glance as she came running in to see him, from the orange grove where she'd been hiding. Then it had been cocktails with the lot of them, blinking back tears when Nigella commented on his lack of a greeting for her.

It was the first time her mother-in-law's acerbic comment pricked.

Butterflies, *no*, it felt like dragons were flying in her belly as she sat at the table with all of them now.

How would Adriano react to the news of her being pregnant? *Of them being pregnant.*

Especially after the strange evening they'd had before he had left four weeks ago.

As usual, he'd exhausted her with his mouth and his fingers, but there had been something more intense to him in those few hours. As if he was equally fascinated and frustrated by her.

Since neither of them was a great phone person, that fraught silence between them had grown thorny and thick over four weeks.

Was it her fault, she wondered, twisting the fake diamond ring on her finger.

Was it her own distracted mind that she'd seen reflected in his edgy words and movements that evening and today?

She had disturbed the easy, harmonious rhythm their lives had fallen into with her lies and her stealing and her secret trips to London. But how could she have not tried to help…

Her gaze flicked to his for a horror-stricken moment.

Did he know? Had he discovered what she had been up to?

Just then, his gray-green gaze collided with hers. And

then it seemed to spear and skewer her as if she were a helpless fish.

Heat and desire and panic and a host of other things she couldn't name flooded her, and she stared back helplessly.

All she wanted was to be held in those arms. To know his touch again. To have him give her that crooked smile that no one else got.

Longing burned a path through her as his attention broke away from her. One of the cousins asked him something.

Damn it, it had been four weeks.

Wasn't she allowed to greet her husband without the audience of his family members? Why did they have to sit down for this elaborate, six-course meal every freaking Friday? And today, of all days?

It wasn't as if Adriano was close to either of his parents. She'd got the sense that he mostly tolerated them and they tolerated his…controlling dictates because he was the source of their continued wealth and jet-setting lifestyle.

So why was he allowing them to see his anger, or whatever it was he was putting out, with her today?

Suddenly, she felt like a Cinderella whose carriage and dress might disappear any moment. Only the clock was malfunctioning and stuck at a minute before midnight.

After what felt like an eternity of letting the Italians around her nearly drown her, she cleared her throat loudly enough that it came to a sudden stop. "Adriano, may we talk please? In private," she finally managed to say.

Gray-green eyes held hers once more, and his pro-tracted silence clearly said he didn't want to.

A cold sweat drenched her.

He knew.

He knew that she was sitting on a pile of lies and half-truths as tall as her.

"I have arranged a grand party to celebrate your... wedding," Nigella cut in. "Late as it is, it has become necessary, Adriano. Everyone is talking about you now. Not just her."

Nyra wasn't sure if she was glad to be released from the end of the line like a floundering fish or angry that Nigella had cut into their angry, angsty eye-fuck across the room.

"What do you mean, Mama?" Adriano said.

"They're saying it's not a marriage at all. That you've kidnapped some barely adult girl from Vegas and are keeping her prisoner as your mistress. And that's why you don't dare show her to polite society."

"One look at her," Federico, Adriano's younger brother and a privileged brat as far as Nyra was con-cerned, said with a laugh, "and they would know she's more maid than mistress, Mama." He dug an elbow into his twin Fabiola's side. "You're the social media queen, Fabi. Can't you release a 'candid' of her and let people see our brother is simply suffering from tempo-rary insanity?"

Across the table, Adriano's chin reared down, shock radiating from his entire posture. He sat back in his chair and folded his arms, the tight lines around his mouth belying his calm facade.

Was he waiting for her to defend herself or to see how much worse his family's taunts could get?

Fabiola's dark gaze swept over Nyra—from her thick curls she'd bound tight in a braid to the loose, off-shoulder sweater, pausing at her bare neck and ears—and then she sneered. "Her hippie hobo look hardly matches my fashionista grid, Federico."

A scoff and a snort came at Nyra from the others at the table.

"She can hardly be expected to match our family in fashion or conduct," Nigella replied to her grown children's giggles. "But what I really don't like is that she won't even make an effort. You're ruining his name and—"

"Basta, Mama," Adriano said, the two words soft and yet pelting through the room as if they were bullets.

To anyone else, he looked unmoved, even bored. Like one of the white marble busts spread over the estate. As if, even dead, they had to shout about the great Cavalieri name, lest anyone forget.

He'd never seen his siblings or his mother attack her so directly. He didn't have an inkling of the kind of stuff they said to her. Because she'd never even hinted at it. The why of it suddenly baffled him.

More importantly though, what he didn't get was that they were bolder today, taking their cue from him. Like a rabid pack that followed the alpha and would tear open something weaker at one command from him.

No, she was not weaker than him, she told herself.

She was younger, had zero power while his thrummed around him like some magnetic field. She didn't have a dime to her name, but she was not weaker. She had survived before he had stormed into her life, had lived through much worse than his family's taunts. Alone.

Whatever this was, she could withstand his temper, the cold burn of his anger.

As for Federico, she'd dealt with men far more dangerous than him. "If you think being a maid is worse than a mistress, Federico," she said, meeting his eyes and letting her mouth curve into a mockery of a smile, "you're well on your predestined way to becoming nothing but a footnote in the great history books of the Cavalieri family. Sorry, but no marble bust for you, buddy."

"I'm not your buddy," Federico retorted with as much disgust as he could pack into the word.

Nyra shrugged, and she thought she saw Adriano's eyes, watching and drinking in every nuance in her face, gleam with something.

Humor maybe. Or acknowledgment.

But when she looked again, desperate for it, all she saw was the killing frost.

Nigella turned her glacial gaze to Nyra, any pretension to warmth gone. "How dare you talk to him like that? Adriano—"

"What is it you think Adriano will make me do, Nigella? I'm not his pet dog for him to give me orders."

The silence that followed was deafening because she'd never retorted before. But things had to change.

It wasn't just her anymore. She wouldn't tolerate anyone speaking to her children like that. Neither could she hide in that apartment.

"Dogs are loyal creatures," Adriano said, raising his glass to his lips.

"I agree," Nyra said, everything inside her quaking.

Did he think her stealing a few trinkets from his mansion made her disloyal?

Okay, for a man with such exacting standards that his stellar reputation in the finance world had reached even her ears, maybe stealing and lying made her disloyal.

But wasn't he going to give her a chance to explain? And why was he doing this in front of everyone?

In the ten months she'd known him, Adriano had never, *ever*, flexed his power to show off or to punch down. It was the very thing about him that had turned her head.

She licked her trembling lips, refusing to show her internal panic. "I guess I should have picked something better as an insult for myself."

Then she turned to Nigella, whose glare should have ground her into dust. "I have no idea why you all are so—" she included the twins in her gaze too "—threatened by me but I'm not playing this game anymore."

A soft gasp fell from Fabi's mouth as if Nyra had given voice to something unmentionable in open company.

"I never wanted your power and position in the family. And your constant venom is...exhausting. But, yes, if you want to arrange some damned party and show me off to the society, I'm willing to try." Then she looked at the man who was watching her with that intense focus. "If that's what you want from me," she said to him.

She didn't know if he could hear her desperation.

A flash of dark humor flashed across those penetrating eyes. "I have already made the mistake of having expectations of you, *cara*. And you dashed them. Quite spectacularly, I might say."

Nyra's belly swooped, as if she were standing in an elevator car whose cords had been cut off abruptly.

Shocked gazes turned to her, then him, like greedy spectators at some bloodthirsty sport.

"What are you talking about?" Nigella asked, curiosity dripping from her tone. "Was I right that she's the thief?"

Every drop of blood fled from Nyra's face, leaving a strange tingling sensation behind.

Adriano folded his napkin and dropped it onto his plate, having barely touched his food. "There will be no celebrations. At least the world hasn't witnessed my temporary insanity, as Federico put it so aptly."

Glee filled Nigella's and her hell-spawn twins' eyes, a glee that they barely hid. "What do you mean, Adriano?" Nigella said, crying fake disappointment, and doing Nyra a favor.

Her own throat refused to work and Nyra suddenly became aware of two things at once. Her stubborn, naive decision to compartmentalize and keep herself limited to a mere sliver of Adriano's vast everyday life had been foolish. Resulting in his family and the world at large assuming that he had hidden her away because he was ashamed of her and what they shared. And the second, more devastating thing, the moment she'd been dreading even as they'd stood in that tacky chapel, had arrived.

Midnight had struck and her carriage, and her pretty dress and her glass slippers…were all about to disappear. And with it, her dark, brooding prince.

Adriano pushed up from his seat and stared down that blade of a nose at her, as if she were an insect that had been helplessly caught under his handmade Italian loafers. In a white Armani shirt that was open at his throat and undone at his cuffs, he looked like the hero of some gothic novel Nyra had read ages ago, before giving them up. She'd had enough angst and grief in her life without reaching for it in fiction too.

"We will not be celebrating because this marriage is over. Nyra—" she thought his lovely mouth had flinched a little when he said her name, but then she was already beginning to feel as if she was floating outside of her body, so what the hell did she know "—will be leaving today."

There was no anger, no heat, no reproach to his words. He said it as plainly and free of emotion and with just as much ruthless finality as he ran his company. Like it was a decision made by his will alone and not a partnership they'd both invested in.

Had it been ever a partnership though? a small voice asked.

"No," she said, the word automatically falling from her lips before she'd given it permission. Her chest rose and fell. Under the table her hands crawled to her flat belly, as if to reassure the tiny life inside. "Don't do this, Adriano, please."

"Bruno will make arrangements for you, physical and financial."

"No, Adriano. This isn't you talking—"

"You do not know me, Nyra. And you've proved that I do not know you. At all."

Ending the marriage wasn't the worst thing he had done to her, Nyra thought, eyes filling with hot, humiliating tears. She bit the inside of her lip so hard that she tasted blood. The pain was so sharp that her brain focused on that instead of the tears.

She held his gaze, even as she was falling apart inside. It was he who looked down finally, before walking away.

The ruthless billionaire Adriano Cavalieri—whose kindness had touched her more than anything else, walked away from the table and left her to be pecked at by the hungry, gleeful vultures of his family.

Whispers and smug announcements and even relieved laughter abounded around her. All of it urging her to run far and run fast and hide. That was what she'd done once before, what she was good at. Finding little pockets of life and hiding in them, instead of living fully.

And Adriano had been such a pocket made of warm touches and hot kisses and wonderful escape.

No, she wouldn't walk away without knowing why he was ending this.

Let Adriano Cavalieri face her breaking heart, and then she would leave with its pieces in hand but her dignity intact.

CHAPTER TWO

BRUNO MENDACI, Adriano's head of security and the closest thing her husband had to a friend, *and* the only one among the vast, devilish Cavalieri clan that she could loosely claim as her friend too, was standing outside the immense double doors of Adriano's study.

A shiver of apprehension ran down Nyra's spine as she stared at the oak doors.

Staring at his tight shoulders, she had a sudden sense that Bruno wasn't guarding the doors so much as he was trying to keep himself out. For an intensely private man, Adriano was close with Bruno, more so than with Federico. Curious as she'd been, she'd never asked him about their relationship.

Bruno turned as Nyra walked closer.

The villa's silence felt extra strange after the dinner. All the various cousins had urgently dispersed, no doubt to spread the latest updates about Adriano ending his marriage, and maybe even sell it to a pap for some cheap payout.

Another breath shuddered out of her.

It wasn't like him to air his personal issues in front of his family. Why, then? Why had he humiliated her in such a way?

"It might be better to not disturb him now, *bella*," Bruno said, his words tinged with both warning and sympathy.

A part of Nyra wanted to heed his advice and hide away. Lick her wounds for the night. Would Adriano, a gentleman if she'd ever met one, have her thrown out if she didn't follow his dictate? Would he order this friend of his to physically drag her out of his palatial villa, like a scene in some soap opera? What if he changed his mind come tomorrow morning? What if he was just angry now and would cool down tomorrow?

Disgust filled her at her own cowardice. "I appreciate your…advice, Bruno. But I'm not leaving without seeing him."

"It might be better if you want to save this."

"He declared to his family that this marriage is over and that I'm to leave. As if I was a…"

Shock painted over Bruno's face.

"Honestly, it's insulting to make me feel like I need permission to see my fucking husband. His or anyone else's."

"Then why did you…do all those things?"

Nyra blanched and hated that she couldn't even meet this decent man's gaze. "If he gives me a chance, I'll try to explain."

"I wish I…" Whatever he wished, Bruno shook his head and opened the door.

Nyra thought she'd heard him whisper *sorry* before she slipped in through the gap. Why was he sorry, of all people?

The immense chandelier with its numerous light fixtures caught her attention first. The architecture of the study was stunning—the two-story space looked expansive enough that Nyra had thought it straight out of a fairy tale when she'd first stepped into it.

It was the only space she loved at the villa. Now she was once again hit by how the dark wood floor-to-ceiling bookshelves that formed a semicircle were reflective of the man Adriano was.

Mystery and adventure and yet also a warm resting place—at least that's what he'd represented to her.

The room smelled of leather and old books and cigars and spice, the latter contributed by Adriano's sandalwood scent and warm sweat. The scent association made her skin prickle with need, images of his powerful body bearing her down into the bed, his muscled thighs holding her hips hostage as he drove inside of her.

Sex with Adriano, slow and tormenting or hard and fast, was always an out-of-body experience. And yet it had always been the silent emotion glittering in his eyes, unspoken even in the utmost moments of raw intimacy that had always sent Nyra tumbling over the edge.

It was the one place where she was always courageous and bold and he was...*hers*.

Only hers, and her entire world.

As she searched through the darkness for the stunning breadth of his shoulders, the crooked tilt of his mouth to one side when he caught her staring at him, the rough cadence of his voice when he crooked a finger at her and beckoned her to him...misery swamped her.

What if it was truly over?

Her gaze caught on the blown-up photos in color scattered haphazardly on the behemoth desk. Her entire world narrowed down to some kind of black hole.

It was her face staring back at her from the pic, caught in a man's embrace. Intimate embrace at that, for his leg was pushed up between hers and his face was buried in her neck. But her eyes were wide-open, almost challenging. The strap of what was clearly a lacy corset top dangled over one shoulder, revealing a breast. Its smooth gold flesh all the more obscene held up by a masculine hand cupping it from below.

Her face and her neck, and her body...but not her.

Shock and something like anger...crashed over her, and she had the sudden urge to grab the paperweight from the desk and toss it across the wall, to break something with her hands.

This wasn't her. Relief crashed down on her, then got swept away by fresh anger.

Could no one tell that the woman in the photos wasn't Nyra?

Adriano should know that Nyra would never wear such a top, not even in the dark intimacy of their bedroom. That she'd turned herself inside out with shyness when the couture designer had forced her to pick from rows and rows of lacy negligees and barely there lacy thongs should have told him.

She preferred cotton underwear and her husband's discarded shirts as sleepwear. On the nights that he allowed her to wear anything at all.

Gold highlights glinted in that woman's hair, while Nyra's had bronze highlights that were already fading, showing her usual mousy brown color at the roots. From how she stood to how she tilted her head to how she wore her hair—everything about the woman in the photos was different from Nyra. Except the fact that she looked just like her.

Nadia...

Tears prickled Nyra's eyes as she ran her fingers over the smooth cheek of the woman in the photo. After years of searching for her, her twin, Nadia, had finally reached out to Nyra a couple of months ago.

Nyra had been sent to live with her great-aunt Olivia after their mother's death. While the old woman hadn't been happy about being landed with a fourteen-year-old and hadn't been the warmest person on the planet, she'd given her shelter and food. The moment she'd turned eighteen, Nyra had left for the US, where Nadia had been sent to live with some distant cousin of her father. Who, she'd told Nyra in those early days when they had still kept in touch through email, was an outright bully and tormented her endlessly.

Then, one day, Nadia had written to her that she was running away from home and disappeared completely. Years of not knowing how her twin was faring had hollowed out Nyra.

Finally, two months ago, Nadia had reached out through an old email account, begging Nyra for help. She'd returned to the UK, she had said, admitting that she was in trouble and needed financial help.

The fact that her twin couldn't make ends meet while Nyra was married to one of the richest men in Italy and rolling around in comfort had twisted her inside out. So, Nyra had turned herself into a thief and a cheat to get her hands on funds.

After three planned meetings in London though, all she'd known was heartache and confusion, because

Nadia refused to come face-to-face with Nyra. Swallowing her disappointment, she'd left envelopes full of cash all three times, hoping her sister would eventually be ready to see her.

Her fingers lingered on Nadia's cheek in the photo now. That this was how she was getting a glimpse of her twin after nearly a decade of separation...tore at her. Caught in a cheap, tawdry photo by someone who had clearly tailed her, thinking she was Nyra.

Was it Bruno? she thought with sudden disgust. Had he been ordered by Adriano to tail her and click these pics of her? How could he have invaded her sister's privacy like this?

And how could Adriano think that she would do this with...another man after everything they'd shared? How dare he?

Suddenly, the cruelty with which he had ended their relationship made perfect sense.

As if he was made of shadows, Adriano drifted into place behind the desk. He might as well have put an ocean between them, Nyra thought, looking across the expanse of it.

Thick, curved lashes hid his expression and she nearly stomped her foot in frustration. Three inches over six feet and with a broad-shouldered frame, he was too much masculinity to take in one glance. Too much magnetism to not get burned.

And she'd been so utterly lost in her own destruction, like a moth inevitably rushing toward the flame. But whatever it had been, it had been real, raw. In a moment of utter self-pity, tears filled her eyes and overflowed.

"Am I to think that the tears represent regret? Or are they of remorse?"

She dabbed them with the back of her hand, telling herself that they were the last she would ever shed over him. "I haven't done anything I regret or have to repent. Except maybe thinking that you're different from other men."

"Ahh…it's a madness both of us contracted, I think. So?" he said, that deep, gravelly voice vibrating with impatience and so much more.

"What, Adriano?" she said, his name falling from her lips like a caress even in the midst of roiling fury. It was entrenched too deep to be plucked out at a moment's notice. "Is there a question you're actually asking me instead of issuing decrees? Tell me, if I don't leave, will you have your rabid family drag me outside by my hair? Will you call the *polizia* and tell them your wife is a thief and a cheat and…what, a slut?"

His chin reared down and he took a step back from the desk. As if her blazing anger was a shock wave he hadn't expected to encounter.

If she wasn't shaking with said anger, Nyra would've laughed at how shock painted his features. There was nothing in the world that could catch Adriano unawares. Nothing that could shake or dent his self-possession.

Had all these months meant nothing to him? How could they, if he thought her capable of this?

"You've been lying to me for months, stealing from my family…"

"Nothing you would have missed. Nothing that would harm anyone. You know that I—"

Laughter escaped his mouth, making him look painfully gorgeous. "Is it true that you've stolen silver candlesticks that have been in the family for two hundred years?"

Nyra's cheeks heated. "Yes. I sold them because I needed the money. I sold the diamond ring you bought me as a wedding present and swapped it with this cheap one," she said, turning the ring round and round on her finger.

The cheap metal had begun to leave a green ring on her skin since she refused to take it off. To take off the one he'd bought her had been torment enough.

Given the state of her marriage currently, the ugly ring of green however seemed like a better fit.

"Why? Why did you need the money?" he said, surprising her with that particular question.

"I..." God, where did she even begin?

"Why refuse an allowance or a bank account in your name or even an expense card if all you wanted was money all along?" Adriano said, not giving her the chance to answer. "Why pretend to morals you don't have?"

The depth of his frustration calmed her rising temper.

Yes, he had jumped to conclusions, but she had laid the foundation of lies for him to build on. This was on her. At least a major part of it. Most of it. "I needed the money urgently, Adriano. And it's true that I made up reasons for—"

"What...to see your lover at a seedy motel in some godforsaken part of London? To run around behind my back?" Something that sounded like pain reverberated in his words. "Or had you begun gathering funds for your exit strategy? Would I have had a grand first anniversary present request to pad it?"

Nyra found herself moving around the desk, toward him, before she had decided to do so. As if she was nothing but a magnet and he her true north.

The familiar scent of him enveloped her senses like a lash, threatening to bind her to him. Her arms trembled with the effort she exerted to stop herself from throwing herself at him.

His chest would be hard and solid and he would hold her against him, hold off the incoming storm. In his arms, she'd always felt safe. From that first night, when she'd asked him to hold her while they slept.

In a life that had been lonely and bereft of touch and warmth for so long, he had been like a blanket made of sunshine.

He stepped back from her, as if her touch, her nearness would taint him.

When she looked into his eyes, there was nothing but a cold, dead frost there. And that confirmation there—that he believed all those loathsome things about her—was enough to kill the last tendril of love she had for him.

"If you want to believe that I cheated on you, that I went seeking this man in some cheap motel in London," she said, grabbing a photo and throwing it at him, "that I undressed for him while you were working in some remote corner of the world, that I welcomed his touch and kisses and let him do all the wicked things you do to me, that I let this man move inside me with the same desire I showed you, then there's nothing more for me to say."

His head jerked up as if she had dealt him a body blow. Beneath his olive skin, a paleness emerged and it struck her like a coiled snake in waiting, shaking her resolve.

She backed away from him, nearly getting tangled in her own feet, afraid of her own neediness and the overwhelming urge to please him, to soothe him, and to court his approval, even as he shattered her heart.

Maybe she hadn't truly loved him then, because leaving shouldn't be easy, she thought, reaching for the damned door handle, eyes blurry with tears.

"Nyra?" Her name fell from his lips softly, with none of the contempt he clearly felt for her.

She thumped her forehead against the thick wood, wishing she could disappear into its grain. "What?" she said, with enough belligerence to sound like a pissed-off teenager. Figured that the little courage she possessed came out when everything around her was burning to the ground.

"It is you in that picture. Why, *cara*?" That he called her that even as he thrust a silken knife into her chest made her want to laugh like a maniac.

If he'd let a hint of doubt seep into his voice, if he had let her see the thinnest crack in his veneer, if he hadn't hung her out to dry in front of his family, maybe she would have turned around and explained it.

But God, she was as sick of living in fear of Adriano and his prestigious family discovering whose daughter she was, of wondering how long the safety of his arms would last.

It was high time she dwelled in reality. For the innocent life in her belly if not for herself.

"Is there anything to explain? Clearly you have decided that I fucked another man," she said, choosing the abrasive words deliberately. Softness had no place in her life anymore. "I hope the image of me, half-naked and writhing against that man, haunts you for the rest of your life."

It wasn't the greatest parting shot, but she felt a blood-thirstiness she'd never known in herself, that she embraced now.

Foolish to think that a man like Adriano Cavalieri wouldn't wipe off the slate and start over again with a more beautiful, accomplished woman, but in this, she would indulge herself.

That the image would torment him as much as he'd hurt her.

CHAPTER THREE

Six weeks later

THE SUDDEN SPLASHING of ice-cold water against his head, prickling his skin and drenching him in mere seconds made Adriano jerk awake from his stupor.

He let out a string of filthy expletives, wondered if he was imagining Fabi's half giggle, half gasp.

Dios mio, where was he and why did his head feel like there was a large metal rod poking through it? What day was it?

"Wake up, *Sleeping Beauty*." Bruno's dry mockery felt like a shout, then he felt his arms under his pits.

Through sheer stubbornness, his best friend lifted him, dragged him into what apparently was his bathroom, because the marble was suddenly cold against his feet.

Adriano blinked and tried to clear his head but hangover was a screw behind his eyes, poking and drilling and…screwing with his balance. He heard Fabi shout that she would make some coffee and then Bruno was stripping him and dragging him again and then there was the ice-cold spray of water all over his naked skin.

With what he hoped was a masculine growl, but was

sure was an unmanly yelp, he turned the knob to blazing hot spray. His skin felt like it was being pricked by a thousand needles but slowly, surely, sanity returned. Along with his location and his current state.

He had checked into his usual suite at George V in Paris three days ago and gotten filthy drunk. The thought of facing work or his family or anyone for another weekend had felt like torment. It was the sixth weekend in a row he had checked into some hotel incognito and gotten filthy drunk.

It was the last thing he'd expected of himself, ever.

As if she was a witch who'd cast a curse on him, Nyra's parting words to him came true. Night or day, waking or sleeping, the image of her in some man's arms...tormented him. The pain of what she had done, the loss of her shy smiles, of her tight hugs and her welcoming body, felt like a physical ache he could only numb with alcohol. It felt as if someone had gouged his heart out of his chest and left a gaping, weeping wound.

For the second time in his life, he had no control over his thoughts, his feelings, and worse, his actions. And he didn't know how to fix it.

Unless it involved seeing her and talking to her...

Is there anything to explain? she'd demanded, such fury written on her face. She hadn't denied that she'd stolen all those things, but the pics...they had shocked her, disgusted her and, finally, infuriated her.

If she was innocent—how she could be with those pics staring at him in technicolor, he didn't know—why hadn't she said one word to that effect?

The band of muscles in his stomach tightened as if trying to expel the discomfort sitting there like a boulder. By the time he dressed and emerged into the attached kitchen, he felt minimally human. And worse than before as far as his emotions were concerned.

Because, for just a second, he'd considered bringing her back even if she had...

Fabi threw herself at him, her skinny arms wrapping around his middle like tentacles, whispering, "I'm sorry."

Adriano ruffled her hair and stroked her back. Over her head, he met Bruno's eyes. He was pouring coffee, and yet his best friend's gaze didn't relent for a second in conveying its message of rebuke and...guilt.

He cut his gaze away—another first for Adriano— unwilling to face Bruno's recriminations. "Fabi, whatever you have done, yet again, I'm sure it is fixable," he said, forcing a patience he didn't feel. "I'll talk to Mama and sort it out."

When his sister looked up, it wasn't the usual naughty expression on her face. She nodded, almost to herself and muttered, "Let's hope you feel the same after you hear everything."

Taking the cup Bruno offered, Adriano took several sips of the scalding coffee. His world tilted a little straighter but not all the way. He was beginning to think it would never be the same without his wife.

"Are you feeling sane enough to listen?" Bruno asked.

"I'm allowed a weekend's privacy. Your job is not to tail me all over the world like a dog," he said, letting his irritation at being caught in such a state slip into his words. "And why the hell are you dragging Fabi around? She shouldn't have to see me in such a...state."

"Since you're behaving the same way Papa does, you mean," his sister said, and then ducked her head.

"I couldn't shake her off," Bruno replied, utterly unfazed by Adriano's attack. "She wanted to be here when I tell you."

"Tell me what?" Adriano demanded.

"Fabi has something to say about the photos."

The coffee cup shattered in Adriano's hand, as if it were nothing but a kid's play cup. Hot liquid scalded his hand on top of a shard digging into his palm. But all of that felt like nothing but a background hum to the rage he felt at his friend's betrayal. He pushed at Bruno's chest with his scalding hand, his control in broken pieces just like the ceramic. "I asked you to burn those photos. How dare you show them to her?"

"I demanded to see them."

Adriano stared at the cut on his palm. "*Dios mio*, Fabi. I know you loathe the air she breathed, but you cross so many lines if you derive pleasure from this mess."

Fabi flinched as if he had struck her. "I know how I behaved toward her was…horrible. I…" She took a deep breath. "I was the one who snooped in her belongings and figured out that she was making those trips to London. I was the one who tipped off Bruno and then he hired that PI. I started it all."

"You snooped through her belongings…" Hot shame slithered through Adriano's chest. How had he not protected his wife from this kind of behavior from his own family? Was that what had driven her to…

"That's not all," Bruno added as if he realized that Adriano was this close to throwing them both out of the suite by the scruff of their necks.

"Apology accepted, Fabi. Now get out."

"No. I was insecure because of how much you seemed

to…prefer her company to any of us. You even forgot my birthday this year." Catching his gaze, she stuttered. "You know what Mama and… Papa have been like our whole lives. You're everything to me, to Federico, even if he won't say it. It felt like she was stealing you from us, Adriano. So, I followed Mama's tune and was a bitch to her, *si*. And she never once called me on it until that day at dinner…" Fabi sniffled. "After she left, I bugged Bruno why, and he told me and… I couldn't believe that you would believe some cheap photos. The reason Mama feels so threatened by Nyra is precisely because she seems to be made of the kind of integrity and loyalty that she has never understood. I can't believe you thought that Nyra would…betray you like that. Anyway, I insisted on seeing the photos and…" Tears poured down her cheeks.

Adriano turned to Bruno.

"It's not Nyra. In the photos," Bruno said, rushing through his words, knowing Adriano was at the end of his tether. "Fabi's the one who spotted the difference. The woman in them, she has a tattoo under her…breast. It's in shadow but it's there, especially when you zoom in on the soft copy. A tiny rose. As far as I know, Nyra doesn't have a tattoo anywhere on her body."

For just a second, Adriano had the insane urge to punch his best friend in his face for knowing that about his wife, for taking her name with such reverence. He'd always known that Bruno had a soft spot for Nyra, but this was a crossing of boundaries and he wouldn't tolerate any man, even his best friend, noticing things about…

Then the blaring truth struck him with the force of a tsunami.

It wasn't Nyra in the photos. She hadn't cheated on him. She hadn't broken their vows, she hadn't...

The relief that flooded his entire being was short-lived, decimated by guilt that clawed its bloody nails across his insides. Sinking against the bench by the foot of the untouched bed, Adriano buried his face in his hands.

The pale tint to her tawny golden skin as she held his eyes, the streak of tears that he'd mocked her for, the hurt pinching her mouth...she'd refused to explain herself, but the truth had been written on her face.

And even knowing how to read it, even knowing her better than he'd ever known another woman in his life, he had failed.

I hope the image of me with that man haunts you for the rest of your life.

Her parting words skewered him afresh, for he now understood the ferocious thrust beneath.

"Who is the woman in the photos?" he said, the cobwebs clearing from his head. One little shift in perspective and the truth blinded him with its simplicity.

"Her twin, Nadia. I sent you her file. They were separated when they were fourteen. Once Fabi spotted the difference, I went back to the PI and located the woman. Nadia has a history of..." Bruno looked hesitant. "Drugs. I'm not sure if Nyra even knows that. She's just been leaving her envelopes full of cash in places that Nadia asked her to. Even though Nadia refused to meet her. The PI mistook her for Nyra at the café and followed her. Their background...you should brace yourself. It's going to be problematic. For you."

I needed the money, Adriano, urgently, she had said, looking devastated.

But he hadn't been in a listening mood. He'd already decided that she was guilty.

"Worse than what I've created?" he scoffed, rubbing a hand over his face.

Bruno dropped the name of a notorious financial embezzler's name into the silence—a man who had ruined thousands of livelihoods through Europe, apparently his wife's father—and the last piece of the puzzle fell into place. A pithy curse flew out of Adriano's mouth.

So that's why Nyra had lied that she was an orphan, why she'd been happy to hide herself away in the margins of his life. But why not tell him that she had an identical twin when faced with those cheap photos? Why not trust him with a little bit of the truth?

Like you trusted her, a voice whispered sarcastically.

"Find her," he said, shooting to his feet.

He had been called a lot of things by the media and his own family, ruthless and tyrannical being the most common, but Adriano never punched down on the innocent.

Neither was he so full of his own ego that he couldn't admit when he made a mistake. This wasn't just a mistake though, but a blunder of epic proportions.

Urgency beat through him as he rifled through his discarded jacket for his phone. "Put as many people as you need on it, Bruno. Make sure you—"

"I know where she is," came Bruno's reply.

Adriano turned to find his friend's steady gaze. A torrent of questions, all fueled by jealousy and possessiveness, filled him, but he held them back. Then came another new helping of shame, because despite the photo, he had a feeling that Bruno hadn't believed that Nyra had cheated on him.

It galled and scraped and burned.

Adriano let his friend see the shame lick at him in a thousand little flames. Maybe that's why they had stuck to each other through everything. To hold each other to a standard above any they'd ever been shown.

"Where is she?" he said, putting on his jacket. "Ask Pascale to get the chopper ready and—"

"She's at my farmhouse, an hour north of Milan."

Apparently, this day held no end of small shocks. "Since when?"

"Since she left," Bruno said, instead of *since you asked her to leave.* A consideration he didn't deserve. "She asked me if I could find her somewhere to stay for a couple of days. Until she could figure out what to do."

"And she's been there all this time?"

Something flashed in Bruno's eyes, but he only nodded.

"Why?"

"Why did I help a helpless woman who had nowhere else to go?" Bruno said, with a soft scoff. "Because you taught me to always do the right thing."

Adriano swallowed and nodded, disbelief and gratitude twining through him.

Why had Bruno believed her to be innocent even when he'd had the proof, while Adriano hadn't? What was he lacking?

He had a feeling that question was going to torment him for a long time.

* * *

Nyra knew it was time to stop hiding at Bruno's farmhouse.

She couldn't return to Vegas or London though. Not in her current condition. Not when she had a hundred and six dollars to her name. Not when she hadn't sold any of her art in a while. She'd been too distracted to paint while stealing and selling things to raise enough cash to help Nadia.

And in the six weeks since Adriano had thrown her out, her head, *and her heart*, were full of regrets and recriminations, with nothing left behind for inspiration.

Should she have explained that it wasn't her in those horrible photos? Wasn't Adriano valid in his anger when he didn't know that she had an identical twin?

But why did he have to be so cold and cruel toward her?

Did she even have the right to indulge in this righteous fury and this reckless tantrum when she was going to be a mother?

Questions pelted her from every direction, as they'd done since she'd arrived at the farmhouse. Sooner or later, she'd have to tell Adriano and demand some kind of settlement.

Life had taught her to be practical if nothing else. He was the father and she wasn't going to simply fade away from his life because he'd ordered her to.

She just needed to muster the courage to face him and fight him, if need be. See him just one more time, and then, never again.

The sound of a car driving up the winding gravel

road toward the farmhouse made her skin prickle with alarm. She stared at the rubbish splashes she'd made on the easel, but for once couldn't care.

Was it divorce papers? Would he serve them himself?

It was a miracle that Bruno had kept her whereabouts a secret for so long. Her husband was a prestigious banker with an illustrious family history. No doubt Nigella would find him the perfect wife this time.

All she cared about right now was that she got what she needed. Even as an eighteen-year-old alone in the world, she'd never asked for handouts. But now, she would fight and bargain and negotiate tooth and nail.

The summer heat was in full swing. She stood up, took a drink of water and wiped her neck with a dirty rag just as she felt a presence behind her. The small hairs on her neck and arms stood up, and a shiver zinged down her spine.

Her body reacted like that to only one man's gaze. Had done so from the first moment he had looked at her. *So he had come himself.*

It took all the courage she had to stay standing on knees that suddenly felt like they were made of pudding. She gathered her bravado, mostly fake, and her dignity, very real, to herself, before she grabbed the edge of the table littered with paint supplies for support and turned.

Adriano stood inside the curving archway of the open barn, blocking all light. Sucking in all the air, exerting his own gravity on her. Pulling her into his orbit.

She didn't mean to do it, but her hands automatically drifted to her belly, the small bump visible beneath the smock she had tied over a cotton sundress. A protective gesture, she realized, in front of a man she didn't trust anymore.

His gray-green gaze followed her hands. Shock made the black swallow the fascinating hues of his eyes. A gaunt bleakness bracketed his mouth.

She braced herself, even as something inside her splintered at his reaction. That he had to find out like this wasn't on her. She repeated that like a mantra.

"You're pregnant," he said, after what felt like an eternity of staring at her. His chest rose and fell, and it was the most agitated Nyra had ever seen this man she thought of as a mountain.

"Glad to see you're sharp as ever," she said dryly, pouring oil into her palms. The rubbing action gave her something to focus on, even though she didn't require the blend she usually used to get rid of the oil paint stains from her fingers.

He pushed off the wall, as if finally, he could trust his legs to hold him up. It was so uncharacteristic of the smoothly confident man she knew that it balanced out her own teetering emotions.

There was nothing he could say that could hurt her anymore. Or touch her in any way.

Bafflement made his mouth slack. He rubbed a finger over his temple and she had the sense of contained but volcanic temper. And a stupid part of her wanted to see the explosion. "You're already showing. How far along are you?"

"Eight weeks."

He flinched, as if she'd launched a missile at him. "So you knew that day…"

She nodded.

"Why didn't you say anything?"

Turning around, she straightened the supplies she'd spread around the table. "And have you throw another dirty accusation in my face?"

His soft grunt was loud in the silence, and she was glad that she didn't have to see his face.

"Is it…? Are you…?"

Fresh anger came to her aid, making her whirl around too fast. "Are the babies growing in my belly yours? Yes, Adriano."

"Babies? As in plural?"

"Twins, yes. And no, I have no proof that they are yours and I honestly don't care to provide it."

A sudden thought made her jerk back and she hit her hip on the sharp edge of the table. She gasped.

Then he was there, his corded arm steadying her. His warm breath hitting her cheek in whispery strokes. The heat from his body was a blanket, beckoning her close. The power thrumming through his frame lulling her into a false sense of security.

All she wanted to do was lean into him and let him carry her away. Where she didn't have to worry about how she was going to raise two babies all by herself. But…that was the easy, cowardly way out.

Murmuring thanks, she stepped away before her base urges won out and defeated her in the process.

As she rubbed the sore spot on her hip, the offending thought came back to her. "I will not under any circumstance go through any kind of DNA testing, simply to prove paternity to you. There's no test that's not invasive and inherently harmful to the babies. I'm a UK citizen and I've been boning up on my rights."

"You have consulted a lawyer?"

"Yes, one of Bruno's friends. I have paid the lawyer a small retainer, which she was generous enough to accept."

His jaw tightened, and a vein pulsed in his temple. No doubt it was at the thought of a lawyer arming her with information in case it came to a custody fight. The very thought sent a cold shiver through her core.

"You're cold," he said, reaching for her hands.

Nyra jerked away. "No. I'm rather hot, actually. It's your being here that's making my body react with fear."

This time, she caught the rearing back of his chin, as clearly as if she'd swung a punch.

A whiteness emerged around his mouth. "You're afraid of me, Nyra?"

She shrugged. "You're a very powerful man who thinks I've wronged you and threw me out without looking back. I've been counting my blessings that your family is too scared of you. Or my alleged sins would have hit the media already.

"And yes, while I'm afraid, I can't be the helpless, starstruck damsel you picked up in Vegas if I want my children to grow up with a healthy sense of security and stability. I know you probably think that you made a huge mistake by not making me sign a prenup, but I want very little in terms of a settlement."

Her chin wobbled. No, there was no place for shame here, and there was nothing she wouldn't do to provide the love and stability she hadn't known in so long. "The lawyer said I should ask for alimony too, but all I want is a trust fund for the babies. You can set it up so it's overseen by someone you trust, like Bruno. If you deny me, then I will wait until they're born and file for paternity claim."

"Why wait?" he asked smoothly, as if they were discussing a merger for his company.

"Paternity can be proved without a doubt then and the courts will order you. I'd rather not have it go to that. And I'm hoping you won't want that kind of publicity to damage the great Cavalieri name."

"Like you've been protecting the Cavalieri name this whole time?" he said smoothly. "By lying to me about who you are?"

She shrugged. "I didn't want my background to become a problem for you. After the kindness you showed me in Vegas and later."

"I wish my kindness," he said, enunciating the words, "had begat your trust, Nyra."

No answer came to her for that fair question.

"So you're claiming that the babies are mine?" he said, the fracture in his temper already smoothed over.

Like that day in his study, a great, overwhelming urge to do violence to his pretty face came over Nyra. She forced herself to breathe through it and fought the rising scream too.

When she turned to him, it was to find him observing her like she was a fascinating specimen, his head tilted to the side.

"Yes. That's what I'm *claiming*, Adriano," she said, air quoting the word.

"Then there's no reason for a trust fund or a lawyer or any other nonsense. You simply need to come home."

Nyra snorted, even as a new fear slithered through

her belly. "Right? Because you believe my word about my babies."

"*Ours, Nyra*. Our babies," he said, so softly, so gently, with her name a caress on those lips that she thought she might break apart. Some steely resolve hardened in his eyes. "And *si*, I believe you."

"Are you sure? Like really sure, Adriano?" She threw the rag aside and started putting the lids on the numerous glass jars of paint, shaking with anger she didn't want to give in to. "Who knows what kind of photographs might emerge a few months from now with the exact date-stamp of their conception? I don't have the energy for your outrage and for being kicked out again. So please, just give me a tiny parcel of your mighty fortune, and a divorce. You'll never have to see me again."

"*Basta*, Nyra," he said, showing the first crack in his smooth, rippleless countenance. "I know it wasn't you in the photographs but your twin, Nadia. Your father was Amal Shah, the Ponzi schemer who stole millions from unsuspecting clients and their pensions across Europe and died in jail. And I know why you stole those candlesticks, why you sold our wedding ring. I'm..." He reached her then, and his fingers, those long, slender, blunt-tipped fingers she knew as well as her own, *trembled* as he stroked them over her cheek. "You should have told me, Nyra. All you had to do was speak one sentence, and I would have taken care of all your problems."

She laughed then, and even to her own ears, the sound was broken, bitter. "Either you're still in shock over the truth of my background or that great conscience of yours is stealing your rationality, Adriano. You're forgetting what will happen when it leaks whose daughter your wife is.

"Wronged people have long memories. Even after all these years, the slightest mention of my father's name in the media or online sends ripples through all the innocent lives he ruined. Posts will go up in forums about how we're hiding away in some exotic place, living like heiresses off of the blood of others.

"Your great family name, your pristine reputation as the most innovative, respectable banker Italy has ever seen will be dragged through mud."

"That is my cross to bear," he said with a rough exhale. "And I would have made sure it never touched you again."

She stared at him in shock. Why wasn't he angry that she'd hidden a truth that could ruin his and his family's reputation? Why wasn't he judging her, like the entire world had done, for whose daughter she was? Where was the contempt and the disgust that she and Nadia had carried like a curse and a taint with them wherever they went in those early years after their father had been imprisoned?

Overnight, they and their mother hadn't just lost their home, but friends and classmates and neighbors they had known all their lives had turned against them. At school, their days had become unbearable. Everyone had assumed so easily that the three of them were not only complicit in his crimes but that they were still enjoying the poisonous fruits of his scams.

Where was Adriano's very justified anger that she'd braced herself about what a headache she'd brought into his life?

Of course, his reaction was nothing like she'd assumed. And where he should have trusted her, he hadn't. Frustration, at him and herself, roiled through her. "One glance at that disgusting photo and you should have known that it wasn't me."

He jerked back as if she had shouted the words at him instead of whispered them. "Nyra—"

"All I want is to raise my babies in relative peace and security. Please, Adriano, you know now the entire, pathetic tale of my background and that I didn't cheat on you. Do this small thing for me."

"No, you're not listening to me." His large hands clasped her cheeks, his words slow, but expertly enunciated. "I want you to come back to our home. To our life together. I want to raise…the babies with you. You belong with me."

Near hysteria came upon Nyra as she registered the urgency, the honesty underlining his words. He thought he could walk in here now that he had proof, and she would simply go back to him?

Beneath the dizziness claiming her, she wished it could be that simple. That her battered, shattered heart would simple scab over and she could go on as if nothing had happened.

But she couldn't.

"You're powerful and arrogant and ruthless, Adriano," she said, laughing at the ridiculousness of his demands, "but even you can't simply turn back time to six weeks ago. I can't go back to you. There is no marriage left, if it even was one in the first place."

"You're being stubborn. Any man would—"

"But you're not any man," she said, poking him in the

chest, "as I've been reminded again and again. You're better than most men."

"Nyra—"

"No."

"Your twin is in trouble. Worse than you might have imagined all these months."

"What do you mean?" she said, fisting her fingers in his chest. "Is she hurt?" The very thought twisted her inside out.

He cupped her shoulders, as if he knew that her knees were close to giving out. "I'm sorry, *bella*. It seems she has a drug addiction problem. All the money you've given her, she used it to buy drugs. She's back to living on the streets."

The bottom dropped out of Nyra's world. After everything she had done to give Nadia what she needed, it was all…lies? Tears prickled behind her eyes and fatigue fell over her like a dank, suffocating blanket. "She's had it so much harder than I did, Adriano. That cousin she was sent to live with…she used to write to me that he was making her life hell. She told me he used to demand that she…work for him if she wanted to live under his roof. Now I realize why she wouldn't see me. Please…don't judge her for this." She didn't know why she even cared what he thought of her twin but it was important to her.

"Tell me something about you both," he said, surprising her yet again. "Something from a happy time."

She blinked, but memories came fast and easy. "As a young girl, I… I preferred to lose myself in drawing and comics. I was quite reserved. I had no friends and never needed any because all I needed was her. She, on the other hand…" A smile curved her mouth, her heart blooming with warmth at the memory. "Nadia was…a bright ray of sunshine, always making others laugh, up for any kind of prank, surrounded by tons of friends. When our birthday would come around, I'd dread it every year because what if she spent it with her friends? What if she found me boring? I mean, it's natural that we might drift apart. But every year, she'd spend the whole day with me. Making me laugh, sharing her presents with me, buying me some kind of art supplies with her allowance. I think she…loved me just as I was."

That sense of faith and utter love she had around her twin returned to her with each word she used to describe that moment. Nyra felt a lightness she hadn't known in…months.

She looked up to find Adriano's gaze studying her with that intensity that licked at her skin like a live flame. But this time, it was tempered by…curiosity. "Thank you for forcing me to remember. For giving me that piece back."

"Thank you for helping me see," he said, with a stiffness she didn't understand. "You love her."

A long breath shuddered out of her. "I do. She's just… unwell and needs help to be that Nadia I knew once."

"I agree."

"You do?" Another shock wave came at her as she searched his eyes. There was nothing but honesty there. No disgust or contempt.

He nodded.

Sudden, intense relief seized her. If Adriano was on her side, she could help Nadia through anything. She could get the girl she'd adored back. Her faith in him even as he'd doubted her in the worst way was…pathetic, but it was there. As solid as the ground she stood on.

"Do you know where she is? If I can just talk to her—"

"Once he discovered it wasn't you in the pic, Bruno went looking for the PI and found her. For now, he's taking her to the local hospital with him. But this cycle doesn't have to repeat. I'll have a team of the best doctors attending to her within the hour. My assistant is on the line with the admin team of one of the best rehab clinics in Europe. She will be taken care of, Nyra, and have the best help to beat this."

"If?" Nyra said, finally getting a grasp of how her husband operated.

"If you come back with me," Adriano announced without missing a beat. "You've done so much for her, *si*? What is this last step?"

"I hate you." The words slipped past the leash she kept on her emotions.

He smiled, and it was the same one he'd given her that evening. Dark and…sad. "No more than I despise myself, *bella*," he said, reaching for her as she stumbled yet again.

Nyra leaned her head against his chest, both to steady herself, and to stop herself from going any further. Soon, her belly would be big enough to provide her a barrier from clinging to him.

She didn't believe, for one second, that he was doing this because he wanted her back in his life.

No, as much as she'd taunted him, Adriano was a man who operated on a strict moral code—an exception among powerful men. It was one of the things that she had adored about him from the beginning. Being powerful had never made him awful to the help, or unaware of his privilege.

Guilt was making him enter a situation in which he wouldn't have the upper hand. But guilt was a temporary emotion. Eventually, it would leave a vacuum behind.

She took in deep breaths, inhaling his scent in the process. And it was the very thing that she needed to avoid that steadied her brain, that gave her fighting ground. "I know how to play this game now that I've seen how your mind works."

"This isn't a game, *bella*."

"No?" If his words pinged over her skin like the open-mouthed kisses that he was so good at, Nyra ignored the sensation. "I… How do you know I won't leave you once my sister is well?" When he'd have provided counterargument, she pressed her finger to his lips. "Yes, it could take months or even years. The one thing I do have is faith in her. However long it takes, she will be free of addiction. And *I will* leave you."

"That is a long time to withhold forgiveness, Nyra," he whispered against her finger.

His Adam's apple bobbed with his swallow, bringing her attention to the strong column of his throat. How foolish she'd been to tuck her face into his neck and call it her safe place.

There was nothing safe about this man for her ever again.

"Oh, is that what this is all about?" she said, pulling away.

The farther she stood from him, the better her defenses were. Even though the sudden motion only intensified the dizzy feeling. God, her throat was parched and she wanted him gone so that she could lick her wounds in private. "I forgive you, Adriano, for thinking I broke our vows in the worst manner possible. I forgive you for thinking that a woman who traded up from taking off her clothes could have no better morals than to spread her legs for any man. I forgive you for acting like you know me, that you see me and then shattering that belief with one swift action. I forgive you for showing me what a naive fool I was to..." Somehow, she held off the soppy declaration. "There, you are free to move on."

And then, whether it was because of heat or exhaustion or sheer shock, Nyra felt a darkness claim her. But before she gave in, she thought she heard Adriano whisper his apologies into her skin, his gray-green eyes full of a terror she never wanted to witness ever again.

CHAPTER FOUR

DUSK HAD FALLEN in sudden bursts that evening, bringing with it a welcome chill as Nyra walked around the terrace of the apartment by Lake Navigli.

The roof garden that had always felt like a safe haven now felt like a cage. But fainting into Adriano's arms put paid to any ideas she'd had of doing this alone.

She'd never passed out in her life before, and doing so that afternoon had scared her just as much as it had him.

The doctor he'd summoned had checked her and pronounced it had been heat exhaustion and cautioned her to hydrate better.

Despite the shock of his arrival, she'd had to reassure Adriano that she had already been feeling dizzy and dehydrated by the time he had arrived. And that he hadn't pushed her to it.

Still, guilt was a powerful emotion and it rode him hard the rest of the day. And in that mood, when he got to that stubborn place, no one had the power to gainsay Adriano Cavalieri. And she'd been shaken enough that when he'd loaded her into his air-conditioned car, after exchanging tense words with the doctor, she'd complied. Her only demand had been that he didn't bring her to the villa. The last thing she felt prepared to do was face his family just then.

She'd promptly fallen asleep, only waking when he'd settled her into the vast bed, *their bed*, and gently pushed her sweaty hair back from her forehead.

Sighing, she had leaned into his hand, grabbed it between hers, rolled over and fallen back asleep. And she knew he had stayed there, at her back, until she'd released his hand, that he'd held her when she'd cried in her sleep.

Her face flamed now, even as the cool breeze licked her skin. She needed to stop acting so soppy around him. Just because he had cared for her this afternoon, acted as if she were truly his cherished, precious, pregnant wife didn't mean it was real.

A soft cashmere shawl landed on her shoulders, gently enough not to spook her.

She stilled, fighting the childish urge to throw it back in his face. She couldn't tire herself, and her willpower, by engaging in silly fights with him. She had to choose her battles wisely.

"Thank you," she whispered, casting him a sidelong glance. And then her gaze got stuck there, on his profile, as it always did.

In the moonlight, his still-wet hair gleamed like it was made of onyx, a little gray peeking through at the temples. A dark olive green sweater hugged his broad chest, trying and failing to bring him to some earthly, casual plane. His lower lip was viciously caught in his teeth. He had a habit of chewing on his lip when he was deep in thought.

The memory of threatening to kiss that stern mouth

every time he went off into some deep thought washed through her, bringing soft heat to her limbs.

God, how was she going to get through the next few months when he was a constant temptation? She'd already learned that some women—of course she had to be one of them—felt extra horny and sexual during their pregnancy.

Just her luck that he would discover that and use it as another carrot stick to control her. Although, she would prefer the other stick he had on him.

An unsanctioned giggle burst forth from her lips at the naughty thought and she stumbled. Instantly, his hand came to her elbow and stilled. As if knowing that she wouldn't welcome a deeper touch.

"I'm glad to hear you laugh, *bella*. Care to share what brought it on?"

"Nope," she said, popping the *p* like an annoying teenager.

She felt his sigh before she heard it. Tension thrummed through him, even if he did his best not to betray it. "Is the exhaustion from the afternoon gone, then?"

"Yes. The nap did a lot of good. As did the juice bar and the juice specialist with fifteen different choices on the menu. Kind of overkill for one person, don't you think?"

"It's more convenience than anything else. I would prefer to never see you faint like that again in the near future. Or ever again."

"Yeah, sure. I'll do my best to keep your peace of mind intact."

"Nyra, I…"

"We didn't finish our discussion from this afternoon."

"Your twin will get every possible care given to her. She's landed in Switzerland and checked into the clinic. They will send us an update every few days. I've told them to add your email to the list."

Instantly, her throat filled up. When she'd begged Bruno to connect her to her twin, Nadia had come on the line but refused to talk. Only her sobs had been audible, and Nyra had conducted the conversation one-sided, telling her that she loved her, that she'd get over this little setback and that she was dying to hug her.

"Thank you for arranging that," Nyra said, clearing her throat. "That's not what I meant though. I had no doubt that you'd take care of all that once you gave your word."

"Such trust in me, Nyra?"

She laughed at his neat little maneuver. "Arranging all this for my sister probably took you one click of your clever fingers. You have the resources, the capability and now the interest in arranging it. This is nothing to you."

"And yet you didn't think of coming to me for help," he pointed out, and this time, Nyra did fall into the trap and wriggled.

In nine months of their marriage, she'd discovered that he wasn't only magnetic and sexy as fuck, but kind and generous beneath that power humming on the surface. But she couldn't trust him. She hadn't been able to trust her own parents to keep her safe.

"When we first met, you wouldn't have cast me a second glance if I opened my considerable, media-icky baggage. The divide between an exotic dancer and a banker was already wide enough."

"You're projecting your fears onto me," he said, sounding angry.

She sighed. "We'll never know how you might have reacted. Ever since my father's embezzlement was discovered and he was arrested, we lost so many friends. And you...you're a pillar of respectability in the banking world. Even after I realized who you were, how bad our association could become for you, I couldn't stop. I wanted you too much." The words rushed out of her. It was a slip, yes, but also the truth. "Not for worldly gain or to be seen with a powerful man. I found you attractive and then interesting. It was a double whammy."

If she assumed that he would tease her for it, or even use it as some kind of upper hand in this battle, she would've been proved wrong.

He lifted his chin in acknowledgment, his lip caught between his teeth. Her gaze lingered on his angular profile, honeyed heat drizzling through her. If she were honest with herself now, his ruthless actions hadn't dimmed his appeal one bit. Which struck her as the height of unfair.

"I should have brought my conditions up before I fainted and followed you here like a dutiful little puppy," she said, wistfully.

"Is that how you see yourself with me, Nyra?" He sounded almost...sad at the picture she painted.

She shrugged, refusing to elaborate.

"Tell me your conditions."

"I'm not sure how your parents will react to this pregnancy, given everything I've done. I refuse to be subjected to their brand of venom through the pregnancy. So leave me here."

"Hiding you here looks like you're truly guilty. For all my sins, I've never backed away from admitting when I'm wrong." He cast her a sidelong, assessing glace. "And while I never meant it like that, keeping you here, separated from the rest of my life made it look like I was ashamed of you."

"That isn't on you," she said, her fair-mindedness forcing her to speak. "I chose to…"

"Why did you never tell me how they treated you when I wasn't present?"

This time, she had no answer.

"I never made you believe that I would be okay with them calling you names to your face, treating you like you were some cheap tart I picked up by mistake, *bella*. Please—" frustration rattled the word as it fell through his tight lips "—do not put that sin at my feet."

"I… I don't know why I didn't come to you," Nyra admitted, even if it made her feel raw again. "It felt like telling to the teacher. I guess I thought you'd…" She cut herself off there. "I didn't dare test the tenuous bond we had."

His jaw locked up so tight that she would need a jack-hammer to break through. A tenderness she didn't want to feel toward him coiled in her chest. He'd doubted her loyalty, even her character, but there was no denying the fact that she had lied to him. A lot. The why she was too exhausted to plumb her own behavior just then. "Not telling you and not standing up to them was both foolish and cowardly. But I'm telling you now and—"

"They will all apologize to you. Will continue to, until you're satisfied."

Nyra stopped so fast that her head spun. "That's…

that's not what I asked for, Adriano. Really, they would just hate me more if you humiliated them."

"That's a problem I will deal with directly this time," he said, taking the ends of her shawl and pulling them tight. He bopped the tip of her nose in a playful gesture, but his words weren't light when he said, "I'm already a villain in your book. Keep your conscience light and free."

Nyra was only capable of nodding.

He turned, taking away temptation with him. "What else?"

"I want that trust fund for my…for the babies," she amended. "You can lock it up however you want."

"For when you leave me," he added, without missing a beat.

"I'm learning to be…smart. For them," she said, palming her belly over the shawl.

"That's…smart," he said, and then grinned.

It was impossible not to smile in return. The prospect of being parents touched every glance and word, every interaction between them.

He would make a wonderful father—Nyra knew it as surely as she knew her own rasping breath. But them together as a couple was a different matter. A mirage that she would never believe in again.

"I have one more condition," she said.

"Tell me."

She bit her lip. "It's more a generous gift I'm trying to trick out of you since you're in a receptive mood."

"No con man or woman would admit to the con before they spring it."

"Hey, I'm still learning," she said, giving him a shoulder nudge. He was so solid that she simply swung in the opposite direction instantly. Even with her growing girth.

His arm snaked out to catch her by the waist, that same flicker of fear dancing in his eyes again. "Careful, Nyra."

There was anger and command and more in his words. That raw, simmering emotion that he never let rise to the surface. Could there be anything more than common decency under his fear for her?

God, she was a pushover.

"Tell me what you plan to con out of me."

"When my sister...whenever Nadia gets out of the rehab clinic, I would like to have her live with me. Provide her with some kind of financial help so that she can make a new start. And—"

"Yes, to everything. I will have a trust fund sort of thing set up for her too. You can review it and see if suits what you have in mind. *Except* having her near you if she gets discharged during the pregnancy."

"What? Why?"

"You're clearly very emotional about her, and I don't want you to distress yourself if she slips up or if your reunion doesn't go as planned. Or if she isn't interested at all in getting to know you. I know that she refused to say a word to you on the call."

That blunt reminder hurt, but Nyra couldn't change her mind. "She's my twin, Adriano. I've tried to find her for years."

"So a few more months won't be that much, *si*?" he threw back seamlessly.

He was right, and yet Nyra was feeling contrary

enough not to want to fall in with his plans. "And what about you?"

"What about me, *cara mia*?"

"You…create emotional distress in me too. Being around you reminds me how naive and stupid I was. How I let you—"

His palm came to rest against her mouth. "Stop it, Nyra. You were not, *are not*, any of those things. I was—" his nostrils flared "—in the wrong. The minute I knew you were lying to me or hedging the truth as it were, my view of you got skewed. I do not handle…" He thrust a hand through his hair. "When I saw those photographs…"

"I don't want to talk about them," Nyra said, slapping her hand over his mouth now. "I…can't have a reasonable discussion about it."

"When, then?"

"Maybe never," she said perversely.

He grasped her wrist, pressing his fingers over the pulse. "Is that all you want of me?"

She swallowed. "Yes. That's all I want of you."

"Bene," he said with a wistfulness she'd never seen in him. Something unsaid tinged the cool night air around them. Something as hungry and bright as her longing for him. "I will leave you to settle in, in peace."

Nyra nodded, feeling bereft at the thought of sleeping alone in that fluffy, cloudlike bed.

In the nine months that they'd been married—three of which he'd been traveling—she had gotten thoroughly spoiled with a comfort she hadn't known in years. Since Nadia and she had been separated at the age of thirteen, to be exact.

Not sleeping alone was a luxury.

In that, she had hit the jackpot with Adriano. The man was a live furnace, his densely packed body giving off heat like no one else's business. And even better, he liked to share that heat with her by wrapping those corded forearms, and those lean, powerful legs all around her.

While she was always cold. He would do an exaggerated pretend shiver every time she tucked her cold feet between his shins and then warm her fingers between his large hands.

But it wasn't her body that he'd warmed on all those nights when he pulled himself away from the bank and his family and came to her. To this apartment.

It was the cold frost that she'd surrounded her heart with that he had melted with his passion, his kindness, his attention.

Only now, when she didn't have it, did Nyra realize how little she had understood what he gave her. And how well he'd protected her against the cold and the world.

Until he had ripped it all away from her in one moment. Throwing her out to the cold world again, with no hesitation.

But now she had her self-respect, as much as it would warm her up in a cold bed. And she wasn't going to give it up in a hurry.

When he bid her good night at the door to their suite, without so much as a kiss on her cheek, tears prickled at the back of her eyes.

God, she was turning into such a contrary, emotional creature but she couldn't help it. After washing up, she went to his side of the closet, grabbed one of his shirts and pulled it on over her bra and panties, then settled under the luxurious sheets.

If she sniffed his shirt like an addict searching for a high for the next hour, what was the harm?

Clearly, for Adriano, this was all about fixing his mistakes. About protecting her during this fragile time. About ensuring that his children were taken care of in the best way, even before they were born.

It was better she get used to doing things alone again.

Adriano crept into the bedroom past midnight like a thief, stalking his own home.

The night-light cast a soft glow on Nyra's bare legs, luring him closer and closer. All he'd wanted to do earlier was to pick her up in his arms, bring her to their bed and prove to her that she wanted him, needed him even, in the only way he knew how.

Contrary to the media speculation and his family's and friends' theories, their relationship hadn't begun with ripping off each other's clothes.

But when it had happened, when, after three weeks of getting to know each other, she had asked him to kiss her and touch her and do more, the connection had been...intense. Life-changing.

Now he wanted to use that passion to cover the distance she was creating between them. And yet he hadn't been able to bring himself to do it.

He sat down at the edge of the bed and fought the urge to run his hand over her limbs. *Dios mio*, what was she reducing him to? Why did it feel like he was being pulled apart when suspicion and mistrust filled her eyes? Why did he care if they'd lost the little, inexplicable spark that had always touched their relationship?

It was better this way, wasn't it? They'd both made missteps, an understatement in his case, but now, this was more rational and out in the open. They both had adjusted their expectations.

When a sudden breeze flew in from the open balcony and goose bumps rose on her long legs, he pulled the kicked-off duvet over her. With a long huff, she turned to her side, facing him.

Slowly, gently, he pushed the thick curls away from her forehead. And saw the tear tracks on her cheeks.

How he detested being her villain...

As for her threat that she would leave him eventually, he would not, could not, allow that. There had to be a solution to fix his mistake. To make her move on.

From the beginning, Nyra had been easy to please, easy to fit into his life around his other, more important commitments. She'd barely made any demands of him, eager for a quiet life, choosing to be left out of the society he ruled altogether.

She'd become a quiet haven for a man who hadn't even known he'd needed one.

He wanted that again. He wanted them to find their places in their relationship again, where he would protect her and give her the stability and simple life she'd wanted. And she would look at him again as if he'd hung the moon and stars.

For all the power he held in his palm though, he didn't know how to win her back.

CHAPTER FIVE

NYRA STARED THROUGH the glass walls of the sunroom, rendered still by terror, as the storm painted the sky with furious lightning. The booming thunder that followed seconds later seemed to shake the very foundations of the high-rise building.

She should probably go in and hide under the duvet. But storms had always terrified her, and the last thing she wanted was to feel trapped inside the four walls.

Where there was nothing but silence. Where she would only wonder what this storm, this day might bring. Where she would miss Adriano even worse than before.

Here, she could witness it and know that it was nothing but a passing phenomenon. Here, the plants she'd tended to with love and care for months would keep her company.

On her return, she'd been surprised to discover that someone had cared for them in the six weeks that she'd been gone. Had it been him? Had he regretted his cruel impulse? Because she was already regretting her grandiose declarations to him about needing distance.

Once, this painful loneliness was all she'd known. Living alone in a city like Vegas with its relentless crowds had been a constant reminder that she was alone in the world. Now, in the aftermath of her relationship with Adriano and how he'd become the center of her universe, the loneliness pricked that much harder.

She wanted to be angry with him that he had taken that too from her, but her anger was like that showy flash of lightning. Burning through her one moment and then fizzing out into nothing after.

It had been mere days since he'd brought her back to this apartment—and not returned per her request—but already, she was losing her grip on the anger. All that remained was hurt and the helplessness he'd made her feel, like a tiny trench he'd gouged in her flesh and left open.

Another stroke of lightning and thunder followed.

Nyra flinched but stood still, unable to step back. Sweat poured down the back of her neck and she blinked back tears. Her fear had no rationale, no grip on her except that it reminded her of the worst day of her life.

Nadia and she running up the stairs to her parents' bedroom, to find her mother cold on the bed.

Shivers coursed through her, as the past held her in its ugly thrall.

"Nyra?"

Only his deep voice calling her name as if from some great distance could shake her out of the stupor.

When she turned, it was to find Adriano standing at the entrance to the sunroom, as dark and potent and beautiful as the storm outside.

Drenched to the skin in his white shirt and black trousers. His jet-black hair was plastered to his scalp, drawing his angular features into sharp relief. Gray-green eyes swept over her, some unnamed emotion whispering there.

Nyra didn't think. Just acted on pure instinct and threw herself at him.

He grunted but caught her, his arms coming around her like steel manacles. Holding her as she needed to be held, all the while murmuring in Italian. Words she didn't understand but had soothed her just like this once before.

In his arms, the last thread of control she held over her fear unraveled. Violent tremors wracked her. A sob fought to be released but if she let it go…there would be no stopping it. She would unravel too and she couldn't. Not in front of him. Not ever.

"Shh…*cara mia*. You're safe," he said, his mouth at her temple, his free hand clasped around her. "I'm here, Nyra. You aren't alone."

Her silent tears soaked into his wet shirt, but at least she held back the sob.

She'd let him hold her just for a minute more, she told herself. Dampness seeped through her sweater and her linen pants, but she didn't care.

Just one more minute.

She didn't look up when he lifted her and carried her out into the living room. Like a squid using its tentacles, she clung to him as he barked orders at the staff.

"I'm getting you wet through, *bella*," he said gruffly, when she refused to dislodge her arms. Settling into an armchair, he brought her into his lap. "I'm not going anywhere, Nyra. Let me get us out of these damp clothes."

She tightened her fingers around his neck. The corded column of his neck smelled like bergamot and rain, with a layer of clean sweat beneath. She breathed in a greedy lungful, the scent filling her with warm tendrils of comfort. If she simply held on to him, without thinking, without talking, it wasn't weak, was it? After all she was pregnant and needed touch.

His large hand stroked down between her shoulders, down her back. "Won't you tell me why the storm terrifies you like this?"

She stiffened and swallowed the answer that begged to be let out. Like a lazy cat, all she wanted was to bask in the warmth of his body.

Her fear had left her the moment he had arrived. Something deep within her that she couldn't shake still associated him with safety. A part of her wanted to demand that he join her in bed at night and give her touch—simple or sexual, that it was his duty to do so.

And he would give it, she knew.

Duty was everything to Adriano.

But even the simplest of touches—not even counting sex between them, was a live flame. And now, a slippery slope. She couldn't risk getting attached to him so deeply again. Not when he might just cut her out of his life at a moment's notice.

Finally, after what felt like a surprisingly long time for them to respond, the staff arrived with a tea tray and a heap of towels. Without looking at him, she took the towel he offered and buried her face in it. Sliding out of his lap, she patted the front of her top and her pants with it, feeling bereft without his touch.

Adriano unfolded from the armchair and rubbed the towel vigorously over his hair. For a second, she nearly grabbed the towel from him so that she could see to the task.

Instead, she poured hot tea into a cup, just to give her hands something to do. She didn't like tea, but since she was trying to cut back to one cup of coffee per day, she didn't have a choice. She didn't pour any for him, giving in to the peevish urge.

The hot tea nearly burned her tongue *and* the roof of her mouth when she took a too-big sip.

All because Adriano had stripped out of his wet shirt and was wiping down his chest. A sight almost worth burning her tongue for.

Thick-ridged pectorals and an equally hard slab of his abdomen dusted generously with hair. His black trousers hung low on his hips as he unbuckled the belt and pulled it off.

The soft whoosh of it filled the room and blistering heat rushed to her cheeks at the memory of that same belt around her wrists and the raw pleasure that had followed.

Her breasts felt heavy and achy, but she put that down to the sudden damp.

When he moved toward their bedroom—with their bed covered in his shirts and sweatshirts that she used to drape herself in come night, she waylaid him.

"Your clothes are in the second bedroom," she said, looking into her teacup. The last thing she wanted was for him to see how weak her resolve was around him.

God, there were months, maybe years of this ahead. How was she supposed to sustain this *I don't need you* act?

Hands on his hips, he turned to face her fully. The definition of his bicep made her want to lick him up.

"I asked the staff to move everything out," she said, responding to his thunderous frown.

"Why?"

"I wasn't sure if you might come by in the middle of the night looking for one of your documents. I prefer not to be disturbed."

He would drop by in the evening—admitting to social exhaustion after a party or a dinner—would drive them both to mindless delirium, and then when she fell asleep, would sit there on the bed for hours into the night, working away on his laptop or reading through documents. His fingers would absently sift through her messy, postsex hair or trail over her bare belly or thighs. Sometimes, he would trace his knuckles over her cheek as she snuggled into his lap sleepily.

Always touching her, even when the sex was over.

As if he couldn't help himself, the needy part of her whispered.

Then he would wake her up around dawn with kisses and caresses and filthy promises, ruin her thoroughly with his mouth or his fingers or his *cock* as he made her say it, then shower and leave before she was even up.

She'd spend her days painting in the sunroom, venture down to the pretty canal district when she got stuck or bored, drink too many delicious coffees and then venture back into her apartment by nightfall, hoping he would show up.

When he traveled, she would stay at the villa with his parents and siblings with the utmost reluctance—the one condition he wouldn't back down on—counting down every minute to when he would return.

That had constituted their marriage.

With hindsight now, Nyra could see it hadn't really been a marriage in the true sense of the word. But it had felt right. And it had been theirs. A cocoon made of touches and kisses and raw intimacy, hidden away from the world. Not a surprise that it had fallen apart, like a castle made of cards at the first puff of air.

"Or you were making sure that I didn't accidentally crawl into the bed with you, purely out of habit?"

There was such…caustic heat to those words that she jerked around. Tea spilled over her fingers at the sudden movement.

With a pithy curse, he grabbed the wet towel and dabbed at her fingers in gentle movements. A ribbon of longing whipped through her as she stared down at his bent head.

Adriano was a master at controlling his emotions, always leaving her to wonder what he would say or do next. When he'd asked her to come to Italy with him, as his wife, she'd nearly fainted out of shock. The fact that they were in the middle of a high-stakes game was the only thing that had kept her moving through the day.

Ten tomorrow morning at the chapel, he'd whispered before walking out near dawn.

They'd known each other for three weeks by then and she'd slept with him the previous night. Which had been a revelation in itself. She'd showed up at the chapel, gotten married and then found herself underneath him in the rear cabin of his private jet, before comprehending fully that it hadn't been a daydream.

She stared at him now as he raised his head, at the vein pulsing in his forehead, at the tight set of his mouth. This was more than he had betrayed in that moment with those photos of her twin splashed across his desk. Did this distance between them cause him as much ache as it did in her?

Her heart gave a thud against her breast, greedily lapping up the fracture in his control. Suddenly, the deep grooves around his mouth, the strain around his eyes became more pronounced to her eyes. "That's not what I…"

"No, *bella*?" A scornful laugh twisted his pretty lips. "I guess you were right that we barely know each other. Because the last thing I expected from you was…this passive-aggressive cold frost."

She went to him then, some foolish emotion urging her feet on. "It's been a week since you brought me back. I still wake up and wonder where I am. What is it that you expected of me, Adriano?"

"I sent my chauffeur to pick you up thrice for dinner. You refused."

"I'm not in the mood for company."

"Just mine, *si*? Because I know Bruno and Fabi have been here a few times in the last week."

"Bruno and Fabi didn't throw me out without a second glance." She regretted the words the moment she said them.

"Nyra—"

"I'm sorry," she whispered, rubbing her temple. "It's hardly fair that I keep throwing that at you but refuse to discuss it."

She was aware of him moving closer by how his delicious body heat swamped her. "We've left 'fair' behind us a while ago, Nyra." His words were full of an aching regret.

She nodded, because he was right. Neither could she forget that she had begun it with her lies.

He tilted her chin up until she met his gaze. "I can withstand this frost of yours, however long it lasts. But I'm not letting you go. If that's what you think this retreat of yours will lead to, no. I will wait you out. You, and our babies, belong with me."

"If it were any other man than you, I would consider that a threat." She laughed. Even to her own ears, the sound lacked any warmth. "See, that's how I think of you. That you aren't any other man, that you're...you. The one man who would never, in a million years, hurt me."

He thrust a hand roughly through his hair, a pained growl escaping his throat.

"It's ridiculous, isn't it? Some of the things we tell ourselves to get through the day."

He sighed. "All I can say is that it's not easy for me."

"And you think the last few weeks have been easy for me?"

"Tell me, *bella. Per favore.*"

"I wake up cold in the middle of the night and look for you to tuck myself up against. I...miss you so much that it's an ache here." she said, pressing a hand to her chest. "And then, when I wake up, I come out of this trance and a knot fists my stomach. Like I have to chase the sensation to figure out what it is and then... I remember what happened between us. All the anger, the hurt and the fear rush back into me. And it's all viciously fresh again."

His hand cupped her shoulder but he didn't pull her closer.

"And seeing you is a hundred times worse. Because a part of me craves the safety you meant to me before all this. Another part hates that I'm so weak with you."

His Adam's apple moved on a hard swallow. "What can I do to fix it? To make us go back to what we were? This isn't good for you or them."

"I don't think there's any going back," she said, pressing her head to his chest with a helplessness she couldn't fight. Because he would always be both the storm and shelter for her. "And I can't find a path forward yet."

Adriano wrapped his fingers around his wife's neck and held her as she trembled from head to toe.

Her hurt, her fear, her helplessness, written so clearly on her face as if he'd etched it into those sharp features with his own hands. It was a humbling point to face over and over for a man like him.

He even acknowledged the fact that a small part of him wanted to walk out on her and her unrelenting stubbornness. Like she pointed out recently, he was a powerful man used to getting his own way.

No, he had to treat this as a test of his own fiber. A series of tests even, the first of which he'd failed abysmally.

He was to be a father in a few months, and the last thing he could afford was to throw a tantrum like he'd done that horrible night. It hadn't been simply tasteless to declare that his marriage was over in front of his vulture-like family. While he hadn't known the extent to which his parents had taunted her, he had known that they hadn't approved of her. And he'd simply served her up into their hostile clutches.

Worse was that that evening had smacked of the very same drama his parents had indulged in, over and over again, in their eternal battle against each other.

He'd meant to hurt her and the admission was galling. To learn that he'd behaved exactly like them was a bitter pill.

So he swallowed his anger—mostly directed at himself—his frustration, of the plain and sexual kind, and stroked his fingers down her neck and her shoulders, wanting to soothe her as much as himself.

There was a strength in her stubbornness, in her refusal to give in, in how she communicated her fear even when she had nothing to fight him with.

She would be a wonderful mother to his children. The thought dispersed his gloomy mood like a ray of sunshine. It was a foothold when he had no control over anything else in his life.

"I apologize for forcing this...confrontation. That wasn't my intention. I hate upsetting you, Nyra. Especially now."

She laughed. "That's not how this works, Adriano. I might be extra emotional because of the hormonal roller coaster, yes, but it doesn't mean you have to treat me with kid gloves."

"No gloves on, *cara mia*. You know how much I like it raw and bare."

She gasped and smacked his chest. "That's exactly what got us here."

"What do you mean?" he quipped, loving the glint of humor back in her eyes.

"I mean it was that time—" she pointed behind him

to the exquisite velvet chaise longue "—on that very couch that got us here."

It had been when he'd returned from a work trip.

He smiled, remembering how he'd arranged her on her knees and arms, pert bottom sticking up in the air, panties locking her ankles. How she'd squirmed and gasped when he'd situated his face below her. And then when he'd finished feasting on her, he'd asked if he could have her without a condom.

Boneless and sated, she'd relented easily enough. And he had nearly blacked out from his climax.

"Don't blame this on me, *cara*. You were on the pill, *si*?"

"Yes, but it's not 100 percent guaranteed."

"So this could have happened even if I had *gloved up*."

"Fine. The two of us together got us here," she said, stepping back. Her gaze landed on his chest and skidded away.

Another ray of sunshine then, he thought, his skin prickling with heat at her sneaky perusal. This desire between them was as strong as it had ever been. That, and the pregnancy were more than enough to work with. For now.

"I have something for you," he said, refusing to put on the shirt she handed him.

The storm had abated outside, bright sunlight now filtering in through the high windows. Strands of it caught the gold in her brown hair and painted golden every inch of her skin left bare by the loose sleeveless sweater. He frowned at the makeshift crop top that had been cut haphazardly at the hem.

And then he understood why it hung loose over her neck and under her arms. It was his sweater that she had ripped beyond recognition. A flicker of warmth came alive in his chest.

Between the hem of the crop top and her linen pants, the swell of her bare belly was such a shocking sight that he stared, arrested. Children had always been such a vague, alien concept to him. And when he'd been confronted by it, all he'd known was shock and pain that she hadn't told him, that he'd driven her away at such a fragile time.

But this…very physical sight of her made it real in a way he hadn't understood until now.

His fingers itched to touch her, to feel the swell, to know the wonder even more keenly. Instead, he fisted them by his sides, resolving to do so only when she invited him.

There were certain things he wanted from her, wanted her to need from him, and that would never change.

"And here I thought you had come by because you know I'm terrified of storms," Nyra said with a self-deprecation that brought his head up.

"Two things could be true, Nyra." He meant to win this battle between them—for it was one—and he wasn't going to give away anything for free.

He *had* rushed here, walked out of a meeting with his board, because of the storm and what it would do to her. "Or three things, actually," he said, casually consulting his phone.

"What do you mean?" she said, her earlier wariness retreating.

"I saw the storm. I also knew that you had a doctor's

appointment this afternoon. And I came to return something that is yours to you."

A flash of longing swept through her eyes before she chased it off. "You're a busy man, and there will be a lot of these appointments. You don't need to attend every single one."

"Your…consideration is appreciated but not needed. I said I will be there."

"Okay," she said, wrapping her arms around her midriff. "What did you want to give me?"

"When you ask it like that, I have to say, a lot of things, *bella*. But I'll wait until you ask me for it. No, maybe until you beg me."

Pink chased up her neck and cheeks, even as she straightened her shoulders. "I will never beg. For anything. From you."

"We shall see," he said, covering the gap she kept putting between them.

When he brought out the velvet box, her whimper was so soft that it cut him. She'd picked the smallest of the lot the designer had presented to them, not knowing that its exquisite cut and clarity made it worth tens of thousands of euros.

"I can put it on," she said, her chest rising and falling. Something danced in her gaze. An eagerness tinged with desperation.

So she was attached to the ring. He hid his smile. It was the only thing she'd ever let him buy her.

"Oh, it looks just like the other one," she whispered.

"I had it commissioned just so."

Another soft gasp, this one full of wonder.

He took her slim hand in his. Pulling off the cheap,

fake one that had left a green ring around her finger, he slid the new one on. "I have been looking forward to putting it back on you," he admitted.

She lifted those beautiful eyes to him, a wet sheen making them glow as much as the diamond. "I hated selling it. I... It was precious to me. It felt like cutting off an integral part of me."

He nodded, not trusting himself to say the right thing.

How insecure he must have been to believe that she had sold it off to finance her clandestine visits to her lover? It sounded so bizarre in his head now, but then... it had taken him out at the knees.

Was it her he hadn't trusted or his own ability to have a healthy relationship, he wondered now with something close to self-loathing.

She ran her finger over the stone, over and over. "Thank you," she said, without meeting his eyes.

"There is one other matter to discuss before we leave for the appointment. Something for you to think on while I'm gone."

"Where are you going?"

He didn't miss how fast the question shot out of her. "Japan. I should be back in two weeks."

"Okay."

"I'm trying to take care of the most critical issues so that my calendar is open later. I plan to keep my workload very light for weeks before the due date and after they're born."

She blinked. "I haven't even thought that far ahead."

"You don't have to, Nyra. That's what I'm here for. Which leads to deciding where we want to live."

"Here," she said instantly. When he stared, she added,

"Does the company need the apartment back? I mean, I can move into a smaller one."

Anger whipped through him but he held it back. "You're full of barbed insults today, *bella*," he said with a grimace.

"I didn't mean it like that. Not this time."

He sighed. "I think I understand what you mean by what I did weighing you down." He went to her then and took her hand in his. Wanting her to know his touch and trust him rather than his word. "This apartment is yours, Nyra. It has been in your name since the day you moved in."

Eyes wide in her pinched face, she looked around. "I...never asked for it."

"It was to be a wedding present along with a couple of other things."

"Oh. Well, it was good enough to keep from me before."

"Is that a complaint I hear?" he said, pouncing on it. Because he wanted her complaints, her past, her anger. All of it. Only if she addressed it could he fix it.

Her chest rose and fell with a sigh. "No, it isn't. You've never asked me to hide myself away. I made that decision."

He didn't probe, as much as he wanted to. "It's not the greatest location to raise a family. There's no garden, no easy access to parks or beaches and the nightlife is too raucous."

"I'm not moving into the villa. Please don't—"

He pressed his finger to her lips. "I won't make you do anything you don't want to."

She smiled against his fingers, her lips warm and soft.

Every inch of him wanted to bend and capture them with his. He nearly shook with the intensity of the urge. "I remember you saying that once before." Her tone turned husky as another memory swirled between them.

Lust punched through him, but this too he kept under check. This time, there was more at stake, more than just themselves. He couldn't simply seduce her into submission.

Before his self-control shattered at her feet, he pulled away. He shrugged on the other shirt she'd brought him, her heated gaze leaving little pockets of want on his skin.

"I will have a real estate agent send you some links. Just…get a sense of what you like. We can tour some of those places once I'm back."

"I'm not sure I would know it even if the right place smacked me in the face, Adriano. It's too big a decision to—"

"Then it's time you learned, Nyra. Learned to tell me what you want and don't," he said, leaning down and kissing her cheek.

The scent of her coiled around him, fisting his cock tight. And for just a second, he felt her leaning in too, her mouth fluttering at the edge of his, her breath a sharp rasping pant.

He pulled away, even if it was the hardest thing he'd ever done.

"It's more than just you and me now. And this time around, I want no lies, no misunderstandings and no hiding."

"I can't promise you any of that."

He stilled at the door. "I know, *cara*. But you know me. I'm a very patient man when I want something."

"And you want this…marriage?"

The hesitation in her tone, the doubt in her words… pained him.

"At any cost," he said, and then he walked out.

And he wondered, for the millionth time, what it was about her that made a mockery of his usual confidence, his smooth rationality.

CHAPTER SIX

"You left him. Now you return, pregnant with his bambinos, and ruin his life all over again."

Nyra's knife and fork clattered to the plate as the words, spoken in a rough Italian accent, whipped her. She looked up from her breakfast in the empty dining room to find Adriano's childhood nanny, Maria, watching her from the end of the long table, her flinty eyes unflinchingly critical.

Nyra took a sip of her orange juice. Her throat clogged with tears, she nearly choked.

Maria had arrived late last night. When Nyra had seen her get out of the chauffeured car, she'd hurried into her bedroom and locked it. It had been a cowardly thing to do, but she hadn't been prepared to face the woman who worshipped Adriano and knew him the best.

She should've guessed that Adriano would send someone to look after her. Maybe even to keep an eye on her, she thought morosely.

It was Maria he had first introduced her to upon their arrival in Italy, Maria who had blessed their union with fat tears in her eyes. Maria, who hadn't immediately dismissed her as a toy that had caught his passing fancy. But... Nyra had always felt like Maria could strip off layers of the armor she cloaked herself in and see the lost, lonely girl beneath.

Pushing her chair back, Nyra stood up and kissed the old woman's cheeks. "It is good to see you, Maria."

The leathery texture of her skin, the smell of lemons and something else, made her stomach slosh. Not in a bad way. More like the indulgent, unstoppable ache one felt in the presence of someone old and kind. And it was Maria's no-nonsense advice Nyra needed.

Had Adriano known that she'd needed someone who wouldn't indulge her *or* criticize her?

Maria took a couple of steps back as if to see Nyra better. Joy replaced the scowl as she patted Nyra's cheek. "You look well, but you're miserable. You miss him."

There it was, what she'd feared. Maria seeing through her defenses.

Nyra swallowed, and under the guise of serving breakfast for the old lady, turned away. She poured herself a little coffee and settled down at the table in front of Maria. Even her tongue-lashing was preferable to silence.

"So, why did you come back?" Maria said, picking through the fruit bowl with a sour expression.

"You don't know what happened between us," Nyra said, even the little bit of coffee she allowed herself daily not helping. "I would appreciate it if you don't blame me for everything."

The older woman cackled. "Of course I blame you for everything. You left. You left my Adriano after making him a vow."

"He threw me out," Nyra burst out. "Humiliated me in front of the whole family. Didn't even ask me if—"

"So you take petty revenge? You think that's what marriage is," said Maria. "Or maybe you think that is what you deserve, to be thrown out like yesterday's garbage."

The words struck her hard enough that Nyra fell back against her chair. Her eyes filled with tears, and she blinked them back furiously. "You think Adriano is not culpable at all?"

"Adriano is proud, arrogant, and does not make it easy to understand him. But he also has no idea what a healthy relationship, much less a marriage should be. What his parents engaged in was…a destructive show. He despises lies and half-truths and petty games."

"I…" Nyra had no response.

"Do you know how many women his mother found for him from the moment he turned thirty—princesses and daughters of cabinet ministers, heiresses…" She let her expansive gestures say the rest. "Adriano would meet each and every one, but there is no…spark. No interest. He tells me marriage is not for him, especially not the kind his society takes part in. And then he goes to Vegas, and brings you home. As a wife, breaking all his own rules. Despite what everyone said, I saw something in you, Nyra."

"What? What did you see in me?" Nyra said, desperate to know.

Maria sighed. "I thought that you could see Adriano. Not the powerful banker who holds so many lives in his hand and who is constantly fixing things for people. I thought you saw the…loneliness in him."

Nyra swallowed and looked away. She *had* sensed the same loneliness in him as she'd felt most of her adult life.

"Or maybe I'm nothing but an old fool and what everyone says about you is true. That all you wanted was a comfortable life for as long as it lasted."

"That's unfair."

"No? Then why let him send you away without a fight? Why hide yourself like a dirty secret in his life for nine months? Why would you not be a proper wife to him? This is not a woman committed to her relationship. This is a woman scared of living the life she has been gifted."

Nothing Maria said was untrue. It was like watching her reflection in the mirror and disliking everything about it. "Why do you say I'm ruining his life?" Nyra asked, a glutton for punishment.

"Because if you leave forever, he could move on, *si*? He could forget about you, forget about his one mistake and move on. Maybe marry some accomplished, pretty socialite, someone from his own world, and have a decent life. A woman who shares everything with him. My Adriano deserves that after everything he has done for others."

Maria left the room as quickly and fiercely as she had. A storm shaking the hollow foundations of Nyra's delusions.

Like yesterday's garbage... The words haunted her for a long while after.

Was that how she saw herself? Had she been waiting for Adriano to come to his senses and dump her this whole time? With her sister reaching out to her, had she known that moment was close? Had she made it true by spinning lies and selling his silver, literally?

Nyra knew she couldn't go on like this. Once, loneliness, loss and sheer powerlessness had been thrust on her. But they didn't have to dictate her life anymore. Neither would those be the gifts she passed onto her children.

This marriage didn't have to be about love, but neither did it have to be a barren, miserable existence. All she had to do was adjust her expectations and they could have a decent life together. Adriano, she knew, would be a good father, and together they would do their best.

They might even flourish without the sticky expectations that came with loving him.

Adriano felt as if there was a hot skewer pounding behind his left eye. He had been up for eighteen hours, and even before that, he hadn't been sleeping well for weeks. His penthouse in Milan was every bit as luxurious as his family home, but he couldn't sleep because his bed was empty.

Because Nyra wasn't there with him, pressing her soft body against his. Tucking those ever-cold feet against his.

He popped a couple of painkillers and made his way toward the boardroom.

Christo, he missed her. And not seeing her, not reassuring himself that she and the babies were okay was a particularly cruel way to punish himself, even after his return from Tokyo.

Pride, it seemed, was a prickly, demanding thing. He'd been resolved to make her miss him, as much as he missed her. At least, physically, if nothing else. Although, in just two weeks, he was ready to crack like an egg.

But now there was this…media shitstorm to deal with, because someone had leaked Nyra's background. It was as bad as she'd feared it would be.

That Adriano Cavalieri, the most preeminent banker in all of Italy, chairman of the prestigious Bancaria Cavalieri—an institution that had been standing for three centuries and represented loyalty and stability—was married to the daughter of a man who had embezzled millions from innocent, hardworking people across Europe.

Adriano had worked at the bank in some capacity for sixteen years, and yet his integrity, his decision-making, his stability, and even *his sanity* apparently, were in question because of who Nyra's father had been.

While he had released a statement to mollify the general public, to inform them that his wife was also an innocent in the financial scandal her father had perpetrated, hell would freeze over before he offered any kind of explanation to his board.

How dare they summon him as if he was their errand boy? As if he hadn't remade their fortunes in the last decade a hundred times over?

He came to a standstill outside the boardroom, finding Bruno standing there like a stalwart soldier. Like him, his head of security hadn't known a moment's respite in three days.

"Any new information on who leaked it to the press?" Adriano asked.

Bruno shook his head. "As far as my sources can dig, no money was exchanged. The lack of a money trail makes it hard."

"Have you checked my parents' movements? And Fabi and Federico?"

Looking startled, Bruno said, "That's…unfair, no?"

Adriano shrugged. "I didn't protect her once. I won't make that mistake ever again," he said, useless anger tiding through him.

The last thing he wanted was for Nyra to retreat even further from him because someone had made her worst nightmare come true. "The security at the penthouse," he said, "you should be there."

"No, I should be at your side. It's not just the board that's getting wild. The chatter online about you and her has been pretty bad. All the old forums have been revived and the anger over her father's actions is as violent as ever," Bruno said. "She's safe at the apartment, Adriano. If she needs anything after the last few days, it's your reassurance that this hasn't changed the status quo."

"*Christo*, Bruno! She knows me."

"Does she? You made me bring her back and you deserted her at the apartment. And you forbid her contact with her twin."

"She's not alone. She has Maria," he said, guilt and anger twinning through him now. Why was it that it never came to him naturally what she needed? Why was he so bad at this…marriage, at this damned relationship?

"Nyra deserves to—"

"*Basta!*" Adriano crowded the other man, not that his half-brother flinched.

Once again, jealousy gripped him in a chokehold. That Bruno understood Nyra and her needs better than he did grated on him like barbed wire around his chest.

That it was because Adriano was wired differently, because some things were beyond him, made it worse. For all that Bruno had been raised outside of the Cavalieri protection or the privilege it brought, his mother had been a kind, generous woman.

Whereas growing up as the heir, all Adriano had been taught was to never show weakness. With all the volatility he'd grown up with, he had simply decided that he wouldn't take a wife at all. Until a waitress with bright eyes had toppled him. "I don't need marital advice, *fratello*. Not even from you," he said, and then pushed the double doors open.

Even facing the wrath of his board members—most of whom had less integrity than he possessed in his pinkie finger, felt easier than the confounding puzzle of how to win his wife and her easy affection back.

But this time, he would protect her, no matter what.

They were barely halfway through the torrent of complaints and advice his board had for him—including immediate divorce proceedings and discreetly packing his wife off to another continent never to be seen again—when the doors to the boardroom were pushed open.

Bruno scowled at this unsanctioned interruption.

A shocked hush fell over the room as their heads turned toward the doors. Adriano's heart rattled against his rib cage.

Dressed in a brown leather skirt that fell a few inches past her knees and a pink cardigan and leather boots, it was his wife. At her ears, diamond studs glinted.

For a second, he couldn't believe it was Nyra at all. With her thick curls running down her back like a silky waterfall, he thought it was her twin. She looked like something out of a glossy magazine, like a supermodel.

Until one's gaze drifted lower.

The slenderness of her frame made her belly stick out. Her body had changed in the two weeks since he'd seen her, and he wanted to curse himself for staying away.

Around him, he could feel the collective focus of the room shift to her bump. *To her.* He thought he might have even heard a couple of gasps, the bolder ones even reaching for their phones.

The small matter of his heir—the next Cavalieri to hold the chairmanship—and that he had remained a bachelor for so long, had been a pain point for the board. He couldn't count the number of times they had thrown their daughters at him.

When Adriano had shocked everyone by showing up with a wife, it had been another disappointment to them. Because he refused to parade her through high society for them to pick at like she was fresh meat.

She had been his secret, his respite, *only his.*

And even after the debacle of their temporary separation—he refused to call it anything else—they had managed to keep the news of her pregnancy out of the media. Now, all of it was moot with her dramatic arrival. He frowned at that uncharacteristic behavior.

She was here, looking like a ripe cherry he wanted to sink his teeth into. Every instinct in him urged him to get her away from the curious, covetous gazes in the room.

"Hi, Adriano," she said hesitantly, her gaze meeting his, oblivious to the grasping attention on her.

Only she wasn't oblivious. With each step he took toward her, he saw the strain of her smile. The tight grasp of her knuckles over the strap of her handbag.

"Surprise," she said, the gap between her front two teeth flashing at him with her wan smile. In the fading sunlight, her golden skin gleamed like some rare metal. Her mouth was painted a vivid red he'd never seen on her and her eyes…clearly made up to look even bigger, shone with a feverish resolve. The scent of her coiled through him—rose and vanilla, and even that felt different, as if it was laced with…something new.

"Nyra," he said, walking around the massive desk toward her. Taking her shoulders, he shuffled her to the side, shielding her with his large frame. "Is something…?" He nodded toward her belly, almost lifting his hands protectively.

His large hands hung in midair uselessly, until he pulled them back to his sides.

"Everything's fine," she said, putting her own palm there.

"Why are you here?" he said, slowly coming out of the shock of seeing her.

She looked healthy and well, he told himself, the knot in his gut loosening. Actually, she looked fucking amazing. A sour sense of defeat curdled in his stomach as he wondered if this was the result of his leaving her alone.

"I wanted to…" Pink crested her cheeks. Her gaze drifted to his mouth and lingered. "See you."

"Why didn't you call? I'd have flown over—"

"I did. Multiple times since the news…came out. I was told you were busy dealing with the scandal." She said it like it was a curse word. "Your personal cell phone went straight to voicemail."

"You tried to reach me," he repeated like a fool, before casting a glance over to his personal assistant. Who lost all color in her cheeks immediately. "It's been a madhouse here, and I don't know even know where my cell phone is."

Nyra's chest rose and fell. "So you didn't tell her to cut me off?"

"Of course not," he said, clasping her wrist.

Her pulse quickened under his fingers. And beneath the resolve and the smile, he saw the fear she was fighting very hard.

Sweat beaded her upper lip, even though it was cool in the boardroom.

She had thought he'd cut her off? Or even that he would throw her out again? His fury at his assistant and himself was so great that he pulled back from her.

And yet she's here, his mind repeated. *She sought you out.*

"Nyra, you know I wouldn't do that, right? Especially in your condition?"

She shrugged, refusing to meet his eyes. And he had a feeling he shouldn't have tacked on the pregnancy. "Is this the shooting squad, then?" She shifted around him to face them, even as he could see the tremble in her shoulders. "Should I stand in front of you and save you?"

Laughter burst out of him. His chest and his throat felt raw from the force of it. He didn't remember the last time he'd laughed like that. Not since she'd started acting strange with the discovery of her twin, in fact.

Her gaze latched onto his mouth, her breath coming in a soft gasp. "I forgot how much I love your laugh," she said, touching his lower lip. For a second, it felt like

the last few months hadn't transpired at all and he had
the old Nyra back.

She pulled away, coloring. "I'm sorry for bringing
this down on you."

"I told you, *bella*. You're not responsible for your father's actions."

"Even if I was the one who leaked to the press my
full identity? Even though I brought this stain on your
prestigious bank and your name?"

CHAPTER SEVEN

ADRIANO REARED BACK, confused. With one shouted command, he had the boardroom empty. But even the expansive space wasn't enough to contain his shock.

The truth of it was written on her face.

She *had* leaked her background, invited a heap of scorn and disgust and judgment from not only the people in her life but across the internet.

"Do you have any idea what you've unleashed?" he demanded, fear for her making his words sharp.

"I do. The vitriol online is...as nasty as ever," she said with a violent shiver. "I wish people would see that we were victims of his actions too. We lost both parents and any security we ever had."

It was the most she'd betrayed about her family and that time. Adriano took her hand and pulled her to the sitting lounge. Her hand was clammy in his, the bright red of her lips emphasizing the paleness of her usually golden skin.

Needing something to do—other than just lifting her into his lap and holding her tight—he pulled out a bottle of water and handed it to her. With a murmured *grazie*, she finished it. His gaze lingered over the long column of her throat and the smooth expanse of skin below, revealing white lace below the cardigan.

A soft thread of desire, laced with something like longing, uncoiled in his stomach. But even the sight of her, here in his boardroom, couldn't distract him for once.

"Why, Nyra?"

She wiped her mouth with the back of her hand, smearing the lipstick in the process. As if the new clothes and the makeup and the attitude were all nothing but a fragile mask. Her eyes wide, her shoulders bowed, she reminded him of the waitress he'd met in Vegas. All sharp angles and dark shadows, but with a brave innocence that shone through nonetheless.

"Won't you sit down?" she said. The fact that she was bracing herself to face this with him made his chest tight. "This might take a while."

He sat on the coffee table, caging her between his thighs. Her throat bobbed up and down.

Her eyes were wide in her face when she looked up. "I... I thought it was better this way. With the truth out in the open."

"You intended to test me," he said, with a growl. Not that he could blame her for her lack of trust.

In another surprising move, she took his hand in hers. Her fingers were long and slender around his thick ones. The splash of pink on her nails, instead of the usually bitten ones, was as much as a shock as all the rest of her. Neither could he remember the last time she'd actively sought his touch.

"Test us both, I think," she said, squeezing his hand tight. As if afraid that he might pull away. Not just from her touch but her.

Dios mío, did she still have no grasp of the power she

held over him? He didn't understand it at all either, but it was there. As real as his heart pounding with concern and pride and lust for her.

"I didn't want it hanging over us, over our future like some sword. So many years of my life, I spent them hiding, ashamed, as if it was my fault that he cheated so many innocent people out of their life savings. I ran so fast, so far that I buried myself in the bowels of Vegas when I was barely eighteen."

He jerked his head up. "You started working in Vegas at eighteen?"

She shrugged.

"When did you start dancing?"

Another flush claimed her cheeks but she bravely held his gaze. "Nineteen. I got a fake ID. It paid way more than anything else."

"But you were waitressing at the poker game," he said, wondering at how late his questions, this discussion, was.

"Just for those few nights. There was a high-paying client that was…fond of me and he requested me personally. The floor manager didn't give me a choice."

"Is that why you pretended we were together that first night?"

She nodded. "You were the only one in the group who intimidated him."

"And if I turned out to be worse than him? *Madre del Mio*, Nyra! What if I—"

"You weren't anything like him, Adriano," she said, a clarity to her voice he hadn't heard before. "When you survive in a place like that, you learn to read people well. Especially powerful men. I knew I could trust you."

He shook his head, the very thought of her caught in a dangerous situation with some power-drunk asshole sending fear skittering through him. Something almost like fate had brought them together, but he couldn't stand how out of his control the entire concept was.

She's here, he reminded himself. *Healthy and swelling with his babies.*

"I could say I'm sorry for doing this, but it would be a lie. I needed to…face this, Adriano. Not just for me, but for the babies."

So that's what the new resolve was about. He should be happy, even ecstatic, that Nyra was nothing like his mother. But he only felt a hollowness.

"And I needed to know that you'd stand by your word."

"You didn't trust me then?" The words felt disingenuous on his lips when her hand was in his. Touching her had always been less about logic and rationality and something more.

"We didn't have any to begin with. It was all mind-blowing sex. Maybe now, we could build it, if not give it unconditionally."

Pulling his hand from her clasp, he leaned back on the coffee table, allowing himself a wider look at her. Allowing her words to sink deep. Although he didn't agree that it had just been sex. And if that wasn't a reversal in his own head… "There's a change in you."

"Yes," she said, biting into her lower lip.

"Do you plan to tell me what it is? Or am I going to discover all your little secrets through someone else, *bella*?"

She looked down at her laced fingers. "Something

Maria said struck a chord with me. It was my foolish pride that threatened you with leaving. It grated on me, still does—" a shiver went through her "—that you thought I was capable of...*that*." She swallowed. "Giving you an ultimatum gave me back a sense of control, but it was only false. What I want more than anything is to give these two a happy, secure future, to break away from all the insecurity that Nadia and I faced. I needed to wake up to the fact that I don't have to be miserable, that I can still build a future with you."

"You don't intend to leave me anymore, then?" he said, his head still reeling from all she'd done, all she was saying.

It was like this was a new Nyra—confident, realistic and smart. Not the wraith who'd clung to him for protection or who had drowned in the pleasure he pulled from her. He didn't know what it said about him that he wasn't sure how much he liked this new version of her.

No, that was a lie. He knew and didn't like how it reflected on him. It smacked too much of how his father's ego would inflate based on how much power he could wield over innocent women.

"I plan to stick it out in the marriage, Adriano. I even came up with a promise to make to you. A belated vow, I guess. Since all we did was exchange signatures in that tacky chapel."

Every cell in him stood to attention. But he refused to ask her for it. Christo, but she turned him into a churlish man-child.

She scooted closer to him on the sofa, a slight grimace crossing her expression at the movement. The outside of her thighs grazed the inside of his, sending a heated flush through him. She raised her eyes, a solemnity to them, and met his.

He kept his palms spread on the coffee table behind him, keeping them out of her reach.

Refusing to be put off, she cupped his knees. His muscles bunched tight at how her long fingers splayed. "I vow to be a better wife to you than I've been before and a good mother, hopefully, to our children."

"I'm not sure what a better wife is, *bella*."

If she was aware that he was mocking her, she didn't betray her irritation. "I mean to take an active role in your life. Be the wife that the mighty Cavalieri bank chairman needs. Learn how to host dinners and talk about high fashion and art and whatever it is your people talk about. Dress in the height of fashion, as I'm expected to. Maybe join the board of a few charities."

She quoted them like bullet points on a list, or like a formula to solve a problem. "I see," he said, without knowing what to think at all.

A wide smile bloomed across her face. "I'm going to start by throwing a party to celebrate your birthday in two weeks. I've already brought your mother on board. Hopefully, that should stop all the rumors swirling about us. The pregnancy and now this scandal, I know it's been a lot."

"Mama?" he said, feeling as if he'd been punched in the head.

She gave another shrug, and a button holding the edges of the cardigan popped. "We had a talk this morning. Or rather I showed up at the villa, demanded she hear me out, and she did. Seeing me so visibly pregnant shook her, I think. She muttered something about you never giving me up now that I carry your children."

"She knows that much about me, I guess," he said dryly.

"Honestly, she gave me the perfect opening with that statement. I made it clear that I wasn't going anywhere and the palazzo was my home. And that our children would be the next Cavalieri heirs. That it's in her interest to be on my good side. I fibbed that I told you about everything she'd ever said to me and that you were mighty upset. The whole time, I nearly peed myself."

"Go on," he said, barely stopping his mouth from falling open.

"It was Fabi's idea actually. You know that she feels guilty about snooping through my stuff, right? She's been visiting me regularly and, wonder of wonders, I think we've become friends. Beneath all the fashionista hauteur, your sister is witty and just as full of insecurities as I am. Isn't it great?"

"Si," he said, barely digesting it all. But Nyra's transformation was so...complete that it caught him too.

"Anyway, she gave me oodles of insight into how to handle your mother. I don't know why I let her cow me. You just need to speak her language. Nigella's nothing compared to some of the men I dealt with at the casino. And the fact that I wasn't running away with my tail tucked between my legs at this new scandal seems to have raised me in her estimation. She's one of those people who likes to know the order of things. And I let her know that I was on the top in this family. She admitted that the only way to weather this scandal will be to show a united front."

His mouth twitched but he held back the smile. "But you're seeking her help for this party?"

Nyra leaned in, smiling conspiratorially. "I actually have no interest in all the small details. She thrives on them. So I thought why not take advantage of the resources I do have."

"All this because…"

"I'm sick of hiding from my own life," she said, swallowing. When he continued to stare at her, she got to her feet. He refused to release her from between his legs though, feeling a juvenile fear that this Nyra was beyond his grasp already. "So, is this acceptable to you?"

"You have no demands of me," he pointed out with a little bitterness.

"You've always given me more than I could imagine in my wildest dreams, Adriano. I'm trying to tell myself to enjoy it. It's a long journey to believing that I'm worth it though," she said, with a shrug. As if she hadn't just revealed her vulnerability in such bald words. "I did have a question for you. Something I should have asked ages ago."

"What is it?" he said, his mouth drying.

Fading sunlight limned her body in profile, tracing each curve with exquisite care. The leather skirt hugged her ass like he wanted to with his hands.

"Why did you marry me?"

He stared at her.

"I mean, *I* was head over heels for you. If you'd shipped me off to some posh flat in Milan and bade me to stay there on tap, I would have. If you put me on retainer for your visits to Vegas, I'd have happily complied."

"I'm not in the habit of paying for pleasure," he said, incensed beyond belief.

She snorted. "That's morality only the rich can afford. And honestly, what we had so far is just dressed up to look like something else, no? It made you feel better to offer me a ring, and I jumped at the security that I haven't known in so long."

It sounded awful, but it was a realistic summary of their relationship so far. And yet it seared Adriano like nothing ever had. He hated to hear their relationship reduced to such stark terms. He'd far preferred the innocent Nyra to this pleasant brittleness she seemed to have acquired overnight. Just to sustain a relationship with him, he wondered with a keen sense of loss.

"The point is I'd have followed you wherever you bid me, until you got bored of me," she said with a breeziness he loathed. "So why marry me?"

It was a question he'd asked himself with increasing frequency of late. He didn't have an answer, only one that masqueraded as such. "I was thirty-four years old. You were twenty-two. The disparity in our ages, the power I had over you, the pull between us, it made me… uncomfortable. Smacked too much of the power my father wielded over innocent women. I told myself marrying you meant I was evening it out somehow. Just a bit."

Her brow cleared. "Not uncomfortable enough to give me up though?"

"No," he said, coming to his feet. He crowded her and she stepped back, her delicious bottom bumping against the glass wall. Her nervousness, for all she'd marched in here like a lioness, made the hunter in him calm. Which, he knew, was a weakness in itself. But until he could make sense of this, he would cling to the order of things. He was like his mother, apparently, however much he had tried to beat it.

He planted his arms on either side of her head and leaned in. Caging her, for she felt like a wisp of smoke to his senses in this new incarnation.

A soft gasp left her as his chest grazed her lush breasts. Despite his discomfort at this new her, the lust that punched through him was the same fierce, feral urge. "Some kind of madness consumed me," he said, near her ear. Her harsh pants were like music to his ears. "It was only when I returned home, put you in the context of my life that I realized what I had done. You put me under a spell. Now shall we seal your vow with a kiss, *wife*?"

He swooped in and caught her lips, needing her taste to anchor him as much as he wanted her desire for him to shake her newfound self-possession.

The kiss was rough, possessive, and Nyra responded like she was dry tinder to a match. Adriano filled her vision, her senses. Even her breath was his gift.

Fresh shivers filled her as his large hands spanned her back, fingertips digging into her. Fear finally leaving her body after thirty-six hours of wondering if he'd go back on his word.

It was the bravest thing she'd done—to leak her identity to the press. And yet she'd never been more scared. For the first time in her life, she'd taken a calculated risk with everything riding on the result.

Her decision.

Her life.

Her future with this compelling man.

Would he still want her when her past touched his prestige? had been a relentless chant in her head. Although the fact that he was too honorable to throw his pregnant wife, *and his future heirs*, on the street was a sad reassurance.

"Open up, *bella*. You've teased me enough," Adriano demanded, nipping at her lower lip. His hands kneaded her hips, stroked over her back, touching her everywhere and anywhere with an urgency that was a sop to her fragile ego.

She groaned as he licked his tongue through her mouth, playing with her, thrusting it in a filthy parody of what she needed elsewhere. All the confusion of the last few days, the cracks he'd made in her heart over the last few months, the heat of his kiss melted it a little. His mouth, so soft for such a hard, inscrutable man, drifted down her jaw, leaving her shaking from her head to toe.

Clinging to his powerful shoulders, Nyra rubbed herself against him like a cat, needing the rough slide of the hard planes of him against her. It had been so long, too long, since she'd felt his need. His possession. His... fracture at her hands.

While it had hurt to reduce their relationship to sex, there was a powerful truth in their physical connection.

She let her hands drift down his chest, loving the tensile strength of him. From the first moment, it was his strength with an underbelly of kindness that had lured her in. A part of her, she thought, would always crave that from him, even as she tried to be stronger.

Strong enough to not need him in that way, to earn

herself a place in his life that wasn't based on sex or emotion or some vague feeling in her belly.

Her palms drifted farther down to the rock-hard slab of his abdomen. Her fingers sneaked in between the buttons on his shirt, eager to feel the rough swirls of his hair. Just as she reached the band of his trousers, Adriano turned her, with a deftness she always found surprising for a man of such bulk.

By the time she could catch her breath, she was pressed up against the cold glass, the edges of her cardigan pulled open. Her lace bra was no barrier, making her nipples pull tight.

In front of her, Milan shone against the night sky in all its splendor. The light from the skyscrapers was the only light inside the office. Her shuddering breath drew a smoky ring on the glass as Adrian roughly pulled the cups of her bra down and filled his hands with her breasts.

His mouth found that spot at the arch of her shoulder and neck where she was extra sensitive. He dragged his teeth down that spot at the exact moment that his fingers flicked at her nipple.

Nyra gave a low moan, pushing herself into him. The imprint of his hard shaft against her bottom made her panties damp.

"Christo, I've missed touching you," he whispered, his lips pulling and tugging at her tender flesh. He kneaded and cupped her breasts, the rough calluses of his palms sending sparks of heat down to her core.

"Please, Adriano," she said, arcing into him. "I need…"

"What, *bella*?" he said, punctuating the question with a tug of her other nipple. Heated sparks arrowed down to her core. And the weight of his body against hers increased. His hands drifted down from her breasts, his long fingers splaying over her belly. Over the tautly stretched skin of her bump.

A sudden stillness enveloped him, the sound of his rough breaths harsh in the silence and he jerked back. A whimper escaped her. Without his claiming touch and his heat, her bare nipples scrunched against the sudden cold. She adjusted her bra, but left the flaps of her cardigan open.

It was the first time he'd touched her belly since she'd begun changing. And she knew it was a shock, as much as it was for her, every day.

Mustering her strength, she turned around to find him pushing a hand through his thick waves, something like panic touching his eyes.

Around her, automated lights came on, ruining the intimate moment with a bright glare. Only now did she see the deep grooves etched around his mouth, the dark circles cradling his eyes.

Guilt pricked her. She had pretty much unleashed the worst-case scenario on him, and he was the one dealing with the consequences. She'd always seen him as larger than life, this…unbending, powerful figure who needed nothing and no one. But that was a disservice to him, wasn't it? To the real man he was, made of flesh and blood and emotions, just like her?

"Adriano?" she said, reaching out to touch him.

He pulled back. "I pushed you against the wall. Christo, Nyra!"

"You did, but your hand was on my belly when you flipped me. Of all the things you had me do in the last year, you never hurt me before. And you won't now."

"In this, you trust me?"

Heat streaked her cheeks. "Yes. Don't ask me to explain it."

"You're truly not hurt?"

"Not in the way you think."

He came to her then, all crackling hunger and magnetic energy, his hands clasping her cheeks. His gaze drilling into her as if he meant to see through to her soul. "How do you hurt, then?"

She leaned in and rubbed her lips over his jaw. His beard was rough against her sensitive skin and so deliciously tormenting. "I miss you in our bed, Adriano. And not just those perfect orgasms you dole out before sleep. I miss...being held by you. Most of my adult life, I've been alone. Until you got me addicted to you. Can we please return to that?"

Hands on her shoulders, he gently pushed her back, his gaze clinging to her breasts. She didn't know whether to smile or sigh. "Your body has changed."

"Apparently that's what happens when you're growing two humans."

"I like it. You're rounder, lusher. Too thin before," he said with a sudden wicked upturn of his lips.

Nyra swatted his stomach with the back of her hand. "Hey! It's bad enough I feel...different in my own skin. None of my old clothes fit and I'm hungry all the time. And horny," she added.

His nostrils flared, and he pulled the thin bow of his upper lip with his teeth. "Now you know how I feel around you," he said, biting his lower lip.

"Oh, please, your body's like a finely honed sword.

If anything, you're aging like a fine wine," she said, snorting.

He gathered her to him then, his arms tight around her. Nyra thought she might expire of this affection he showed her in rare moments. "Horny, *bella*. I'm always horny around you." As if to underline his statement, he pressed closer, and the hard outline of his shaft against her belly made her breath falter.

Then he pulled away, but his mouth remained at her temple, and for a breathless moment, she felt utterly cherished. Wanted. *Needed, even.* "You're…beautiful, *mia cara*. Even more so, swelling with my children inside you."

His fingers sifted through her hair, the tops pressing into the base of her neck. "So why did we stop?" she said, burrowing into his neck.

His chuckle moved through her, filling her with a fizzy decadence. "Other than the fact that I'm too exhausted to satisfy you the way I want to? The whole board is still waiting for me outside the doors. I'm possessive enough to not want them listening to the sounds you make when you come. You're very loud."

"I don't want to go back to the apartment anymore," she said, clinging to his warmth. "I know you have security there to keep the hounding press away, but please don't send me away."

"It is the best place for you right now."

"No, I want to be here. Wherever you are."

"Nyra—"

"That day after he was sentenced, the crowd came at us outside the courthouse in London. I slipped and fell and someone stepped on my hand. It was the only rea-

son I got away. Nadia…spent an hour looking for me."
She took a shuddering breath. "I don't want to be alone,
Adriano. Neither do I want to be around your family
right now. Their discomfort at being hounded wherever
they go because of me is completely justified."

His arms tightened around her and his mouth lingered
over her temple. "*Bene*. I'll have someone bring you
to the penthouse here. Eat and rest. I'll join you later."

Looking up, she traced a finger gently over the dark
circles cradling his eyes. "You're the one who needs
rest and sleep."

"*Si*. But after I deal with what you've unleashed."

"You aren't angry?"

He shrugged. "You're right that secrets like that will
come out eventually, and then our children might have
been affected. I just…would have preferred less doubt
and worry for you at this time."

"That's not something even you can arrange me for
me though," she said, smoothly pointing out that for all
his power, there were some things beyond his reach.
Like her heart. "But knowing you're on my side makes
all the difference, Adriano."

Swallowing at how easily she unmade and remade
him, he held her close for another minute.

CHAPTER EIGHT

NYRA WOKE UP to the sounds of the shower running. She blinked and instantly searched the other side of the bed.

The sheets were cool and unruffled while her side of the bed looked like it had been hit by an earthquake. A quick glance at her watch on the nightstand told her that it was nearly two in the morning.

She'd eaten dinner alone, again. Only this time, it was at the penthouse in the skyscraper that belonged to the bank rather than at the castle. After dinner, she'd just drooped and wilted, waiting for Adriano.

Her body had been beyond exhausted, the relief after three days of stress and tension taking her out at the knees.

Sitting up in the bed now, she turned on the night lamp and stared down at herself. Another one of Adriano's dress shirts tented over her belly. She'd long ago discarded her bra. Her hair had lost whatever silky sheen it had been given after her hasty shower and letting it air-dry. Wavy and tangled, it was out of control.

She braided it quickly and grabbed the overnight bag she'd packed. Her fingers were cold, her sleepy brain slow to respond as she unbuttoned the shirt. Shrugging it off, she pulled on the beige-colored satin nightie she'd picked only yesterday afternoon.

Picking lingerie and sheer, lacy nightwear under Nigella's gaze had been an exercise in embarrassment. But it was the only way—having Nigella call her personal shoppe—to get her hands on new clothes for this new image she was building.

Her choice had still been the most modest of them all, with the satin fabric simply draping over her curves.

Standing, Nyra studied her profile in the full-length mirror that had been hung directly across from the king bed. Pregnancy had given her skin that healthy glow, and eating well and sleeping on time the last couple of weeks had taken care of the rest.

She looked…pretty, if not ravishingly beautiful as she'd hoped. Her finger skidded across her mouth when she tried to apply lip gloss as a sudden, horrifying thought struck her.

Why did Adriano have a mirror right up against the bed in his bedroom? Was this his love nest?

The lip gloss tube fell from her hand and promptly rolled under the bed as she looked around the luxurious room with suspicious eyes.

For all that he had rarely been caught in tabloids with a partner, even before they'd met, she had first-hand knowledge of how insatiable her husband was. It had been months since they'd been intimate. Rightly or not, he'd thought she'd cheated on him.

What if he had already…

"Nyra!"

Flushing, she turned.

Adriano stood at the entrance to the bedroom, clad

in nothing but a towel around his hips. The white of the fabric contrasted richly against his olive skin. Heat prickled over her skin, as she followed the trail of a waterdrop down the thick ridges of his chest and abdomen.

"You look like a ghost," he said, coming to her. The scent of his soap made her flesh shiver and ache instantly. "What is it, *bella*? Was it a bad dream?"

When he laid a hand on her shoulder, she jerked back. "Have you…"

"Have I what?"

"Have you been with another woman in the last few months, Adriano? When you thought I was…"

His jaw tightened and a vein ticked in his temple. "No."

Relief poured through her in shivers. Turning toward him, she wrapped her arms around his waist like a child. Though the damp heat of his skin and what it evoked was another matter. "I'm sorry."

His heart was a steadying beat at her ear. Though he didn't put his arms around her or press his mouth to her temple. If anything, he stiffened in her embrace. "We've already established you have no trust in me. There's no need to apologize."

And yet he sounded angry. No, hurt. *He was hurt.* That wasn't possible.

Hurt required attachment and expectations and some sort of affection. All they had was lust and this determination to be good parents now.

"You have a mirror right up against the bed and your assistant of nearly fifteen years blocked my calls. And you thought I had betrayed you."

Suddenly, she could feel an echo of the pain he must

have felt in seeing those photographs of her twin, naked and writhing in another man's arms.

His humiliating her in front of his parents had blinded her to his pain.

She didn't know if she could ever forget how easily he had thrown her out, but she thought she could forgive his jumping to conclusions.

"I couldn't bear it if you even looked at another woman, if you…let someone touch you or give them the right to touch this body." She dug her teeth into his chest, feeling a near savage thirst to mark him as hers. "I couldn't stay then, not even for the babies."

"Shh…" he finally said, one hand coming to the nape of her neck. Those long fingers bracketed her neck possessively, an adornment she liked more than diamonds. "My assistant," he said, as if knowing not to bring the woman's name to his lips, "had no right to block you and has been dealt with severely. I apologize for causing you that extra stress."

"Fabi said she used to be your preferred partner at any number of society galas and parties."

His sigh ruffled the hairs at her temple. "Because I didn't like playing games with women I had no interest in. As my assistant, she was a safe choice." Like an ice cube rolling down her skin, he marched those fingers down her spine. And then he was winding her braid around his fingers and tugging, exerting just the right pressure on her scalp.

It dripped like drops of molten honey down her limbs. Every inch of her pulled taut with anticipatory pleasure.

Nyra gave her own hands free rein, tracing the thick ridges and valleys of his muscles. The power thrumming through this man, the thick length pressing against her thigh…it was all hers. How had she never realized the bounty the universe had given her, for once?

She would never take it for granted, ever again.

"And you never…before we met?" She knew she was pushing it, but she wanted this topic closed. Just thinking of how naive she'd been in not seeing his appeal to other women seemed foolish now.

"Never. She's under my power and protection. I'm not my father."

The steel in his words put paid to the final niggle in her head. "Will you fire her, or should I?"

"Where has this lioness been all these months?"

She hid her face in his chest. "Don't remind me. I was…foolish and naive. Your mother was right about me."

"*Basta, cara!* I liked that woman," he said gruffly. "She was brave and honest."

Her heart inflated to dangerous proportions. It was the first time he'd admitted that their relationship had had more than just sex as its basis.

She pressed a kiss to his chest, then raked her fingernail over the flat nipple. His chest hair tickled her palm. Sudden tension filled his powerful frame.

"The mirror?" she said, looking up.

He laughed. "You're quite the suspicious little thing, aren't you?"

"It's not just men who get jealous and possessive," she said, raking her nails down his abdomen.

A hiss left his mouth.

She flushed as her gaze fell on the clear outline tenting the towel.

But before she could touch him, he shifted her so that they were facing the mirror. Behind her, he was all rough, rugged planes and masculine magnetism. Framed by the gilt-edged mirror, they looked like they...belonged together, she thought, with a shiver.

Their eyes caught and held, heat arcing around them like a coiled lash.

His erection at her back prodded her bottom even as his hands lazily drifted over her shoulders, grazed the sides of her breasts and then settled on her belly. "Remember the time I took you in the greenhouse?"

"You nearly shattered my orchid after I had just repotted it."

He grinned. With his wet hair flopping onto his temple and his smile weaving crinkly lines at the corners of his eyes, he was a different man from the one the world saw. The one that had dismissed his entire board with one word that evening. The one that dealt with the forgotten scandal involving his wife and the mud raking that followed with harsh measures.

Maybe only she got to see this side, she thought, with a giddy joy. And maybe this passion and the trust they would build could be enough.

"You wouldn't let me press you against the glass even though I told you no one can see us. Then when..."

"When you kept edging me without letting me come, I promised to let you do whatever you wanted in front of a mirror if only you gave me relief," she finished, feverish tingles breaking out across her skin.

His hands cupped her breasts, the nipples poking through the satin. "*Si.* It was delivered here by mistake."

Nyra threw her head back as he pinched one peak. "Okay, have at me, then."

His teeth and tongue played havoc on the sensitive spot at her neck, while his fingers drove her wild. "Maybe some other time. Right now, I think I prefer the bed."

"What?" she said, straightening. "Why?"

His palms cradled her belly protectively. "I should curb my more dangerous intentions for you for a while, *si*?"

She covered his hands with hers, loath to lose this one real, concrete thing between them. The pregnancy was already doing a number on her emotions. "No *si*. No *bueno*. Adriano, I'm not fragile. Whatever you want, I'm up for it."

"Nyra—"

"This is a fresh start for us. And maybe it's not a big deal to you, but I went to a lot of trouble to please you and—"

"What trouble?" he said, widening his eyes exaggeratedly.

With a huff, she pushed out of his embrace and glared at him. "Now I feel like I'm truly married."

His mouth twitched. "Such temper, *cara*!" Reaching out, he traced one finger from her neck down to her chest. "Look how prettily it paints your chest and neck…"

Then he prowled toward her like some great predator. He hooked one finger at her neckline and tugged until the nightie ripped straight down the middle.

"I just picked this from too many," she said, holding the torn edges together. "I got my nails done, got waxed to an inch, got a facial and picked out a whole new wardrobe so that you're not ashamed of me."

He froze, his gaze a stormy gray now. "I never claimed I was."

"There's a reason we've never been out in public even once in all these months. I didn't even meet your—"

"You never asked to meet anyone."

"I'm not blaming you," she said, rubbing her finger over his lower lip. "It suited me to hide in the corners of your life. I think I was almost waiting you out, waiting for you to come to your senses."

"What does that mean?"

She shrugged. "Doesn't matter. But all that's going to change now."

"I like you in my shirts, *bella*, or like this, with nothing on."

Before she could draw another breath, he bent that proud head down and licked her nipple. Electricity shivered down her spine. She sank her fingers into his hair as he played with the bud, licking and tugging and finally, closing his lips around it and sucking.

Shaking, Nyra half gasped and half moaned as his fingers gently cupped her belly and then delved down into her folds.

His curse rang loudly in the silence.

"You're dripping," Adriano said, laving the wetness and tapping on her clit.

"For you," she said, holding on to him for balance but also hoping he would launch her into the sky like he usually did. "I've missed you so much, Adriano."

He shifted his mouth to her other breast, his breath

a sharp stroke against the waiting bud. "Never again, Nyra. You will never be deprived again."

And then with his mouth alternating between her nipples and the valley between her breasts, and his finger strumming her folds, thrusting through her core, pinching her clit, while his filthy words of praise drenched her skin, he pushed her to the edge of the cliff and launched her into a thousand fragments.

Nyra came, sobbing and keening and crying, his name falling over and over from her lips.

When she returned to the ground, trembling from head to toe, it was to find the cool sheets at her back. On his knees and hands, Adriano was watching her, filling her entire vision.

She clasped his cheek, loving the rough bristle of his stubble against her palm. "I wanted to seduce you," she said, her eyes flickering between his. "You didn't come to see me after returning from Japan."

"I wanted to," he bit out, skating his mouth over her palm.

"I want this to work, Adriano," she said.

"I know, wife. And it will." Then he leaned down, his shoulders bunching tight when he stopped short of giving her his entire weight. "And you don't have to go to these lengths to seduce me, *bella*." His pelvis came down and Nyra instantly opened her thighs.

The rough, weighty press of his cock against her damp core made their groans ring out together. "All you need to do is ask me for this. For whatever you want."

She threw her arms around his neck and pulled herself

up. Her already sensitized nipples scraped deliciously against his chest hair. "Then, please, come inside me. I'm desperate." And then she took his mouth.

He tasted like toothpaste and whiskey and him…

The kiss went to incendiary from the get-go. Heat flushed and prickled under her skin, as he plundered her mouth with the same desperate need she felt.

Nyra writhed against the sheets, anchoring her hands in his hair as he moved his mouth down her jaw and then blew a soft puff of air over her nipple. The peak tightened and arched toward him.

She tugged at his hair hard. With a chuckle, he closed his lips over it and she was riding the gates to heaven on a wave.

The suck and pull of his clever lips made her core weep and gush. A curse rattled off his lips when his cock felt her damp folds. "You're so ready for me, *bella*."

"I am," she said, clinging to him.

He played with her breasts a little more, bringing her right to the edge, all over again. Just when she thought she might expire from the little mirage hovering out of reach, he pulled her up to lean against him.

Her chest heaving with rough pants, Nyra took a few seconds to register how he had positioned them. Her damp back slid against his hairy chest but it was only one point of attack. His hair-roughened thighs bracketed hers and against her lower back, his cock was trapped. The scent of his soap and sweat wrapped around her like a coil.

"Give me your gaze, Nyra," he said, kissing a line along her shoulder blades.

Pushing sticky tendrils back from her forehead, she looked up.

In the mirror, gray-green eyes trapped her, as surely as if he was a hunter who'd set a snare for her. And the lure was this erotic picture of them together framed perfectly in the mirror.

The ceiling lights were in full brightness and they danced over her skin like gold drops. Her breasts were full with peaked nipples, and his long fingers on her belly, made her swallow. With his broad shoulders and long, powerful limbs and all those clenched muscles around her, he should have minimized her. Instead, against the contrast of his body, anchored by the naked desire in his gaze, she felt beautiful.

Seen. Known.

"Will you sit for a painting like this, Nyra?" he said, nuzzling her neck, his fingers beginning the ascent of her desire all over again.

"If you join me," she said, throwing her head back.

His smile was a dark gleam in the mirror. "I shall convince you," he said, digging his teeth into her shoulder.

And then his hands were everywhere, his mouth was everywhere. Nyra stopped trying to keep track of what he was doing to her and simply gave in to the assault.

Her second orgasm came and went, spinning and hurling her around as if she were a speck of light in the cosmos. Or even an exploding star.

The pleasure was so intense that she started sobbing at some point.

Every muscle in her body felt stretched, wrung out, but Nyra hung on to him, knowing he still hadn't sought his satisfaction. "Enough, Adriano. Let's take care of you now. *Por favore*," she said, turning and rubbing her swollen lips against his jaw.

He chuckled, and the sound went straight to her sensitized core. "Do you still think I don't appreciate you, *bella*?"

Taking his lips in a soft kiss, Nyra held back the things she couldn't say anymore. "I will never complain, ever again."

His fingers strummed her folds and then her popped clit, sending a weak arrow of pleasure through her. She whimpered, her spine feeling like it was made of Jell-O. "You're ready for me, then?" he whispered.

"Always," she said.

"Keep your eyes open."

Nyra blinked and watched as he lifted her to sit on him as if she were a feather. Then he adjusted her thighs, and suddenly, she was glad for the flexibility and strength her daily yoga practice had given her.

"Now take me inside, *bella*. Easy and slow."

Clutching his forearms, sensing his raised tendons with her fingers, Nyra pulled up and then drove herself down onto his cock. After all these months, she'd forgotten how the stretch and breadth of him felt inside her. Pleasure and just a pinch of pain drenched her.

A feral moan ripped from their mouths, joining into an erotic symphony.

One corded arm sat under her breasts, holding her impaled against him, while he sent the other to cup her cheek. His kiss was brutal in its need and so soft in its delivery.

"Is this dangerous enough for you, Nyra?"

She giggled. And even that sent a fresh arrow of sensation where they were joined, pleasure shorting out her synapses.

Of course, she should have known that her extracompetitive husband would take it as a challenge.

And in this new position, it felt like he was right in her heart. She'd barely taken stock of all the new, raw sensations strumming through her, when he said, "Give me your gaze."

She looked up, and there she was, indecently stretched out and splayed against his lap. Sweat made her skin gleam with a sheen, and her mouth was swollen, as were her nipples.

Every inch of her screamed his possession with pride.

With one hand on her throat, she moved the other down to touch the place where they were joined. Licking her lips, holding his gaze, she stroked the root of him.

A fiery jolt speared her from that place.

His filthy curse, a guttural groan and a slight thrust were her rewards.

Her sated body pulsed with renewed desire as she repeated the motion. Something about seeing Adriano reach the edge of his control—seeing his lower lip slacken, the green becoming richer in his eyes—made her feral with possessiveness.

She repeated the motions with her fingers, skimming over whatever she could reach of him as he spun those wicked hips into slow, shallow thrusts, making her eyes roll back in her head. Moving inside her, reminding her how glorious it could be but not giving her enough.

"Will you come for me again?"

"I can try," she said, sensations shimmering into life under her skin all over again. "I worried that…"

"What?"

"That you might not want to try all these things

anymore. I prepared myself for a loveless marriage but this…you and I and this intense physical connection… I worried that all you saw anymore was a liar. And your children's mother."

His teeth dug into her shoulder and the hiss of pain made fresh sparks pop at her core. It was punishment, but she didn't care.

"I'll always want to do wicked things to you, *bella*. Your changing body only makes me hungrier." As if to prove his point, he played with her nipples.

Burying her fingers in his hair, Nyra moaned.

And then he was urging her to move, setting a slow, soft pace. Splayed open like that, his every thrust hit some deep, incredibly soft spot, making her moan. Her thighs burned as she pulled up and pushed down, matching his pace and then upping it because the spring in her lower belly pulled tauter and tighter the faster she moved.

That spot sent out reverberations of pleasure, skewering her.

Praise and curses fell equally from Adriano's mouth, urging her on the last inch. Soon, she was clenching around his hard length, and breaking apart. Her climax a wave bringing her under.

Aftershocks wracked her as he gently pushed her onto her knees and hands. And she watched him in the mirror, shamelessly, this glorious man of hers.

And his naked hunger was etched on every plane and ridge of his body.

He met her eyes in the mirror and his thrusts got rougher, faster.

Nyra watched, her heart thudding in her chest a thousand times faster, as his climax hit and soaked her insides.

He bowed around her body, even in that moment of utter escape. As if he meant to protect her, even from himself.

Tears pooled and overflowed, and when he wiped one with a shaking hand and inquired if she was okay, she said he had ruined her once again.

And some worried part of her found solace in the fact that maybe this passion would be enough to sustain their marriage.

CHAPTER NINE

THE LAST THING Adriano wanted was to attend a party with people he'd had no choice but to endure all his life. Especially since he and his family and Nyra had spent the last two weeks in the spotlight, while he took the necessary steps to make it clear to the press that his wife and her twin were in no way connected to the financial scandal their father had perpetrated.

Finally, when Nyra faced the cameras herself to give out a statement to that effect and also announced a charity trust for victims of financial scams that she would spearhead, the story lost its initial focus.

Once again, his quiet but fierce wife had shocked him.

But her resolve to create a new role for herself in his life was not a laughing matter. Hence the party.

Granted, he didn't mind spending time with Bruno, or Fabi, or even Federico, who was showing signs of cleaning up his act, but his parents and their society friends were another matter.

Toxic backstabbing was the only phrase he would use to describe most relationships in that crowd. And now his wife had planted herself in the middle of it all.

Neither did he want to put on a performance of his

marriage for a crowd of hungry vultures who, even a month ago, thought Nyra was trash he'd picked up from the back streets of Vegas. Or a week ago, believed she was the thieving daughter of a career criminal who should be discarded, even if she was pregnant.

In no more than two weeks, the announcement of their pregnancy and her reaching out to his circle had of course achieved a one-eighty among the same crowd.

The woman was on a mission. Even refusing to leave the penthouse without him, claiming he needed her at such a stressful time. Though he'd done no more than shower, shave and catch a couple of hours of sleep after that night with her.

Something had changed between them—for good, ostensibly, but he wasn't sure. Then there was the fact that he wanted her out of the city and the easy clutches of the media. "To protect his reputation from the scandal you've caused," Mama had said, thinking he was out of earshot. For a second, he'd seen the fear flash through Nyra, that he would tell his mother that she'd been the cause of it directly.

For all that she promised him fidelity and devotion and a fresh start, she still didn't trust him. And he hated it with every breath in him.

Now, as he jumped off the chopper and walked the corridors through the main level of the yacht, curiosity began to overtake the exhaustion he'd felt on arrival. Soft jazz, from one of his favorite low-key artists, crooned through the speakers, instantly loosening the tension he felt in his shoulders. That she'd remembered the artist's name from when he'd played it in their suite in Vegas…put a smile on his lips.

And this was a record he didn't even own.

Grabbing a champagne from a passing waiter, he drank it in one gulp and grimaced. Before the staff could throw a second glance in his direction, he climbed the stairs to the upper deck.

Among the guests crowding the sky lounge, he noted his parents, on opposite ends.

HIs mother, as usual, was flirting with his father's oldest colleague, and his father, on the other end, was entertaining a very eager, very young wannabe actress Adriano recognized from her various colorful media scandals. Then there were his sister and brother and friends…and colleagues he barely tolerated in work.

His gaze drifted through the crowd, considering and discarding people until it landed on…her. He'd initially whizzed past the figure in red. Something about the nervous way the woman pushed her hair behind her ear caught his attention instead.

It was his wife, with her thick curls straightened into wispy layers that barely touched her shoulders.

She had cut her hair.

Christo, why did the loss hit him as if he were a boy whose favorite toy had been donated to the shelter?

It is only hair, he told himself, fighting rising frustration.

The red silk dipped so low in the back—barely held together—that if one had the interest, one could simply catch a glimpse of her delicious bottom. Given the man she was dancing with was a scoundrel who thought making promises and debauching women, married or single alike, a sport, it would be no surprise if he pawed her.

Whatever it was the rogue said, leaning his mouth

quite close to her ear, she laughed. It was a genuine sound, full of that huskiness that Adriano loved. Like the world's richest miser, he wanted to hoard it all for himself.

The man grinned, pulled back and turned her in his arms.

Adriano got a glimpse of her front. And cursed low.

The dress dipped just as low in the front, almost baring her skin to her stomach. Then the fabric gathered and fell in thick folds, all the way to her ankles, with a thigh-high slit on the side.

Diamonds, large and flashy, winked from her throat, wrists and ears. Even her makeup was different, with subtle gold eyeshadow making her eyes pop like jewels, even viewed from this distance.

Finally, with a gracious smile, she pulled away from the man.

Adriano's breath came just a little easier.

She flitted through the rest of the crowd, the red making her glitter among boring blacks and navy blues, laughing and entertaining whoever accosted her. And a lot of men did accost her. Some out of curiosity—this was after all their only chance to get a close eyeful of the scandal Adriano Cavalieri had willingly courted. Some because this Nyra, with flirty smiles and smart quips and subtle arm touches, was too stunning to resist.

Some because they wanted to test her, and him, through her.

She looked beautiful, sophisticated, like one of the numerous socialites and heiresses his mother had picked for him through the years.

I'll be a perfect wife to you, Adriano.

She was perfect. This was what his parents had wanted for him. This was what his own lifestyle demanded. This was what society expected from him and his wife.

And it was all wrong.

This was not the Nyra he wanted, the Nyra he'd secretly married, away from the eyes of the world.

Nyra became aware of Adriano's presence minutes before he made his actual appearance.

Every inch of her bare skin, and there was a lot on tasteful display tonight, prickled with warning and pleasure. The small hairs on her neck stood to attention, and a sweet hum thrummed through her, pooling low in her core.

The last time she and her husband had talked had been on the phone two nights ago, and it was to indulge in phone sex. Because she'd admitted that she was restless and horny, and Adriano was a man who viewed it as a challenge to his title, if he didn't see to her satisfaction.

While his softly filthy words had pushed her to climax, the restlessness hadn't quite left her. She'd still lain awake long into the night, wishing she could wrap herself around him. Wishing he would hold her.

Not that she'd admitted that part to him.

Now she could feel his gaze run down between her shoulders, following the deep cut of the gown. Her body, tired and socialized out, came alive with a thrumming buzz, as if he'd planted one of those erotic chips under her skin and activated it by remote.

Relief and anticipation were such strong currents running through her that she laughed a little too loudly at something her companion said. A snake charmer type if she'd ever seen one.

The handsy scoundrel grinned down at her, his extrawhite teeth making her retinas hurt. She sighed.

Her husband was more than an hour late, and for a few moments, she'd been worried that Adriano might not even show up. "Oh, you know how much Adriano hates this kind of fake schmoozing," Fabi had said, in a throwaway comment upon arriving a couple of hours ago.

When Nyra had stared at her in shock, she had tangled her arm through hers. "But clearly, he let you throw this huge party for him, Nyra. It's not like mother or father ever celebrated his birthday growing up."

"They didn't?" Nyra had asked, suddenly feeling as if she'd stepped in a minefield that was Adriano's relationship with his parents. Blind, at that.

"Nope," Fabi said, and drifted into the gathering.

All evening, doubts had crowded her mind. But she'd committed herself to this path and she would see it through.

Suddenly, the memory of her father throwing extravagant parties for big shots he was courting, with her mother playing happy hostess, came to her.

Adriano might not personally like parties—he was as much of an introvert as she was—but this kind of socializing and networking was necessary for his social standing. Wasn't it? Especially since she'd called his loyalty, his dependability, his honor into question by mucking it through her own background.

Whatever harm she'd caused his standing, and it was a lot according to his mother, she was determined to do her part in smoothing it over.

"I think you've danced long enough with my wife," a sudden voice said behind her, dislodging the snake charmer's hand from around her waist.

Nyra blew out a sigh. Apparently, the fact that she was pregnant didn't dissuade the man. But she hadn't learned the sophistication of how to disentangle herself from him without causing a scene.

All evening, he'd flirted outrageously with her, even though Nigella said he was interested in Fabi and that she should encourage his pursuit of her sister-in-law. Not that she could see the spirited Fabi liking the smarmy fucker.

"You're frowning, *cara*. Maybe you prefer your previous partner."

The thin thread of irritation in those words made her head snap up. Adriano's mouth was pursed in displeasure, that thick vein in his temple standing taut.

A slow, dizzying heat unspooled in her veins as she leaned back to better take in his thick brows, that blade of a nose and the sensuous mouth. The scent of him filled her lungs and it felt like the first free breath of her day.

Behind him, the lights from the lakes and cottages suddenly shimmered brighter. Everything around her felt more beautiful, more alive, now that he was here.

It took a few moments for his words to sink through the instant haze of desire he spun around her senses. "What? Of course not," she said, laying a hand on his chest.

Unlike every other man here, he'd already discarded his jacket and tie and rolled the cuffs of his white shirt back. She clutched his wrist with her other hand, the contrast of thick muscle and hairy texture giving her the tactile pleasure she'd needed all day.

She wished he would pull her closer and let her feel the solid warmth from his body.

When he simply stared at her, she said, "The only reason I entertained that snake oil salesman is because Nigella said his family was important to yours." She wisely left out the whole arrangement for Fabi thing, not wanting to start a mini family battle in the middle of her party.

His lips twitched, and the rigid tension with which he held himself broke. Although he didn't fully smile. "That is an apt description of him." His fingers tightened over her waist. "I thought you were taken in by him, the way you clung to his every word and laughed."

"The only reason I laughed so much is to hide my shaking knees. I could sense you around, Adriano. And you still have the effect of making my knees quake just by landing your gaze on my flesh."

The gray of his gaze shifted to a glorious dark green, like rain-washed leaves in the deep of autumn. Shock flickered there along with something else. Why did he always look so amazed when she admitted how his one glance could affect her? It was the one place where she'd always been honest with him.

Leaning in, not caring how tacky it might be to cling to her gorgeous husband in front of everyone, she kissed his cheek. His stubble met her lips and she had to rub her thighs compulsively. Remembering how he had inflamed her inner thighs with the same stubble. "Happy birthday, Adriano."

"*Grazie*, Nyra."

He held still when she went on her toes and wiped at the smudge she had left. "Just so you know, I'm leaving a little behind."

He frowned.

"So that all these women know that you're taken. By me."

He laughed then, and finally, it was one of the genuine things that he gave her. The sound burrowed into her, making a cozy nest in her chest. Something more than the ever-present thrum of desire uncoiled in her belly. A sweet sense of anticipation for more. An intense longing for something deeper than just desire.

"Shall we mingle and greet everyone?" she said, struggling to keep it out of her face. Her desire was something Adriano always wanted, but this…this neediness was different. "They've all been waiting for a while."

"You look different," he said, completely ignoring her request with that signature arrogance that she found both annoying and arresting. "I had hoped operation Nyra was done."

Her nerves jangled. "Bad different or good different?"

"Different," he repeated, some of that arrogance seeping into the way he scratched his brow and studied her. "The dress, the hair, even the makeup, it's all different. It's much more skin than I've ever seen you show in public."

"Is that a problem?" she said, something of the survivor in her creeping into her words.

His chin tilted up, in equal challenge. As if he wanted that creature to come out. "Do you think so?"

She colored. Adriano was possessive but he'd never judged her for her choice of profession or her clothes or her lack of sophistication, ever.

So what was it about this exchange that was putting her on the back foot? She was exhausted from the week of planning this with his mother. "Nigella says everything I wear and say and do reflects on you and your reputation."

His frown deepened. "And what statement is it that you want to make?"

"That I'm equal to anything they expect of your wife. Of the mother of future Cavalieri heirs."

"You sound like her, *bella*. As taken with the legacy and legitimacy of things as this society is." He didn't quite mock her, but his contempt shone through each word.

"Is it wrong if I want to cultivate the good opinion and friendship of these people, some of whose children will grow up alongside ours?"

"You don't need it. And our children certainly don't."

"But as your wife—"

"As my wife," he said, pulling her impossibly closer. Their chests brushed and a breath shuddered out of her at the quick graze of his erection against her belly, "You could rule them all, *cara*. I would not have you pretzel yourself, courting their approval."

"I don't want to rule anyone, Adriano. I want to make friends in this world of yours. I want to wipe the stain I bring to this marriage, to our children's lives. I want to use this power you talk about to do some good eventually. When I mentioned that charity, I wasn't blowing hot air to look better."

"I have nothing against that," he murmured, his tight hold of her sending vibrations that pooled at her core. "And I knew that you meant it."

With one sentence, he made everything between them a thousand times deeper and more real. She had to clear her throat to make words, to clear the wanting gripping her. "Fabi said you're not a fan of parties. But you're… not just bored or displeased. You're almost angry. May I ask why?"

"I'm not angry."

"And now you're lying to me," she said, exhaustion hitting her like a sledgehammer. She swayed and he caught her.

"You're exhausted, *bella*."

"Yes, arranging a party of this size takes energy. Especially in the way that pleases your family. Even if it means just sending minions on a hundred errands. The decision fatigue is real."

"Forgive me for being a cranky bastard, *cara*. You clearly—"

Whatever he'd been about to say was cut off as Adriano's parents joined them with another couple in tow.

From there, small talk ensued and the Adriano that accompanied her for the rest of the evening wasn't the one she wanted.

"I'm glad to say there's hope for her," Mama said, coming to stand by him on the upper deck. "Her willingness to correct her past, and your own mistake, goes a long way."

Adriano swallowed the biting retort that rose to his lips. The last thing he would do was to ruin Nyra's hard work by getting into an argument with his mother at the tail end of the party. Bad enough he'd behaved like a grumpy bastard for most of it.

But her condescending tone grated on him. "You do know that she's pregnant with twins, *si*?"

Below them, under the glittering glass deck, Nyra was now surrounded by a group of women from the board of some charity foundation. Even from here, the exhaustion pinching the corners of her mouth were visible. But she wouldn't listen to a word of his entreaty that it was okay to leave. "You're running her ragged, having convinced her she needs to make reparations. My wife doesn't owe anyone a thing."

"She's already beginning from a place of…weakness when it comes to our society. She needs to have her finger on everything before the babies come. Then there's all the arrangements we need to make with nannies so that she can continue the work she's started here. There were at least two charities that she showed interest in. I plan to get her on board immediately."

He gritted his teeth. "She will need time to recover from the pregnancy. As for nannies, that is a decision she and I will make together. Your advice on all things parenting, while appreciated, is not required."

She turned to stare at him, only now catching the growl in his words. "You will decide on nannies, Adriano?" A scornful laugh escaped her.

He straightened to his full height. "*Si.* And all this…" he said, moving his hand over the guests and the yacht and the party. "I will indulge it only as long as Nyra wants it."

"What does that mean?"

"It means our marriage is nothing like yours and Papa's. And I will light this entire society on fire before I let you mold her into another version of you."

"Adriano!" Mama said, paleness creeping in under her skin. "You dare to speak to me that way..."

"I think the question should be why I left it so long. All you and Papa did in your marriage is one-up each other. Affairs, lies, cheating, scandals...a parade of nannies for me and a cluster of illegitimate children spread along the coast. Papa didn't even leave one of the nannies alone." His gaze fell on Bruno, who had looked up at them just then. A shake of his head followed, because of course, his half brother could read Adriano's tension from his body language. But this was something he should have done ages ago.

His parents had misunderstood his aversion for this kind of discussion—where he had to caution them for their behavior—as his apathy for how they treated his wife.

He faced his mother. "My children will not be raised by a string of strangers, will not be used as pawns in a game of drunken, cheating bluff. Will not be left alone at a cavernous suite at some luxury hotel at the age of five, for a whole day and night. Until Maria came back to look after me, I didn't know what it was to be touched and hugged. And loved." His voice broke at the last word and he felt...as if he'd been punched in the head. Never once had he admitted to himself the effects of his parents' sheer negligence of him.

"Adriano—"

"No," he said, cutting her off.

Even the glitter of tears in his mother's eyes didn't dissuade him. If she did feel regret, it was too late.

"Whatever Nyra wants to try and become, your job is to support her and walk her through it. You have no say, no power when it comes to my marriage, my wife or my children. If not, I know how to make you and Papa behave."

"Adriano, please—"

"Now, let's not drag this out into one of your drama specials, Mama," he said, bending and kissing her cheek. "After all, my wife worked quite hard on this party, *si*?"

The mild rose scent she'd always worn squeezed his heart. As a child, he'd adored her, craved her attention, cried for her deep into the night. He'd begged, and then bargained, with a God he didn't even understand, for her to see him. For her to love him.

Until he had had no choice but to harden himself against that kind of dependence on her or his father. Or anyone else for that matter. It was only Maria's presence, and later Bruno stubbornly pushing into his life, that had stopped him from becoming a complete island. Desolate, alone.

Suddenly, he could see the damage all of it had wrought on him.

His skin prickled and when he looked down, he caught the gaze of the woman who had paid the price for that damage. It was his own incapability of trusting her and himself and their bond that had damaged their relationship. He saw it now.

And yet Nyra stared at him with such faith in her eyes that he felt renewed hope for himself.

Maybe it was time to see his birthdays as something worth celebrating. For Nyra and for their future together, if not for himself.

CHAPTER TEN

IT WAS PAST midnight when Nyra dismissed the two women from the catering staff who had assisted her in the gourmet galley. The chef had barely hidden his laughter, which had begun as contempt for her pitiful attempts, but this was one thing she'd wanted to do by herself. Even if it took her forever.

Finally, the yacht was empty, free of even family.

Adriano was nowhere to be seen though. For just a moment, she wondered if he'd left with the rest of the guests. But he wouldn't just abandon her. Would he?

She emerged from the galley onto the lower deck and looked past the glass walls that kept out the chilly breeze. In the dark, a new kind of magnificence greeted her, with lights from elegant villas and charming villages shining on the dark waters. The yacht's sleek exterior gleamed, reflecting the colors of the earlier sunset.

She'd barely had any time to explore the expansive space, busy with the arrangements all morning, then getting ready—which took far too long these days with hair and makeup, and then greeting guests as dusk fell.

Balancing the fine china plate precariously in her hand now, she walked up the spiraling staircase toward the sky lounge. Even after all these months, the reach and flex of Adriano's wealth was a shock to her. Like the existence of this yacht.

But then, he was a man who was as miserly with personal or family details as he was generous with his caresses. Her toes sank into the thick carpet, while the cold glass scraped against her bare arms in a welcome slide.

She'd kicked off her heels, but the dress was an annoyance. Thanks to the breeze, her hair had long ago won the fight against everything that had been used to tame it. When she'd caught her reflection in the gleaming chrome of the appliances in the galley, she'd grabbed a clip and put it up.

On the main deck, the air was filled with the gentle lapping of waves against the hull, creating a soothing rhythm. If only it could soothe the confusion and worry that dogged her like shadows.

All evening, she'd sensed that Adriano wasn't pleased with her efforts or the party or anything to do with the evening. Catching fragmented phrases of his conversation with Nigella had only confirmed her suspicion.

Whether it was Nyra's attempt at the party or something else that displeased him, she had no idea.

After a week of losing herself in this new life that only seemed to have moving targets, all she wanted for tonight was to show him that she was worth the scandal she'd brought on him, worth the drama and pain she'd caused in his life. That she appreciated him.

For a second, the weight of all that she'd taken on threatened to crush her. It felt as impossibly daunting as the dark silhouettes of towering mountains that surrounded the lake. Forget the physical toll of the party today— the socializing and the laughing at inane comments, pretending that she didn't see the censure in some gazes was mentally exhausting.

But she had made her bed—a very pleasurable one when her husband was in it, and she was determined to make the best of it.

If only she knew how to reach Adriano. Because clearly, whatever she had done today to please him hadn't remotely had that effect.

No wonder she'd spent months limiting herself to one corner of his life. Her husband was powerful, ruthless, kind and beneath it all, a mystery.

Her breath caught in her throat as she stepped into the master suite on the top deck, which was forbidden to the guests.

Large panorama windows lined one entire side of the suite, offering sweeping views of the lake and the mountains beyond. Sheer curtains drifted lazily from some cool draft overhead.

The centerpiece of the suite was the lavish king-size bed adorned with sumptuous white linens and an array of plush pillows that looked like a fluffy cloud. A hint of fresh flowers scented the air.

On the other side was a chic sitting area featuring furniture elegantly upholstered in velvet. The lighting, she noticed, was carefully designed to accentuate the suite's luxury without detracting from the beauty outside.

And here, sitting in the largest armchair nursing a glass of whiskey, was her missing husband.

Nyra slid the plate onto the side table before approaching him. Just being alone with him made her heart skip a beat. She came to stand in front of him, between his legs. "Adriano..." she ventured but he remained unmoving.

Unable to fight the urge, she sank her fingers into his thick hair and tugged.

He looked up then. Thick lashes blinked slowly and his gaze focused on her hair. His fingers gripped the glass tightly as if he were stopping himself.

"You cut your hair," he said.

She touched the short, wavy locks that were already tumbling out of the hold of the clip. "It's easier to manage this way."

"I liked it better when it was long."

"Oh." Dismay filled her because she hadn't given him a single thought. Only that she needed to give herself a makeover, inside out. Something fresh to change how she saw herself. "If you really want me to, I'll grow it back. But with the pregnancy and everything else, it is easier this way."

"Bene," he said, looking down into his drink. When she didn't budge, he said, "Go to bed, *cara.*"

"You're drunk," she whispered, the shock of it making her frown. She refused to pull away from him however. "You never drink."

"It's my birthday, *si*? Only a mild buzz."

"I'll keep you company, then," she said, running fingers down the back of his head, past his neck and then farther down to his shoulders. Slipping her fingers in under the unbuttoned collar of his shirt, she found warm skin and taut muscles.

He groaned—a sound that went straight to her core—when she kneaded the muscles with firm fingers. His head dipped to rest against her belly. Nyra increased the speed and strength of her movements, dipping lower into his back and coming up again.

The solid planes of his back, the heat of his body hit her bloodstream as if he were an oral drug she was addicted to.

His whiskey tumbler clanked down on the table as his own hands came to grab her hips. He turned up his head, pushing her back a little. His forest-green gaze pinned her to the spot. "I don't want our children to be raised by a string of nannies and childminders who will, at best, treat them as nothing but a cushy paycheck."

It was the last thing she expected him to say. Neither was the delivery soft or easy. Some great emotion pulsed beneath each word. Suddenly, his fractious conversation with his mother looked different in her head. To her, it had always seemed like a mild irritation with his parents. But what if it was something deeper?

Damn it, why hadn't she asked Maria when she'd visited. Though she wasn't sure if she'd have told Nyra anything without Adriano's express permission.

"I understand," she said, swallowing. His shoulders bunched with tension under her fingers, but she refused to give up the anchor. "And I agree with you."

"Mama said you're interviewing nannies and a whole team of people for the nursery in the next few weeks."

"Yes, to help out as I need them. Twin babies are a lot of work, Adriano."

"And you know this how?" he asked, almost belligerently.

Smiling, she clasped his unshaven cheek. "From all the materials I've been reading. The classes I've been taking. Of course, modern medicine is amazing but giving birth and the recovery after is still a big deal. More so with multiple births."

He frowned. "I didn't know that you've been researching all this."

"What do you think I do with my days?"

He opened his mouth and closed it. No doubt to swallow the swift retort. For once, she wished he had let it rise.

"Anyway, we barely have had any time to talk about what comes after the pregnancy." She sighed. "Can I please sit down? My feet are killing me."

Instantly, he moved back and she settled down on the coffee table with a groan she couldn't catch. While she wasn't huge yet, her back twinged at the end of a long day.

Dark eyes drank in every nuance in her face. "Give me your feet."

"That's not necessary."

"I'm in a beastly mood, *cara*. It might be a good idea to indulge me, *si*?"

"Am I allowed to enquire the reason for this beastly mood?"

"No."

"Even if I wonder that I'm the cause?"

He glared at her, but his gaze held such greed, such hunger, such naked emotion that Nyra was drenched in it. There was something agonizingly addictive about being the one person who got this less than civilized version of Adriano. The real Adriano. "You're only partly responsible."

"That makes me feel much better," she said, pursing her lips. "I'm desperate to be in your good graces."

He said nothing, even though that was a supreme effort at flirting on her part.

Holding his gaze, she shifted back on the coffee table. It was quite a feat to raise her feet into his lap without sliding onto the floor in an undignified heap. Really, her center of gravity was a ride these days.

The moment his elegant fingers touched the arch of one foot and pressed, shivers of relief filled her. Leaning back, she threw her head back and let out a soft moan.

God, the man was deliciously clever with his fingers, whether it was her comfort or pleasure that he teased out. Tension released from her as he pressed and kneaded with just the right amount of pressure, giving both her feet equal attention.

And something about his bent head, about the spread of his long fingers on her feet, the utter devotion with which he applied himself to her comfort…unraveled the tight lock she kept on the darkest parts of her past.

"I remember my mother telling us how much fun but hard work Nadia and I were in our early years," she said after several minutes of simply enjoying his touch. "She used to say I was the easy baby, and that Nadia was a diva even back then. But I think she loved us both the same."

His head jerked up. "You've never mentioned her."

She shrugged, swallowing the sudden lump in her throat. "If possible, I don't like to think much of the past. This pregnancy and everything that I unleashed…it's bringing it all back. The good and the bad."

"I wish you hadn't. Especially since it rakes up the painful past."

"It is done, Adriano. And honestly, I don't regret it. I

only feel sorry that I threw Nadia to the wolves too. With me being your wife and constantly in the spotlight, she will be recognized the moment she steps into public. I took the decision out of her hands and, given how fragile she already is… I'm scared of how she might react." This guilt had been eating away at her nonstop. What if Nadia hated her for this and never wanted to see her again? It wasn't just her babies that Nyra wanted to be strong for. "I've been so selfish—"

"No." His eyes might as well be daggers pinning her in place. Not that she wanted to get away. Her lips twitched when she realized he was outraged, on her behalf.

"You jeopardized the little security you had with me to look out for her, Nyra." His words pinged over her skin like little light charges. "If she gets angry, she'll forgive you."

"But what if—"

"She is safe, *cara*, for now. When she is recovered, we will look after her. And we will explain to her that you had no choice. That it is better for both of you this way."

"You will help me, then?"

"*Si*. As long as she gets better."

That he didn't shove her worry for her sister aside or give her false reassurances made warmth bloom in her chest.

"What happened to your mother?"

"She overdosed a year after Papa was arrested and we lost everything."

His fingers crawled up her ankle and rested there, as if she might slip out of his grasp if he didn't. As if he could sense how hard this was for her. "If you would rather not talk about this, I understand, *cara*. I do not wish for you to distress yourself."

While the wary concern in his words for the pregnancy itself—as if it was a separate thing from her—pricked, she knew it was high time she did talk. For the same reason he thought she shouldn't. "I've never talked about them with another person, not once in all these years. It's as if parts of me have calcified along with the memories. I want to purge this, Adriano. Be whole for them, if possible," she said, placing one hand on her belly. "For Nadia when she gets better."

"You're not responsible for her well-being, Nyra. Your primary concern should be—"

"Is it true that Bruno is your half brother by your father?" she said, annoyed by his tone. When he nodded, she mirrored his action. "Is it also true that you found him as a teenager, beaten up by some street gang, and brought him home with you?"

"Who told you that?"

"He did, this past week. After I probed incessantly."

"You should come to me with such questions."

"Yes, but Bruno's so much more…approachable and available."

"I'm a jealous man, Nyra." The rotating whiskey tumbler in his hands caught and reflected shards of golden light onto his face, and the beds of his nails were stark white with how tightly he gripped it. "While I know that neither you nor Bruno see each other that way, such a friendship is…hard for me to bear."

Nyra realized, with a stuttering heartbeat, that this was Adriano opening up to her. "It is simply a fondness," she said huskily.

He raised his hand, palm out. "I don't care what it actually is. Your confidences are mine, *bella*."

A part of her bristled at his authoritative tone but something more held her back. This was what she wanted to build, didn't she? This kind of trust where they could actually verbalize what they expected from the relationship. And really, if the shoe was on the other foot, she would hate for his uptight assistant to have his confidences.

She didn't want that woman even in the same room as him.

"Okay. I will try to come to you with these questions. Or anything else."

He held her gaze. "Bruno's mother was my nanny before Maria. Fabi and Federico, on the other hand, are not my father's children."

"Oh," she said, shocked by this new piece of the puzzle. Suddenly, his reaction to those photos of Nadia with some man, thinking it was her, made even more sense. "I'm... How did they come to be raised as Cavalieris, then?"

"They were eight when my father found out. He threatened to throw them out and disinherit them. Fabi came to me with tears. I had already made some good investments and was beginning to build a reputation for myself in the bank. My father had never been much of a leader anyway, chasing after every woman he came across. A few choice words from me about his debts and he backed off."

No wonder his relationship with his mother was no better than the one he shared with his father.

"So you're responsible for looking after all of them?"

"I don't deserve a medal for protecting two innocents."

"How do you think I would want to do any less for
my twin? For one who wasn't as fortunate as me? Losing my parents, our house, the little security we had,
being tormented as *his kids*…all of it became a hundred
times worse when Nadia and I got separated. I love her
more than I've ever loved anyone." A shuddering breath
left her lips.

One hand clasped her cheek and Nyra pressed into it.
The words came easily then, as if they had been waiting
all this while to be released. "Mama always had trouble
sleeping, and whatever the consequences of Papa's actions, she told us every day how much she loved us. So
I tell myself that the overdose had to be accidental. I
was sent to live with a great-aunt in London and Nadia
to some distant uncle in the States."

She sniffled and his fingers tightened on her feet.

"I was twelve and so many things happened back
then that all the memories are hazy. But some of the
good ones are when Mama would recount stuff about
us as babies. All of us would sit together and look at
pictures. Usually, Nadia and I ended up giggling in her
lap. I wish she were here so I could ask her, you know."
She looked at her fingers, willing herself to come back
to the present. "All the literature I've been reading says
it's better to have help, even if it's just an extra pair of
hands once in a while. And since I don't have any family and we do have the resources—"

"You have me," he said, pulling her leg up and kissing the ankle.

She giggled, even knowing that he'd done it on purpose. Kissing her where she was extremely ticklish to distract her from echoes of the painful past. "The mighty, powerful banker that all of Italy fears will change stinky diapers, sing lullabies and do feeds in the middle of the night?"

"*Si*, I will. What else?"

His words were filled with such wonder that her heart stuttered. Words escaped her as she beheld this powerful man eager to know what else parenthood would entail. Would he ever cease to surprise her?

"Nyra?"

"Right. Feeds and burping, walking in the middle of the night to get them to sleep, changing diapers and doing it all over again. I read on some forum that one girl infant would only sleep on her father's chest." She patted his broad chest and his soft smile was like a beacon guiding ships into port.

"I would like to have at least one daughter, then," he said.

Nyra's heart melted. "And that's just keeping them healthy and safe. There's talking to them, singing to them, playing with them, exposing them to the world, bit by bit. Letting them stretch their wings even if it means little hurts but teaching them that we're here to hold on to."

"You're scared?" he said, perceptive to the last.

"Terrified," she admitted, the spike of fear so real that she shivered. If she thought he would take her into his arms then, she'd have been sorely disappointed.

He was in such a strange mood that she didn't know what to expect. And it underlined how little she really knew about the deeper, real parts of him, and how much she wanted to know all of him. If only to soothe him in this mood as he did for her.

Like asking her to talk about a good memory with Nadia when the present overwhelmed her.

"Of what?" he said, his eyes flickering between hers.

"Of not doing it right. Of…not being enough, for them."

Of not being enough for you. That she might wake up one day and be thrown out again by him because he'd discovered that she was nothing to him.

"That you worry about getting it right is proof enough that you will, *bella*. And if you do get something wrong, you'll love them enough that it won't matter."

"And you know this how?" she said, throwing his question back at him.

"My parents." No elaboration, nothing.

The two words stood in the small space between them like minor explosives. Ticking away, on and on. Nyra had never been so scared of what she might say that would set them off.

"Adriano—"

"And when you do get something wrong," he said, cutting her off, "I will be there to tell you that you're doing it wrong."

"How predictably arrogant of you," she said, grinning. She knew those explosives would go off at a later time if she didn't push it. But she was too greedy, too gone for this easy intimacy that was just as raw as making love.

His smile was a baring of teeth while his gaze drank hers in.

"Wait, I almost forgot," she said and shot to her

feet. Too fast. A sudden dizziness claimed her and she swayed.

Hands on her hips, he steadied her. His eyes were nearly wild with panic, an expression she'd never seen in him. No, it had been the same when he'd declared that their marriage was over in front of everyone.

"That's twice now you're swaying on your damned feet," he said, steadying her. "Do you need a keeper 24/7, *cara*?"

"It's been a long day and I shouldn't have stood up so fast." She pressed her forehead into his chest. "I'm fine now. You can let me go."

He didn't, for a long while. His heart thundered against her forehead, far too erratic, while his fingers dug a little harder into her shoulders.

Did he know how his rough breaths and rougher touch betrayed him?

Nyra took every little thing he gave her. That his concern was solely for the babies—clearly, he was one of those men who was made to raise a family—couldn't ruin the moment for her.

After what felt like hours, he released her.

Her legs shook, for a new reason now, as she walked across the lounge. When she brought it back to him and placed it on the coffee table, he stared at it as if it were a suspicious…alien thing. Granted, the chocolate cake did look a little crooked.

When she'd have moved to the opposite side of the table, he held her in place with his hands on her hips. She couldn't help leaning into him with a sigh.

"What's this?"

"It's a chocolate cake. A pathetic-looking one but one all the same."

"Ahh… I see that now."

Covering his arms with hers, she pinched his abdomen. Not quite possible when it was a slab of rock though.

"Why have you brought me this sad-looking cake is the question I meant to ask."

"I baked it. For you. I…wanted to give you something for which I didn't dip into your own bank account. Five minutes in, the chef tried to discourage me. I think his heart was breaking at my lack of even basic baking skills."

Behind her, Adriano stilled. Seconds piled on as Nyra waited, her breath hovering somewhere in her throat.

Embarrassment flushed through her as he continued to be silent. "I'm sorry that I don't have something more…sophisticated. I did start painting something for you but I didn't have time to finish it."

Untangling herself from him, she grabbed the plate and looked around for a trash bin when he took it from her, nearly dislodging it from the plate in the process. He held it close to his chest, as if it were precious and regarded her with twinkling eyes. "I see the hungry glint in your eyes, *cara*. But this is mine."

She laughed and wished she could snap a pic of him like this to hide away for herself. Blinking back sudden tears and fighting the sweeping rush of something else, she looked around. "I forgot to bring a lighter. I did manage to secure a single candle from the galley."

He handed her a sleek navy-colored lighter.

Under his curious gaze, Nyra stuck the candle into

the cake, which threatened its whole existence a little more, and lit it. Grabbing his hand, she pulled him until he was bending over the table by her side and handed him a knife. "Make a wish, Adriano."

And when he blew out the candle, she sang for him. Out of tune and at a very bad pitch. Then she fed him a bite of the cake.

His eyes widened. "How deceptively like you, *cara*. It tastes like heaven. *Grazie mille* for my birthday celebration, wife."

Nyra stared at him as he grabbed the knife and cut another piece of the now crumbling cake, a sudden lightness to his movements. All week, she'd been desperate to make him happy, to show him that she was committed to them.

But instead of the grand party and the transformation she'd forced on herself and all the hundred new things she was learning to be, the pathetic cake had done it.

When he brought the piece of cake to her mouth, the moist chocolate exploded on her tongue. When he bent down to lick a crumb from her mouth, sweeping molten heat through her, she stole a kiss from him.

And when he pulled her close and dragged his mouth up her jaw to her temple and pressed a soft kiss there, she did the thing she promised herself she would never do again.

She fell in love with him, just a little. But this time, it was with the real man. Not the billionaire who had offered her protection and escape from a lonely, horrible life all those months ago. Or even the man who had promised to never doubt her again.

But this man, with his authoritative demands that belied his aching touches, with his soft confessions about what he wanted from her, this man who always strove to do the right thing…

She was falling in love with the real Adriano and she didn't know how to stop it. Because that way lay expectations, and she'd been burned too many times already.

CHAPTER ELEVEN

ADRIANO FED THE last piece of the cake to Nyra. A crumb danced on her lower lip, inviting him. Leaning down, he licked it off.

"It tastes even better on your lips, *cara*."

Gripping his jaw to hold him, the minx caught his lips in a kiss that sent dizzying heat through every limb.

It was this very passion, this naked, artless hunger of hers, that had once lured him in and then bound her to him forever. Now it was underscored by something else, the rough tug of her teeth over his lower lip tinged with raw desperation.

The taste of which he had known all evening. And his harsh words to his mother—while there was no resolution and would never be—had purged something from deep inside him. Just like Nyra said she was trying to do. It made him feel lighter, to see this woman and everything she brought to his life with fresh appreciation.

With a harsh groan, he swept his tongue through her mouth, pulling her closer. All evening, he'd watch her flit from man to man like a colorful butterfly, and it had scraped him raw to see her bestow her smiles and wit on them.

And now to know that she was his in this abandon—only his, all her secrets, all her desires—soothed him.

She was soft and warm in his hands, and the rough slide of her curves against his body was both a thrill and a torment.

Lust beat at him in relentless waves, but something else, something softer pulsed beneath it.

A long overdue picture was emerging in his head of Nyra as a girl, as part of a twin bond, as a teenager, a survivor and the woman he knew now. Of how the world had let her down and he had been part of that very world too.

Of how she was finding her way to herself through this marriage, through their own strife and now through impending motherhood.

Of how bravely she had taken on the very same people at the party this evening who had, and would, mock and judge her behind her back for months to come.

All to carve a place in his world for herself.

The tightness in his chest, it seemed, was tenderness. Even affection.

He'd felt something similar for Fabi, Bruno, even Federico, but this was different in a way he couldn't explain to himself. Neither was it something he'd ever wanted to express. At least until now.

Maybe because he'd spent the first half of his life craving it from his parents, and the other half teaching himself to not need it.

Until he'd met the now-trembling woman in his arms in Vegas, he'd written off passion and marriage, and this...sense of belonging to something bigger than him.

So much for his best-laid plans and his arrogance, believing that life would pan out exactly as he'd planned. Now he had a wife who could turn him upside down with one small act, and he was about to be the father of two innocents.

Every facet of himself that Nyra unlocked was as much a surprise as she continued to be herself.

And he still didn't trust this...expansiveness he felt in his gut. Didn't dare let it rule him. Because there were no equations he could calculate, no rules he could follow to minimize the risk, to even the odds.

No way for him to know when he might be left alone in the darkness again. It was all so out of his control and he wasn't sure if he would ever give himself over to it completely. To her completely.

But he would let nothing touch it, ever again.

"Don't move," he whispered into the soft skin at the arch of her neck.

"If you leave me here for too long," she said, reluctantly releasing him, "I might fall asleep standing."

He studied her with a growing frown. Dark shadows cradled her overly bright eyes, but he was loath to let the evening end. He wanted to devour her. Leave her as knocked out as she'd made him feel with that cake. "Do you want to go to bed?"

"I know it's *your* birthday but I was hoping to get a present out of it too," she said cheekily.

Lust beat a tattoo through his body. "And what is it that you want?"

"There are only two things I want anymore. Food and sex. Either I'm hungry or I'm horny. While I have several sources for the first, the second—"

He pressed his finger to her lip, knowing the soft

kitten was flexing her claws with him. "Which one do you want now?"

She licked his finger pad before sucking it into her mouth. His erection turned so painful that he cursed.

Releasing his finger, she pouted prettily. "The latter."

"Keep talking," he said, going through the cabinets around him.

"Apparently, some women can get extra horny during pregnancy and I'm clearly one of them," Nyra said, tracking his movements like a laser pointer. "Also, I was thinking we should just like…front load a lot of it now, y'know. Who knows how much time and privacy we'll even get once these two arrive?"

He chuckled, finally spotting the thing he wanted. "Front load a lot of sex?"

"Yep. Like really glut ourselves on it. So that I can live off of the memories."

"Memories? I'm not going anywhere, Nyra," he said, and then proceeded to cut the bodice of the dress with the scissors.

Eyes wide in her tired face, she watched him as he cut strips of the red fabric off. A gasp escaped her. "Adriano?"

"I hate this dress."

"It cost thousands of pounds and it's by that designer that everyone's salivating over and—"

"Not a fan, *bella*," he said, continuing the snip-snip until it fell away from her body, leaving her in a nude-colored bra and matching panties. The latter was a flimsy piece of lace so high cut that he could see the shape of her through it. His mouth watered.

"Not a fan of the dress, the makeup, or the hair," he said, discarding the scissors with a flick of his wrist.

Her look of helplessness turned into a glare. A sigh whistled through her lips, as if she was accepting defeat. "Is there anything you liked about tonight?"

He ran a finger over the lace of her bra and watched in fascination as her breasts rose and fell. "Your changing body fascinates me endlessly, *cara*."

Her throat bobbed in a swallow, and the pulse at her neck invited his attention. "That's not an answer."

He pulled the strap of her bra with one hand while tracing the seam of her lace panties with the other. "Something tells me you picked these. For me."

Her tongue swiped out. "Yes."

"They're perfect. They're you, Nyra."

"Is there so much of a difference, Adriano?"

"*Si*. For me. I don't want you to turn into one of them," he said, going to his knees.

She trembled as he grabbed her thighs to steady her. Little beads of perspiration danced over her upper lip. And he knew she was as excited as he was for this.

"One of whom?" Her voice went deep and husky as he pressed a kiss to the swell of her belly and trailed down.

He pulled at the seam of her panties with his teeth and the flimsy thing tore apart.

Finally, her fingers sank into his hair and tugged hard. "It's your birthday. I meant to do this for you."

He grinned and laced his fingers over her ankle. There was so much of her he wanted to kiss, needed to brand.

Slowly, so as not to disturb her balance, he lifted her

foot and placed it on the chair he had vacated. Opening the deepest, prettiest parts of her to his greedy gaze.

"Holy hell, Adriano," she said, her breaths serrated pants now. "I must look…obscene."

"You're pretty, *bella*, everywhere." He ran a finger over the strip. "As for a birthday present, how can I not taste you when you went to all this trouble?"

"I don't know if I'll do it again. Get waxed like this. It hurt. The technician kept saying it's the perfect precursor to labor pains."

He kissed the under curve of her belly even as he traced the intimate shape of her with his fingers. "Why did you do it this time?"

"I wanted you to find me irresistible."

Burying his nose in the fold between her thigh and hip, he breathed in her scent. It was deeper here and as arousing as her mouth on his cock. "Did I tell you that I was supposed to be in Vegas for only one evening?"

Her gasp was music to his ears. "But…you stayed for three weeks. And the first evening, all we shared was a glance when I greeted you with overt familiarity at the end of the game."

"*Si.*"

Her nostrils flared. "You stayed because of that?"

"Because I found you hot. And I found you intriguing and smart and irresistible. These," he said, scraping his teeth down her upper thigh, "small things you do, they get me hot. But not the way you imagine. I've never found society's idea of beauty or perfection attractive, Nyra."

Her huffy breath told him how she much she liked

him using his teeth on her. "How does this get you hot, then?"

"That you would go to this effort for me. That you openly ask me for sex gets me hot. That you want me and don't play games about it gets me hot."

She remained quiet for so long that he looked up. From his position at her feet, her face framed by her breasts, the lush curves of her body...everything about her was entrancing. Everything about her felt like a bounty he didn't deserve.

"I...don't know any other way to want you," she said, looking both bemused and alarmed.

His heart gave a loud thump. "I know. Because I want you the same way." He let go of her ankle slowly. "You're steady?"

"Feels like a trick question." Her accompanying laughter turned into a serrated gasp when he ran his thumb down her folds.

Her thigh muscles quaked under his hand and those panting breaths turned into shuddering gasps as he ducked low and tasted her. Her grip of his hair tightened mercilessly.

She tasted like tart honey and he wanted more. He wanted all of her confessions and all of her moans and all of her. And he had a feeling his hunger for her, for everything *about* her, was bottomless.

Cursing, he fed a finger into her sheath and then two, and when she started chanting his name, he laughed and caught her clit with his lips. He filled his other hand with her plump ass, steadying her, even as she swayed, her hips dancing, chasing his mouth.

His shaft turned rock-hard as her tight wetness

clenched his fingers tight. A sob escaped her mouth and echoed out into the lake as she came.

Like a storm, leaving him drenched and still craving more. From that first moment.

Nyra couldn't imagine she could feel any more turned on, after Adriano had sent her off the cliff with his mouth and fingers.

But as he lifted her leg and pushed into her from behind, his entire body cradling her like a warm, weighty blanket on the bed, she felt a butterfly whisper of need down there yet again.

His left hand, reaching under her head, clasped her cheek with a gentle reverence even as his hips drilled into her.

Every thrust pushed her own awareness deeper until all she knew and felt was him. The scent of his sweat filled her nostrils and she breathed deeply. Here she knew the man she had married. Here she knew herself too.

"Touch yourself, *cara*," he whispered, his rough exhales coating the shell of her ear.

"Can't," she said, feeling muscles she hadn't known existed before.

"*Si*, you can, Nyra." Then lifting her hand from where she'd dug it into his thigh, he brought it to her folds. His strokes slowed as he strummed her popped clit, her fingers tangled in his. She moaned at the lack of friction and he painted her skin with his laughter.

"Please move," she demanded, biting his forearm.

Fresh tingles sparked at her core as she glanced down

at the eroticism of their laced fingers delving into her and coming away damp.

"See? Like that. Come for me, *cara*. I need to feel you clenching me before I can let go."

Nyra continued stroking her clit, the sensation as new and addicting as anything else that Adriano made her experience.

And in counterpoint, his thrusts gathered speed and soon, she was toppling all over again and he followed.

He came with a roar that reverberated through her body, and Nyra blinked back tears. Here, in that moment, she knew that he cared for her, as much as he could.

Adriano jerked out of the mindless stupor his climax had left him in when he felt something flutter under his fingertips. Raising himself on his elbow, he realized it came from... Nyra's belly. He quickly turned on the ceiling lights at the lowest setting.

His heart threatening to jump into his chest, he spread his palm softly, reverently. And then it came again.

That movement. The babies, one or both, was kicking.

"Nyra?" he said, to the softly dozing woman in his arms.

Her mouth was lax, her hair sticking to her temples with sweat. He had tired her out with his demands, after an already exhausting day. Although, she'd egged him on, saying they had to make up for the past and the future.

A flood of tenderness burst in his chest as she fluttered her eyes open and gave him a weak smile.

"Hmmm?"

"The babies…"

She placed her hand, palm down, next to his, the tips of their fingers touching. Wonder filled him, at this new sign of the life they'd created. In the blink of an eye and a shattered breath, it went from a vague pregnancy to two real people. "Yeah, they can get quite rowdy in there. In fact, I worry if they don't make themselves known every couple of hours."

"Does it hurt?"

She yawned and covered her mouth. Something that looked like sheer, indescribable joy shone in her damp eyes. "No. Sometimes it tickles, sometimes it's so sudden that I'm awake and alert. It's like they're playing football in there. At night though, it's a lot. So I just sit up and talk to them."

"Talk to them?" he said, wonder in his throat.

She shrugged, trying to push up against the bed into a sitting position. He gave her a hand and gently pulled her upright.

"Yeah. I do it for me. Just telling them how much I love them. How eagerly I'm waiting to meet them. And how loved they are…" She wiped the lone tear tracking down her cheek. "Everything in the same vein pretty much."

He bent down and kissed her belly. Her fingers in his hair felt like an extra benediction. And then he whispered everything that came to him on a wave of such pure, unconditional love as he'd never felt.

Nyra's fingers drifted over his shoulders and she vibrated under him. With curiosity, he guessed. When he looked back at her, her smile was so broad that it should have illuminated the entire room and the dark surface of the lake beyond.

"What did you say to them?" she said, her voice a thready whisper.

"That they're very lucky to have you as their mama. And that I would do my best to love them just as much."

She sniffled and brought their laced fingers to her mouth. Slowly, she kissed his knuckles, more tears running down her cheeks. "I don't think you have to try, Adriano. I think you already love them as much as I do."

"Your confidence is very much appreciated, Nyra," he said, putting an arm around her.

She ran one hand over his chest and wrapped one arm around his back. "You doubt yourself? Even though all your siblings adore you."

He heard the hesitation in her voice. "I don't want to simply do my duty by these two. I want to love them. I need them to know that they're cherished and wanted."

"And you think that's not possible for you," she stated far too matter-of-factly. But she couldn't help how her dismay punctuated each word.

"I'm sure you have gathered by now that my parents aren't exactly what you call nurturing, *bella*. If anything, they're the opposite. And when you grow up, wishing your parents were different, wondering what you had done wrong to receive not the least bit of care, you create a shell around you. And the last thing I want is for my own children to feel that shell. To think I'm incapable of the emotion I never got to taste."

Her arm tightened around him and she buried her face in his neck. "You won't. Anyone who worries so much about getting it right will inevitably will," she said throwing his own words back at him.

He smiled, and yet it felt as if there was viselike clamp around his chest. "There has been a revolving door of my parents' lovers through my life. Some far kinder and more caring than they themselves have ever been to me. Like Bruno's mother. She was my nanny."

Her soft gasp against his neck urged him on. Even as he stiffened at what else he had to say. But he would say it. He had to. "I've even caught them at it a couple of times. Involving some foolish, innocent party just to take petty revenge on the other. And what I felt was beyond contempt. And when I saw those photos of Nadia…" His chest rose and fell and with it the woman draped over him.

He braced for her to jerk away or to shut him up or shrug it off. But her heart thundered against his, as if trying to reach out.

A cold shudder moved through him. "I reacted so badly. I…was not myself. I became that boy who was so hurt that I wanted to lash out and hurt in return. I lost the common sense I pride myself on. In that moment, I forgot everything I knew about you. I didn't have to know about your past or your twin or any of that to know that you would never do that. That you would never… just as much as I would never do that to you."

"Adriano—" she finally said, eyes red rimmed.

"Forgive me for that lapse, Nyra. For acting like a cruel bastard."

"Please—"

"It wasn't you that I didn't trust. It was myself, my

gut, my instinct that I didn't listen to. I made you feel so unsafe and dispensable and…none of that is true."

Her mouth touched the corner of his lips, her scent a cocktail of sweat and sex and her musk. It anchored him when guilt and shame would have carried him away from her. "You're forgiven, Adriano. Completely."

"That easily, *bella*?"

"You regret what you did. And you have tried so hard to show me that you were wrong. Will you forgive me for lying to you?"

"*Si*. Just…no more secrets."

"*Bene*," she said.

And then he was pulling her into his lap because he desperately needed to seal that promise with touch. It was less smooth than he'd have preferred, but they were laughing as she tried to maneuver herself into his lap and he thought laughing with her was even better than sex. Then he kissed her like he couldn't stop. Like she was air itself.

Because she was.

They were panting and shaking when she pulled back. Her eyes searched his. "You truly don't want me to become an accomplished society wife? You don't care if I walk around in torn-up sweaters and with messy hair? If all I do is raise our children and paint things that no one wants to buy?"

The doubt in her words made his heart ache. He clasped her cheeks. "I don't want you to change yourself in any way to please me. Or for this marriage. If you do want to change something for yourself, I'll support you all the way."

She pressed her cheek to his chest, and he ran his

palms over her smooth thighs. "Thank you, Adriano. I have everything I could ever want in life."

And then, like a kitten, she fell asleep on him within seconds.

Adriano didn't know how long he sat like that, with Nyra's body a warm weight in his lap, her face tucked into his neck, the sound of her soft snores the only sound in the room.

When he tried to adjust her so that she would be more comfortable, her arms tightened into steel bands around him.

He smiled and smoothed a sweaty curl from her temple.

He thought there had been an *almost* at the end of her sentence. No, he knew there was because she'd shied her gaze away, afraid of betraying herself.

And the fact that there was something she found missing from their lives was untenable.

He wanted Nyra to have everything she ever wished for. Because she was everything he'd never known he needed.

CHAPTER TWELVE

"WHAT?" ADRIANO ROARED in the middle of the board-room, startling a bunch of clients and businessmen into silence.

"She fell," Fabi repeated, her voice nearly hysteric.

He reached for the back of the chair, bile rising up through his throat. He didn't have to ask his sister who "she" was. There was only one person who could cause such worry in Fabi's voice and now, in Adriano.

"How is she, Fabi?" he said, somehow forming the words. "What happened? Where is she?"

His sister rattled on so fast that only every other word came through the bad connection. He fought the urge to scream at her down the line, knowing it would only distress her even more. "Breathe, Fabi. And tell me what happened. Slowly, *per favore*," he said, begging now.

A few moments of silence later, Fabi said, "I should've told you first that she and the babies are fine. It was a minor concussion and she's been under observation the whole time. In fact, now that I think about it, Nyra is going to kill me for calling you. But I was so scared, and I knew you'd want to know."

Gratitude and relief crowded in, choking the fear out of his body. Adriano cursed, rubbed his hand over his temple and prayed to the god he'd never believed in for patience. "I am glad you called. Hey, Fabi. Did I tell you that you are my favorite sibling?"

She giggled down the line, relief powering her laughter more than humor or affection. "She made me promise not to tell you. I've grown fond of her, and now... I broke the promise."

For just a second, all his insecurities, all his fears that he couldn't give Nyra everything she deserved came back, pummeling him.

No, he told himself, pushing those fears back. He was being ridiculous.

Nyra was six and a half months pregnant with his children. She was thriving, and happy, if uncomfortable most nights. And days. She had such a thin frame with barely any hips and his two daughters—God had granted him one wish of his—were growing so rapidly, that they were putting too much strain on their mother's pelvis. She had been advised bed rest for the last month.

The only thorn in an otherwise content marriage was his wife's worry for her twin. Nadia had finally started calling her twin for a weekly chat from the clinic. After he'd intervened and told her how much Nyra missed her and how she needed to clean up her act if she wanted to see her sister and her nieces in the future.

It was the hardest thing Adriano had ever done—to not ask Nyra how her sister was faring. Or why she still looked so worried even after several chats with her sister.

And now this...

It had killed him to go away on this trip to Japan again for two weeks, but Nyra had reassured him that she was fine with Fabi and Bruno and Maria for company and that she would rather have him by her side when the babies came. So, he had reluctantly made the trip a week ago.

"What did she make you promise?" he asked softly, dreading the answer.

"It's about her twin," Fabi said, after another prolonged silence that twisted his nerves into painful knots.

Adriano pressed his head to the wall in front of him. Of course, this had to be about Nadia. It was only her that Nyra would go against his wishes for. The one person, sometimes it seemed to him, that Nyra loved more than anyone in the world.

Definitely more than him. If she loved him at all, that was.

And he...*he loved her with every breath in him.* Enough to forgive her anything and everything if only she was safe.

"What about her twin, Fabi? You might as well tell me the whole story."

"Will you promise not to be mad at Nyra? I mean, I helped her because I understand her pain."

He sighed. Apparently now his wife had an army of allies. "I won't be mad at my six-months-pregnant-with-twins wife," he said, a humorless laugh punctuating each word. "Just tell me what happened."

"Nadia left the rehab clinic. I think she ran away and she came to the villa. To see Nyra."

His breath stuttered in his throat. "When?"

"Almost to the day after you left. And I can assure you that Nyra didn't know. She was...shocked to say the least. She looks so much like Nyra, Adriano. Except for the pregnancy, I mean. No, except, around the eyes, actually. Nyra has kind eyes."

"And?" Adriano prompted. Though he could imagine what had happened. Nyra must have told her twin that he would be out of the country. And it was the chance her volatile twin had been waiting for.

"After the shock, Nyra was crying and sobbing and hugging her sister," Fabi continued. "And I thought this was good, you know. But then…"

Adriano bit his lower lip hard to stop himself from losing his temper with his sister.

Finally, Fabi spoke again. "Right away, she started talking about how Nyra should leave you. How cruel and ruthless you are. And how not only had you thrown Nyra away once, but had Nadia locked up because you wanted to isolate Nyra. She said you threatened her about talking to Nyra…" Fabi sounded both alarmed and horrified. "Her conspiracy theory against you went on and on. It scared me to hear all the stuff she said about you and Nyra, about how much she was urging her to leave you, to run away with her."

It felt like his heart was now permanently lodged in his throat. He knew that Nyra would never do something as foolish as running away with her drug addict sister. But the thought of her in pain at what her sister had become…pricked him sharply, as if it were his own.

"What happened today, how did she…fall?"

"Nyra told Nadia she would meet her at this café. And she asked me to come along. When we arrived, Nadia started arguing with her immediately. Demanding that she give her the cash she asked for if she was going to ditch Nadia anyway. Then she saw that Nyra had alerted Bruno. Nyra was holding her hands, begging her to go back to the clinic, that it was the drugs making her talk like this. Nadia jerked away so fast that Nyra fell and hit her head on the footpath. She lost consciousness for like two minutes. And in the scuffle, Nadia ran away."

"And she's okay now? You aren't lying to me?"

"No, Adriano. She's fine but she won't stop crying these…silent tears. She…needs you here."

Adriano told his sister that she had indeed become very wise and that, yes, he would be on his private jet in a half hour. Only when Fabi hung up and he reached the privacy of his suite did he lean back against the door, nearly sliding to the floor on shaking knees.

She was fine, he told himself over and over again.

He needed to be strong because she needed him. Whatever else he might be feeling now—anger, fear and this…knee-buckling love for her—they were all his to bear and manage.

His wife and her well-being would always come first.

Nyra was lying on the comfortable chaise longue in Adriano's study at the villa, watching boats lazily drift over Lake Como, with the background of pretty villages. The afternoon felt eternal from her unmoving spot.

Rain was pelting outside mercilessly, matching her gloomy mood.

She pulled Adriano's leather jacket close around her shoulders, even though the last thing she felt was cold. All she wanted was to drown in the scent of him, and the leather jacket still had a whiff of him. She shifted restlessly. At her lower back, there was that persistent twinge, arrowing down to her pelvis.

It would be better to lie down in her bed, but she

didn't want to leave the cozy room with its large fireplace and books. Here, she felt surrounded by him.

For the millionth time, she picked up her phone, her finger hovering over his number. Cursing, she jerked away and switched the display off.

Anger at herself washed through her. What right did she have to call and inconvenience him when she hadn't heeded his advice in the first place? He had told her, again and again, that Nadia would only distress her in her current condition. It was almost as if he'd known what would happen.

At least she'd stopped crying over her sister's actions and stopped panicking about how much worse it could have been, if not for Fabi's and Bruno's prompt action.

As if sensing the fracture in her composure, the babies gave a swift kick, nearly up into her chest, making her gasp and laugh.

While she would always wonder about Nadia, she had enough sense now to see the new sister she had acquired. Just this morning, on an impulse, she had hugged Fabi, overwhelmed by affection for the younger woman. Who had burst into tears and admitted that she had been so terrified that she had called Adriano and confessed everything.

Now Nyra was waiting for her husband and the black temper he surely was going to be in. Not that she didn't deserve it. God, she would bear it happily—make all the promises he demanded of her, if it meant he would hold her after giving her the tongue-lashing she deserved.

Rubbing a hand over her lower back, she put her feet on the ground and was about to shift her bottom when her nape prickled.

She turned so fast that she made herself dizzy. The reward, six foot three inches of masculinity, stood under the archway. Her heart rabbited in her chest and every inch of her longed to run across the study and throw herself at him, like she'd done once.

The only thing she would manage in reality, if she even got up to her feet now, was to waddle toward him. With his thick brows tying into a frown—his penetrating gaze sweeping over her, from her hair to her toes as if looking for proof of her misadventure—his posture told her not to dare something like that.

So she stayed there and simply looked at him to her heart's content. Just seeing him here, under the same roof, was enough to lighten her grief just a little. And that's what, she realized with a sudden flare of understanding, it meant to love him.

"I know you're angry with me," she finally said, tired of waiting for him to come to her. "And I will take any punishment you give me, but you should know that I did not lie to you at any point. Except after you left. Even that was omission rather than a lie."

"That's a concession you will make for yourself, then?" he said, his silky tone hiding something far more volatile.

"What point would it serve to worry you?" she said, hoping he could hear the truth in her words. "I didn't know that she was coming, Adriano. She had three more months left at the clinic. I didn't even dream that she was going to run away. All I told her was that you were going out of the country on a trip, and that too, because she asked me about you." She rubbed at the stupid tears filling her eyes with the back of her hand. "She must have been planning it for a while, and I…didn't even realize that she was using me. I know you'll call me foolish for trusting her. I just wish…"

He came to her then, all brooding angles and volatile energy packed into that strong, powerful frame.

Before she could get to her feet, he knelt before her. Making her head swoon with both joy and a sudden flooding of grief.

Hand on her belly, Nyra spread her thighs apart so that they straddled his hips. She longed to kiss him, but her face was wet with tears and snot and sweat.

"Where did you hit your head?" he asked, a whiteness emerging around his lush mouth.

His words sounded like gravel, like they were coming from somewhere far, muffled by some great force on the way.

Nyra had the sudden realization that it was emotion that had changed the tenor of his voice. For a second, she considered laughing it off, but something about the feral look in his eyes arrested the impulse. She lifted her hand and pressed on the still-painful bump on the right side of her head.

"Bend your head," he said.

Dutifully, Nyra did. Long fingers gently probed the edges of her bump, without causing more pain. "They said everything was okay with you? And the babies?" he said again in that far-off voice.

Nyra was hit with another swift realization. It wasn't just any emotion that was choking him, it was fear. Fear that he might have lost her, or that she might have been hurt worse or that she might have been in pain.

Fresh tears—God, did she do anything other than cry these days—filled her eyes. "It was an accident. We were arguing…and she was angry with me. I told her I would bring cash so that we could get away and when she realized I had lied and asked Bruno to be present…" She studied her fingers, replaying the scene in her head one more time. "Neither did I take any risk. I realized immediately after she showed up that she needed to go back to the clinic. She was in bad shape, Adriano. All I wanted was to send her back so that she could get help. The only action I could have taken, in your absence, was to call security on her when she first showed up at the villa, and I couldn't. I just couldn't."

"I'm not going to scold you, Nyra," he said, his own voice cracking.

It only made her cry harder. "She's my sister and she hates me now and she thinks I've betrayed her and…"

Finally, he took her hands in his and raised them to his mouth. "I am sorry that she hurt you like this. I'm sorry that I cannot change this for you." His throat moved up and down in a hard swallow. When he looked up, his eyes were bleak. "Fabi said she urged you to run away with her? That she said I threatened her and that I intended to separate you two all along… I interfered, yes, Nyra. I only did it because I knew how much you wanted to talk to her. All I told her was that the sooner she got better, the sooner she would get to see you. That just speaking to her regularly would cheer you up. She asked to come here without finishing the rehab and I said no. That in your current condition, it was not good for you or her. I never intended to keep her away from you forever, Nyra. Never."

He raised such anguished eyes to her that Nyra's tears stopped. In the face of his pain, hers felt like nothing.

She quickly wiped her hands over her cheeks.

"Of course, I know you didn't threaten her. She is very sick, Adriano. You tried to tell me that and I didn't listen. She is not the sister I knew as a child. Nadia was bright, rational, kind. The woman who came to see me is someone else. You cannot think for one second that I believed any of that?"

"When Fabi told me what happened," he said, "I couldn't breathe. All I could think of was you, Nyra, and the babies and…us. I realized how foolish it was that I didn't tell you."

Her heart stuttered in her chest. "What? What didn't you tell me?"

"How much I adore you, my sweet wife. How much I love you. How much…" Again he took her hands in his and kissed her knuckles gently. "You are my world, my stars, my sun, my entire universe, Nyra. You and these babies and our family… I cannot imagine my life without you. And I feared that I would not know how to love you. That I would not deserve your generous…"

She pressed her palm to his mouth. "There is no deserving in love, Adriano. That's what you have taught me. Even after I came back to you, even after I made my vow to you, I still kept thinking that I had to earn your love. A place in your heart. But it doesn't work like that, does it? Even without admitting it to yourself or saying it to me, you have loved me, in the way you know, from the beginning. I just didn't see it because, like you, I didn't know it. And seeing Nadia again, in the condition she is in, I realized how foolish my fears were. I realized how stupid it was to pass even a single day without telling you how much I adore you. I loved you from that first minute when I leaned toward you and breathed in your scent, Adriano. You are the storm and the shelter for me."

He jumped onto the chase longue while Nyra giggled, pulled her into his lap and pressed fervent kisses over her face and her jaw and her temple and her neck. His arms were tied around her and his breath came in rough pants.

"You want to know what your punishment is, wife?"

"What?" she whispered, drowning in the scent and feel of him.

"Since you have shaved ten years off my life, I will not leave your side for a moment for the next two months."

"Oh, really? Because sitting on my ass all day is boring."

He laughed then, and with wonder in her heart, Nyra traced the lines that laughter drew around his mouth. With love shining in his eyes, he was even more gorgeous. "It's punishment, *bella*. You're supposed to not like it."

She shrugged. "You could teach me about the finance world and I could teach you how to paint. And together, we could learn how to knit some booties for the babies."

He groaned and caught her mouth for a fast, hard, breath-stealing kiss. "I was hoping we could front load all the good stuff before they get here."

Nyra laughed and stole another kiss right back, her heart jumping with joy. "I love you, Adriano."

"Say it again," he demanded.

And she did, over and over again, while he paid the tithe for it in kisses and languid caresses that turned the gloomy rainy afternoon into something altogether hot and bright.

EPILOGUE

Two and a half months later

MAYA AND MIA CAVALIERI came into the world two months later, nearly tearing down the walls of the private hospital with their screams.

For all that she'd been advised bed rest—which her hawklike husband instituted as if he was a military commander going to war—fortunately, the birth itself had been a relatively easy one.

"*Relative* being the operative word," Adriano had said drily, when Nyra had said it. "Seeing you in labor pains is not an experience I'm looking forward to ever again, *cara*," he had said, pressing a kiss to her forehead.

"Oh, really," Nyra had said with a scoff. He, on the other hand, was busily wiping her temples with a wet washcloth while the nurses bathed her daughters. "I braced myself for at least two more."

He frowned, his own face streaked with sweat. "I know you didn't enjoy the pregnancy enough to want to go over all of that again. Especially the last two months."

"No, but I'm not the one who gets all worked up about doing it bare."

To her utter amazement, as if the bounty she'd already

been handed wasn't abundant, her husband blushed. Dark red streaks painted his high cheekbones.

Nyra smiled.

The nurses and the midwife and the doctor—having heard her shameless comment, turned away with twitching lips.

His nostrils flaring, he bent down to kiss her mouth. The kiss was so tender, so sweet and so painfully raw that she clung to him even when he pulled away. "Then I will control my greedy impulses, *cara mia*. I would not see you in so much pain again."

"Wait, Adriano," she said, tugging him closer. "I was joking. Not another set of twins, but maybe we could have a boy. That way, we get to experience both."

"You amaze me every day, Nyra Cavalieri. And *si*, a son, or another daughter, if that's what happens. I want whatever brings you joy. I have so much love to give, *bella*. It is a wonder in itself since it is all consumed by you."

She blinked at the raw emotion swimming in his eyes. "I love you too."

"I have another piece of good news for you," he said, searching her eyes.

"Yeah?"

"Last week, that overnight trip, I went to see Nadia."

A sob kicked up in Nyra's chest and she held it off by pressing her hand to her mouth. She'd held on to so much hope, but in this moment, it felt threadbare. She swallowed again to speak past the lump of ache in her throat. "How is she?"

"She's doing very well. That relapse two months ago…someone from your past contacted her after they saw your profile in the news. It sent her into a spiral. She said it was the reason she was so angry with me. She thought it leaked because of me."

Tears swam in Nyra's eyes. "I… I was the cause then."

"No," Adriano said firmly. "She said you'd say that, and I'm to tell you that she will be very angry with you if you blame yourself for any of this. That you've had your journey back to yourself, and she's starting her own. With you by her side." A soft smile broke through his somber expression. "I finally saw the glimpses of the girl you talk about so much, Nyra. I saw the Nadia you love."

A soft cry escaped Nyra at his potent, sweet words. "What else, Adriano?"

He held her hand tightly, his gaze tracing her tears as if they hurt him physically. "She said she feels like she's been through the final obstacle. From what I could tell, she's doing really well."

"Oh, Adriano," Nyra said, laughing and crying. "That's such good news. Do you think she…might want to see me sometime in the future?"

"She promised to come see you and her nieces in a couple of months. She asked me to tell you to hold on for her, just a little bit longer. She even kissed me on the cheek and said I better look after you properly."

"You went to see her for me." Wonder fizzed through her at the lengths this man would go to for her. "You've been visiting her regularly from the beginning, *si*?"

He nodded. "She's your sister. And that means she's family. When I couldn't, Bruno has been going. I think they've become…frenemies, as he called it."

Nyra laughed so hard that she thought she might expire from sheer joy. Reaching up, she clasped Adriano's cheek and pulled him down for a kiss. "I don't know how to say thank you, Adriano. I'm…humbled and grateful and…"

"I don't want your thanks, *bella*. Only your love."

"It is all yours, my love."

His gaze filled with fresh tears. "Everything I have to give is all yours, *mia cara*. And now, theirs."

Before she could steal another kiss from her husband, the hungry, angry wails of her daughters had them jerking to alertness.

Nyra took Maya, her oldest, and held her to her breast, while Adriano cradled Mia.

And seeing his proud eyes full of tears, his large, powerful arms cradling that tiny bundle, made her heart overwhelmingly full. She had everything she had ever wanted in her life.

Nyra kissed this man who knew every inch of her heart, knowing that she and her daughters would be treasured for the rest of their lives.

* * * * *

STILL THE GREEK'S WIFE

EMMY GRAYSON

MILLS & BOON

To Laura, who dared to dream again.

To Ashley and Mom, for sharing their stories
and helping me bring Tessa to life.

To those who shared their mobility challenges
through blogs, social media, and more.

I learned a lot from you. Thank you.

CHAPTER ONE

Rafe

I'VE NEVER CONTEMPLATED murder before. There are more logical and efficient methods of dealing with people. Having a net worth of one point seven billion euros at my disposal gives me more options than the average person.

But as I watch my wife smile up at a strange man on a Paris sidewalk, my fingers tightening on the wheel of my car as he leans down and kisses her enthusiastically on the cheek, I evaluate several possibilities. Hiring an assassin wouldn't be hard. Or I could shove him off the top of the Eiffel Tower.

I'm not jealous. I'm angry. I've never tolerated anyone breaking a contract. That includes my wife, even if our marriage was a contractual arrangement in name only. The same contract that included a two-year infidelity clause. Perhaps that's why she's asking for a divorce just four months into our marriage. To pursue a relationship with the blond-haired man now gesturing wildly. His animated antics remind me of a circus clown. And Tessa...

My chest tightens. Tessa looks beautiful. Dark blond hair falling thick and loose to her shoulders. A light blue dress that follows the slim curve of her torso before flowing into a wide skirt that stops at the knees.

Awareness creeps over me at the sight of her bare legs. I've never seen her in anything but dresses, long skirts, or flowing pants. Seeing her at my brother Gavriil's wedding four weeks ago had momentarily jolted me out of my usually apathetic state. The sight of her moving confidently with the aid of forearm crutches as she talked and laughed with strangers had kindled a flicker of pride in me. She had always been forced to stay on the sidelines by her overly protective mother, an observer of life rather than a participant.

Not anymore.

The man reaches down and hugs her, wrapping his arms around her waist with an intimate ease that propels me out of the car in the blink of an eye. I resist slamming the car door and close it quietly so I can continue to observe as I cross the street, my eyes fixed on my cheating wife.

When I walked into my bedroom the night of our wedding and found her letter on my pillow, there was a single moment when I felt like a hand punched into my chest and hollowed it out with one clawing scoop. A sensation that had happened only twice before. One I knew I needed to shove away and bury before it became a problem. I focused on the facts as she stated them in her letter: she was taking advantage of our arranged, in name only marriage to live independently in Paris and wished me the best in my future endeavors. A cold, blunt conclusion to a letter written by someone I had once considered as close to a friend as I'd ever had. No discussion, no warning.

I have never gone after a woman. I certainly wasn't going to pursue one who had displayed a cunning I'd never seen beneath her supposedly quiet demeanor. I thought I was offering her an opportunity to move out of her parents' home, a new life with the kind of wealth and luxury most people couldn't begin to imagine.

But she wanted nothing to do with me or my money. Marrying me had apparently given her the fortitude to leave her former life behind. So I did what I do best; prioritized what

I needed to accomplish now with an eye on the future. The wedding was over. I had what I wanted. Our marriage convinced her father to sell me the luxury real estate brokerage firm he inherited, a firm with decades of prestige and a mountain of debt that would have crippled Nolan Sullivan without my help. Investing in that project, along with my other work, kept me focused.

Until three days ago when a petition for divorce was delivered to me at my private island villa just a short boat ride away from Santorini's shores. I'd read it on my balcony, from where I could see her modest house. The same house where I'd proposed seven months ago, months before I knew anything about Lucifer's mad scheme.

A knot twists in my chest at the memory. Tessa had been sitting on a balcony in her wheelchair looking out over the ocean, her face so sad it had tugged at me. It had hit me then that I had seen her looking that way many times over the years. That offering marriage would not only get me what I wanted, but maybe offer her something more than the mundane existence she lived in.

I'd sat down next to her, outlined what her father and I had talked about. It hadn't been until I'd asked her if she would be my wife that I saw the hope in her eyes, the hope and something more than casual affection. Something I had responded to, felt in that cavernous pit of nothing. Then shut down just as swiftly.

It doesn't matter, I remind myself. None of it does. If she wants a divorce, I'll give it to her. I have no interest in being tied to someone who doesn't want to be married. I saw what that did to my mother.

But I need Tessa to agree to carry my last name for a little longer. Just eight more months and I will officially inherit everything my father left to me, including the company I was raised to lead. A company the old bastard tied to the condition of me being married for at least a year.

Tessa doesn't know yet about the stipulation in my father's will, the one that demands we must reach our first anniversary or I forfeit my entire inheritance. I didn't know myself until just over a month ago when I attended my father's will reading. Gavriil had wasted no time in marrying a journalist to hold on to his share. My other brother, Michail, whose existence I hadn't even been aware of until recently, cursed our father and stormed out of the lawyer's office.

I, on the other hand, had already fulfilled the first stipulation of my father's will, even if I hadn't known it at the time I'd slid my ring onto Tessa's finger during an intimate yet lavish ceremony hosted on our island off the Santorini coast.

But there's a second clause, one that is now in jeopardy because of Tessa's decision to file for divorce. If we don't reach our one-year anniversary, I lose everything. And, will or not, her trying to break our contract after less than a half a year rubs salt in a wound I hadn't even realized existed until I'd read the letter from a high-profile lawyer in Athens.

Goals. Tasks. Concrete things I can assess, measure, attain. This is what I excel at. Not emotions or social engagements or marriage. This whole mess also proves that the philosophy I've lived my life by is accurate; alone is best.

I reach the other side of the street.

It's time to remind her what she has to lose, both with her flagrant affair and her ridiculous request.

Tessa glances my way as the man releases her, then does a double take. Her eyes widen, but there's no panic or shame in the golden-brown depths. Just surprise. Anger jolts through me at her lack of remorse.

"*Bonjour*, Mrs. Drakos."

Her lips thin into a tight line. "Hello, Rafael."

Touché. I despise my full name, and she knows it. I also

despise how I have to intentionally bite back a smirk of admiration.

"Is this your husband?"

I turn my attention to the blond buffoon who's looking back and forth between us like he's at a damn tennis match.

Cold anger fuels my next words. "I am."

Instead of turning and running like any sensible man would when confronted with their lover's spouse, the idiot reaches out and grabs my hand.

"It's great to meet you. Your wife is amazing. Just amazing."

He's gushing like an overexcited teenager. Annoying as it is, it gives me a moment to reassess the situation. I'm not sure what I witnessed on the sidewalk. But a tender embrace between lovers seems less likely given his enthusiasm.

I pull my hand out of the man's clammy grasp. "I think so, too."

Tessa's quiet snort surprises me, as does the arched look she gives me when I glance down at her.

"I don't even know if I'd be doing this without her," the man continues, seemingly oblivious to the tension between Tessa and me. "I thought about the Eiffel Tower, but Tess thought the gardens were better, and they really are."

Theos, does the man ever shut up?

"She even helped me pick out the ring."

The pressure in my chest eases as I realize Tessa is helping this man propose to someone else. A pressure that surges back seconds later as I glance down and realize Tessa's left hand is bare.

I think back to my brother Gavriil's wedding. Our one interaction was brief. I never looked at her hands. How long has she not been wearing her ring?

It shouldn't matter. But it does. Another symbol of her intention to break our agreement.

Our eyes meet. Pink suffuses her cheeks, but she doesn't look away. I pointedly glance down at my hand and the silver ring glinting in the last rays of sun streaming down the street. She follows my gaze, her nose wrinkling in a frown when she sees the ring.

"God, sorry." The man shoots me an embarrassed smile. "I'm Nathan. Nathan Jones. Katie's boyfriend."

The last puzzle piece falls into place. Katie, Tessa's sister, also disappeared the night of our wedding. I struggle to contain my irritation. It had taken just one phone call to find out Katie had accompanied Tessa to Paris. My sister-in-law was not in my good graces.

"Hopefully fiancé before the night's out." The smile Tessa gives Nathan pokes at me like an irritating insect. "Which speaking of, you're going to be late if you don't get going."

Nathan glances at his watch and swears. "Off I go!" He kisses Tessa's cheek again, pumps my hand before I can step back. "Nice to meet you, Rafael." He's gone before I can correct him.

Leaving me alone on the sidewalk with my wife, who's biting down on the insides of her cheeks to keep from laughing.

"You couldn't have corrected him?" I narrow my eyes at her. "You know I despise Rafael."

"It's an elegant name," she counters.

I never realized the sharp disparity in our height before. Gavriil's wedding was a blur, one where I fought dual demons of trying to crack my heart open just enough to stop my brother from rushing into a marriage of convenience with his sworn enemy while keeping my distance from Tessa. Simply seeing her had unsettled me. Given that I had just tried to have a heart-to-heart with Gavriil for the first time ever, I needed time to retreat and stitch myself back together. But that had meant a quick greeting from several feet away.

Now, as I stand within arm's reach, I realize she's nearly a foot shorter than me. I gaze down at the familiar heart-shaped face, the large caramel-colored eyes and full lips softening the defined cheekbones and elegant jawline. A stunning face, one made more arresting by the newfound confidence radiating from Tessa's petite frame. A faint fragrance teases my nostrils, something light and floral with an underlying sweetness.

"You're right."

She blinks. "What?"

"Elegant." I tilt my head to one side. Two can play at this game. "Just like Contessa."

Her brows draw together as she glares at me. "Mine's not elegant. It's ridiculous."

"Noble and graceful," I counter, enjoying the heightening of the flush in her cheeks.

She huffs. "What are you doing here? I thought we were meeting tomorrow."

I take in her dress, the rosy hue of her lips. That awareness hanging in my chest takes root, spreads. I've always thought Tessa was attractive, with a haunting quality that drew me to her side on more than one occasion. A kindred spirit. A notion that made the idea of marrying her to solidify a merger with her father's company acceptable. The few times I'd envisioned anything about our marriage, it had always been simple: quiet conversations, existing in each other's presence with a level of comfort I've never experienced with anyone else.

There's no comfort in this moment. No, now there's desire. Not the subtle attraction I've kept a firm grip on for the past couple of years as I observed the woman Tessa was growing into, but something that sinks deeper beneath my skin and kindles a spark.

I mentally step back. There's no room in this marriage for any emotions that could turn it from a mutually beneficial arrangement into something messy. I'm also acutely aware of the smoothness of her skin, the brightness of her eyes. Hallmarks of her youth and the thirteen years that separate us. It never bothered me before. But it does now as my eyes drift down to the swells of her breasts, as I wonder how she'd feel in my hands—

I look away. It's just the surprise of seeing Tessa in a different light. That and simple human biology.

"Negotiations concluded sooner than I expected. I'd like to take you out to dinner."

A V appears between her brows. "Why?"

I give her a tight smile. "We have business to discuss. We're in one of the premier food capitals of the world. We might as well enjoy ourselves while we talk about an unpleasant topic." She glances down at her dress. Jealousy tightens the muscles in my neck. "Unless you have somewhere to be."

She stares at me for so long I wonder if she's going to answer. Then, finally she shakes her head. "I was just going out to a bistro. I can go tomorrow."

Victory surges through me. I've learned through countless mergers, negotiations and takeovers that once someone has agreed to the first step, the finish line is already within reach.

She squares her shoulders and lifts her chin, as if readying for battle. I smile down at her. She can fight all she wants. But before I return to Greece, I will have won the war.

CHAPTER TWO

Tessa

I GLANCE AROUND the dining room of La Tour d'Argent. The simple ivory-colored tablecloths and caned chairs keep the focus on the food and the view outside the floor-to-ceiling windows. The Seine River curves through Paris, a dark blue ribbon dotted with boats. The towers of Notre Dame are backlit by the sun sinking toward the horizon.

The kind of restaurant one would take a date.

My eyes flicker to Rafe, who's seated across from me perusing the menu. Once I would have given anything to be on a date with him. The man who captured my imagination as a child with his dark intensity. Who transformed into an unattainable, romantic hero during my teenage years.

The man I fell into what I thought was love simply because he was the only man who ever noticed me.

The ache in my chest grows as Rafe's eyes cut to me. I know what he's doing; evaluating me, trying to see if there's any chink in my armor he can use to his advantage. Why he wants me to stay, I have no idea. It's certainly not because he wants *me*. I'm not going down the road again of thinking hope and love can conquer all, at least where Rafael Drakos is concerned. That dream died the night of our wedding when I overheard exactly what he thought of me and our arranged marriage.

The events of the last hour have taken their toll. Exhaustion pulls at me. Sharp pricks of pain shoot up my calves. Nothing I haven't faced before, but it's more challenging tonight. Going to physical therapy this morning and then using my crutches tonight, coupled with the psychological stress of having my soon-to-be ex-husband unexpectedly show up outside my door, has taken its toll.

Still, I force myself to sit up straight, to casually raise my glass of wine and take a modest drink of my rosé. I've gotten much more comfortable asserting myself and telling people around me what I need. But I refuse to be vulnerable with Rafe.

I stare out the window at a tourist boat drifting down the river. This restaurant was on my list of places to try this summer. But instead of reading over the menu or enjoying the sight of Paris at night, my awareness is laser-focused on him.

Am I aching because I'm nervous of why he's here? Why he's finally sought me out after all this time when he barely said two words to me at his brother's wedding? Or is it because a part of me wants to cling to him, to what I thought our future could be, even though I know I have to let go?

"How are you enjoying Paris?"

Irritation pierces my melancholy thoughts. "As much as I appreciate the attempt at small talk, let's not pretend, Rafe. You invited me to dinner to discuss our arrangement."

He tilts his head to the side, that smile still on his face. But it doesn't reach his eyes. No, this is classic Rafe: calm, cold, calculated. He has a reason for being here, and it's not me.

The ache deepens.

"I don't recall you being so direct."

"I've changed a lot."

"I noticed."

His eyes darken as his gaze sweeps down over my bare shoulders. I freeze. Tension charges the air between us as his eyes rest on my breasts, then travel over my arm to where my fingers are wrapped around the stem of my wineglass.

Then his gaze snaps back to mine. God, I feel pathetic. There's no warmth in his stare, no fleeting hint of desire. There's just ice.

"You're here because of the divorce papers."

"I am."

The waiter appears with Rafe's bourbon and a plate of artfully arranged brioche toast points covered in ricotta cheese and topped with spring peas and bacon, all resting on sprigs of rosemary. I focus on the art of the food, the relaxing aromatic scent of the herbs that reminds me of walking through the ancient forest of Fontainebleau with Katie that first month. Nothing but soaring trees, sandstone boulders, and the calming scent of pine as I'd relished my newfound freedom.

Better to think of that than linger on the fact that Rafe and I are officially enjoying our first meal as husband and wife. I barely ate anything at our sham of a wedding reception. I was too sick to my stomach, too heartbroken at what I'd overheard, to eat anything.

Calm. I serve myself a piece of brioche and bite down, savoring the flavors with a quiet hum of appreciation.

"I received your petition for divorce."

I swallow too fast and cough. Rafe presses a glass of water into my hands.

"And?" I finally say after I clear my throat and barely resist glaring at him.

"You truly want a divorce?"

"I wouldn't have sent the papers otherwise."

He stares at me for so long I know he's testing me. Using his legendary ability to stay silent to get me to talk. To reveal something that will unveil an elaborate plot.

But there is no plot. Nothing sinister. When Rafe proposed to me, he told me upfront it was a business arrangement. He wanted the real estate firm my father had inherited after the unexpected deaths of my grandfather and aunt the year prior. A firm that had been in our family for over fifty years, hence my father's reluctance to sell even if it meant hanging on to something that could ruin him.

My lips twitch. Apparently holding on to things that aren't good for us runs in the family.

I set the water glass down and resume eating, ignoring Rafe's hard gaze. I knew what he was offering when I said yes. I latched on to the lifeline he had offered with both hands, as someone drowning grabs on to a life preserver without bothering to see who's towing them to shore. Entertained some idiotic notion that, over time, he might come to feel something more and that, in the interim, I could be happy with the unique friendship we'd developed over the years.

Until our wedding night. Until that horrible moment when I'd passed by the library during the cocktail hour and over-heard Rafe and his father talking. Realized that whatever fairy tales I had concocted were just that: fiction.

Yet it was also the last tie, the last thing tethering me to my past, to my own fears and doubts. I'd gone back to my room, packed my bags, and even arranged my own trans-portation back to Santorini with a staff member who was thankfully discreet. Each move away from my old life had been like shedding a shackle, the weights dropping off the farther I went. It helped temper the dull throb of a heartache years in the making.

Coming to Paris was the first thing I've truly done on my own. I spent the majority of the last four months building a new life, one where I depend on no one but myself.

I have my sister, Katie, of course, and a few friends I've made. I have my own apartment that's half the size of the bed-room Rafe had designated for me at his villa. I wake up every morning excited to face a new day and see what it brings instead of knowing the exact schedule of every waking moment. A schedule created by an overprotective mother who cared more about keeping me safe than letting me potentially fail.

I also have Tessa's Interiors. My heart swells as I repeat the name in my mind. My own interior design firm. It's already growing faster than I expected. Out of my first three clients, two are accessible design clients. The kind of projects I had hoped to specialize in one day, never anticipating I would get to try my hand at them so quickly. Combining my love of design with creating functional spaces that represent my clients is a dream come true.

In Paris, I'm not dependent on others for my own happiness. I'm making my own. And I'm not about to surrender that to my so-called husband.

"Do your parents know?"

Irritation makes the pain in my calves dig deeper as a hard ball settles in my stomach. I'm twenty-eight years old. I don't need my parents' permission to live my life.

"I haven't told them, no."

"Have you talked to them since you left?"

I drop the piece of toast I just picked up and sit back with a sigh. "No, I haven't." I don't mention how my mother blew up my phone the first week after I left, leaving dozens of voicemails and hundreds of text messages until I changed my number. "Contrary to what everyone back on Santorini believes, I'm an adult. I have my own place, my own business and my own money to keep me going until my company is more secure."

"That would be the trust fund left to you by your mother's mother."

Of course he knows every detail of my life. "Yes."

He cocks his head to one side as he raises his glass to his lips. "A rather small amount."

I don't bother to hide my snort. "Two million euros would

mean a lot to almost anyone else in the world. And the interest is enough for me to live on, even without my business, for decades if I live within my means."

"You could have more."

I curl my fingers into a fist. "You can't offer me what I want."

His brows knit together. "I'm one of the wealthiest men in the world. Of course I can."

God, Gavriil was right. His older brother is truly incapable of seeing anything but facts and dollar signs.

Too late, I realize I said the first part out loud. Heat floods my cheeks. "I..."

"What was Gavriil right about?"

Rafe's voice is silky, just as smooth as the bourbon in his glass as he holds it up to the light. Nervousness makes my throat dry. I grab my rosé and take a long drink as I mentally prepare myself for what needs to be said.

"That you only care about Drakos Development."

One corner of Rafe's mouth quirks. "Care is a strong word."

"Regardless, there's no room for anything else in your life." I pause, fight past the resurgence of pain I tried to bury four months ago. "Including a wife and children."

His eyes snap to mine, that pale blue swirl of ice and mystery that enticed me when I was young and stupid. That lingered in my heart after the quiet conversations he engaged me in at the dinners, galas and fundraisers our families attended.

That I mistook for something more than business.

"The contract clearly states—"

"I know what it states." I try to keep my tone even, my voice steady as I fight against the demons I thought I had conquered. The ones urging me to just accept what was already offered, including a loveless marriage with a strict no-children clause.

"I've changed my mind, Rafe."

His blink is the only outward sign he's heard me. "You signed, Tessa."

"I did." For all the wrong reasons. "But I've changed my mind. Living in Paris has opened my eyes to what's possible for me when I'm not locked up on Santorini."

The flash of fury is unexpected. He leans forward, his gaze fierce. "Locked up?"

A shiver creeps down my spine at the lethalness underlying those two words.

"Figure of speech," I murmur.

Just like that, the anger is gone, replaced by that aloofness no one can break. Did I imagine it? Am I still so desperate for some sliver of his attention that I'm spinning stories in my head?

He sits back, picks up his bourbon again. "Care to elaborate?"

The waiter comes by with another glass of rosé. Normally I stick to two glasses for an entire meal. But tonight seems like the perfect night to throw those rules out the window. I drain the last of my first glass and hand it to the waiter, deciding how much I want to share.

A shudder passes through me as I remember how involved my mother was with my care. Involved doesn't begin to scratch the surface of what I've come to realize was an unhealthy obsession, a role she poured herself into until there was nothing else. Caring for me was her entire identity. One I didn't fight for the longest time because I wanted to keep the peace, even if it meant sitting off to the side and watching life pass me by.

But it wasn't just some altruistic form of guilt that kept me tethered to my former life for so long. There was also the fear. Even on the days I felt trapped, the alternative of making my own way was overwhelming. Frightening.

My stomach rolls just thinking about my past fragility.

"My parents found it hard to let me live my own life," I finally say. "My mother carried a lot of guilt over my accident. I did, too, so I tried to keep the peace for a long time." I shrug. "Then one day I realized I was unhappy with letting them make most of my choices."

There's no point in telling him about my mother dissolving into a fit of screaming hysterics at the thought of me traveling to Paris alone last year to visit my sister, an incident that resulted in me canceling my trip to make her stop and assuage my own remorse for even attempting something without her. It also dragged a deeply rooted resentment to the surface where I could no longer ignore it. My mother may have started out with good intentions with her obsessive control. But at some point she had become unhealthily fixated on her mission of keeping me shielded from any further harm.

Shielded and protected. Smothered and imprisoned.

My eyes flick to the glittering spire of the Eiffel Tower in the distance. After sunset, the tower lights up, a glimmering beacon every hour on the hour until midnight. Even though I can see the tower from my attic apartment, I'm constantly seeking it out. Some call it cliché, others boring or the most overrated landmark.

To me, it's beautiful. A symbol of adventure and romance, of new beginnings and timelessness. It may have taken some horrible circumstances to force me to do something with my life.

But I did it.

"So my proposal came at an opportune time."

I tap one finger against the base of my wineglass. Rafe won't understand emotions. But intelligence, shrewdness? Those are qualities he respects.

"Yes."

Another blink. "I see."

Damn it, why do I feel guilty when he says that? Why does

it matter one whit given that he married me for the company my father inherited after my grandfather and aunt passed away in a car accident earlier this year?

"So once you had your freedom from your parents, you left."

"Yes." A bald-faced lie. I left because I heard him telling his father the only reason he married me was to get his hands on my father's firm. The company Rafe's father, Lucifer, had tried to buy numerous times from my grandfather. A point Rafe made with a cold, cruel smugness that had stabbed me straight through my naïve heart.

My marriage, this potentially grand love affair I'd concocted in my adolescence, wasn't just a business arrangement. It was revenge, all to one-up the man Rafe and Gavriil both hated.

I'd known I was nothing more than a means to an end. But to hear it stated in such callous terms, to realize revenge was more important than what I had thought was at least a friendship, had killed the girl I used to be.

But, I reminded myself as a couple passes by, the man's arm wrapped possessively about the woman's waist as he places a gentle kiss on her forehead, it was a good thing I overheard everything. Who knows how long I may have clung to the idea that our relationship could change? How long I would have gone without realizing all the other things that could be?

"You want children now?"

I look away from him. It's too painful to look into his eyes. To remember how I once used to dream about a child with his eyes when my dreams were an escape. Before a doctor told me those dreams could be a reality.

If I'd needed any other sign that I needed to end my marriage, that had been it. I'd contacted the judge the next day.

"I've always wanted them." A smile tugs at my lips as I

remember the moment my new doctor finally answered the question I'd avoided asking for so long. "I just didn't think I could for the longest time. Katie said a doctor told my mom I probably wouldn't be able to have kids right after my accident. But my current doctor says I can." Giddiness bubbles in my chest. "There have been a lot of advancements since my accident."

"Why did your mother not follow up with a doctor sooner?"

My smile turns sad. "Because my mother and I are, or at least were, a lot alike. Not knowing the answer and living in her little bubble was safer than having her worst fears confirmed."

Although it crossed my mind that maybe my mother hadn't pursued anything because it made it easier to keep me by her side, to pretend like I would always need her. The only reason she agreed to my marriage to Rafe was because my father put his foot down for the first and only time.

The two things that seem to motivate my parents: money and guilt. I will break that pattern, starting now. I'm not touching the bank account Rafe set up in my name. And I'm not letting guilt keep me tied to a marriage I no longer want.

The sounds from the restaurant amplify as silence falls between us. Cutlery clinking on porcelain plates. The rise and fall of voices as several different languages drift on the air. The quiet creak of a chair as someone shifts in their seat.

And the sound of my own heartbeat thudding in my throat so hard it hurts.

"That is your only reason for asking for a divorce?"

Not even close. "Yes." I swallow against the discomfort of lying. "There's no one else. I'm not trying to alter yours and my father's agreement in any way, although from what I can tell the sale is final. Nothing can change that."

"No," Rafe agrees.

"The only timeline in there was the two years before we

were allowed to…" Bile rises in my throat. When I'd read the clause about no affairs for two years, I'd framed it as having two years to show him how much I loved him. I want to shake some sense into the woman I was. "So there's no reason for us to continue on. I'm invoking the provision allowing one of us to change their minds, especially if their future wishes no longer align with the other party's."

More silence. Long seconds that stretch out into what feels like an eternity as I face down the man I thought I'd be with forever. The man I thought might be able to fall in love with me.

Idiot.

"I'll sign."

I breathe out. It hurts, how easily he can let us go. But it's just another reminder I never should have agreed to this in the first place. And at least there's relief in knowing this will be over soon. That I will finally be able to move on and embrace my future.

"Thank you."

"On one condition."

Apprehension pricks the back of my neck. I should have known it wouldn't be that easy. "Oh?"

"The divorce won't be finalized until after our first anniversary."

CHAPTER THREE

Tessa

PANIC CRAWLS UP my throat. Eight more months? After wasting twenty-one years of my life under someone else's thumb, eight months feels like an eternity. Especially knowing I can have the things I thought might be out of my reach. Things like a family of my own. Children. Things the man sitting across from me wants nothing to do with.

"Why?"

Rafe's face hardens. Even knowing him as I do, my body tenses. I've rarely seen him like this, every muscle in his body wound tight, anger lurking beneath the surface. So many people think Rafe feels nothing.

But they just don't know where to look.

"Lucifer's will stipulates that for me to inherit my share of Drakos Development, including all European and Asian holdings, I have to surpass our one-year anniversary."

My mouth drops open. "What?"

Rafe's father had barely paid me any attention. Something I'd been more than fine with. The man was an odious, selfish toad who lived to satisfy his own desires and make his sons miserable.

"That's insane."

Rafe's smile is small but lethal. "On that, we agree."

My mind races as I sit back in my chair. "So Gavriil and Juliette…"

Rafe nods. "My requirement was to reach our first anniversary. Gavriil's requirement was to marry within a year of the will reading and stay married for a year."

Hurt cuts through me. Gavriil and I have been friends since my family moved to Santorini. With our house being perched on the shore and within a three-minute boat ride of the private island Lucifer Drakos had built his lavish villa on, it had been easy for Gavriil to ride over with the housekeeper when she came to Santorini to do the shopping or visit with friends. It had been on one of those visits that Gavriil had seen me sitting outside on our porch and asked why I was in a wheelchair. After I told him I'd fallen off a wall, he'd asked if he could try it sometime in the innocent way so many children see life. He treated me like a person instead of someone to be handled delicately or ignored. We'd been best friends ever since.

Or at least I thought we had. Him not telling me about the will, about his real reason for marrying Juliette, stings. I'd even started to view Juliette as a friend. She was my third client ever, and the largest account to date.

I bit down on the inside of my cheek. This is part of what I need to work on when it comes to business. Keeping things professional. Not letting personal feelings get in the way. To be more like my husband.

The thought has me choking back a laugh.

"Gavriil didn't tell you?"

I narrow my eyes at the slight taunt in Rafe's voice. "No."

"Interesting." He glances at me over the rim of his glass. "If you and I hadn't been married, I imagine he would have asked you."

I stare at him. Then I laugh. "Gavriil?" I finally say, my sides hurting from laughing so hard. "Are you joking?"

"I don't joke."

The cold delivery of that statement has me laughing harder. I grab my napkin and press it to my lips. It takes a moment, but I finally wrestle myself back under control.

"Marrying Gavriil would be like marrying Katie."

The slightest crinkle appears at the bridge of his nose. "How so?"

"Gavriil is the brother I never had. It would be like incest." I suddenly remember the other man at the wedding. Tall, hulking, like a lumberjack stuffed into a tuxedo. But he had been surprisingly kind and fun to talk with. It had taken me a moment to realize why he felt so familiar.

The eyes. The same pale blue as my husband's.

"What about your other brother?"

Rafe stills. "Other brother?"

"Michail."

I can feel the fury whip across the table before Rafe pulls his mantle of apathy back on and shuts me out.

"Gavriil told you about him?"

"I met him at the wedding."

"Ah." He downs the rest of his bourbon and sets the glass on the edge of the table. "What about him?"

"I didn't realize you had another brother."

"I didn't either until just before the will reading."

"Are you…" My voice trails off. Rafe never had much of a relationship with Gavriil. From what Gavriil had shared, Rafe essentially ignored him ever since he stepped foot inside the Drakos villa after his mother died and he was sent to live with Lucifer. Whenever I saw them together, I noticed the distance between them, as well as the lack of emotion on Rafe's end and the lingering hurt and bitterness Gavriil held on to.

"Are you okay with having another brother?"

One shoulder rose and fell in a subtle shrug. "It's inconsequential. He has no interest in Drakos Development and has chosen not to fulfill the requirement to inherit."

"But what about…" I pause, then decide to go for it. What do I have to lose by holding back at this point? "What about getting to know him?"

Two blinks this time. "Why would I?"

Pain squeezes my lungs. Pain for the man in front of me who cares about nothing, who exists solely for the purpose of his company. Pain for the numerous relationships he's dismissed.

Including our own.

But this is good, I remind myself. *A clear answer he's not the one for you.*

One day, that will be comforting. One day, I will look back on this moment and know it was the best thing to ever happen to me, second only to my decision to move to Paris.

But right now, it just hurts.

"I don't want to wait, Rafe." I breathe in deeply, exhale harshly. "I'm ready to move on with my life. Surely you could break the will."

"I haven't explored that option yet." His gaze is intense, penetrating. "My proposal is much simpler."

"Yes, but longer."

"Is being married to me for eight more months such an abhorrent thought?"

If it were anyone else, I'd almost think I'd hurt him. Would imagine I saw a slight downturn of his lips, a tightening around his eyes. But as this conversation and my past behavior have proved, my interpretations and feelings about Rafe can't be trusted.

"It has nothing to do with you, Rafe." *Liar.* "I just want to move on with my life."

"Even if we were to proceed," Rafe says quietly, "Greek

courts take an average of a year for a hearing, not to mention another year to make a decision."

"Yes, but when a close friend of my father's serves as a judge, matters can be expedited."

His eyes narrowed. "How quickly?"

"Two months."

Two months instead of two years. Twenty-two more months of freedom. Of shedding the remnants of who I used to be and embracing who I can become. An entrepreneur, a lover, a wife, a mother.

It's enjoyable, watching Rafe unsettled for a moment as he processes this revelation. The signs are subtle: a quick blink, the tensing of his jaw that's barely visible beneath his neatly trimmed beard.

"Is it worth the hassle?"

I used to subscribe to that mindset. Nothing was worth the hassle, especially if it resulted in my mother crying as she apologized yet again for falling asleep that day instead of going outside to play with me like she'd promised. Each teardrop added to the weight of my own shame I'd carried like a yoke around my neck for more than twenty long years until I was drowning in guilt and tears.

After living that hell for so long, calling in a favor from a family friend and going through expedited divorce proceedings seems more than worth the hassle.

"It is to me."

Darkness shifts in his eyes. Before I can analyze it, the waiter appears with a platter of Coquilles Saint-Jacques and a plate of grilled asparagus on the side. The sea scallops, baked in half a shell and drizzled with Gruyère cheese and cream sauce, smell heavenly.

Yet I can barely stomach taking a bite as my heart gallops in my chest. I'm past the point of wanting Rafe to somehow reveal that he's missed me. I hate that he's so close, that we're sharing what should be an intimate and enjoyable experience between a wife and her husband, but is instead a meal charged with undercurrents of pain and exhaustion.

"What would it take for you to agree, Tessa?"

I pop one of the scallops into my mouth, barely register the delicious taste of shellfish soaked in butter.

"What are you offering?"

His blue gaze narrows. Years of training keep me from rolling my eyes, but just barely. I told him what I want: a clean break. He's the one trying to persuade me to stay.

"Money. I have over a billion at my disposal."

I stab another scallop with my fork. "I told you, I have enough of my own."

"People can always use more money."

I pause with the fork halfway to my mouth.

"Yes." I say the word quietly before giving him a small, sad smile. "My father thought the same thing."

Nolan Sullivan spent his whole life in the shadow of his older sister. An existence that, coupled with my accident and my mother's choosing to focus her life on me instead of her husband or younger daughter, had fashioned a distant man who found no joy in life. The one thing that made him get out of bed in the morning was money, as if he earned enough of it he might one day also earn his father's respect. Perhaps even his love.

I'd seen the pleasure on my father's face, the relief at learning my grandfather had entrusted the firm to him upon his and my aunt's death. A pleasure swiftly defeated by shock when the lawyer told him how deeply in debt Sullivan Legacy Properties was. I know he'd rejected Rafe's first offer to simply buy the firm. Had cited that the company had been in our family for four generations. Rafe had countered with his offer of marriage.

He'd talked to me only once after I accepted Rafe's proposal. I'd been on my balcony, the same place where Rafe had sat and presented his proposal like a business presentation, staring out at the lines and ridges of Drakos Island. My future home.

My father had asked me if I was happy about marrying Rafe. The question had surprised me. My father rarely asked me my opinion on anything. So I'd simply said yes.

"I'm glad."

And then he'd walked back inside. The last time I'd seen him had been during my wedding reception when he'd sat at a table with my mother with a perpetually full glass of wine in front of him and a glazed look in his eyes.

Probably mentally reviewing the astounding sum Rafe had paid to purchase Sullivan Legacy.

"Something for your business then."

My spine stiffens. "What?"

"Your interior design firm. You've only been in business for a couple months. Plenty of opportunity for—"

"No. Thank you."

He's watching me now, his unnervingly direct gaze tinged with curiosity. I pause, trying to figure out the best way to phrase my next words. To stay strong and not let him glimpse the insecurities that still haunt me.

"As I move on with my life, I want to make a clean break. No ties to Greece, or anyone from my past." *Including you.* "I also want Tessa's Interiors to succeed on its own merits. On the work I put into it. Using my trust fund to get started felt like a compromise to begin with. Accepting handouts from my…" I look down at the table, unable to look him in the eye. "From my husband would negate my independence."

His shoulders stiffen. Now he's frustrated. Rafe and his brother Gavriil are renowned for their ability to make deals, to come up with mergers and sales most people in the property development community can only dream of. Stymying him shouldn't bring me pleasure. But it's interesting seeing this side of him, watching as he tries to come up with something to appeal to me.

The only thing I want is something I have no interest in receiving from Rafe. When I have a family of my own, I want it to be with someone I love and who loves me in return. Who won't place business above all else. Who will look at me and see me, want me, for who I am and not what I can bring to the table.

Rafe continues to stare. He's mentally analyzing what he knows about me and trying to come up with something, anything, to persuade me. It's not fair on my part to be upset at his lack of feelings toward me. He never once led me on.

I just wanted it to be different.

"We've always gotten along well, Tessa."

Gotten along well.

Bland, banal, boring.

I take another sip of my wine as I think about Nathan. Yes, the man is essentially a puppy in human form with his huge smile and affable personality. But I've seen the way he looks at my sister, the little things he does because he knows it matters to her. And on one embarrassing occasion, I walked in on him pressing my sister against a wall as he kissed her like she was his last breath of air. Nathan had been mortified. Katie had laughed until tears rolled down her cheeks.

And I… I'd been slightly embarrassed. Amused. But beneath it all, envy had coursed through me like poison. I don't want to be Rafe's brother's friend who happened to be a convenient wife. I want passion. Romance. Love.

"Yes, we have."

"I don't like making threats."

I arch a brow. "So don't."

"But I will if my hand is forced." His voice is deadly calm, his eyes glittering. "If I were to lose my role as head of Drakos Development's European and Asian divisions, thousands of people would be at risk for losing their jobs."

Oh, yes. Pile on the guilt. Not like I don't suffer from enough of it already.

I sigh. Would eight more months of marriage really make that big of a difference?

Yes. Perhaps if he hadn't come to Paris and had simply written or emailed, I could have agreed. But seeing him here now has put fresh cracks in my healing but still broken heart. I just want this to be over. Surely there's some other way for him to work around this condition with the will. It's so archaic in nature, so controlling, it's almost laughable.

"Tessa."

Hearing my name on his lips has me gripping my wineglass so tight I'm afraid I might snap the stem. It pulls at my heart, but it also tugs at that part of me that was awakened nine years ago. The first time I saw Rafe through a woman's eyes. I can still see him kneeling next to me on a moonlit balcony, silver light glinting in his dark hair as he gave me the faintest of smiles. Can feel the warmth of his fingers sliding over my skin when he took my hand in his. It lasted all of a second.

But that one second changed everything.

My pulse kicks up as an idea glimmers at the edges of my mind. Faint at first, but then it solidifies, takes shape even as the rational part of my brain tries to squelch it.

It's ridiculous. Foolish. It would be doing the exact opposite of what I just told myself I needed. Yet the more I think about it, the more tempting it becomes. Yes, it would potentially be putting my heart on the line. But I've proven to myself I'm so much stronger than I ever thought possible. And even if I occasionally struggle, the end result would be more than worth it.

"There is something."

I can almost feel his sense of victory as his mouth tilts up at one corner.

"Name it."

I square my shoulders, raise my chin and look him straight in the eye.

"I want you to be my first lover."

CHAPTER FOUR

Rafe

A WAITER PASSES BY. The couple behind me are talking about some tour they went on that failed to meet their expectations. Out of the corner of my eye, I see a boat cruising down the Seine, its upper deck crowded with tourists.

The world marches on despite my wife asking me to take her virginity in exchange for delaying our divorce.

A virgin.

Knowing how closely Maeve Sullivan monitored her daughter, it shouldn't be a surprise that my twenty-eight-year-old wife is a virgin. But sex is not something I've given much thought to where Tessa was concerned. It was something I deliberately didn't think about. The difference in our ages, the sweetness of her personality that contrasted so sharply against the cold darkness of mine, made any type of physical attraction seem obscene. Having Tessa agree to the "in name only" clause of the contract had been a relief, even if the thought of her taking a lover after two years left me unusually ill-tempered.

It had been the right thing to do. I wasn't going to consign her to a lifetime of no physical intimacy. Not when I had resolved to let her live her life and not dim it by subjugating her to my cold, barren existence.

My shock shifts, melds with a dangerous possessiveness. The same possessiveness I experienced when I saw her with

Nathan rears its head once more. Heat fills my veins as blood rushes straight to my groin. I go hard in an instant at the thought of having Tessa in my arms, undressing her, being the first to ever see her, touch her, taste her. Need to take what's being offered, to satisfy the hunger I had denied far longer than I had realized—

Paúō. This right here is a reason why such an insane proposal is out of the question. I'm not thinking with my brain.

I pick up my glass so I have something to hold on to, something tactile I can focus on.

"Is this a joke?"

"I think I would have remembered losing my virginity," she replies wryly.

If I'd thought my irritability at the possibility of her taking a lover down the road bad before, it's nothing compared to now. Thinking about another man daring to touch her, let alone look at her...

Thankfully our waiter interrupts my devolving thoughts with the third course: duck fillet, shallots with *caillette* sausages, and a mustard sauce. I stare at the food, at the artistic swirl of mustard on the edge of the plate, at the sprinkling of some dark purple powder over the duck that makes the colors of the food pop against the white plate.

The details swirl, blend together as her words echo in my mind.

...my first lover.

I pick up my fork, wielding it like a weapon against the insanity she has just proposed.

"What would be the terms of such an arrangement?" I finally ask.

She shrugs. *Shrugs*. I'm not prone to emotional reactions. But less than an hour ago I was tempted to commit murder. Now I'm tempted to reach across the table and shake Tessa by the shoulders.

I should have stayed in Greece.

"I hadn't thought that far ahead."

Ah. I mentally pounce on the bit of logic she dangles in front of me. She threw something out, a wild idea she knew I would never pursue, so that I would agree to an immediate divorce.

"Once you come up with terms I can review," I reply, calm now that I have a better understanding of the reason behind her request, "then I'll consider it."

Her eyes widen. "Do you ever just go with the flow?"

"No."

Disappointment clouds her face. She looks back down at her plate. For the first time in a very long time, I regret my lack of spontaneity. My inability to let myself feel. That a childhood filled with pressure and anger and cruelty molded me into the man I am today. One who can't forge stable, long-lasting emotional connections with anyone. Hard to do when I have almost no emotions to give.

Case in point: Drakos Development. The company everyone assumes is my end goal. My reason for existing. Except in the wake of Lucifer's death three months ago, I've been left with a horrible realization.

It means nothing to me. The company I was groomed to take over, the one I have dedicated almost every moment of the last forty-one years of my life to, is nothing more than something to occupy my time. Without Lucifer dogging my footsteps, watching with bated breath for his firstborn to fail, I was motivated to work, to pursue, to lead.

But when I accompanied Gavriil to California after Lucifer's passing and stood with him on a hotel ballroom stage, heard the passion in his voice as he spoke about upcoming projects up and down America's West Coast, I knew. Knew the company could go under tomorrow and I wouldn't care.

Yet another thing that widened the ever-growing chasm

between my brother and me. Not that we had a good relationship to begin with. We had almost nothing, save what had been our mutual interest in Drakos Development.

Now we don't even have that.

I swirl a bite of duck through the mustard sauce as I resist the weight trying to press on my chest. It's only natural, I remind myself, to experience apathy toward something one cared about after loss. Even if the loss was not unexpected, and even if the person who died was a detestable human being who deserved a far worse fate than passing away surrounded by luxury, it's still a loss.

In a few months, I'll feel differently. As I settle into my new role, as I grow and expand the company under my own terms, it will get better. And even if I don't feel anything at all, I'm capable of moving forward. Emotions have no place in business.

But if Tessa doesn't agree to wait until after our anniversary to pursue the divorce, I'll have my own substantial wealth, my investments and properties…and nothing else. My mother has been dead for years. Even when she was alive, she kept her distance from both her husband and her son, going so far as to move to Madrid to live out her final days. I have no relationship with the brother I kept at arm's length for over twenty years. If I can't make amends with Gavriil, a sibling I've lived and worked with, I see little point in trying to establish a relationship with Michail who clearly stated he wanted nothing to do with the Drakos name.

The weight presses down harder.

"I stay married to you through whatever date you set," Tessa says suddenly, "between now and one month after our first anniversary. In that time, you agree to introduce me to sex."

It takes a few seconds for her words to sink in. It wasn't an empty challenge or a last-ditch attempt to make me leave.

Tessa is serious.

My imagination grabs the reins and takes a hard left into a vivid image of me sliding that blue dress down, revealing her bare breasts, her breathing erratic as I trail my lips from her mouth down to her jaw, then lower still over the elegant column of her neck.

"Is that it?" I reply, mentally applauding myself for keeping a steady voice as I try to dismiss the pictures filling my mind.

Try and fail, as I see myself kissing the swells of her breasts, then sucking one nipple into my mouth as she arches against me.

She frowns. "What else is there?"

God, I would laugh at her naivete if it wasn't alluring in its own way. Her blatant confidence entwined with her innocence is intoxicating. The few women I've been with over the years—I hesitate to even call them relationships—were in it for the same reasons I was: mutual pleasure. Satisfying urges, spending some time with an interesting companion, and then parting ways. I liked them, enjoyed our interactions. But there was always that safety net of distance. Physical desire without the interference of unnecessary emotions. No risk of falling into the type of hell that had been my parents' marriage.

Yet just a few minutes with my wife, seeing her and the woman she's become in our months apart, has left me throbbing with lust. But her innocence is also the lifeline I need to grasp on to. A reminder that her inexperience is a severe detriment. She might have developed considerable grit since coming to Paris. But if I know one thing about Tessa, it's that her heart is far too big for this world. I have no illusions that I'm her prince in shining armor. A woman like her, one who can't hide the stars in her eyes or how brightly they shine when she thinks no one's looking, deserves to have her first time be with someone who can at least give her the potential of a future.

Even if the thought of it being someone other than me is enough to make me set down my knife and pick up my bourbon.

Focus on the bourbon. The duck. The damned chandelier. Anything but her.

"How many times, for example," I say as I raise my glass to my lips.

"Given I've never done this before, I'm not sure what's reasonable."

It is only through sheer willpower that I don't snort the bourbon out my nose. She's not trying to be manipulative or amusing. She's simply stating facts.

The strength of my reaction is a telling sign that the control I exude in my life would be nonexistent. If there's one thing I have left that is solely mine, it's my control. I will not cede that, not for anyone.

Turning her first time into a business agreement is also an issue, one that leaves me with a vaguely nauseous feeling in the pit of my stomach. The same feeling when I proposed and I'd told myself I was doing the right thing, not just for the sake of the company but for Tessa. That anything was better than her sitting in that house day after day with no one but her controlling mother and a housekeeper for company since her sister had left for university in France. That the friendship we had established over the years would be enough.

I lied.

I had known, even then, that Tessa would want more. Deserve more. Even though I felt more for her than most, I would never be able to let myself feel enough. The last time I tried, it nearly ripped me apart.

"Tessa—"

"Garçon?"

I frown as Tessa interrupts me to signal our waiter.

"Tessa?"

"Oui, mademoiselle?"

She ignores me as she smiles up at him. "I'm leaving early."

The heat spreading through my body has nothing to do with lust and everything to do with irritation. "I thought we'd finish our meal together."

"I gave you a lot to think about. I think it's best if we take some time apart to consider options." She pulls out a silver clutch and hands the waiter a card before I can intervene.

"No, I'll—"

"After I finish the house for Gavriil's mother-in-law, I have another client lined up," Tessa says with a sharp smile that warns me to stay quiet. "This is a business dinner. I'm paying."

Like hell. "No."

"It's not up for negotiation, Rafe. And," she adds with a ferociousness I never would have expected from her, "I'm taking a taxi home."

I blink. I'm not used to people talking back to me. Ever. Especially not a woman who just a few months ago looked at me like I'd hung the moon as we recited vows to stay with each other in sickness and in health and all the other empty promises that fill up a wedding ceremony.

The waiter leaves. Tessa reaches behind her and grabs her crutches.

"It would be faster if I drove you."

"I don't care."

She winces. Warning flares.

"Tessa, if you're in pain—"

"I am, Rafe, but it's normal." She sighs as her shoulders droop. "Part of the additional physical therapy, part of this…" She waves a hand in my direction. "It's a part of who I am."

It hits me then how little I know about her injury, that I

have no understanding of how it's impacted her life. Remorse keeps me seated in my chair as she straightens. Regret for all the times I sought her out at events, talked with her yet never bothered to ask about the deeper parts of her life. Just because I have no interest in sharing pieces of myself doesn't mean the same was true for her.

She slips her arms through the cuffs and grabs the handles, standing with a fluidity that speaks to how much she's been using the crutches.

"We've talked through some serious subjects. Before you impulsively say no—"

"I never do anything impulsively," I grind out. "I just don't think this is the right thing for you."

Her shoulders are thrown back, her movements confident as she turns away.

"You're running away again."

She freezes. Then, slowly, turns her head to look down at me.

"If you want to call it that. I, however, see it as removing myself from an embarrassing situation and from the company of someone who's taking away my choice."

I frown. "What?"

"I'm twenty-eight years old, Rafe. Yes," she says, raising her arm slightly to show me the crutch, "I'm partially paralyzed. I'm a virgin. But that doesn't make me helpless or stupid."

"I never said you were."

"'I don't think this is the right thing for you,'" she repeats. "You don't have a say in what is or what is not best for me. If you don't want to agree to my terms because of your own reasons, that's one thing. I may not like it, but I'll respect it." She leans down, color high in her cheeks, eyes sparkling with anger. "But don't you dare take away my choice. Ever."

She moves toward the elevator. A few people glance at her.

One outright stares until I catch his eyes and glare at him. He pales, looking back down at his table so fast I'm surprised he doesn't have whiplash.

She walks into the elevator and presses a button. The doors start to close. Her head comes up and for one moment, our eyes meet. Pink still stains her cheeks. Her chin is still raised up in the air like she's about to do battle.

But it's the hurt in her eyes, the embarrassment, that guts me.

Then the doors close, leaving me with lingering discomfort and a sense of loss. Like once again I just let something vital slip through my fingers.

I force myself to drink the rest of my bourbon slowly. Take a bite of the triple chocolate torte with hand-whipped mousse the waiter brings out. Tell myself over and over again that I'm doing the right thing.

Only to have the possibility that she's right and I'm letting my own concerns and guilt override her wishes circle back and slap me in the face.

I never saw Tessa use the crutches back in Greece. I had just always assumed she preferred to move around with the support of her wheelchair. I only knew about her accident because Gavriil told me shortly after he met her on one of the few occasions we talked while Lucifer was away. About how she'd been playing along a wall, slipped and fell, sustaining an injury to her spinal cord that left her partially paralyzed.

But when I saw her at Gavriil's wedding, so happy, so assured, it had been yet another indicator that I hadn't bothered to look past the surface. That I had taken so many things about Tessa at face value.

Like this proposal. I should have asked why. Why does she want me to be her first lover? Does she understand I can't offer her more than what I already have? I was thinking with an entirely different part of my body, one that is still painfully hard even after her departure.

I should feel guilty. She's young. Innocent, both figuratively and literally. Yet as she reminded me, she's no longer a teenager. She's a grown woman who's accomplished a great deal.

...don't you dare take away my choice.

The longer I sit, the more I contemplate the possibility that I dismissed her idea too quickly. I'll fulfill the terms of Lucifer's will. Tessa will get her divorce. And she'll get whatever she wants out of this newly proposed arrangement. As she pointed out, she's a grown woman more than capable of making her own decisions. She uprooted her life, moved to another country and is cultivating her own business.

If we talk, if she can explain her reasons to my satisfaction and we can agree to mutual terms, then perhaps there is a way for this to work.

The alternative if I say no is she pushes through with the divorce, I lose my share of Drakos Development and everything Lucifer willed to me.

And Tessa finds someone else to be her first.

Like hell.

The strength of my reaction surprises me. But it's understandable. Right now, Tessa is my wife. One day, I will accept that she will move on. Find someone who can tell her all the sweet things she wants to hear, cuddle on the couch, take her out to restaurants like this. Give her a family.

A noise rises above the din of the restaurant. One no one else can hear. But I can, clear as if it were happening now instead of twenty-three years ago. Soft, muffled cries. A child crying into a pillow as he mourns his mother with no one to comfort him.

No one except a spineless brother standing just outside

his door, his hand on the doorknob even though he knows he can't open it. Can't risk what will happen.

A cold wall slams down. I will never be a father. Unlike Lucifer, I'm fully aware of my own weaknesses, including that any children of mine would deserve far more than I am able to give them.

I need to take the rest of the evening to think. Even though I'm not having Tessa sign an actual contract for me to take her virginity, I need to write out terms, see everything in black and white. Complete a final review on my concerns about her emotional vulnerability and any other potential conflicts.

As much as I don't care to admit it, I also need to review my own ability to stay detached. I'm not at risk of falling in love. It's not something I would ever allow to happen. But I have concerns about this craving Tessa has ignited. I need to be sure that when the time comes for us to part ways, I won't let petty jealousy or possessiveness interfere.

I glance over my shoulder. The bell towers of Notre Dame stand tall and proud against the darkening French night sky. They've survived generations of war, fire and humanity creating its usual havoc.

I can survive this challenge. Survive, conquer, control.

Tessa's scent lingers in the elevator as I leave, a light blend that makes me think of strawberries and violets. It stirs my blood as anticipation courses through me.

I've never lost a negotiation. I'm not about to start now.

CHAPTER FIVE

Tessa

THE FIRST TIME I imagined myself to be in love with Rafael Drakos, I was nineteen years old. I'd known him since I was seven and my father moved us from a small town outside of Dublin to Santorini. As a child, he'd intimidated me, dark-eyed and brooding. He rarely interacted with Gavriil or me. It didn't bother me. Gavriil preferred to keep his distance from the man he described as having a block of ice for a heart. I got enough moodiness from my father and his never-ending quest to earn my grandfather's approval, so staying away from the older Drakos brother wasn't hard.

Until that summer when I went to my first event at the Drakos villa. A birthday party for Lucifer. The massive estate, set on a private island I could see from our front porch, was just a short boat ride away from Santorini's famous caldera. The mansion dwarfed our home, playing host to Corinthian pillars and too many balconies to count, all of them offering unobstructed views of the sea. There was beauty there, but also opulence, so much that I felt smothered by the sheer luxury of it all.

My mother had insisted on pushing my wheelchair up the ramp and into the main hall, a cavernous room lined with Greek sculptures that should have been in museums instead of someone's private home. Most people gave me looks of pity. A few whispered behind their hands, as if being in a wheelchair meant I couldn't hear. Gavriil hadn't come down yet. Lucifer had made a beeline for my father as soon as we'd entered. He'd coveted Sullivan Legacy for years and wasted no opportunity to speak with my father.

Despite my parents' tense marriage, my mother had sensed my father's rising irritation. She'd wheeled me off to the side and told me to wait while she went to serve as a buffer between Father and Lucifer.

So I'd sat, as I often did. Observing. Waiting for a few acquaintances to arrive who didn't let my wheelchair stand as an obstacle between us.

Until a glimpse of the sea just beyond a balcony had called to me. I'd wheeled myself outside and up to the railing, only to belatedly realize I wasn't alone.

"Good evening, Tessa."

That voice…to this day, I sometimes wake up to the memory of that voice sliding over my skin, sinking deep into my veins and winding its way through my body. My first experience, I would later realize, as a woman responding to a man.

I'd started to look behind me. But before I could crane my neck back, Rafe had shifted out of the shadows and knelt down next to my chair. He made small talk about the weather, recently completing a diving course with the CEO of some company he wanted to buy, asked me about my nonexistent social life.

When he had glanced back toward the ballroom, it gave me a moment to appreciate the details I had seen before but never noticed. His face was narrower than Gavriil's, but the blades of his cheekbones were just as sharp, his black beard cut to precision along the straight lines of his jaw. He possessed the same pale blue eyes as Gavriil and his father. For so long, I had imagined them as Gavriil had, tiny glaciers existing inside a man who might as well have been made of stone for all the emotion he displayed.

But that night, as he looked back at me with that hint of warmth, I didn't see a man of stone. I saw a man living behind a shield. A man I suddenly suspected had far greater depths than the child I had been would have recognized.

My mother had come out moments later, her voice shrill with nerves as she'd lectured me on not straying too far away from her. I'd been mortified. But Rafe hadn't run away. Instead, he'd taken my hand in his and bowed over it. His touch, warm and firm, had lasted for a single heartbeat.

One heartbeat was all it took to fall for Rafael Drakos.

After that night, I couldn't shake the impression he made on me. I never threw myself at him or found excuses to be with him. That smacked too much of desperation. But when we found ourselves at the same event or ran into each other in Santorini, I savored every moment I had, every bit of conversation.

Once, I'd found it romantic. Now it just adds to the layers of humiliation slowly suffocating me as I move down the street with my market bag thumping against my hip.

He wasn't wrong. When I realized he was going to say no last night, I left. Ran away, as he put it, to be alone with my humiliation and anger.

The humiliation is something I'll get over. Being rejected, especially by the man you pined over for nearly ten years and imagined yourself to be in love with, is embarrassing. Toss in that I had spun quiet dreams of him falling for me in the months leading up to our wedding, only to hear him tell his father just hours after our wedding ceremony that he would never fall in love, and I had every right to flee.

But the anger, the helplessness… I pause to catch my breath. Helpless anger is far worse than…anything. There is no power. No control. Only feelings that can do nothing but suffocate you.

The same anger that drove me to say yes to Rafe's proposal. Had I not had that anger festering inside me from not getting to visit Katie the year before, I'm not sure I would have said yes, even with my decades-long crush. Something I realized on my wedding day after I'd fled to my room. I'd let Rafe's offer be the catalyst for change instead of making the choice myself.

Rafe still hasn't called or texted. Either he's contemplating my offer or, the more likely scenario, he's gone back to Greece.

Good riddance.

I've reserved today for rest, to get myself back into a good place. A quick trip to the market, a light lunch, hours of lounging on my bed or the terrace with a book. Tomorrow morning will be designated for work. And the afternoon will be something fun, something I can look forward to when thoughts of Rafe and his rejection of my proposal weigh me down.

Notre Dame, I decide as I turn a corner and my building comes into view. I can't remember how many times I've been inside since I came to Paris. I'll wake up early and continue my work on the schematic designs for Juliette's house. Applying the skills I learned in my program to renovating a stunning home on Washington's Olympic Coast isn't just a dream. It's satisfying, knowing I'm helping Juliette create a home for her stepmother that she'll be able to move through with confidence.

It's also the kind of project that will enable me to pursue other passions down the road, like taking on designs for clients needing accessible designs who wouldn't be able to afford them. I've known since university that accessibility design was an area I wanted to focus on. But living in an apartment that wasn't designed for someone like me has made me more appreciative of all the privileges I grew up with. That and having two potential clients who had needed those changes, but had to decline my proposals because of cost.

I won't be able to help everyone. Not even close. But I can do something.

Buoyed by my plans for the next two days and thoughts of my future, I mentally map out tomorrow afternoon if the morning is successful. I'll go to the cathedral first, navigate the long aisles, the dark little coves flickering with candles lit by prayers of the thousands who will have streamed through that morning. Then wrap up with a visit to Shakespeare and Company on the Left Bank. Definitely use the wheelchair so I can take as long as I want to wander through the shelves on the main floor and pick one, two, or even half a dozen books to take home.

Perhaps, after an afternoon to myself, I will somehow work my way around to accepting putting off my divorce long enough for Rafe to receive his inheritance. In the moment, all I could think of was myself. But condemning Rafe to losing out on his entire life's work, not to mention the uncertain future Drakos Development's thousands of workers would face in the aftermath of such a huge change, feels selfish.

I don't want to. Resigning myself to another eight months of purgatory feels like forever. But it's the right thing to do.

The scent of freshly baked baguette wafts up from my bag and eases some of my tension. Paris's open-air markets are a wonderful place to spend a morning. I can find anything from fruit and gourmet cheese to flowers and spices. The Marché de Grenelle, with its colorful stalls arranged under the Métro, offers not just the usual consumables, but random goods like books and clothing.

I glance down at the bag slung across my body. Beneath the bread, fruit and wedge of goat's cheese is an impulse purchase. One I questioned at least three times as I maneuvered my way through the crowds.

But beneath the self-doubt, I'm glad I bought it. Rafe may not want me as a lover. Fine. But someone will. When that time comes, I want to feel as sexy and confident as I can. Until then, I can enjoy my gift for myself.

"Tessa!"

I bite back a sigh and glance over my shoulder as a young man darts out of the lobby.

"Hi, Thomas."

Thomas bounds up to me. With his shaggy brown hair and lanky build, he is the epitome of what I imagine a college boy from California to be. He's here on a summer study abroad program, a detail I learned when I ran into him in the lobby his first week here. Since then, every time he sees me, he peppers me with questions about my life in Greece, what it was like to live in Ireland before that, my favorite things to do in Paris. It would be endearing if I hadn't glimpsed the interest in his eyes or turned him down four times to "just grab coffee."

Even if I wasn't married, the kid is easily seven to eight years younger than me. I have zero interest in being some college student's French fling.

"Let me get the door for you."

He holds open one of the glass doors to our apartment building. I nod my thanks as I maneuver inside. Accepting people's offers for help during my first couple of months in Paris took some getting used to. My mother had maintained almost exclusive control over my wheelchair whenever we were outside the house, meaning I never had the chance to see those offers of support. I'd mostly used my crutches in the privacy of my own room, as my mother claimed it made her nervous I could fall again. Moving around the City of Lights on my own had been freeing but also challenging at times. The assistance given to me by random strangers helps me stay independent.

"Can I carry your bag for you?"

"No, thanks." I smile at Thomas over my shoulder as I head toward the elevator. "It was a light shopping day. Thanks, though."

"I don't mind. Really."

Sometimes, though, offers for help can be challenging. I appreciate when people see me struggling and step in to assist. But when someone is acting like Thomas, pushing even after I've clearly said no, it's hard to be polite.

"I know, Thomas. But I'm fine. Really."

I feel a tug on my shoulder. Irritation surges through me as I look back to see Thomas wrapping a hand around the strap of my bag.

"You look exhausted, Tessa. Just let me help."

I start to swing around, but he pulls at the same time I turn. The movement throws me off balance and I stumble, one of my crutches sliding out from under me as my weight shifts to my left leg. I can't stop my cry as a sharp pain shoots up my calf. I twist and manage to lean into my fall, sliding across the tile floor as the contents of my shopping bag fall out.

"Tessa!"

Thomas is at my side, hands reaching for me as I grit my teeth against the pain.

"Thomas, if you touch me, I'm going to bean you with one of my crutches."

He stands back, hands up in the air, eyes wide. "I'm sorry. I'm sorry," he repeats. "I was just trying to help."

I close my eyes, wincing against the pain still circulating through my leg as I slowly sit up. Nothing broken from what I can tell. But God, that's going to leave one heck of a bruise on my hip.

"I know, Thomas." I sit there on the floor, catching my

breath as I force myself to relax, to get my body back under control. "But next time someone tells you they don't need help, listen."

"I just—"

"Wanted to help," I echo wearily. "I know. And I declined your first offer. Why did you keep pushing when I said no?"

I open my eyes to see Thomas staring down at me, a mixture of regret and confusion on his face.

"I…" He blinks at me. "I just…"

"I know," I say gently. "Thomas, I really appreciate you offering to help. I do. Sometimes I need it. But if I say no, can you please listen to me next time?"

He stands there, looking absolutely miserable, as I slowly maneuver myself into a kneeling position. I reach down and grab my errant crutch, silently cursing as I look at my morning's shopping strewn across the floor.

"I can…" He pauses, looking around at the mess. "I'd like to help you clean this up. Please?"

"Thank you." I hiss out a breath and stay on my knees, waiting for the pain to subside. "That would be helpful."

Thomas darts around the lobby, picking up bread and cheese, a somehow unbroken jar of stone fruit compote, a bunch of herb leaves, and…

I sigh as Thomas picks up a scrap of red material off the floor.

"Is this yours…"

His voice trails off as the material unfolds, revealing a barely there nightie made of scarlet lace. It's a pointless piece of clothing, one I certainly hadn't expected to find in the stalls of the Marché. But when I saw it, I imagined myself in it, the lace barely covering my breasts as I watched Rafe move toward the bed, his eyes devouring me as he slowly stripped off his shirt to reveal a muscled chest.

That's a much more pleasant image than the sight of

Thomas holding up the nightie with a slightly scandalized expression on his face in the middle of our apartment lobby.

"Thomas—"

The door to the lobby swings open as I stand back up. A shadow fills the doorway, the face obscured. It doesn't matter. Whether it's his broad shoulders or his scent or just his sheer presence, I know exactly who it is.

Great. Fantastic. Could this morning get any better?

"What's going on here?"

I wince as Rafe's voice cracks through the lobby like a whip. Thomas grips the nightie as he whirls to face Rafe.

"Who are you?"

I bite down on my lip as a very inappropriate giggle builds in my throat at the sight of Thomas squaring off against Rafe. The two are similar in height. But Thomas lacks Rafe's sheer presence, the confidence that rolls off him as Rafe pinpoints him with an icy gaze.

"Thomas, it's okay."

Thomas shifts to stand between me and Rafe. It would be sweet if the whole situation weren't so absurd, like watching a gazelle stare down a furious lion.

"You know him?"

"I'm her husband."

I see Thomas's shoulders fall. Guilt intrudes. It's ridiculous, I know. I've never once led the boy on. But I still feel bad as he turns to look back at me with a crestfallen expression.

"You're married?"

I raise my chin, determined to keep at least some semblance of my dignity intact despite this whole mess.

"I am."

Thomas's eyes flicker down to my left hand.

"You're not wearing a ring."

"She just told you she's married." Rafe stalks toward

Thomas. Before I can open my mouth, he rips the nightie out of Thomas's hands. "Stay away from her."

"Rafe!"

He ignores me, advancing toward Thomas so that he has nowhere to go but backward until he slams into a wall.

"If you ever come near my wife again, I will track you down and make your life a living hell."

My jaw drops. Thomas stutters out some inane reply before dumping my groceries on a sideboard table and making a beeline for the stairs. He avoids even looking in my direction as he takes the steps two at a time.

Silence falls. Seething, I navigate over to the table and balance with my hip so that I can repack my bag. I grit my teeth against the pain still pulsing in my leg.

"Why are you here? Again?" I snap as I shove the greens inside.

"To talk with you about your proposal."

His matter-of-fact tone grates over my nerves even as his words make my breath catch.

God, get it together, Tessa.

"You didn't have to be so mean."

"It doesn't take a genius to figure out what happened here." His voice is just over my shoulder now and, despite my irritation, awareness slides down my spine. "That boy has a crush on you."

"Yes, he does."

"He didn't know you were married."

Accusation sharpens his words. I shove aside a niggle of guilt. I have nothing to feel guilty about.

"No one I've met in Paris knows I'm married." I brace, then hold up my left hand, waggling my fingers before refocusing on shoving food back into my bag. "It's easier that way."

"Easier for who?"

"For me," I shoot back.

The lobby goes quiet again, save for the rustle of produce and the tiny grunt that escapes my lips as my leg spasms again.

"You fell."

I tense. Then, finally, "Yes."

"Did he cause you to fall?"

"Rafe—"

He appears at my elbow, not close enough to disrupt what I'm doing, but close enough that every cell in my body responds to his proximity. To the memory of what occurred between us last night.

"I asked you a question, Tessa."

My head whips around and I stare up at him.

"I heard you, Rafe. Don't talk down to me because your ego's bruised for some obscure reason. Yes, Thomas caused me to fall. No, you can't kill him and bury him in a quarry somewhere. Yes, I'm in pain. Thank you for asking." I reach out and wrap my fingers around the nightie still clutched in his hand. "And that's mine."

The bastard doesn't relinquish his hold. No, he arches a brow and stares down at me, indiscernible emotion flickering in his eyes.

"Who did you buy it for?"

My thighs clench. I steady myself as I toss back my head and meet his gaze head-on.

"Me."

His eyes darken. The air between us charges with electricity. My breathing grows ragged as he leans down slightly. God, is he going to kiss me?

"We need to talk."

His voice is still measured, controlled. But the underlying huskiness sinks into my skin as warmth pools between my thighs.

"Okay."

"Not here."

I look away first, not wanting him to see how much I'm feeling right now. How much I'm desiring him. "Where?"

"Come with me and find out."

I swallow hard. It's hard for me to picture Rafe inviting me back to his hotel or some other location with a bed just so he can divest me of my virginity and send me on my way. Although at the same time, I think with a tiny smirk, he's known for his efficiency.

No, the most likely scenario is that he wants to talk through terms and conditions. Negotiate in a setting where he's in control. I'd prefer the comfort of my apartment. But I'm also learning when to pick my battles, when to push and when to accept that things might need to go a different way.

"All right. Let me put my groceries up and get my wheel-chair."

"You still use it?"

I nod. "Some days are good for crutches. Others aren't, especially if I'm tired or hurting. Or if I might be moving around for a long time."

"I'm coming up with you."

I narrow my eyes. "You think so?"

"Yes." His gaze darts to the stairs where Thomas vanished moments ago. "Just in case."

I roll my eyes. "Well, you can take the stairs and meet me up there. The elevator won't fit both of us."

I turn away from him and move toward the elevator. *Elevator* is a generous term, given that it can barely fit two people. But the elevator is what made me living in this building possible. It's slow and occasionally makes a grinding noise that has me questioning if it's going to just randomly stall and strand me between floors.

Yet I love it. I love everything about this building, from

the old marble floors to the wrought-iron railing, all the way down to the quirky foreign exchange students.

The elevator door slides open. I move into the tiny compartment and turn around to see Rafe standing just beyond the threshold, his expression hard.

"You think I'm overreacting."

"Yes."

"He knocked you down."

"He did."

I want to tell him how much it means to me that he cares, that he wants to protect me. But I also can't stand back and let others fight my battles for me anymore. I did that for years. I'm not going to slip back into old patterns.

"Rafe," I say gently, "it was an accident."

"Just because it was an accident doesn't mean he gets a free pass."

I sigh, caught between agreeing with him and not wanting to see Thomas penalized for what happened.

"Yes, he made a mistake. Had he been dismissive about it, or cruel or careless, I would agree with you." I put my hand up to stop the door from closing. "But he wasn't, Rafe. He was apologetic and, before you showed up, I think he truly realized what he had done. People make mistakes, but they can also fix them."

His glower deepens.

"Perhaps. But people can also simply be people. They can fail."

CHAPTER SIX

Tessa

THE ELEVATOR DOORS CLOSE. The car rises, so slowly and with an occasional grinding noise that makes my jaw tense. Exhaustion from the whirlwind of the last five minutes has me leaning against the wall for support. After what feels like an eternity, the elevator finally reaches the top floor. The doors slide open to reveal Rafe leaning casually against the doorway, the lingerie thankfully out of sight. Maybe he threw it in the trash. I'm too tired to care right now.

I move past him, keeping my eyes focused on my door and off my husband's dark, brooding handsomeness.

"Did you take the stairs two at a time?"

"I should have waited at the bottom in case it crashed."

"It's not the Ritz," I shoot back over my shoulder, "but it's functional."

I jam the key into the lock and twist. The door swings open and I walk into my own version of paradise.

Ever since I first walked into what the Realtor called "the apartment under the eaves," I knew a sense of calm I had never experienced before. From the white crown molding and tan wood floors, to the small fireplace with a mirror hung above it and the huge windows with dormers that looked out over the city, it was love at first sight. Every morning, I'm treated to a view of Paris's rooftops dusted with the rose gold of sunrise. All I have to do is glance out my living room window to see the Eiffel Tower. The tiny balcony off the bedroom I've converted into my office is just big enough for a tiny table and chair. My bedroom used to be a linen closet long ago, the bed extending out of a wall made up of numerous shelves. The entire apartment is half the size of my bedroom back in Santorini.

I love every square inch of it.

I move into the small kitchen and set my bag on the counter, conscious of my husband glancing around my space as I put groceries away. Evaluating, analyzing, assessing. He can look all he wants. I know it's not the luxury he's grown up in all his life. I doubt he'll understand the value of my surroundings, the peace it's brought me even as I've adapted to a different style of living.

I brace myself against the counter and pull the bag holding my wheelchair out of the closet.

"May I carry that for you?"

I stiffen. After my experience with Thomas and the lobby, my nerves are stretched tight. But I also know if it were anyone else offering, I would accept it.

"Thank you."

I hand him the bag. Surprise passes over his face. "It's light."

"Thirteen pounds and foldable." I grab my crutches and head for the door. "Much better than that massive thing my mother used to push me around in."

"Wait."

I glance back over my shoulder, confused by the sudden intensity on his face. "What?"

"Where's your wedding ring?"

My stomach drops. I yanked the ring off in the taxi on the way to the airport the night of our wedding and shoved it into a spare makeup bag I'd had tucked in my purse. I hadn't put it back on since, couldn't even bear to look at what I'd once seen as a symbol of possibility. Of love conquering all odds.

"In my purse," I finally say with a nod to the black bag hanging from a hook by the door.

"Bring it."

My fingers tighten around my handgrips. "I'm not wearing it."

"Not yet."

A different tension builds between us as we face off.

"Why is it so important to you?" I finally ask.

He moves toward me, each step ratcheting up my heart rate until it's pounding so hard I wonder if he can hear it in the quiet of my apartment.

"You're my wife."

"For now."

His eyes harden into shards of blue ice. "For now," he repeats. "If I'm even going to entertain the possibility of your proposal, you will wear the ring."

I want nothing more than to walk to my balcony and throw that ring as far as I can. An urge, I acknowledge with no small degree of irritation, that would only shoot myself in the foot.

"I'll put it on if we reach a mutual agreement."

"Done."

He grabs the purse and offers it to me. Grudgingly, I take it. He reaches around me and opens the door, his eyes never leaving mine. I'm the first one to blink, the first one to look away. Foreboding whispers across the back of my neck as I make my way out into the hallway. An apprehension that I've just agreed to something that will be harder to walk away from than I can comprehend.

The car ride is short and silent. I frown as we pull up outside the glass pyramid in front of the Louvre.

"We're negotiating here?"

"I reserved the Denon Wing for an hour."

My jaw drops. "You did what?"

He stares at me for a moment before getting out of the car. I watch in stupefied silence as he gets my wheelchair out of the trunk and unfolds it before opening my door and extending a hand. I want to take it, which is why I don't and instead shift myself from the car into the wheelchair.

We enter the museum and are quickly whisked past world-renowned paintings and sculptures to the Denon Wing, an ornate hall that plays host to crown jewels, sculptures by Michelangelo, and a trove of Da Vinci paintings. Our guide speaks quietly with Rafe before heading back toward the reception desk.

Leaving us alone among priceless works of art.

"Did you do this just to prove how much money you have?"

Rafe's lips twist into a cold smirk. "No."

I whisper the word *liar* in my head instead of saying it to his face. I don't think for one second he did this out of the kindness of his heart. But I can't help but feel awed by the art surrounding us. I'm surprised, too, how intimate it feels to be viewing works like a famous Greek statue or a Rembrandt painting without anyone else in the wing.

Rafe seems content to let me set the pace. I take my time, making use of the lack of other guests and plenty of room to stare at oil paintings, ancient statues and other incredible works.

It's not until we're in the domed room that houses the infamous Mona Lisa that he speaks again.

"Why Paris?" he asks quietly.

I stare at the iconic painting, the hint of a smile, the cool confidence in the eyes. My mind is racing nearly as fast as my heart. I don't know why he's asking these questions. Why he's acting like he cares now.

"Haven't you heard? Everyone wants to go to Paris."

I swear I can feel the warmth of his body on my back, as if he's standing just a breath behind me.

"Why did you come here?"

After you fled our wedding.

He doesn't say the words out loud. But they're there, a phantom hovering between us. I hinted at my reasons last night. I don't want to share. But I also have a feeling that if I don't give him something, he'll go back to Greece and fight me every step of the way on our divorce.

"Last year, Katie came back from her first semester at the Sorbonne. She talked about Paris so much I found myself yearning for a place I'd never seen." Even now I can see her at Christmas as we'd unwrapped our gifts, describing the little store in a street market in Le Vésinet, eyes glowing as she'd talked a mile a minute. "I wanted to go by myself. But every time I would bring it up, my mother would tear up or just cry until I told her I wouldn't go."

"She controlled you."

I blew out a harsh breath. "Yes. I don't know how much was about control and how much was about fear that I would fall again. Metaphorically speaking," I add with a slight smile, trying to take the edge off the dark turn in our conversation.

"Does it matter when the end result is the same?"

There's something in his voice that tells me he, too, has been at the mercy of someone else's erratic emotions before. Probably his father. A man who made my mother look like a saint.

"I finally stopped bringing it up. Katie tried to whenever she would call, but I told her to stop, too, because it just made things worse. But the desire was still there.

"The day we got married, I realized I had said yes for the wrong reasons. I was angry at my parents, especially my mother, for being so overly protective to the point that she was controlling my life. It was a miracle that she didn't try to dissuade me from marrying you." I sigh. "I'm sorry, Rafe."

He arches one dark brow. "Sorry?"

"I used you."

"One could argue I did the same to you. Proposing marriage to get your father to finally agree to a merger my father had been trying to talk him into for nearly twenty years."

"Yes, but you were upfront with me about your reasons. I wasn't."

"Is that why you left?" he asks as he closes the distance between us and crouches down, much as he did that night at his family's villa when I saw him as his own person instead of Gavriil's older brother. "Out of guilt?"

I start to tell him what I overheard, the horrible words that stripped away any last remaining hope.

But what's the point? What will it change?

"Yes. That and the need to have my own life, one I built myself."

His eyes crinkle slightly as he gives me a crooked smile. "How did you do it?"

My eyes drift down to his mouth before I can stop myself. "What?"

"How did you leave the island?"

"Oh." My tongue darts out and I wet my lips. "Your housekeeper, Sybil, arranged for a boat back to Santorini. I bought a ticket to Paris and called Katie on my way to the airport. She was staying with my parents for the wedding."

I'd always loved my sister. But that night, as I'd sat in the back of the taxi and sobbed out my story, a new bond had formed between us. She'd listened to me for a solid five minutes before she'd cut me off to ask where I was. When she learned I was en route to the airport, that I was actually following through with my dream of going to Paris, she'd told me to give her fifteen minutes. She'd called me back in ten with a suitcase in the back of a taxi. She held my hand as the plane lifted off and Santorini faded from view, a light-strewn speck against the black blanket of the sea at night.

"And now you're here."

"And now I'm here."

"Why did you ask me to be your first lover?"

The impact of his question hits me out of nowhere, so blunt and unexpected that I answer without thinking.

"Because I know you. I've known you for years. You're also, conveniently, my husband." I hesitate, wondering if I should voice the rest, then decide to throw caution to the wind and just go with blunt honesty. "I know you never really saw yourself getting married or having kids. But I want a family of my own one day. In order to achieve that, I'll have to date and…"

My voice trails off. This is awkward, telling my husband that one day I plan on sleeping with someone else.

"I know how babies are made, Tessa."

His dry tone erases my guilt.

"I've never dated. Our kiss on our wedding day was my first and only kiss."

His eyes widen. "What?"

"Don't pity me." I hold up a hand. "Please. Unless I count your brother—"

"What?"

I lean away from the harsh change in his tone.

"What? Gavriil kissed me when I was nine years old—"

"Which would have made him twelve," Rafe snaps as he moves to the other side of the room, "old enough to know better."

I roll my eyes. "Can you focus, please? He was a kid. It was a dare. It lasted less than a second. My point is I have no experience and absolutely no confidence in my ability to date, let alone find someone I can spend the rest of my life with. I know some people are going to be put off by my mobility—"

"Those people aren't worth your time."

"No," I agree, touched by his defense, "but it doesn't make it any less hurtful. If I have experience with sex, if I'm introduced to it by someone I know and trust, it will give me more confidence when I start dating. It might help me find the person I want to spend my life with."

The words roll off my tongue, bitter and cold. Less than a year ago, I wanted Rafe to be that person. Heck, just a couple months ago, I still wanted it to be him. It wasn't until the wedding I finally accepted that wasn't going to happen.

I sigh. "Look, Rafe, I—"

"I accept your proposal."

It takes a moment for his words to sink in. When they do, all I can manage is blank stare.

"I… Is this a joke?"

"No."

I frown. "Is this you being impulsive? Because last night you told me—"

"My knee-jerk reaction was impulsive." The way he says the word sends a delicious shiver down my spine. "It surprised me. But on further reflection, I made an updated and more practical decision. You get what you want, I get what I want, and we both receive mutual pleasure as a bonus."

I can't help it. I lean back into my chair and laugh.

"I'm sorry," I say as he stares at me. "Only you could turn something like sex into something so…businesslike and efficient."

He smiles. Truly smiles. One that makes the sharp contours of his cheekbones even more prominent as his teeth flash white against tan skin.

Did I think I could keep my emotional distance? Because if just a smile makes me feel this breathless as it sparks a heavy, tingling sensation between my thighs, I can only imagine what actual sex might do to me.

"Applying business principles to sex is actually an excellent idea."

"I'll have to take your word for it."

His chuckle rolls through me, a deep sound that reverberates through my body and settles in my core. My breath catches as he crouches down in front of me.

"Think about it, Tessa. If I were to simply kiss you here," he says as he leans forward and lays a finger on my mouth for a second, the warmth of his skin pressing against my lips, "as I did on our wedding day, it might give you a moment of passing pleasure.

"But," he continues as he moves his finger from my mouth and traces a slow, teasing path down the side of my neck, "if I kiss you here, taking my time, paying attention to every gasp, every little movement you make, it will be far more pleasurable for both of us."

I sway toward him even as panic slivers into the desire pumping through me. When I had this mad thought less than a day ago, I knew I was attracted to Rafe. He's the only man I've ever had a sexual fantasy about. It's not like there were many candidates to choose from. It's hard to fantasize about men who barely glance at you, and Gavriil has always been a friend, the brother I never had.

Yet even in my daydreams, there was the safety of inexperience. Of innocence sugarcoating what I imagined sex would be like.

Reality check: it's nothing, absolutely nothing, compared to the flames slowly burning inside me.

"How do we proceed?"

Is that my voice? Breathless, almost sultry?

"There's eight months left until our anniversary."

The spell he wove is broken as he slips back into the Rafe I know, his voice level, his face smooth. It doesn't matter. Now that I know what truly lurks beneath the surface, I'll never be able to look at him the same way again.

"I'm aware."

"I have numerous demands on my time. Given the nature of our agreement," he says with the hint of a smile on that last word, "I think it best if you accompany me to Corfu for the next few weeks."

Desire flees, replaced by a tightness that threatens to strangle me. My breathing quickens as I fight to stay composed.

"Tessa?"

"I'm fine," I lie. "I'm just very busy myself. I'm doing professional renderings for Juliette's house, and one of the new clients I'm working with wants to move fast on the programming phase."

He cocks his head to one side. "I'm unfamiliar with interior design. You could tell me about the phases you work through on our flight to Greece."

Warmth blooms in my chest at the fact that he has even a cursory interest in my work. My father never bothered to ask, and my mother only looked at my work long enough to say "That's beautiful, dear," before turning the conversation to something else.

But going back to Greece... I swore I wouldn't step foot there for at least a year, if not longer. Greece holds nothing for me right now except painful memories.

"In the interest of efficiency, we could just go back to my apartment," I half joke.

His eyes heat as his expression intensifies.

"Efficiency is important. But it's not my primary focus when it comes to this arrangement."

God help me.

His eyes sharpen as he watches me. "Is there a reason you don't want to go back to Greece?"

I look away. "Paris has become home to me. I can't imagine waking up and not seeing all of this."

What I don't say is that Greece represents everything I want to leave behind me. And the man in front of me is a huge part of that.

Doubt creeps in. Should I just tell him I'll wait eight months? That he can go back to Greece without me and I won't pursue the divorce until after our anniversary?

No. I asked for this, and by some miracle, Rafe is agreeing. He wants me to go with him to Corfu, not Santorini. I won't be running into my parents there. With the stages I'm in for my two primary projects, I can work almost anywhere. I'll miss my cozy studio with its postage stamp of a balcony. But it'll be waiting for me when I come back. As will the rest of Paris.

"No. No reason." I smile. "Where do I sign?"

He offers me his hand. I'm catapulted back to another time and place, one where Rafe's earthy, smoky scent wrapped around me with an intimacy I'd never experienced. A night when I pitched headfirst into love.

Resolve hardens in my veins. I remind myself of all the reasons why loving Rafe was a bad idea. Of why a marriage between us will never last. I use them as a shield against any wayward emotions and instead focus on the growing sensations of desire. The blood flowing through my veins, the heaviness of my breasts, the crackle of awareness across my skin.

When I accept his hand, I concentrate on the physical feelings, savor them as his fingers wrap around mine.

"May I help you stand?"

Shock renders me speechless. I blink up at him, surprised and touched that he's asking. Confused by this display of feeling. Empowered that, unlike Thomas, he's giving me a choice.

I nod. I secure my chair and then hold out my other hand.

My tongue grows thick in my mouth as I give him instructions. "It's best if I put my arms around your neck."

He leans down, his eyes focused on mine. I slide my arms around him, the movement bringing our faces within inches of each other. He pulls me up in one fluid motion. One hand settles on my back while his other arm encircles my waist and pulls me flush against his body.

His tall, lean, hard body.

"Given the unique nature of our contract, I suggest a kiss to seal the deal."

I glance around the gallery. "What if someone comes back—"

"They won't."

He speaks with such casual dominance that I can't do anything more than nod. His eyes stay locked on me, the unbroken contact almost more intimate than the feel of my breasts pressed against his chest.

And then his lips cover mine. Warm, firm, a kiss that fills me as I lean into his embrace, my hands gripping his shoulders as I surrender myself to his touch. It's intense yet tender, teasing and light.

It's perfect.

I sigh, my lips parting slightly beneath his. His muscles tense beneath my hands.

And then his mouth opens. I gasp as his tongue teases the seam of my lips. He takes advantage and grazes his teeth across my lower lip. Sensation shoots through my body, leaving my nipples hard and my lower belly tight as I arch against him, feel his hardness pressed against my thighs. The world fades. Everything fades as I grip his shoulders, hanging on to him for dear life as my body responds to our mutual desire.

Finally, he breaks the kiss, slowly easing me down in my chair. I sit there, my mind whirling. It's been just under twenty-four hours since Rafe walked back into my life. In one day I've gone from thinking I would be divorced in a matter of months to proposing a business arrangement that revolves around my husband introducing me to sex so he can inherit a multibillion-dollar company from his depraved and deceased father.

It sounds impossible. But so did my moving to Paris. Living on my own. Starting up my own business. Judging by how incredible our first real kiss just was, our agreement is going to exceed my wildest expectations.

So long as I can keep my heart locked up tight.

Rafe walks behind my chair. I know what he's pulling out of the small pocket on the back. He circles back around, my purse in hand.

"The ring."

I stare at the purse for a long moment. Then, slowly, I extend my hand. I pull out the little black makeup bag and unzip it. Diamonds set into the silver band glitter up at me. Rafe holds out his hand. I avoid his eyes as I set it in his palm.

He kneels in front of me. Tension wraps around my head and squeezes, pressing in on my temples as a burning sensation builds behind my eyes. There's absolutely nothing romantic about what he's doing. It's merely a formality, a stipulation of a contract.

I tell myself this over and over again as he takes my hand in his and slides the ring onto my finger.

It doesn't stop the ache.

"I'll take you back to your apartment to pack."

Rafe thankfully turns the conversation to my company as we move back down the hall, asking questions about the process of redesigning a room versus a house, how I work with clients requesting changes for accessibility. It relaxes me enough to make the ride home bearable.

But it's not until he drops me off at my apartment and I close the door behind him that I'm finally able to step back from the emotional cliff he dragged me to. A cliff I nearly allowed myself to slip over once more.

Hesitation nearly makes me speak. But I stop myself. I want this. Want it for myself, for my future.

I move to my balcony. Sadness seeps in as I look out over Paris one last time, knowing tomorrow my view will not be of terra-cotta chimneys and lattice balconies, but of an impossibly blue sea and thick-branched olive trees standing guard on rocky cliffs.

But beneath the sadness is a restless excitement. I know Rafe can't offer me anything beyond this. We are destined to live separate lives. But right now, he wants me, too. And I intend to take everything he's offering.

CHAPTER SEVEN

Rafe

I WATCH TESSA out of the corner of my eye as I walk her through the massive living space on the first floor of my villa in Corfu. Since we left Paris, with a quick stop by her apartment for her to pack, her tension has noticeably increased.

Her smile slipped as we boarded the private plane at Charles de Gaulle. Her hands gripped the armrests of her seat as we took off. My few attempts to engage her in conversation about her business fell short as she murmured half answers and kept her gaze on the window. When my pilot announced that we were getting ready to descend into Corfu, her lips thinned into a line. Her expression didn't alter on the limo ride through Corfu, even as we passed elegant Venetian mansions with soaring arched windows and the long, pillared portico of the Palace of St. Michael.

Even now, as she glances around the luxurious surroundings of what will be her new home for at least a couple weeks, she looks trapped. Hunted.

I don't regret many things. Regret has no place in business. It is one of the few, perhaps the only, useful lesson Lucifer taught me. As I watch Tessa's eyes dart around the room, as if she's seeking an escape, she reminds me of a frightened animal about to leap away.

When I envisioned our arrangement, I pictured taking my

time, introducing her to the pleasures of sex while I dictated the direction of our affair. It gave me an opportunity to wrestle back some of the control she'd taken from me by negotiating such an incredible clause.

Yet seeing her like this, I realize I underestimated the impact it would have on her. I don't fully understand her reasons for hating it so much. But I don't need to. Her reasons are her own. Just like when I make a decision, I don't owe anyone an explanation. Being CEO means I get to make the decisions.

"I can have the plane take you back to Paris."

She whips her head around. "No." She exhales slowly. "Honestly, this is good for me."

"It doesn't look good."

Her laugh sounds forced. "Probably not. But I can't go my whole life avoiding the fact that I spent almost my entire existence here."

I know the sensation she's describing. It's the same one I experienced the day Lucifer's secretary called to let me know he had passed. Except unlike Tessa, I have yet to find a purpose in that freedom. Perhaps it's too late for me. Forty-one years is a very long time.

She turns to face me then. Her face is determined, her breathing more even.

"I will make this work."

I'm struck by the stark difference between the woman in front of me now and the young woman I knew before our wedding. The one who watched the world go by with a sad hunger that pulled at me, tempted me to reach out when no one else had come close to making me feel anything.

But the woman my wife has become doesn't need me to seek her out and keep her company. She's thriving on her own. A notion that stirs both admiration and that distant sense of loss.

"I trust you'll inform me if you start to feel differently."

At her nod, I move toward the hallway. "I'll show you to your rooms."

I take her on a tour of the villa, pointing out features like the massive kitchen, the library, the terrace with the infinity pool that looks out over the sea. As a child, I despised Lucifer's grandiose spending. But as we move through massive doorways and utilize one of several elevators, I'm grateful for it. As I watch Tessa out of the corner of my eye, I get a small glimpse of the world she's grown up in. One she's now trying to change through her work.

A small smile tugs at my lips. I already knew her to be a kind woman. But knowing she's resilient, determined, and is using that kindness to benefit others stirs a deep pride. One I've never felt for anyone or anything in my life.

We continue down the hall toward the eastern end of the villa, stopping in front of a pair of white doors.

"Welcome."

Her eyes widen as I open the doors. White walls gleam against the contrast of a slatted wood ceiling with exposed beams. A four-poster bed sits against one wall, angled toward double glass doors on the other side of the room that open out to a private balcony with a soaking tub and stunning views of the sea. A bright blue fainting couch sits in an alcove on the far side of the room with a bay of windows behind it and views of the olive groves.

"It's beautiful."

"Coming from an interior designer, I consider that an especially high compliment."

She flashes a smile at me. "You're welcome." She moves into the room, navigating her wheelchair with ease. "Where is your room?" The words are barely out of her mouth before a blush stains her cheeks.

"I stay on the second floor. There's an elevator at the end of this hall if you're using your wheelchair."

She frowns. "Is the master suite not on the bottom floor?"

Old anger surges in my chest, then abates just as quickly. "It is. I utilize an office space."

"Why?"

Irritated, I moved toward the doors. "Because I do."

Instead of backing down as I would have expected her to, Tessa turns and moves closer, following me.

"I remember seeing pictures of this place when your father first bought it. Right before…" Her voice trails off.

"Right before he was kicked out of his own company for threatening an old woman and nearly stealing her home from her." My smile is cold and humorless. "Your point is?"

I know that I'm being abrupt. Even a touch cruel. Despite officially holding the title of wife, however, Tessa does not need to, nor have the right to, know the intimate details of my life.

She tilts her head to one side, watching me, as if trying to decide just how far to push me on this. At last, she looks away with a shrug.

"It's none of my business."

"No. It's not."

Her head whips around, her eyes widening for a moment before a shutter drops down over her face. I blink. This is how she looked last night in Paris when she first saw me. Distant. Removed.

"Well, I'm sure you have things to attend to. Thank you for the tour."

She's dismissing me. Me. I open my mouth to argue, then realize it would only be sabotaging myself. I have an opportunity to exit with no more conversation on a subject that is best left closed.

I incline my head to her.

"Dinner is at seven in the main dining room."

I turn and walk out. I have plenty of work to focus on.

Tasks that need my attention. But as the afternoon progresses, I find myself returning time and again to our exchange. To how quickly I dismissed what should have been a simple question, one that makes even more sense when I take her profession into account. I responded from a place of emotion. I find it odd that after years of suppressing, of existing in a space of neutrality, that Lucifer's death would shake my ability to stay calm and controlled. Something I will need to examine at a later date as I wrestle myself back under control.

A couple hours later, I closed my laptop and stand. I've accomplished a lot. But my focus has been off, drifting on more than one occasion to the woman just one floor down. When I proposed her coming back with me to Greece, I had assumed it would be easy to do the work I needed to during the day and focus my attention on Tessa at night. Instead, thoughts of her plagued me through conference calls, reviewing reports and drafting up several letters of correspondence.

Tomorrow, I decide as I walked through the villa, I'll go to our office in the city center. Physical distance will be useful. Tonight, though, I plan on continuing what we started when we sealed our contract with a kiss.

Tessa is waiting for me in the dining room. There's an odd tightening in my chest at the sight of her sitting there, and how right she looks there. For once, the room doesn't feel like a prison. I sat at that table for far too many events when Lucifer still ran Drakos Development, sometimes with an iron fist, other times with a lackadaisical attitude as he pursued his latest desire, from women to properties to vacations.

When I do finally inherit, I intend to sell all of the properties Lucifer left me. I have no interest in residing in the spaces he lived in, utilized for his years of debauchery and cruelty.

Yet to stay somewhere else feels like a surrender, as if I'm acknowledging his memory affects me to any extent.

"Good evening."

She looks up at me and smiles. "Hi."

I sit down next to her. "How was your day?"

She blinks, as if surprised by my question.

"Good. Progress on Juliette's house. And," she says with a proud smile, "I made headway on another new client proposal." Her face falls when she sees my frown. "What?"

"Didn't you say that you already had a client you were working with after Juliette?"

"Yes, and I actually just got another referral."

I frown. "How are you going to manage that by yourself?"

Some of her excitement dims. I've never regretted telling anyone exactly what they need to hear. But as doubt creeps into her eyes, I mentally chide myself for not stopping and crafting a better response.

"I won't be taking on any more. But this client…" Her voice trails off. "She's the reason why I wanted to start my own firm."

"What do you mean?"

She hesitates, then pulls her phone out of her pocket. "I love designing. Sometimes it's a simple change or upgrade. Other times it's a complete overhaul." She taps something on her screen. "And sometimes, it might be the first time someone gets a home that's truly made for them and their abilities."

She hands me the phone. I swipe through the photos. An old, rambling farmhouse that looks to be one step away from disaster, with steep stairs, a slight pitch to the floor and a sagging roof. I know nothing about design. But from what little I can see, it should be condemned, not redesigned.

I say as much as I hand the phone back to her.

"It's been in her family for generations." She smiles as she looks down at her phone. "Just outside of a village in southeastern France."

"Given the state of the house, I'm surprised your client has the funds to fix this."

"She received a grant." Tessa doesn't meet my eyes. "There's also a charity that's providing some support."

A suspicion forms in my mind as I stare at her. "Tessa."

"Don't." She looks at me then, her face hard even as her heart shines in her eyes. "This is a big part of what I want to do with my company, Rafe. To help people."

"An admirable goal. But you also have to think about it from a business perspective. Maybe hire some help instead of giving away your services for nothing."

"With what I earned on that Paris apartment and what I will earn from Juliette's house and the penthouse in London, I have plenty."

"But you can't run a business on charity."

Her lips thin. "I don't expect you to understand."

Her words deliver an unexpected blow. It shouldn't matter. She's behaving foolishly, leading with her heart instead of the numbers she's no doubt ignoring. But, I remind myself, she's an adult. Capable of making her own decisions and, judging by the way she's refusing to meet my eyes, more than aware that she's making poor choices.

Perhaps another opportunity will come up in the coming weeks to discuss. To steer her toward efficiency and practicality rather than trying to save the world. She won't like it, but I'll also be including a generous settlement in her account when our divorce is finalized. The account I know she still hasn't touched. Another thing that shouldn't bother me. How Tessa chooses to fund her life is none of my concern.

"Have you thought about redecorating the villa?"

Her question catches me off guard. "Excuse me?"

"The villa," she continues, as if she hasn't heard my voice's sudden drop in temperature. "It's a beautiful structure. With the right upgrades and renovations, it could really be—"

"Once I receive my inheritance, including this villa, it will go on the market as is."

Her eyes widen. "Why? You could do so much with it—"

"I have no interest in doing anything with it other than turning a profit."

Her eyes narrow. "Is that all you ever think about? How much money you can make?"

"It's the only thing I know or care to know."

I can feel her disappointment. I dismiss it, telling myself it doesn't matter.

"There's more to life than money."

"And there are plenty of villas I can purchase with the money I earn."

"Is it because your father—"

"Don't."

I don't bother to soften my order with a smile or some other nicety. Tonight appears to be about setting boundaries. Clearly defined ones so we don't have this issue again. I mentally step into the void, that place where nothing exists except me. A place where I have total control. Where no one can reach me, including her.

"The subject of Lucifer is off-limits to everyone, and that includes you, arrangement or no. Are we clear?"

She stares at me for so long I wonder if she's going to say anything. Then, at last, she closes her portfolio and puts it in her lap.

"Crystal."

She wheels back from the table, turns and leaves the room. I sit there, staring down the length of the table. The room seems a touch darker, memories of the past surging in the shadows to fill the emptiness left by my wife.

My butler, James, appears with a bottle of wine and two glasses.

"Is Mrs. Drakos not joining us, sir?"

"No." I keep my eyes away from the door that Tessa just left through. "Tired from traveling. I'm dining alone."

He nods his head and sets one glass on the table. I watch the ruby red liquid splash inside. Focus on the details instead of the emotions until they're quiet enough for me to push them back down where they belong.

I remember creating the void as a child. I couldn't have been more than five or six. I remember stepping into it for the first time after one of Lucifer's screaming matches that left my mother in tears and me cowering in her embrace.

One of the last times I remember her hugging me before she withdrew from my life. Became a cold wraith that flitted through the villa until one day, she simply left.

The void is what kept me strong all these years, immune to anything and anyone. I utilize it not just for my own sake, but for others', too. People like Gavriil, even if he doesn't know it. The void was the only thing that kept me from breaking, from going to my brother and offering the comfort and support I had wanted to, an action that would have resulted in Lucifer tossing Gavriil back out onto the streets.

People like Tessa, who look at the world with stars in their eyes that blind them to the reality of who people really are inside.

For decades, the void has been unbreachable. But as I pick up my glass of wine, I have to work to dismiss the guilt tugging at me through the walls I usually maintain. Yes, I was harsh. Tessa has never experienced that side of me, not fully anyway, in the years I've known her.

Better for her to learn now, though, before we continue with our agreement. If she truly wants to follow through with our arrangement instead of ending up in a long, drawn-out legal battle, she'll have to accept me and who I am.

With a man like Lucifer for a father, it's only understandable that I have a little bit of the devil in me.

CHAPTER EIGHT

Tessa

I STARE AT my screen, rereading the same email for the fourth time. I've managed to push through most of the day by focusing on work. Juliette's house is a pleasure to work on. I did a video conference with her earlier, including a walk-through of some of the rooms I had questions on. Seeing the spaces and hearing Juliette's enthusiasm for everything I proposed gave me a much-needed boost to my gloomy mood.

The house in France, however, the one for the client I'm essentially doing for free... I'll never admit it to Rafe, but the scope of the project is starting to become clear. And God, it's going to be rough.

When the woman wrote to me sharing how her husband had passed away before he had been able to make the improvements he had promised as old age had stolen her independence, I had resolved to find a way. Yes, on some level, I know Rafe is right. It's foolhardy. I don't even know if the inspection I've ordered will find that the house is savable.

But as I read the inquiry that came through my website, her desperation was evident. "I feel trapped," she'd written. "I'd like to live my remaining years as best I can, but I fear it's too late."

I felt each and every one of those words. And, I think angrily as I exit out of my screen and push back from my desk,

I don't give one wit about Rafe's outlook on business. I can survive without Tessa's Interiors. I started this business because it was something I enjoyed and something I could bring a unique perspective to. I would rather try and fail than make a profit at the expense of people who could use a business like mine the most.

Screw you, Rafe.

He hadn't sought me out last night after I'd left the dining room. Seeing that side of him, the one I'd heard Gavriil talk so much about but had never witnessed in its entirety, had been unsettling. Rafe and I were nowhere near compatible. I must have had a moment of insanity to agree to his proposal.

Not insanity, I correct myself as I shift from my office chair into my wheelchair. Desperation. I roll myself out onto my balcony and look out over the sea. This is one of the few things I've missed living in Paris. Being able to go out and smell the salty air, hear the distant cry of gulls, the lapping of waves on the beach.

Maybe I'll set aside some funds from my next project and schedule a couple trips to some of France's beaches. I haven't been to Normandy or the south. The south is especially appealing given that Katie and I both earned our scuba diving certifications a couple months ago. Maybe when I get back, I can talk her into a girls' trip to celebrate her engagement. She texted me photos yesterday of her proudly wearing the ring.

I didn't tell her where I was, just that I had left for a short trip and promised to tell her everything when I got back. When she pressed for more details, I'd encouraged her to enjoy her engagement and being with a man like Nathan who adored her.

My heart twists my chest. I'm happy for Katie. Truly. She was mostly ignored by my father and barely acknowledged as my mother devoted herself to my care. It's a miracle she doesn't resent me. Although our parents' lack of interest gave her a freedom I never had. A freedom that kept us on friendly terms, but without the kind of deep, fierce love we have now.

I am happy for her. It's just hard to ignore the whisper that I may never experience what she has. And after Rafe's and my disagreement last night, I wouldn't be surprised if he booked his plane to fly me back to Paris before I can experience sex.

At this point, I wouldn't fight him on the terms of the divorce if that happens. I can handle eight months if it means finally being completely free of my past and moving forward. Not just with my life in Paris and my business, but getting out, meeting new people and maybe finding someone who wasn't an arrogant ass.

A knock sounds on my door. I tense. "Come in." James, the butler, enters. I smile at him. "Good evening."

He gives me a slight smile in return. "Good evening, Mrs. Drakos."

I barely manage not to wince at the sound of my married name.

"You're invited to dinner on the rooftop tonight."

"On the rooftop?" I repeat.

"Yes, madam. Mr. Drakos has invited you to join him at eight."

My heart jumps into my throat. Not what I was expecting at all. "Are you sure?"

James gives me another slight smile. "Confident, madam. You two are the only ones here."

"Of course."

I wait until he leaves before going back into my room and moving over to my closet. I assumed I would only be here a couple of weeks and packed light. A few sundresses and some loungewear. I shouldn't want to dress up for the man who so quickly dismissed me yesterday after reminding me that I had absolutely no stake in his life whatsoever.

But I want to look good. Not for him, but for me. So I can

navigate whatever is going to happen with the confidence I've developed over the last few months instead of slipping back into old patterns and letting my insecurities rule me.

I pull out a red sundress Katie convinced me to buy on a shopping trip on the Champs-élysées. I brush out my hair, add a touch of perfume behind my ears, and then pick up a book I've been meaning to read for the past few weeks, a romantic comedy with family drama, ghosts and a star-crossed romance to distract myself.

After an hour, I finally make it through the first chapter, interrupted by constantly glancing at the clock and the door.

Disgusted with myself, I set the book on my nightstand and reach for my crutches. I've spent most of the day in either my office chair or my wheelchair. It'll be good for me to get up and move around.

I also resolve to utilize the impressive personal gym James showed me this morning. One of the reasons why I've been able to shift to utilizing the forearm crutches far more than I ever did at home is because of the incredible physical therapist my doctor in Paris paired me with. I'm not going to lose progress just because I'm distracted by my coldhearted husband.

I make my way to the elevator a few minutes later and merge on the top deck. I stop, confused by the sight before me.

The deck is incredible, a stone terrace edged by plants and strategically placed lighting that make the lush flowers seemingly glow in the dark. One side of the terrace is lined with endless lounges, plump cushions and even plumper pillows offering a place for someone to sit and enjoy the views of the sea, the olive groves and the rooftops of Corfu in the distance.

But it's the table that has me confused. The small table in the middle of the terrace, draped with a white tablecloth and topped with a small bud vase with two red roses and a single candle.

"Good evening."

I turn around. My heart catapults into my throat. Rafe is standing just a few feet behind me. The sleeves of his dark blue dress shirt are rolled up to the elbows revealing tan skin and muscled forearms. His black pants follow the long length of his legs. There's no sign of the coldness, the anger he displayed yesterday. He's regarding me with that half-amused smirk I've seen him sport so much since he walked into the restaurant and upended my life less than forty-eight hours ago.

"Hello."

He gestures to the table. "Shall we?"

I stay where I am.

"I hope you can understand my confusion."

He nods. "While I stand by my words, my reaction was strong yesterday. Consider this a peace offering."

I notice what's missing: the actual apology for his overreaction. But I also recognize that he's offering me something he probably doesn't to most people: a truce. If this were an actual marriage, I would call him out on his lack of remorse. But it's not. As he made perfectly clear yesterday, this is a business arrangement. Nothing more. I can either accept what he's offering, or walk away and fly back to Paris.

The temptation to do just that is strong. But I would be shooting myself in the foot. I'm attracted to Rafe. *Very* attracted. Even if he and I disagree on the fundamentals of life and business, I know him. He knows me. Just having those years between us lessens some of my nervousness.

His impressive physique certainly helps, too, a naughty voice whispers in my ear.

"Thank you."

I move to the table. He pulls out my chair, waits until I'm seated before he circles around. He nods and James materializes from a corner of the terrace with a bottle of wine and two wineglasses.

"Mrs. Drakos?"

This time I'm not quick enough to contain my flinch.

"Yes, please. Thank you, James."

He pours the wine and then leaves as silently as he arrived.

Rafe picks up his glass. "Not used to your married name?"

"No. I've been using my maiden name in Paris."

"I noticed."

He says the words matter-of-factly. There's an almost one hundred percent chance it doesn't even bother him that I don't use his name.

"How was your day?"

"Productive. Again." I start to tell him about Juliette's house, then stop.

"What?"

"Nothing. It's just…shop talk. Sometimes I get very excited and forget most people have no idea what I'm talking about."

"I'm interested."

His words lodge somewhere in the vicinity of my heart. I meet his gaze and, for the first time, I'm grateful for his blunt way of speaking. I know that when he tells me he's interested, he truly is.

I tell him about the schematics, the work involved in breaking down each part of my proposal to Juliette into further detail and getting more explicit with things like materials, design and the work involved.

"A far more intricate process than I realized," Rafe says as James places salads in front of us.

"What about you? How was your day?"

Rafe blinks, as if he wasn't expecting the question.

"Busy."

"Are you working on anything special?"

His lips curl, but the smile is humorless. "Just work."

I start to ask a question, then stop, remembering how yesterday went. I don't want to pry, even if the flatness in his voice makes me curious about what's going on at Drakos. Makes me wonder why he seems so disinterested in the company he's devoted his life to.

"What is it?"

"Nothing."

"No lies. Remember?"

The words are gentle, said without the tension from yesterday.

"I always got the impression that Drakos Development was...well, everything."

"It is the focus of my life." He looks out over the sea. "Although when I compare my level of commitment to the company against Gavriil's, I find mine wanting."

I can't help but smile. "Gavriil is certainly passionate."

Rafe's eyes land back on me. "Just the one kiss?"

"Just the one," I reply with a small smile. "It doesn't even begin to compare to the kiss he gave Juliette on their wedding day." My smile dims. "I'm surprised he didn't tell me. That it was all for the will."

Rafe looks at me for a long moment. "He was in a hard place. Judging by the last time we spoke, his marriage is no longer just for the inheritance."

I blink at him in surprise. "Are you defending him?"

He arches a brow. "You sound surprised."

"It just... I know you two never had the best relationship."

"We never had a relationship at all." Rafe's smirk is cold, bloodless. "As I'm sure he told you."

I don't bother denying that Gavriil has vented to me on numerous occasions about his brother. But I also think Gavriil got at least some of it wrong. There's a reason lurking somewhere in the past, something that made Rafe turn away.

"At least he had you." Rafe gives a slight shake of his head. "Never a friendship I would have imagined."

I think back to the first moment I met Gavriil as he'd leaned over the low-slung stone wall, golden brown hair falling over pale blue eyes, and asked why I was in a wheelchair. His bluntness had been refreshing compared to my coddled existence.

"Gavriil was the first person to ask what happened to me."

A furrow appears between Rafe's brows. "That was a positive experience for you?"

"It was then. Even now, it just depends on the day. Sometimes I don't mind answering questions. Other times it's hard. But back then…" I pick up my wineglass and gently swirl it. "It was like everyone just pretended like we were normal. Like I wasn't in a wheelchair or going to see a physical therapist. Your brother walked right up to me and said, 'Why are you in a wheelchair?'"

Rafe makes a huffing noise that sounds almost like a laugh. "Not surprising."

"He wasn't being rude or mean. We were kids. He just wanted to know. He was the first person, aside from my sister, who saw that I was different and didn't either make fun of me or pretend like everything was just fine."

Rafe is quiet as James comes out and delivers our main course: freshly caught fish drizzled with butter sauce and served on a bed of fingerling potatoes.

"May I ask what did happen?"

I pause with a fork full of fish halfway to my mouth.

"You don't have to answer."

"No," I agree, "I don't. Before we move to Greece, we lived in Ireland. My father was working for a real estate firm. Slowly climbing his way up. I vaguely remember my parents arguing about moving to Greece. My mom didn't want to leave her family, his family, the area they grew up in. It didn't help, too, that my mom was home with Katie and me. I remember her being tired all the time. Tired and sad because my father was gone a lot trying to convince my grandfather and aunt to promote him." My throat tightens. "There was a day my father went into Dublin for a meeting. Katie was up a lot the night before. Normal toddler stuff, nothing dramatic. My mother was exhausted. I wanted to go out and play. She asked me to wait, to just give her a couple hours to sleep."

I can still remember my frustration, indignation that I was once again waiting for my mom to stop messing with my baby sister or get up from a nap. I feel it as though I'm there right now in the living room, watching her quietly snore on the couch as I creep past.

The guilt is also fresh, just as bitter and heavy as it was twenty-one years ago when I woke up in the hospital and realized my family's lives had been changed forever.

"We lived on the edge of a moor. It was beautiful. This endless expanse of grass and shrubs. That day it was misty. I pretended like fairies were lurking in the mist. I wanted to go out and walk along the stone wall that ran along the back of our property.

"I can still remember climbing up on the wall, holding my arms out as I placed one foot in front of the other. A big girl, navigating the wall on her own. I slipped. I only fell about ten feet. But I sustained an injury to my spinal cord. One that left me partially paralyzed below the waist. I'm fortunate to have as much control and feeling as I do."

Silence falls. Rafe is watching me with that cold, dark gaze. Except the longer I stare, the more I see. The slightest softening of his eyes. A tensing of his full lips. A touch of pallor beneath his golden skin.

"I'm sorry, Tessa."

I breathe in deeply, knots of tension loosening as I accept a rare gift of compassion from my husband. "Thank you. I don't remember much of my life before the accident, so it's been a part of me for so long that most days, I don't think about it. But my parents do. Ever since that day, nothing has ever been the same."

Suddenly aware of the depth of what I've revealed, I start to say something, anything to relieve the tension. But the shrill ring of Rafe's phone saves me from having to come up with something. He glances at the screen and frowns.

"Excuse me."

He steps away. I let out a harsh breath before taking a long sip of wine. Out of the corner of my eye, I see his lips thin, his face tighten. Even if he doesn't carry the same personal passion that Gavriil does for Drakos Development, the company is still his first priority. A good thing to remember and motivation for me to guard my heart.

I may like Rafe, care for him. But we will never be on the same page when it comes to what's important in life.

"Yes. Fine. Do what needs to be done."

He hangs up and comes back to the table.

"Apologies."

"No." I wave him off. "Business comes first."

Something flickers across his face, an emotion I can't place. But neither of us pursue it. We've reached some sort of an impasse, quality that is far more pleasant than the tension we experienced yesterday. The rest of the meal proceeds smoothly, partially due to the exquisite meal and incredible dessert.

"You're not going to stay for your first lesson?"

My heart surges into my throat as heat sweeps through me. "What?"

He stands and moves with a predatory grace that makes my breath catch. He stops by a lounge and turns, one corner of his mouth curved up in a taunting smirk as he gestures toward the cushions.

"Join me."

I hear the subtle command in his voice, try to fight the way my body responds to the deep melodic tones of his voice.

And fail miserably as I find myself standing and moving slowly toward him. Drawn toward the banked fire in his eyes, the hunger that emboldens me even as I tremble inside at what's to come. Nervousness, excitement, anticipation, it all swirls together as I stop a foot away.

Slowly, he reaches out and grabs my waist. I slide my arms out of my crutch cuffs and lay them against a nearby chair. Rafe eases me down onto the lounge, his hands firm yet infinitely gentle. The pressure of his fingers on my skin sends pleasurable bolts of sensation through my body.

He sits next to me and pulls me closer. Our breaths mingle as he lowers his head, pausing just above my lips. My pulse pounds so fiercely I wonder if I'm about to pass out.

"Rafe."

There's a question in the way I say his name, a hesitation. I don't know what he has planned, what's going to come after this. I do know that I'm standing on the edge of a precipice. One wrong step, and I could lose my heart to a man who will never allow himself to return my feelings.

"Tell me you want this."

Another command. But one that offers a way out. I stare into his eyes, pale blue fire.

And make my choice.

"Kiss me."

The words are barely out of my mouth when his lips capture mine. I moan as one arm wraps around my waist, his hand pressing against my back and pulling me tighter against his body. His other hand delves into my hair, his fingers cradling the back of my head as he deepens the kiss.

But this time I'm not just going to sit back and let him initiate. I slowly run my tongue along his lips. He groans. Our mouths open, tongues delving, breaths melding. I can't tell where I end and he begins as he urges me closer, like he can't get enough of me.

My hands slide up his chest, over his shoulders, then wrap around his neck. My fingers slide into hair, the silky strands a delicious contrast to the hard planes of his chest. Driven by desire and newfound confidence, I gently tug, rewarded by a growl as he grips my hips and hauls me onto his lap.

I gasp as my skirt rides up. The only barrier between his hard length and my core are his pants and the thin material of my underwear. I shift my hips, moaning as the most incredible feeling spirals through me.

But before I can experiment further, Rafe pulls back. His hands hold me in place so that all I can feel is that wonderful, torturous pressure.

"Rafe," I beg, trying to move, to feel more.

He doesn't answer. At least not verbally. No, instead he brushes a kiss over my forehead, one that calms some of the heat racing through me even as it stirs an altogether different feeling in my chest. A tenderness that is both beautiful and unwanted as he trails his mouth over my cheek and down my jaw.

I should stop him. I wanted fire. Foreplay. Sex. Not this sweetness, this romance that makes me want things I can't have.

I shudder, trying to keep myself under control as his lips trail down my neck toward my shoulders. I knew this was a possibility. That I might struggle to keep sex separate from how I used to feel about my husband.

Used to? a little voice taunts in my head.

He grazes his teeth against the dip in my shoulder, reignites the fire. I embrace it, letting my head drop back as I focus on the physical sensations.

His fingers slide up my neck and into my hair a moment before he turns my head. He kisses me again, a searing kiss I feel in every nerve ending in my body.

And then he pulls back.

"Is that it?"

He chuckles. "For now."

Disappointment chases away some of my contentment. "But…that was just a kiss."

One brow climbs up. "If that only ranks as just a kiss, I'm going to have to improve on my technique."

I lightly thump his chest with my fist. "You know it was good."

"Good," he repeats with slight disdain. "I prefer the best."

"Given that you're the only man who's truly kissed me, you are the best."

"Minus my brother."

I roll my eyes. "I never should have told you that."

"I'll have to remind him to keep his lips off my wife the next time I see him."

His teasing words have the opposite effect. He says "my wife" so casually. Yet in just a few months, we'll be divorced.

"Well," I say, striving for a light tone as I slide off his lap, "if that's all for tonight, I'm going to go to bed."

I avoid his gaze as I reach for my crutches. He waits until I'm standing before he speaks.

"Tessa."

I swallow hard before I look at him, trying to project a confidence I don't feel. "Yes?"

"We can stop this at any time."

He stands, sliding his hands into his pockets. The fire is gone, replaced by the familiar ice I'm accustomed to. The lover has disappeared. In his place stands the billionaire developer who can switch feelings on and off in the blink of an eye.

I knew what I was getting into when I proposed this. Just like I knew what I was getting into when I agreed to marry Rafe. I ran away then. I'm not going to run away now.

I raise my chin up and smile. "I know. I'm enjoying myself. Hopefully you are, too."

"Yes. But this isn't about me." He advances toward me. "You're upset."

I shake my head, dislodging more of my hair from its updo. "No."

"No lies, Tessa." His hand comes up, then falls back to his side. "Not to me. Not to yourself. Arrangements only work if both parties are honest with each other."

Arrangement. A cold word. Businesslike. One that yanks me out of the emotional quagmire I've stumbled into and pulls me back to reality. There is nothing waiting for me on the other side of this. Not with Rafe, anyway.

But if I can keep my head, if I can enjoy what he's offering, explore my sexuality with someone I trust, there's only endless possibility waiting for me at the end.

"I want to be here, Rafe. I'll tell you if that changes."

I turn and walk away.

CHAPTER NINE

Rafe

I GLANCE OUT the window of my limo as it pulls into the circle drive of the villa. Yes, I'm hoping for a glimpse of my wife. It's been two days since our rooftop dinner. Two days since what I referred to as Tessa's first lesson, one that left me clinging to the last vestiges of my self-control.

The morning and afternoon after our dinner, it was understandable that I didn't even glimpse my wife. I had plenty of things to focus on, worked to accomplish, and I knew the same was true for her, even if I didn't agree with her methods or how she was conducting her business. But that night, she had sent word through James that she would not be joining me for dinner, pleading exhaustion.

Fine. I could accept that. Except last night was a repeat of the same. When I failed to see her this morning before I left for a meeting in town, I concluded that my wife was avoiding me.

Like so many things with Tessa, it shouldn't provoke me. But it does.

She had seemed more than satisfied by our encounter on the rooftop. Unfortunately, it had left me wanting, too, craving her as I had never craved another woman.

James appeared. "Good afternoon, sir," he said with a slight bow.

"Good afternoon, James. Is Mrs. Drakos in?"

"Yes, sir. She's in the gym."

I take the stairs down to the lower level. A few empty rooms occupy the space down here, including the state-of-the-art gym that Lucifer had installed but never used. If I recall correctly, it was for one of my father's numerous girlfriends who imagined herself to be the next social media darling of the fitness world. A short-lived notion, especially after she chose to pursue a much younger millionaire over my father who was nearly three times her age.

I walk by the wall of glass that separates the hall from the gym, look up, then stop. Tessa is facing away from me, her legs straddling a weight bench as she slowly but steadily lifts two dumbbells overhead. She's wearing nothing but a red sports bra and black shorts molded to the curves of her backside and thighs. As I watch, entranced, she reaches the peak of the lift, holds the dumbbells aloft. The muscles in her back quiver but hold steady. Then, just as slowly, she lowers them back down.

Another glimpse of the woman my wife has become when she had the freedom to spread her wings.

I enter the gym, calling out a soft greeting so as not to startle her. Tessa glances over her shoulder, giving me a cautious smile.

"Hello."

"Hello." I glance around the gym, taking in the high-end rowing machine, the rack of free weights and the mirrors lining two of the walls. "I'm glad someone is finally utilizing the space."

"I'm supposed to be working out several times a week, if not almost every day." She slowly puts her dumbbells on the floor. "It's been great having this here."

She's distant. More so than she was when she came up and saw that romantic tabletop set for two the other night. My attempt at an olive branch. As angry as I was with her for pushing our first night here in Corfu, I overreacted. Offering her dinner had been a way to smooth things over between us, to get us back on track. My suggestion of completing her first lesson had been spur of the moment, driven as much by desire to taste her again as to advance our arrangement. I hadn't expected her to withdraw afterward.

"If you ever need a workout partner, let me know. I'm usually up by four."

She smiles as she shakes her head. "It is my fervent hope that one day, Rafe, you will simply do something because you want to, not because you have to."

I don't know how to respond to that, so I focus on something I can do. A small refrigerator hums in the corner, fully stocked with bottled water. I grab one and hold it up. At her nod, I walk over and hand it to her. My fingers brush hers. The heat of her skin is noticeable after grasping the cold bottle. A spark arcs between us. Her gaze snaps up to mine as she lifts the bottle to her lips.

Théos, the simple act of her drinking from a bottle makes me hard. A bead of sweat slides down her chest, disappearing between her breasts. The need to taste her is a hunger I've never experienced before.

She sets the bottle down and then looks up at me with her caramel-colored eyes. Her gaze drifts down to my growing hardness. My blood heats as her lips part and she sucks in a shuddering breath.

When she looks back up at me, the lust in her eyes is tinged with an endearing shyness. One that makes me pause despite the strength of my own desire pumping through me. I want her. I want her so bad it hurts.

But I can't ignore the dark voice whispering in my head. The one that whispers Tessa deserves far better than a man like me.

I barely bite back a groan as she sinks her teeth into her lower lip.

"I think now would be a good time for lesson number two."

All rational thoughts fly out of my head. I walk to a point just behind her and straddle the bench, easing myself down until I'm just behind her. My hand settles on her stomach. The sound of her inhaling, coupled with the heat of her skin searing my palm, sears itself into my brain. I pull her back against me, press my hardness into the curves of her backside. When she pushes against my erection, I have to steel myself against the urge to just take her right then and there.

I could have taken her up on her offer in Paris. Taken her back to her apartment, introduced her to sex in that one night, and then come back to Greece. My inheritance secure and no further dealings with the woman who would soon be my ex-wife.

Except even just the thought of doing so felt...wrong. Tessa deserves more. I can't give her what she needs when it comes to marriage. But with this, I can take things a step further. Push my boundaries just enough to give her an experience she'll never forget.

Even when she moves on with her life. Another man.

I grasp her chin with my other hand and turn her head so that I can capture her lips with mine. In this moment, she's mine. Mine and mine alone. No one else has touched her like this. Has made her shiver or moan. Has made her arch against them.

She's mine.

I know it's just the heat of the moment, the animalistic desire that surfaces any time I think of her being untouched. Still, I temper my approach just enough so that I don't slide too deep.

I lightly caress her bare stomach, my fingers inching higher until they're just beneath the band of her sports bra. I wait for a moment, give her space to tell me no.

Then continue higher when she murmurs her discontent at my lack of progress.

I slide my fingers beneath the material, feel my body tense as the weight of one bare breast brushes my skin. A shudder passes through me. I break our kiss long enough to grab the band of her bra and pull the material up and over her head.

Leaving her topless in front of me.

Our eyes meet in the mirror. She's so damned beautiful it hurts. Eyes wide, lips parted and swollen. Firm, supple breasts bare to my gaze. Long strands of her honey-blond hair slipping from her ponytail, giving her a wild, untamed look as uncertainty flickers over her face.

I watch us in the mirror as my hands come around and gently cup her breasts. The nervousness disappears as her head falls back against my shoulder and she moans, leaning into my touch. I lightly drag my thumbs across her dark nipples. Nearly lose my control as they harden into peaks beneath my gentle strokes.

"Rafe," she moans, pushing her breasts into my hands as she presses her hips back against my groin.

I band one arm just below her breasts and give into temptation, letting my other hand drift down to her waist. I tease a finger along the waistband of her shorts. She freezes, her breath coming fast and short as she watches me, her eyes fixated on my hand as I slide down her stomach. My fingers graze lace.

And then there's nothing but her. Hot, wet silk against my skin as she shudders in my arms and moans my name. I tease her with light caresses and gentle touches. Savor each and every noise she makes, smiling as she tries to press harder against my hand.

I drag it out as long as I can. Until the torture becomes too much for both of us.

I lean back, keeping her pressed against me. God, she spreads her legs for me with such trusting innocence it nearly undoes me. Doubt stabs through the haze of my lust. What right do I have to touch her? To take her like this when I can offer her nothing but pleasure? It's never mattered before.

But it matters with her.

"Rafe?"

I shove my uncertainties aside. "Tell me if it hurts."

She nods, slowly but without hesitation. The trust she places in me shakes me, heightens my senses as I slide one finger inside her. Her breath rushes out as her body clenches down on me. It only takes a few strokes before the thrust of her hips becomes faster, more frenetic.

"Rafe... I..."

"Just let go." I kiss her neck, her cheek, graze my teeth across the shell of her ear. "Let go, Tessa."

She listens. A moment later she peaks, coming apart in my arms.

Her eyes drift shut as she sags against me. I stare at our reflection in the mirror. Tessa, the woman I once thought of as a haunted shadow, lying half naked in my arms with a smile of contentment on her face. Me, sitting on a weight bench holding my wife like I never want to let her go.

Except I'll have to. I'll have to release her to find her own happiness in the world. With someone else.

My arm tightens around her waist. I need to take a step back from this, from our so-called "lessons." Regain my equilibrium and remind myself that while there's a certain level of affection to be expected, I can't be courting disaster by getting emotionally involved with Tessa.

Tomorrow, I tell myself as I give in to the urge to press a kiss to her hair. Tomorrow I'll step back. For both our sakes.

But right now, I'm going to savor the unexpected pleasure of holding my wife.

CHAPTER TEN

Tessa

I SLOWLY WAKE UP, blinking through the grogginess that's clinging to me even after a decent night's sleep. The price to pay, I suppose, for finally having my first non-self-induced orgasm.

I stretch my arms overhead and smile. My doctor told me there might be a possibility of not having complete sensation. I wasn't sure what to expect. But Rafe made it so easy to trust him, touching me, making love to me with his mouth and fingers. The sight of him watching in the mirror, his blue eyes on fire as he brought me to a level of pleasure I'd never experienced, had sent me not only to new heights of desire, but new levels of confidence as a woman.

Except, I remember with a cold dash of memory, for the aftermath. He held me, kissed my hair, cradled me as if I were made of glass. But as soon as he stood, that mask dropped back into place. He told me he had a meeting and wouldn't be joining me for dinner. And then he left. Aside from my flushed face and the delicious, lingering sensation of having been made love to, there was nothing to suggest that I had just had my first brush with sexual intimacy.

He handled it the way he should have. Had he dragged it out, whispered vague promises he never intended to keep, it would only make my ability to keep my distance more challenging.

Still, it left me with the feeling of being dropped off a cliff. So I threw myself into work. Again. Doing what I had accused Rafe of doing as I sought to distract myself.

Unfortunately, focusing on work had only introduced a new worry. That perhaps I had bitten off more than I could chew in starting my own business. Working on one project at a time was one thing. Working on two with a third waiting in the wings was something else entirely.

Rafe's advice, that I should consider hiring someone to help, resurfaces. As much as I want Tessa's Interiors to be mine, if I truly want to grow, I'm going to have to change my mindset. Frustrated with myself, and even more frustrated with Rafe that he *might* be right, I look away from my desk and out toward the sea.

It's beautiful here. The tension that gripped me between Paris and Corfu has disappeared. Ironic when I think about it. In trying to distance myself from my past and avoid anything that might remind me of the years after my accident, I had actually been holding on. If I had said no to Rafe's request to accompany him to Greece, I wouldn't have had last night. I wouldn't be gazing out over the cerulean waves, the olive trees, the brilliant sky.

I sigh. It was so much easier to move on in Paris, with no reminders, nothing familiar for me to fall back on. There was only forward.

But this trip, I'm coming to realize, is good for me in so many ways. Showing me how to accept my past, live my present and look ahead to the future.

I glance back at the sketch pad lying on the table next to the lounge. In between schematics and materials, I took a few breaks. But instead of picking up my book, I sketched, mentally redecorating the rooms James had given me a tour of the afternoon I had arrived. Before Rafe had made it clear he had zero interest in doing anything but selling his father's house.

I only met Lucifer a handful of times. I loathed the man, so I can only imagine what growing up with him had been like. From the snippets Gavriil told me about how Lucifer treated him, it's no wonder that Rafe is a block of ice. It's probably the only way he survived.

A shudder crawls down my spine. When I have children, I will never let them go a single day without knowing how much they are loved, as my father did. I will endeavor to never suffocate them under the weight of my own guilt and insecurities, like my mother did.

I pick up the sketch pad and flip through it. The rooms themselves are beautiful, with the colors and flooring serving as surprisingly solid foundations. Clean. Timeless. It's the ostentatiousness of the furniture, the paintings, that overwhelms. As if Lucifer bought the most expensive things he could find and stuffed them into rooms.

Which, I think with a snort, is probably exactly what happened.

Rafe, however, is about efficiency. Progress. Yet as I'm coming to know a different side of him, he also has that undercurrent of passion, that attention to detail. He says nothing matters to him. Yet I see the way he looks out at the sky, the trees and especially the ocean. As if in the busy pace of his life, the view of nature calms him.

I don't even know if he's aware of it himself. It makes me wish that he could trust me, just one room, show him what could be possible and maybe even give him a glimpse of a side of himself he hasn't listened to. May not even be aware exists as he marches forward with his schedules and checklist.

Maybe tomorrow. Given the argument that came out of our discussion before, I have no interest in reintroducing that tension. Or pushing him.

A knock sounds on my door. "Come in."

My body tightens as Rafe walks in, dressed in a white polo shirt and tan slacks. Even in neutral-colored clothing, the man looks like a Greek god.

"Good morning."

His face is smooth, but there's a hint of warmth in his voice as he approaches me, hands tucked into his pants pockets.

"Good morning. How did you sleep?"

I give him a small smile. "Are you genuinely asking, or is this your way of looking for a compliment?"

His teeth flash white against his tan skin, so quick I might have missed it had I blinked. A slight pressure builds behind my eyes at the side of his genuine smile. I wish he would smile more.

"I was genuinely asking after your welfare. But compliments are acceptable too."

I roll my eyes as I glance away. But I noticed my sketch pad lying open. Trying to move as casually as possible, I reach over and start to close the pad.

"I slept well—"

"What is that?"

I slam the cover shut. "Just sketches. Doodling."

"That looked like the master bedroom."

My body tenses. His face is back to being blank, his voice emotionless. I have no sense of direction, no indication of what he's thinking or feeling.

I raise my chin. I lived years like this. Always watching, waiting for a sign that I was going to do something to upset my mother, to make my father turn away. Always anticipating, always on edge.

No more. If Rafe is upset that I drew some sketches, then he can go jump in the sea.

I open the sketch pad and hand it to Rafe.

"I worked late last night. Sometimes reading calms me, but other times it's sketching."

He examines the pages, taking what seems like a ridiculously long amount of time evaluating each design. His fingers glide over the pages, moving with that same slowness that I once chalked up as methodical.

But now, with the memory of how he used those fingers on my body yesterday, I no longer see the movements as efficient. No, it's sensual, the way they move over the paper, lingering, grazing.

I bite my lower lip. God help me, if one session of heavy touching can reduce me to this, what will the actual event do?

"These are good."

I blink in surprise as I try to hold back a smile. Try not to let him see how much the simple compliment warms me.

"I'm glad you like them." I lace my fingers together. "I wasn't trying to invade your privacy. I just saw the rooms and—"

"I'm not accusing you. As you are aware, my relationship with Lucifer was not a pleasant one. And as I said at dinner, I should have handled my response better."

"Thank you." I hesitate, then decide to take the plunge. "I could have handled my response to your feedback on my business better, too." I swallow my pride. "If you have time, I do have a couple questions. Structuring a business as it's growing. Don't look so smug," I snap as he looks at me with a distinctly masculine gleam of triumph in his eyes.

"Are you saying I was right?"

"No, I'm saying I have questions."

"I'm good at what I do, Tessa."

"I know. My reticence has nothing to do with you. It's… me. I let my parents, especially my mom, rule my life for so long."

"And you're afraid that if you ask for help, you'll be falling back into an old pattern."

A tightness I didn't even realize I have been carrying slowly eases from my chest. "For someone who says he doesn't do emotions, you're very perceptive."

"Psychology is a science. One made up of research, data, statistics. Patterns. I can understand those. Plus," he says as he watches a gull fly up high in the sky before diving back down toward the water, "without being able to observe and make my own conclusions about how people are thinking or feeling, especially going into a deal, I would not be effective at what I do."

It's incredible how he rationalizes everything down to science, to numbers. But I know that there's far more to this man than he lets himself or anyone else believe.

"You've accomplished more than you are giving yourself credit for, Tessa."

Just like that, he turns it back on me. I swallow hard. "It doesn't feel like enough."

"You've been on your own for four months."

"And ever since I was seven years old, I've lived someone else's life. Not my own. It feels like I've wasted the last twenty-one years."

"Stop." He's looking at me now, his expression firm. "The work you're accomplishing now, what you've done, is because of the experiences you've had the past twenty-one years. Not to mention that for eleven of those, you were a child."

"But—"

"But nothing, Tessa." His eyes are hard, glinting with an inner resolve that makes me grateful I've never been on the receiving end of his true fury. "Parents make mistakes. They fail. Your mother's obsession with keeping you safe to the point of isolating you from the outside world is a reflection of her, not you."

I stare at him. I want to ask. Want to know just what Lucifer did to him that turned him into a man who sees so much yet keeps everyone at arm's length. Who insists he has no soul even as he reaches deep into mine with his perception, his caring.

"Don't dwell on the past," he says quietly. "Move forward."

My breath comes out in a rush. "All right. Let's start with questions. Work our way up to having you take a look at my business structure and plan."

I shift, my hands grazing my portfolio. Inspiration strikes. "Actually, how about another arrangement?"

His eyes heat as he sweeps me with a lingering gaze. "The last one has certainly been beneficial for both of us."

"You may not like this one," I reply as I try to keep my attention focused on now and off how his hands felt on me. I tap the portfolio. "You let me redecorate one room, and I'll let you review my business proposal."

Even though he doesn't move, I can almost see the gears turning in his head. Weighing, assessing.

"Budget?"

I mentally tally what I want to do. "Ten to fifteen thousand."

"Significantly lower than I would have expected."

"It's not a complete overhaul. More updating. Making use of what's there and swapping out what no longer works. Most of that cost would be new furniture, artwork, things like that."

His eyes narrow. "What do you charge by the hour?"

"Seventy-five."

His eyebrows shoot up. "An hour?" he repeats.

"Yes."

He scoffs and shakes his head. "You do need my help."

"I'm an entry-level designer. I'm not going to charge people two or three hundred euros an hour when I'm just starting out."

"Except you do good work. You should charge it for it."

My mind turns to my other client. The one outside of the little French village.

"There are ways to meet the needs of the population that you want to help the most."

My eyes fly to his. It's unsettling how he knew exactly where my mind went. "Why do you want to help me?"

He pauses, as if he's not quite sure how to answer himself.

"I enjoy it. Organizing, identifying problems, coming up with solutions. It's the best part of what I do."

Surprised, I ask, "Not the property development? The acquisitions?"

"I mentioned the other day that Gavriil lives and breathes Drakos Development. I go through the motions out of habit. I've known nothing else my entire life."

"So what would you do? If you didn't have Drakos?"

"There is nothing else. There never will be."

My lips part. My heart aches for him, for a man so talented to simply relegate himself to an existence that brings him no joy.

His phone rings. He glances down at his screen and narrows his eyes.

"Something wrong?"

He shakes his head. "The Acropolis Museum is trying to get in touch with me."

"The Acropolis Museum?" My eyes widen at his nod. "What do they want?"

"They're hosting a gala fundraiser tomorrow night. They want me to attend."

I lean forward, propping my chin in my hand. "I feel like there's more to the story of why a world-renowned museum is calling you." I bite down on my lower lip as he glares at me.

"I made a donation."

"How big of a donation?"

"Drop it, Tessa." His phone rings again and he swears in Greek.

"You should go."

He looks at me and frowns. "No."

"Why not? It's good publicity for Drakos Development. Not to mention their museum looks incredible."

He cocks his head to one side. "You've never been?"

"No. I should add it to my travel list." A list that's growing longer with each passing day.

"I'll go." I start to smile, but he holds up a hand. "On the condition you attend with me."

Excitement races through me. "Really?"

"I wouldn't have asked if I didn't mean it."

My excitement vanishes as nerves flutter in my stomach. "Won't it look odd, though? With how intimate our wedding was, I don't think a lot of people even realize we're married."

He shrugs. "My personal life is none of their concern. I'm only asking if you want to go."

I can't remember the last time I went to a party. My mother only allowed a few large-scale events a year for my "safe-keeping." The thought of going without her keeping a stranglehold on my leash is very appealing.

As is the idea of finally having the chance to redeem what happened all those years ago the night I fell in love with Rafe.

Thought you fell in love.

"I'd like that." I wrinkle my nose. "I didn't bring anything fancy enough for a gala, though."

"Give your sizes and preferences to James and he'll have several dresses sent over for you to choose from."

"Okay. Thank you."

For a moment, I think he's going to lean down and kiss me. But he simply nods and leaves the room, leaving me alone with my sketch pad and the sounds of the sea just beyond my balcony.

CHAPTER ELEVEN

Rafe

THE STRAINS OF a string quartet drift over the outdoor terrace of the Acropolis Museum. The pillars of the Parthenon are visible on top of the Acropolis hill, the marble lit up with golden light as the sun sinks below the horizon. Waiters in tuxedos navigate the crowd of people dressed in expensive finery as they balance trays filled with *tiropitakia*, prawn *saganakia* and juicy olives. Tour guides stand off to the side, ready to whisk gala attendees up to the top of the Acropolis for moonlight tours of the Parthenon and the Temple of Athena Nike.

The kind of event I find, and have always found, to be a waste of my time. I donated money because I like the work the Acropolis Museum does. I despise my own heritage, but I understand the importance of protecting history and legacy. Whether it was the comfort of seeing artifacts and treasures preserved for thousands of years or just having an escape whenever my father surprised me at the villa here in Corfu, I spent countless hours in this museum. It's a place of refuge.

But one I prefer to enjoy in private, I think irritably as a young woman jostles my arm on her way to the bar.

I had no intention of coming. But when I saw the awe on Tessa's face when I told her who was incessantly calling me, followed by her enthusiasm for my attending, the answer had been clear. Discovering how much her mother had suppressed her over the years—I'd almost go as far as saying imprisoned—and seeing how much she was enjoying her new life, saying yes was the right thing to do.

My eyes shift down to the woman at my side. Not because I haven't brought a date to a company event in years. Even though people were aware of our marriage, Tessa's appearance sent a flurry of gossip through the room as soon as we walked in. I've seen more than one person look at her crutches, too. What would it be like to always live under such scrutiny? To have people look, hold up their hands as they whisper behind your back?

Yet here she is, standing confidently by my side even as she gazes around like she's never seen such beauty in her entire life.

Just as I can't recall the last time I felt like this about a woman. She's beautiful. The gown clings to her body, highlighting her narrow waist and following the lines of her legs. A slimmer fit, she told me in the limo, that wouldn't interfere with her crutches. Her wheelchair is also easily accessible, stored in a spare room just outside the ballroom in case she gets tired or off balance with so many people around.

She questions her ability to run her own business, to persevere. Yet she's constantly adapting, moving forward. She doesn't give herself enough credit.

"Rafael."

I tense, then slowly turn. Gavriil is walking across the ballroom floor toward me, his wife Juliette at his side. My brother looks almost nothing like me, with a thicker build and dark brown hair gifted to him by his mother, a hotel maid Lucifer seduced and abandoned.

The eyes, though…his eyes are the same pale blue as mine.

"I didn't realize you were attending, too."

I hear the cold in my own voice, see Gavriil's eyes narrow slightly.

"When the museum was struggling to get ahold of you, they called me. We were already in the air when they notified us you were coming." He looks down at the dark-haired woman by his side. His face changes, softens. "And Juliette's never been to Greece."

Gavriil smiles down at his wife. Seeing the change in him is jarring. When I last saw him at his wedding, he looked cold, determined. But now, as Juliette looks up at him with emotion shining in her eyes, he looks happy.

Envy twists through me. An envy I have no right to feel. I'm the only person who knows what Gavriil went through when he joined our household, what Lucifer put him through to prove himself. An eight-year-old boy left alone in the wake of his mother's death with no support. Certainly no love or compassion offered to him as he grieved in a new place surrounded by a luxury he couldn't even begin to comprehend after growing up in the slums.

And why was he left alone? a nasty voice whispers.

"It's so good to see you in person, Juliette," Tessa says with a smile. "You look beautiful."

For a moment, I see a possibility before me. One where my brother and I are married, our wives are good friends, our conversations not overshadowed by our history.

And then the moment passes. I'm glad my brother has found happiness. But I have no interest in delving into a fantasy world I know will be gone sooner rather than later.

Juliette turns to Tessa. "Have you had a chance to dive?"

"Dive?" I repeat.

A light blush stains Tessa's cheeks. "Katie and I got certified for scuba diving three months ago."

Gavriil grins. "That's awesome."

He leans in and gives Tessa a hug with an ease and familiarity that stirs jealousy in my chest. If I'm being truthful with myself, I envied their relationship for years. How easily

Gavriil could talk to Tessa. The relationship she built with him as I kept him at arm's length for both our sakes.

"Thank you. Adaptive diving," she says to me. "Once I'm in the water, I can do almost everything myself. I just can't get in and out without some help."

"Still," I say, feeling like an echo of my brother, "it's an accomplishment."

"It was. It's like a whole other world under the water."

The music starts up again, a slower number set to sultry music that filters through the warm summer air. Gavriil holds out a hand to Juliette.

"May I have this dance?"

The smile she gives him is so sickeningly sweet I barely stopped myself from rolling my eyes. Tessa grins as she watches Gavriil sweep Juliette into an elaborate turn.

"He always did like to show off," I say dryly.

She doesn't respond. I follow her gaze, see the longing as she watches the dancers. A longing I feel deep inside my bones.

"Would you like to dance?"

She looks up at me, a hesitant smile on her lips. "I never have."

"Neither have I."

She laughs, a light, joyful sound that fills my chest.

"As much as I want to, dancing for the first time in front of a room full of people I don't know is a little much for me."

I detest the idea of dancing. But I loathe the idea of her sitting on the sidelines even more.

"Follow me."

We move to the elevator. I've spent countless hours here over the years. The elevator doors close, leaving me alone with my wife for a precious few seconds. Her scent, that same delicate blend of daisies and strawberries, teases me. I glance down at her and nearly give in to the urge to kiss her when she smiles up at me.

But I don't. I've come too close to crossing the line already. I worried about Tessa not being able to keep herself emotionally removed during our affair. Yet the more I spend time with her, the more I taste her, the more I wonder how difficult it will be to let her go when the time comes.

I lead her through the pillars and statues of the Archaic Acropolis Gallery. The lingering heat left over from a scorching day hits us as we walk out of the air-conditioned museum and onto the glass floor of the atrium. Above, the museum's second floor juts out from the building.

And below, beneath our feet, lies thousands of years of history.

"Wow."

I glance at Tessa out of the corner of my eye as she stares down at the mosaic tiles of an ancient floor. Her eyes are round with wonder, her lips curving up as she takes it all in. Farther ahead, an opening in the floor gives a stunning view of the ruins of homes and workshops just beneath the museum.

"Thank you, Rafe."

I give her a slight smile. "You're welcome."

I glance around, but we're alone on the atrium's bridge. The music is faint but still audible.

"I'm not sure what to do." She glances down at her crutches. "I thought about taking dance lessons, but I haven't found the time yet."

"Is there anything you haven't planned on doing?"

"No," she says with a laugh. "It's like the whole world is opened to me. I want to do it all."

Moonlight makes her hair glow and her smile radiant. For once, I don't want the comfort of that emotionless void, the knowledge that will guide my choices and actions. No, I want an ounce of Tessa's excitement, her zest for life, her drive to push past everything that has held her back and succeed.

Yes, the potential for her to fall, to suffer, is far greater. But seeing her now, like this, I also get a glimpse of the rewards that life is bestowing upon her. Rewards I have never experienced.

"Can you maneuver at all without the crunches?"

She shakes her head. "I can support some weight. But I need something to brace on."

"What about me?"

I can almost feel her inhale, blood starting to pump harder through my veins at the side of her eyes darkening.

"That might work. Just don't drop me."

"I won't."

I let her come to me, let her set the pace of what she's comfortable with. I know the amount of trust she's placing in me. And try not to let it affect me too much.

When she's right in front of me, I wrap an arm around her waist, wait for her to slide her arms out of the crutches and lean them against a nearby wall. I hold out one hand, my body tightening as her fingers slide across my palm. Her other hand slides up my chest and presses against my shoulder.

"May I have this dance?"

She smiles up at me.

"Yes."

I sway back and forth, gently at first, letting us both get used to the motion of our unique dancing. Her feet graze the floor as I slowly turn.

"This is amazing." Her eyes crinkle at the corners as she gives me an impish grin. "Faster?"

I oblige, moving around the terrace with her body pressed firmly against mine. She responds to my movements, following my lead even if she leans in to my hold. The rest of the world fades away as I dance with my wife in the Greek moonlight, acutely aware of her scent, her breath whispering against the base of my throat, her breasts pressed against my chest.

I tighten my hold. I don't want to let go. The thought blazes through my mind, leaving a burning trail in its wake.

Just in this moment, I tell myself. Not forever. Just for now.

The music winds down. Applause sounds from the rooftop. We stop, still pressed together. Tessa's eyes drop to my mouth. I lean down, anticipation building in my chest.

"Rafe? There you are."

I've never been upset with my brother. A rarity, I'm sure when it comes to siblings. But right now, as my head whips around and I glare at him over my shoulder, I'm furious.

"What?"

Gavriil slows, holding up his hands. "Whoa, I didn't…"

His voice trails off as he catches sight of Tessa in my arms. His eyes widen, then narrow as he glances between her and me. My arm tightens around her waist. I don't like the protective look in his eyes.

"The head of fundraising wants to speak with you."

I nearly growl at the edge to Gavriil's voice.

"Go."

I look back down at Tessa. She smiles up at me. "This is important."

Her words penetrate my haze of anger and possessiveness. I carry her over to her crutches, keeping her steady as she slips her arms back into the cuffs. Once she's stable, I step back.

"Are you coming?"

She shakes her head. "I think I'll stay out here for a little bit. Enjoy the view," she adds with a gesture to the ruins beneath us.

I stalk toward the doors of the museum, conscious of Gavriil at my side, disapproval radiating from him.

"Say your piece and be done with it."

"I'm just surprised at the difference between you and Tessa compared to my wedding."

"You disapprove."

"You married her for her father's company and then didn't bother to chase after her when she left. Of course I disapprove, especially when I wonder what game you're playing with her now."

I know what my little brother thinks of me. Have known it for years. But tonight, for the first time in a long time, it cuts deep.

"She's an adult. It was her choice to go."

Gavriil's hand lands on my arm, pausing me in my tracks. My eyes flick down to his fingers, then back up to his face. A clear warning to let go. One he doesn't heed.

"Why are you doing this?"

"What?"

"Dancing with her, showing her off at a gala in front of hundreds of people?"

"She's not something to be shown off," I grind out.

Gavriil's eyes narrow as he releases my arm. "Has something happened between you two?"

An image of the gym flashes in my mind; Tessa bare from the waist up, her nipples swollen, her breathing erratic.

"Why is it any of your concern?"

"Because she's my friend."

"A friend? Or something more?"

Gavriil's eyes narrow to slits. "You do realize my wife, the woman I love, is just inside that ballroom?"

"A woman you could barely stand a month ago."

"A woman who drove me crazy, yes, but who I respected and now love. I can be in love with my wife and still love Tessa for the friend she is." He stabs a finger at my chest.

"You may not remember when I first arrived at the villa. God knows you barely acknowledged my existence."

Regret surges up, ensnares me and pulls me down. I remember all too vividly walking in those doors, seeing my eyes looking back at me from the face of an eight-year-old boy with his chin thrust in the air and his lips pressed together as he tried not to cry. I wanted to go to him, to protect him from the hell I knew Lucifer had waiting for him inside his gilded villa.

Had I done that, Lucifer would have made good on his threats. Any chance Gavriil would have had at a decent life would have been ripped away from him.

"I had no one in that house. No one," Gavriil repeats, his voice vibrating with years of suppressed anger. "When Tessa and her family moved to Santorini, she was the only person who would talk to me. We spent hours outside, playing, talking. She was my lifeline. So yes, I will protect her, even from my own brother. I don't even understand why she's here if you two are going to be divorcing."

"That's…" My voice trails off as coldness sweeps through me. "You know?"

Gavriil has the good sense to look somewhat embarrassed. "Tessa told me."

"When?" My voice comes out as a snarl, more animalistic than human.

He hesitates, then runs a hand through his hair as his breath comes out in a rush. "The week before she sent the petition."

Betrayal cuts through me. This is the price to pay for opening myself up, for letting myself feel something for my wife.

"You care for her."

My head jerks up. "I've always cared for Tessa."

"No, this is something different." His eyes widen. "Do you—"

"No." My smile is cold, humorless. "How can a man like me even come close to being capable of loving someone?"

"Tell yourself what you want, but I know what I saw back there."

I lean in. "It doesn't matter what I do or don't feel. You saw her back there. Saw her smile. Her happiness."

Gavriil nods. "That's what I'm saying. I—"

"Now look at me. Who do you see?" Gavriil falls silent. "You see it." His eyes dart to the side. I lean in closer until he has no choice but to look at me. "I see it, too, every time I look in the mirror. He stripped me of the ability to be anything more than a man with a heart of ice."

Gavriil flinches as I toss the words I've heard him say multiple times over the years back in his face.

"You and I may be forever at odds, little brother, but the one thing we can both agree on is that even if I were capable of loving someone, Tessa deserves better than me."

CHAPTER TWELVE

Tessa

I TAP MY fingers nervously against the armrest of my wheelchair as I sit outside the door to Rafe's room. What started out as an incredible night turned bad so quickly I barely had time to catch my breath.

I lingered on the atrium bridge for quite a while, trying to get myself back into a place of neutrality after our heated dance. That Rafe had even noticed me watching Gavriil and Juliette dance and picked up on my quiet yearning had meant something to me. So, too, had me being his first dance partner.

And then there was the matter of the dance itself. Something so simple yet so sensual it had stoked a slow flame that crept through my veins and continued to smolder long after Gavriil had come to fetch him.

Except he hadn't returned. Nearly fifteen minutes later, Gavriil had sought me out to tell me that Rafe had left. He'd been uncharacteristically somber and, when I pressed for details, simply said that he and Rafe had a disagreement and he had said some things he shouldn't have. I sent Rafe a text, but all he'd answered was that he needed to get home and had arranged for the limo to come back to get me whenever I wished to leave. I'd swapped out my crutches for my wheelchair and spent the rest of the evening with Gavriil and Juliette. Juliette had been thrilled to talk about her house and my business, although I'd caught her more than once shooting a concerned glance at her husband. Finally, when people started to leave, I took the limo Rafe had arranged back to our hotel, conscious of the empty seat beside me.

Rafe booked us a room at the Hotel Grande Bretagne, the most luxurious hotel in Athens. The two-bedroom suite included a marble bathroom, ornate furniture, and a balcony overlooking the Acropolis hill. When I wheeled myself into the room, I was greeted with the comforting glow of a lamp that has been left on and an empty sitting room. Rafe's door was firmly closed.

I resolved to stay in my room, give Rafe space. But his abrupt retreat, combined with Gavriil's uncharacteristic behavior, ate at me. So now I'm sitting outside the door to his bedroom, working up the courage to knock.

I changed out of my gown and into a lounge set from a shopping trip with Katie all those months ago. A sleeveless silk top and matching pants in burgundy. Simple, but elegant, the cool material against my skin a much-needed contrast to the heat I hadn't been able to get rid of since our dance.

I raise my hand to knock. Then I freeze. I still feel raw after our dance, vulnerable. Is me being here now the best thing for him? For me?

But, I tell myself as I raise my hand again, if it were anyone else, I would be checking on them.

I knock. Silence greets me.

Doubt creeps in. I debate returning to my room, but before I can make a decision, footsteps finally sound on the other side of the door. Rafe opens it. My breath catches in my chest. He shed his black tuxedo jacket but is still wearing his white dress shirt and black pants. The top two buttons of his shirt are undone, giving me a tantalizing glimpse of skin and dark curling hair.

"Tessa."

His voice is flat. Unease ripples down my spine.

"I just wanted to check on you. You left the party."

"Yes. Gavriil and I had words."

"That's what he said." I tilt my head to one side. "Are you upset with me, too?"

He braces one shoulder against the doorway and stares down at me. "It was disconcerting realizing my brother most likely knew about your intent to divorce me before I did."

My stomach clenches. "Rafe—"

He turns his back on me and walks away. "It doesn't matter," he says over his shoulder. "It doesn't change anything."

I hesitate on the threshold. And then move into the room, closing the door softly behind me.

"I'm sorry, Rafe."

He moves to the small balcony and looks out over Athens, his body stiff.

"I would ask that for the remainder of our arrangement, you not share any details with anyone else."

"I didn't tell him about…"

Rafe glances over his shoulder, one eyebrow raised and almost a challenge.

"The other part," I finish lamely.

"My debauching you? Your discretion is appreciated."

Irritation chips away at my compassion. "Look, when I talked to Gavriil, I was trying to get his perspective. To make sure I wasn't jumping to conclusions or making a hasty decision."

He looks back out over the ocean. "He said you talked to him a week before you sent the divorce papers."

I will not feel guilty. I will not feel guilty.

"Yes. I hadn't heard from you since I left. And then at the wedding you acted like I didn't exist. There wasn't any anger, there wasn't any sadness, there was just…nothing."

"Nothing," he echoes. "That's the state I usually exist in, Tessa."

"I know. Although I don't understand why."

"Why doesn't matter. It's simply how it is."

The irritation digs its claws deeper into my skin. "Do you never ask why?"

"I do when it matters."

"Well, the why of this matters to me." I stop my wheelchair next to him and look up. "You say you and your brother have no relationship, but I see the way you look at him sometimes when you think no one's looking, like you want to talk to him and figure out whatever mess happened between you two. You notice that I want to dance and find a way to make it happen. You say you're not capable of feeling even as you demonstrate that you are on a regular basis. I don't understand why you keep insisting otherwise."

Silence falls between us, broken only by the distant sound of traffic. Then, at last, he speaks.

"Gavriil and I have never been close. He thinks that's because I chose not to forge a relationship with him, that I'm incapable of doing so. He's right. But at one time, I wanted things. Family, a friend."

Foreboding forms a hard ball in the pit of my stomach. "What happened?"

"When Lucifer told me I had a brother and that that brother was coming to live with us, he also issued an ultimatum. He told me that if I attempted to befriend Gavriil, he would make life extremely difficult for both of us."

The awfulness of what Lucifer inflicted on his sons slices through me.

"I imagine it's the same speech he gave my mother. When I was around five years old, she withdrew. Turned into a cold woman who never showed me an ounce of affection. For the longest time, I assumed it was me."

Five. When he was five years old and lost the love of the one person he still had in his life.

"I was so angry with her that I shunned her. She eventually moved to Madrid, and only visited occasionally until she passed right before I graduated from university. It wasn't until after her death that I realized Lucifer had probably given her the same talk he had given me about forging a relationship with Gavriil."

I press my lips together to keep the tears at bay. This isn't about me. It's about Rafe and the horrible manipulations of a cruel, selfish man who forced him into this state of existence, one where emotions had been suppressed to the point he now believed himself no longer capable of experiencing them.

He moves away, just a couple steps, but clearly putting distance between us. He sits down on a lounge chair and leans back with a casual arrogance.

"Contrary to popular belief, I am capable of feeling. But I've lived so long in this space devoid of emotion that even when I do feel something, I don't know what to do with it. Usually," he adds with a slight smirk, "the emotions are not positive ones. A flash of fury. A burst of anger. Emotions that are better left under wraps."

I approach the lounge slowly. As I look closer, I see the subtle signs of how deeply the past is gripping him. The tightness in his jaw. The pulse throbbing in his temple. The cold flatness in his eyes that now seems more like a man trying to hold himself back than someone who simply doesn't have a heart. That he left the gala and came back home after his disagreement with Gavriil is a hint that he cares far more for his brother than he's ever allowed Gavriil to see. Perhaps even more than he's admitted to himself.

I put the brakes on my chair and slowly ease myself from it onto the end of the lounge. I scoot closer to Rafe, bracing myself for him to tell me to leave. But he doesn't; he simply watches me. When I'm close enough, I reach up and lay my fingers on his temples. He stiffens beneath my touch, then gradually relaxes as I start to massage his skin.

"Sometimes I dream about my accident," I murmur as I rub at the tension beneath the skin. "How frustrated I felt that Mom was spending all of her time with Katie. Even then, she tended to focus on one thing or one person, pour most of her attention on the new baby. Maybe that's why my father was always working. My grandfather and aunt barely paid him attention. Neither did my mother. He had nothing but work." I shift my fingers slightly, continue to rub soothing circles as I talk, the activity calming me hopefully as much as it's comforting him.

"I remember seeing Mom asleep on the couch. I knew Katie was in her room napping. Mom had promised me that she would take me outside to play that afternoon. But she told me the same thing the day before, and it hadn't happened. So I went out on my own."

I smile slightly. "We lived in a beautiful stone house. We weren't that far out of Dublin, only thirty minutes or so. But to me it felt like we lived in the wilderness. There was a stone wall at the back of our yard. It dropped off on the other side down to a creek. I remember my heart slamming into my ribs when my foot slipped. I remember a sharp pain that cracked through me right before I slipped into a blissful blackness. My next memory isn't until a day or so later, when I woke up in my hospital room to my parents arguing."

I can hear the echoes of that argument. The fury vibrating in my father's voice. The helpless anger in my mother's.

"My father was accusing my mother of not watching me closely enough. My mother was accusing him of not being around enough to help, let alone care about his family. When they realized I was awake, they stopped talking. It's the last time I heard them say anything about the accident, unless we were talking about a surgery or physical therapy.

"To this day, they blame each other. I know my mother also blames herself." I pause, swallow hard. "Her tendency to become hyperfocused turned into hypervigilance. That turned into control. Controlling where I went, what I did. Everything to keep me safe." Despite my anger, I feel a twinge of sympathy. "She once told me she would never fail me again. Toss in my feeling guilty that I disobeyed her in the first place and went out to play when she was asleep, and you have a family that has been living on guilt and blame for the past twenty-one years."

"Is that why you stayed?"

I can feel the hum of his voice beneath my fingers as I continue to massage his skin.

"A large part of it. I felt responsible. For years, I went along with what my mother said because…" My throat tightens. "I wanted redemption. If I listened now like I hadn't before, maybe one day I would make up for all of the trouble I had caused."

"You were a child, Tessa."

"I was." I mentally push away the guilt that tries to surge up. "Something I've come to accept. I made a mistake. So did my parents. Although I can't blame them for all of it. I didn't stand up for myself."

"Again," Rafe repeats as his eyes capture mine, the intimacy of our locked gazes making my breath catch, "you were a child."

"Until I wasn't." I smile sadly. "Guilt and fear kept me trapped just as much as my mother's control issues and hypervigilance."

He leans forward and captures my face between his hands.

"Yes, it's a part of you. But look at what you've done. You," he says with an emphasis that makes my eyes grow hot. "You started up a new business, you're living on your own, scuba diving," he adds with a slight shake of his head and a small smile, "learning how to navigate a new city, a new language. Your life is far richer than mine has ever been."

I grab on to his wrist. "The reason I share all of that with you, Rafe, is because you can still make a choice. You don't have to let the guilt over what happened with Gavriil keep you in this prison you've created for yourself."

He starts to pull away. "Tessa, I'm happy that you have found so much joy. But not everyone does in this life."

He leans down and kisses my forehead in such a way that I know he's preparing to send me back to my room. I inhale, then slide my hands up his chest and around his neck with a boldness I fake every step of the way.

His eyes darken almost instantly. "Tessa."

My name is a warning. One I ignore as I lean up and kiss him. For a moment, he doesn't respond. But when I tease his lips with the tip of my tongue, he groans and hauls me against him, plundering my mouth with lips, teeth, tongue. He devours me, leaves me speechless.

"Tessa."

My body ignites as he growls my name, the sound reverberating through my lips. Every cell attuned to his every breath, the beat of his heart, the rise and fall of his chest.

I pull back just a fraction, still close enough I can feel his breath feathering across my lips.

"I've waited long enough." My hands slide up into his hair. "Make love to me, Rafe."

CHAPTER THIRTEEN

Rafe

HER WORDS UNLEASH the stranglehold I've been keeping on my desire. I slide my hands up her legs, the cool silk sending my pulse skyrocketing as I pull her hips against mine. I fist my fingers in her hair, tilt her head back and kiss her. She returns the kiss with that deep, trusting passion that shocks my foundation and sends me perilously close to the edge I've kept myself away from for years.

I break the kiss long enough to whisk her top over her head. The sight of her breasts, bare again to my gaze, sets me on fire. I cradle the full weight of one in my hand before lowering my head and capturing a dusky peak between my lips. The first suck has her arching against me as she cries out my name. The second makes her press her hips against mine, a move that has me groaning at the exquisite torture of her pressing against my hard length.

I make love to one breast, then the other, feeding off her sighs, her moans, her increasingly frantic movements.

"Rafe." I feel her hands tugging at my shirt. "I want this off."

I chuckle against her skin and sit up. "Demanding."

Pink washes over her cheeks, but thank God she doesn't stop. She pulls the shirt over my head and leans forward, pressing her heated skin against me. The intimacy of the contact, her arms winding around my back and holding me close, shocks me. I've never sat with anyone like this, bodies pressed together, simply savoring the contact between us. I can feel her heart thudding against my chest, smell that delicious floral scent of her shampoo.

I wrap my arms around her and bury my face in her hair. Inhale.

"Tessa… I need you to be sure."

There's no going back from what we're about to do. The thought of her being with anyone else is enough to drive me insane.

But I have to give her one last chance before we pass the point of no return.

She leans back, her eyes luminous and warm. A distant warning bell clangs. I can see something more in the caramel depths. Emotions Tessa shouldn't be feeling. Emotions I shouldn't be responding to.

"I want this, Rafe." She leans up and presses the softest of kisses to my lips. "I want you."

I banish my concerns as I reach up to cradle her face and kiss her deeply.

"I need you to tell me if anything hurts. Not just with this being your first time, but anything else."

Her lips curve into a grateful smile. "I talked to my doctor."

I arch a brow. "About losing your virginity?"

"Yes," she says with an adorable lift to her chin. "I wanted to do it right."

I can't help but laugh as I gather her close and kiss her as I bring one hand up to cup her breast again. I drink in her moan as I run a thumb lightly over her nipple and savor the shudder that racks her body at my touch. She's so responsive I could spend hours just exploring her body and see how she responds to every little touch.

"From where I'm sitting, you're doing absolutely everything right."

"My doctor did say…"

Her voice trails off and I can feel her slight withdrawal. My hands slide down to her waist and I lean back so I can see her face. She glances down. I slide one finger under her chin and slowly lift her face so she can see me.

"You don't have to be embarrassed, Tessa."

"It's not even embarrassment," she says quietly. "She said there may not be as much sensation, or I may not…"

She swallows hard.

"May not what?" I prompt as I graze my fingers over her cheek in a gesture I hope soothes some of the tension gripping her.

"May not get…you know," she says, gesturing to her thighs. "It might be hard for you to…push in."

"Do you remember when we were in the gym?"

She gives me a look that has me biting back a smile. "Yes."

"You were so wet for me, Tessa." My voice grows husky as I remember how her body clenched around me. Just the thought of sliding into that incredible heat sends a shudder through me. "I don't know what this first time will be like. But we'll go slow. Enjoy. You tell me if it hurts. I have no doubt that we're both going to sleep very well tonight."

She sucks in a deep breath and nods. "Okay."

I reach out, grab one of her hands and guide it to my groin. Her eyes grow wide. Her hand wraps around me and I shudder again.

"Careful. I don't want this to end too soon."

Her slow smile is full of wonder. "Really?"

"This is how much I want you, Tessa. You. All of you."

Her eyes sparkle with unshed tears. "Make love to me."

I grab hold of her thighs and anchor her against me. "Hold on." I stand, sealing my mouth over hers as I carry her from the terrace into my room. We don't even come up for air as I walk over to my bed. I sit down on the edge with her wrapped around me, scooting back until I'm sitting against the headboard. I can't remember the last time I kissed anyone like this, the motions hot and heavy one moment, then tender and lingering the next.

Never. I've never enjoyed a woman like this. And I know, deep in my bones, I never will again.

Finally, I tear my mouth away.

"Lay down."

She obliges, stretching out so that her incredible body is on display against the silk sheets, her blond hair glowing like a beacon in the dim light. I move between her legs, the act of nudging her knees apart winding my body so tight it's all I can do not to strip her and take her right there.

Slowly, I hook my fingers in the waistband of her pants. She watches me, eyes fixed on my face as I ease the material over her hips, down her legs, and then toss it onto the floor.

All she's wearing is lace. Red lace that reminds me of that damned nightie I ripped out of the hands of the young man I wanted to toss out onto the street for even daring to look at my wife.

"Beautiful."

I lower myself, kiss her most sensitive skin through the material. Her breath catches, her hips arching up to meet my touch. I tease her, soft kisses and licks until her breathing is ragged and color is high in her cheeks.

"God, Rafe, please."

I grabbed the waistband of her panties and pull them down, tossing them onto the floor before settling between her legs once more. I inhale the scent of her, intoxicated.

"Beautiful," I repeat.

And then I lower my head.

Tessa

I cry out as Rafe's mouth closes over me. The intimacy of what he's doing to me, the sheer pleasure stirred by his tongue running up and down my skin, his teeth grazing me, his lips kissing and sucking, drives me crazy. My hands grab on to the sheets, my fingers hanging onto the silk as heat spirals through my veins. There's a pressure growing between my thighs, a lightness in my chest, the two combining, whirling around inside me until I don't know how I can possibly hang on, how he can keep going when I need—

The light bursts inside me as I cry out Rafe's name, ripples through me like a fast-moving wildfire, consuming everything inside me.

At last, I sag against the bed, my head spinning as I suck in a deep breath.

"That…that was…"

I feel the bed shift under me. I hear a faint rustling. And then my eyes fly open as Rafe settles his naked body on top of me, his hardness resting against my core as his bare chest presses against my breasts.

"Was what?" he prompts with that faint smile.

"Better than anything I've ever done for myself."

He stares at me for a second, then throws back his head and laughs. "God, Tessa, you make me laugh."

His words warm my already heated body.

"You should laugh more," I say, striving for a casual tone as I brush a lock of hair off his forehead. "It's a good look for you."

His eyes darken as I graze my fingernails over his skin.

"Give me a moment."

The absence of his heat as he leaves the bed stirs a longing that goes far deeper than simple lust. I shove it aside as I watch him pull a packet out of his suitcase. Intrigued, I watch him rip it open and sheath his hardness inside a condom.

"I haven't been with anyone in over a year." He walks back to the bed, each step ratcheting up my heartbeat as he draws near. "And my last tests were negative. But this will keep us both safe."

I nod even as loss pulses beneath desire. Knowing that the man who was my first love will not be my last. Not if I'm going to move forward with my life and live it the way I want.

The sadness vanishes as he lowers himself back on top of me. The heat from his body seeps into my skin and sets every nerve ending on fire.

"I need to be inside you."

I swallow hard even as I nod. He reaches between our bodies. His hardness nudges my still-tender skin. My eyes widen as I feel him start to push inside.

"Rafe…"

He freezes. "Do I need to stop?"

His voice comes out strangled, his jaw tight.

"No. Just…" I glance down at where our bodies are pressed together. "Are you sure you're going to fit?"

He lets out a strangled laugh.

"Let's find out."

He pushes deeper with an aching slowness that stirs some of the lingering embers still smoldering beneath my skin. There's a pressure, then a sharp bite of pain.

"Oh!"

He gathers me in his arms, kisses my forehead, my cheeks.

"Hold on to me, Tessa. Just hold on."

I breathe in, gritting my teeth against the pain. Rafe continues to gently kiss me, stroking one hand up and down my side with the occasional whisper of my name.

Gradually, the pain subsides, leaving behind a sensation of fullness. Curious, I shift my hips.

Rafe freezes. "Tessa…"

"That feels good."

"I'm glad," he groans.

"Does it hurt for you, too?"

"A very different kind of pain, I assure you."

I run my fingers up and down his back, savor the feel of the muscles stretched tight beneath his skin.

"Show me what comes next."

His eyes turn molten. He pulls out, then eases back inside me. The friction builds as our bodies move together. Our eyes lock on to each other, our gazes holding as my husband makes love to me.

The pressure builds again, deeper this time. Rafe's thrusts quicken as his breathing intensifies. I climb with him, try to match his rhythm, savor the way our bodies feel together.

"Rafe…"

"Let go, Tessa. Just let go."

Higher, pulses throbbing, blood pumping, hearts pounding.

And then I soar. Up and over into a place of utter pleasure. Rafe follows a moment later, groaning my name as he holds on to me like he'll never let go.

As we drift down, he eases himself off me. I try to grab on to some thread of rational thought, to prepare myself for him to get up from the bed. But instead, he turns on his side and pulls me into the circle of his body. I relax into him, into the comforting weight of his arm across my stomach.

I don't know long we lay like that. A few seconds, a couple minutes, half an hour.

"You were right," I murmur.

"I usually am."

I shake my head as I roll my eyes. "Thorough is the way to go."

He chuckles. Silence falls again. Then, a quick inhale of breath.

"Why did you leave?"

Of all the things he could have said, that was the least of what I was expecting.

I trail my fingers over his arm. "A few reasons."

"Like what?"

"Rafe—"

"Tell me, Tessa."

I think back to how my confiding in Gavriil struck a nerve. Of what he alluded to about how his mother leaving affected him. There's a pain there, one I never would have suspected in the man I knew him to be before Paris.

But one that makes sense in the man I've come to know these past few days.

"I overheard you and Lucifer talking in your study. I was passing by when I heard him say my name. I eavesdropped," I admit. "I heard him asking you if you thought I would be able to have children."

"He was a cruel bastard, Tessa. Whatever nasty things he spewed that night mean nothing."

"It wasn't what he said," I whisper. "It was what you said."

Rafe tenses at my back. "What?"

"When he asked about children, you said it didn't matter because we wouldn't be having them regardless. That you had resolved not to have a family and our marriage would only ever be in name only."

I'd steeled myself for it. It doesn't stop the slice of pain cutting through me as if I were still sitting outside the study door in my wedding dress, tears rolling down my cheeks.

"Lucifer got angry with you. Furious, actually. You told him he should be proud of you for not having a heart. For not being capable of loving anyone, just like him. That you didn't and would never love me."

Why did he have to ask? Why did he have to ruin the aftermath of our lovemaking by bringing up the past? The pain?

I start to roll away. Rafe's hand clamps down on my waist and he rolls me back toward him. He grips my chin in his hand and lifts my head so that I'm looking at him.

"My not wanting children has nothing to do with you, Tessa. And I…" He hesitates. "I care—"

"I know." I truly do. "It just…at the time, I never thought I would get married. Never thought I would have a family of my own. You offered me an escape and I latched on to what you offered without thinking things through."

He stares down at me. I force myself to meet his gaze even as guilt constricts my chest. Can he see the omission lurking beneath the surface? That I once believed myself in love with him and latched on to his proposal like a besotted fool?

"I would not be a good father. I'm not a good husband. I don't have the emotional capacity to serve in either role. I should have had that conversation with you before we married."

"There are two people in this." I lay one hand on his cheek. Something flickers in his eyes. "I could have said something, too. Should have. But I did what you've been cautioning me not to do; latched on to the fairy tale and didn't stop to think about the ramifications."

He blinks, his lips parting as he exhales.

"Tessa…if I could—"

"But you can't."

I don't want to hear empty platitudes or meaningless promises. Rafe has been nothing but honest with me from the beginning. If I had been as transparent as him, we would have never made it to the altar.

Although I can't regret it now. Not after everything that's happened. Not just between us but with my life. Marrying Rafe gave me a courage I hadn't even realized I'd had. If I hadn't said yes to his proposal, I'd like to think I would have eventually made a move on my own.

But I also know it's entirely possible I would still be languishing back on Santorini, staring out over the sea and wishing for a different life.

He gets up and pours us both a glass of brandy from the bar in the corner of the room. As I sit against the headboard, enjoying the spicy taste and flash of fire on my tongue, he brings my wheelchair in from the balcony and puts it next to my side of the bed. Touched, I stare down into my glass.

"Tessa—"

"It's okay, Rafe." I look up and offer him the brightest smile I can. "I promise."

I don't tell him that I wish things could be different as he sets our empty glasses down and rejoins me in bed. That as we lie together, skin to skin, I can feel the soft whispers of old feelings on the edges of my heart. There's no point in sharing that.

"This…" He pauses, as if searching for the right words. "This doesn't feel right."

I caress his shoulder, his biceps, then drift my fingers over his chest. Farther down over the ridges of his abdomen to his hardening length.

"It feels right to me."

"Tessa," he groans.

"Make love to me again, Rafe. Please," I whisper.

CHAPTER FOURTEEN

Rafe

I WAKE UP to sunlight warming my skin. I breathe in deeply, my body heavy. I can't remember the last time I slept so deeply. But I also can't remember the last time I made love four times in one night.

Thinking about the last time, when Tessa got on her hands and knees and allowed me to hold her hips up with my hands as I drove myself inside her, has me hardening almost instantly.

I reach out for her. My fingers cross nothing but cool silk sheets. My eyes fly open. The room is empty.

Slowly, I sit up. This is good. A show of Tessa keeping what's happening between us physically separate from any emotional developments.

It's a good thing, I repeat to myself. A knock has me standing and pulling on a robe before I go to the door and open it. Tessa is right outside the door in her wheelchair, a silver tray balanced across her lap. She's wearing a plain yellow sundress, her hair damp and falling over one shoulder. She gives me a shy smile, one that arrows straight into my chest.

"Good morning."

"Good morning. I thought you might like some breakfast."

I glance down at the tray. "You brought me breakfast?"

She shrugs. "It's the least I could do after last night."

I stand back and let her past, slightly amused that I'm being served breakfast by the woman who I thoroughly seduced multiple times over the course of the evening.

She moves to the table on the balcony and I take the tray from her, setting it down and pulling up lids on dishes of eggs, bacon, and Greek yogurt topped with honey and plump strawberries.

"Thank you." I glance outside and note the sun has barely cleared the horizon. Another glance at the clock in my room has my eyebrows raising. "How long have you been awake?"

"An hour or so. I had a lot of work to do," she adds lightly.

I sense the slight distance between us, the deliberate establishing of a barrier as I sit down across from her. Even though it's a good thing, part of me wants to talk to her, get a sense of how she's feeling after our night together. But I have no desire to make her first morning after making love a tense one. Especially when my questioning after our first round of lovemaking made her relive a painful moment.

I mentally curse Lucifer. He had been furious ever since he'd learned of my proposal to Tessa and realized I had done what he had failed to do for years—acquire Tessa's family's company. Yes, it had been a smart acquisition. But besting my sire had been a satisfying revenge after decades of torment.

A revenge I've now realized hurt someone who didn't deserve any of the pain I inflicted with my carelessness. Another sign that, despite my growing affection for my wife, I'm not the right man for her.

I mentally shift my focus away from the ghosts of my past and concentrate on something I excel at.

"Later today, I can take a look at your business plan."

"Thank you." She murmurs the words without looking up.

"Something on your mind?"

She stirs a dollop of honey into her yogurt. "I was thinking about going out this morning and didn't know if you'd like to join me."

My brief flash of pleasure disappears as quickly as it reared its head. The idea is tempting. No conference calls, no proposals to review, no site visits. A morning to enjoy the company of my wife.

Just the fact that I want to is a red flag that I need to step back. That I'm at risk of feeling more than I should.

"Unfortunately, I can't. I have an hour or so to look over your plan." I keep my voice even, businesslike. "After that I have a conference call, and our flight to Corfu departs at noon.

Her face falls before her expression smooths out. I know I've made the right decision. I need to maintain distance. Even if I feel like a bastard for hurting her. Again.

We finish the rest of the breakfast in silence.

Tessa

I walk out onto the dock of Rafe's villa, excitement pumping through me as I take in the speedboat tied up at the end.

"Good morning!" a man calls to me from aboard the boat.

"Good morning," I call back. "Are you Emerson?"

"Yes. Tessa?"

"Yes. Thank you for coming on such short notice."

When I woke yesterday morning in the circle of Rafe's arms, my body sated and my soul content, a different kind of desire hit me. I suddenly wanted what I had been resisting ever since Rafe agreed to my proposal; the slow, rambling road to intimacy. I didn't just want to spend the next few days in bed.

Well, I amend with a small smile as I near the boat, I do. But I also wanted to spend time with my husband. To get to know the man I shared far more in common with than I realized. Someone who was hurting, living with the guilt of his past.

My smile vanishes as I remember how quickly he retreated from me. It's only been a day, but he's kept his distance, from sitting on the opposite side of the plane on our flight back to Corfu to spending the night alone in his room at the villa.

It hurt. I poured myself into work, spending most of yesterday afternoon and evening jumping back and forth between Juliette's home and the farmhouse.

But this morning when I got up and rolled out onto the balcony, saw the calmness of the ocean, I could suddenly think of nothing else but slipping beneath the waves.

I glance once more over my shoulder. The villa is stark white against the vivid blue sky. My eyes wander over the balconies, the portico.

Nothing.

My stomach sinks. The woman I was six months ago would never have dared to ask Rafe to spend a morning with me. She certainly wouldn't have pushed past the first rejection to try again. But I did, texting him shortly after I booked my dive. He never responded.

I turn my back on the villa and focus on Emerson, on the boat gently bobbing on the surface of the sea and the familiar sight of scuba diving gear on deck. Excitement fills me.

"Just the one dive?"

"Yes. I haven't been diving since I got certified other than practicing in a pool, and I can tire easily."

"Then you're in for a treat." Emerson steps up onto the bow and extends his hand. "If we set out now—"

"Tessa."

I freeze. Then, slowly, I turn, lightness filling my body until I feel like I could fly as I watch my husband walk onto the dock.

"You came."

The blank mask slips, giving me a glimpse of the inner battle he's fighting as his eyes dart between Emerson and me. "I did."

I want to go to him then, wrap my arms around him and kiss him. Something a wife would do when her husband accepts an invitation.

A real wife, I remind myself. I inhale deeply to calm the tingling sensation in my chest.

"Rafe, this is Emerson. He's a divemaster based out of Corfu."

Rafe nods to Emerson. His fingers curl into fists, then flex outward as his gaze locks on to the boat. "One of my meetings was unexpectedly canceled."

My smile dims almost as quickly as it appears. "I told Emerson you weren't coming, so I don't know if there's any gear for you on board."

"Actually," Emerson says, "you called just as I was leaving, so I left all the gear on board. I didn't want to be late."

Rafe looks back at me. His gaze softens as one corner of his mouth curves up. "Let's go diving."

Twenty minutes later, the boat is anchored and Emerson is double-checking our equipment.

"We're good to go."

Emerson helps me sit on the back of the boat and get my legs in the water before going to grab his own gear. Rafe stands next to me, his wetsuit clinging to his muscular physique as he eyes the water.

"It's going to be worth it. I promise."

"Definitely different from the budget meeting I had planned."

I snort. "This sounds way more fun than a budget."

"That's just because you haven't sat through a rousing experience with our head of accounting." He stops, then crouches down next to me, keeping his gaze on the horizon. "Why did you invite me?"

I nearly brush it off with some careless remark. But then I remember Rafe opening up to me in Athens, sharing his painful past. My resolution to remain invulnerable to my husband no longer seems like a show of strength but of weakness. One where instead of taking risks, I'm once again pursing the safe route.

"I've dived once since I got certified with Katie. This is my first ocean dive." Butterflies flap wildly in my stomach as the boat rocks. "I wanted to share it with you."

He tenses next to me. "Why?"

I hesitate. "Because it felt right."

Before Rafe can reply, Emerson reappears. He gives us a couple of instructions before he steps into the water, sending up a plume of spray as he submerges. He surfaces a moment later and smiles.

"Ready whenever you are."

I look up at Rafe. "Ready?"

He blinks, almost hesitating as he stares into my eyes. "Yes."

I pull my mask down, put the regular in my mouth and slip into the water. The sea closes over my head as I sink a couple inches beneath the surface. Rafe jumps into the water next to me. Emerson holds up the okay sign and, at Rafe's and my nods, gestures for us to start descending.

When I was getting certified, this was one of my favorite parts of the dive. The slow descent, the feeling of weightlessness. Not having to be aware of where I was placing my crutches or if there would be a bump as I navigated my wheelchair. I could simply move with a freedom I hadn't experienced in decades. An almost magical sensation of flying, swimming above an underwater world few people see.

I splay my arms and legs out as I slowly drift down. We

near the bottom. My breath catches as I survey the colorful splendor below me. Stunning coral and a rainbow of colors. Fish darting in and out. A turtle nibbling on strands of sea grass. I glance every now and then at Rafe and Emerson, always making sure they're within sight. But for the most part, I just swim, enjoying the world around me.

At one point, I see Rafe staring down a seahorse, one that darts within inches of his mask, then back, then forward again. I smile around my regulator. He glances at me and arches a brow behind his mask. But he's enjoying himself. I can tell as he moves through the water, pausing here and there to watch some creature or examine a bit of coral.

It's odd, seeing him not only in a place so foreign, but so relaxed, so removed from the hustle and bustle of daily life. Odd and enjoyable.

The dive is over far too quickly. Rafe climbs up onto the boat, shutting his vest and tank before turning to help me onto the back platform. Emerson stays in the water until I'm secure on the boat.

"What did you think?"

Rafe glances at the water. "Enjoyable."

"Really? You saw fish and turtles and seahorses. And all you have to say is enjoyable."

"Very enjoyable."

I smile because I can see how much more relaxed he is, saw how engaged he was as he navigated the ocean floor. A smile he returns, his eyes unexpectedly warm with appreciation.

"You're a natural."

Pleasure sweeps through me. "Thank you."

"You're welcome. I haven't been diving in years, but even when I dove every week for an entire summer, I never moved with the confidence and grace you did."

His words fill me as that edge I've been trying to avoid ever since he walked back into my life looms right in front of me. All those years I pined for Rafe, imagined that he saw me as no one else did, formed the foundation of my feelings for him. A foundation I decided must have been constructed of starstruck youth and desperation.

My eyes grow hot as I look away. Infatuation and inexperience may have played a part. But that feeling that Rafe saw more than most, that he paid attention to the person I was inside?

I was right.

The boat ride back to the villa is far too short. As Emerson docks the boat, I'm faced with a question I'm terrified to answer. Has Rafe ruined me for another man? Will I ever be able to share my body, let alone my heart, with someone else after the past few days?

Days, my brain reminds me as Rafe stands to my side, a hand at my back as I move from the boat to the dock. Think about how he's acting these past few months. The years you've known him. A couple days doesn't change the fact that you two have very different expectations for your future.

"Thank you."

I glance up at my husband. "For what"

"Getting me out. Doing something different."

"You're welcome."

Between the sun and the swimming and the emotional wringing I've put myself through, I suddenly want nothing more than to get up to my room, rinse off, and then soak in the Jacuzzi tub until lunch.

"What are your plans for the rest of the day?"

"I hadn't thought much beyond a shower."

"What do you say to another boat ride?"

I smile. "As much as I enjoyed diving, I'm not up for another dive trip."

"Not diving. An afternoon on a yacht."

"A yacht?" I repeat.

"With who?"

"Me."

My heart skips the beat. "You know how to sail a yacht?"

"It helps that it's powered," Rafe says with a smile.

I want to say yes. Or rather, my heart does. My brain is still screaming for me to step back.

"Why did you change your mind?"

"Because I don't know how much time we have left," he finally says.

His admission hits me hard. We're both thinking the same thing. That after last night, there is no reason left for me to stay. The sense of loss even just thinking about leaving tells me that it is probably time to go.

Just a little more time, my heart whispers. Just a little more.

CHAPTER FIFTEEN

Tessa

THE YACHT IS a catamaran, with living quarters strung between the two hulls and a massive white sail stretching toward the horizon. It's a stunning boat with a lounge deck up top, complete with the plump pillows for sunbathing. The main deck boasts the galley with an outdoor dining space, the rails lined with more lounges and cushions. And down below, an en suite with a cozy bed and walk-in shower.

I lift my head from where I'm sitting on the sundeck to watch Rafe at the wheel just a few feet below me. As in everything he does, he looks confident, at ease with his surroundings even as his eyes constantly sweep the horizon.

"When did you take up sailing?"

"Two years ago." He glances up at me, his eyes shielded by his sunglasses. "The CEO of a business I wanted to acquire was an avid sailor." He gestures to the yacht. "So I bought it, took lessons, and when he came to Greece, I took him out on the yacht."

My jaw drops. "You bought a yacht and learned how to sail just make a business deal happen?"

He smirks up at me. "It worked."

I watch his hands expertly move the wheel as he navigates us toward a private cove. When he had first walked down with me to the dock and I'd seen the boat, I'd been excited, thinking that finally here was something Rafe did to relax. Something he enjoyed.

But with Rafe, it was once again about business, and only business.

I roll over on my back and adjust my sunglasses. It didn't matter. Shouldn't matter, I silently correct myself. It does matter because my feelings are still there. I'd been lying to myself when I thought I was getting over him. Being in Paris provided the necessary distance for me to suppress what I felt, pretend that I was getting over him. My time here in Greece has revealed otherwise.

In fact, I think with a soft sigh, my time here has deepened what I started to feel ten years ago. There's nothing to do about it. He's made it perfectly clear he has no interest in a real marriage, and allowing himself to return my feelings. And I will not live any more of my life for someone else.

Even if it means breaking my own heart when I say goodbye.

I push away the negative thoughts and focus on the sun warming my body. I have this last day. One last day to be Rafe's wife in full and enjoy both the physical pleasure and moments of connection we've experienced because of it.

A cove embraces us as Rafe sails in, steep stone walls cradling a blue well. Rafe drops the anchor just off the beach before disappearing into the galley.

"Hungry?"

"Very," I call down as I reach for my crutches.

I meet Rafe on the deck and smile at the food he's arranged on the table, complete with glasses of wine, slices of tomato covered in mozzarella and shredded basil, toasted crackers with tzatziki, and the delicious aroma of gyro meat drifting up from a bowl.

"You can cook."

"More like I can pull food out of the container my chef sent," Rafe says as he pulls back my chair.

We help ourselves to the generous lunch.

"How did you decide on diving?"

I bite into a piece of tomato, chew for a moment as I think.

"Because it scared me. It was my first weekend trip away from Paris. Katie already had plans to go to Switzerland with some friends on one of her university breaks and invited me to come along. I wasn't going to go. I was worried I would just slow her down." I smile. "But she insisted."

"You two have grown close."

"We have. She could have been resentful or even angry at how much attention my mother gave me and not her. Instead, she just embraced me. I took her for granted."

"But you don't anymore."

"No," I say softly. "Not anymore. We were there at the lake, and some of her friends wanted to go on a hike. The trail wasn't accessible, so I opted to stay behind. Next to the café was a diving shop. The owner came out and started talking to me. I told him how much I love to swim. He suggested diving. At first I thought he was joking. But then he started talking to me about it working with other people who have mobility challenges and disabilities. And I was on a calm lake that was the perfect place to explore diving."

He tilts his head to one side. "You were scared."

"Terrified. Moving to Paris was one thing. But tackling something physical that I had never even thought of as a possibility? Plus the risk of failure is a little different when you're under the water."

"But you love it now."

I think back to that first moment, when I sank under the water and took my first breath.

"It was…freedom. I could move. I didn't have to think about what was accessible, if I could move my wheelchair here, rest my crutches there. I could simply just go. Even though sound is amplified under the water, it's a different type of noise. Like a constant shushing. Peaceful."

"Thank you for sharing it with me today."

I smile at him. "Do you think you'll do more of it?"

"Perhaps."

I try to hide my disappointment at his answer. I know he enjoyed it. But nothing's changed.

Nothing will change, I remind myself. Enjoy the moment. Focus on the now.

We enjoy the rest of our meal. As the sun dips down toward the horizon, I glance up at the sundeck.

"What do you think about dessert up there?"

"All right."

I can't get a read on his mood. He's engaged with me throughout dinner, paid attention to everything I've said. He's not as distant as he has been, but there's definitely a wall between us. As if he, too, is anticipating what's coming next.

Rafe helps me navigate the stairs up to the sundeck as water gently laps against the hull of the boat, then disappears back downstairs. He rejoins me a moment later with the drinks and a plate of gourmet chocolates circled by raspberries and strawberries. We sit, sipping our wine and savoring the sweetness of dessert as the waves turn golden orange, then dim to a violet hue.

"Do you remember that party nine years ago? Your father's birthday party. It started to rain halfway through and the lights went out."

His lips tighten. "All too well. He was furious, as if the weather itself had decided not to listen to him."

"I went out on the balcony when I first got there. I didn't realize you were out there."

He glances over at me, his eyes moving up and down my body. "I remember. You were wearing a pink dress."

My mouth drops open as warmth blooms in my chest. "You remember that?"

"I do." He pauses. "Before you realized I was there, you looked sad."

I smile slightly. "Yes. That was most of my life. But not now."

No. Not now.

I set down my wineglass. His eyes sharpen as I place my hand on his chest and push him back.

"I want to taste you."

His lips part as his gaze darkens. "Tessa…"

"Please."

His chuckle is strangled. "How can I say no?"

I grab the hem of his shirt and pull it up over his head, running my hands up his muscled chest before I gently push him back. He lies down on the cushions and watches me as I slide my fingers under the waistband of his shorts. I slowly pull them down, anticipation climbing higher as his hard length springs free.

I toss his shorts to the side, then sit back and look at him.

"You're staring."

"You're impressive."

Another huff of a laugh, one that morphs into a groan as I wrap my fingers around him. Silk, steel and heat. Feminine power fills me as I move my hand up and down, feel him swell in my grasp.

I release him long enough to move between his legs, bracing my arms on his thighs. The moan he makes when I drag my tongue from root to tip makes me feel like a goddess.

"Tessa," he growls.

I take him in my mouth, feel the muscles in his legs bunching beneath my hands as his hips thrust against me. I experiment with how fast I move, loving the rapid pace of his breathing when I move quickly just as much as the long, drawn-out groans when I move slowly. Savor the taste, the feel, the intimacy.

He starts to sit up.

"My turn."

I raise my head. "But I'm not done."

His eyes are molten. "Now, Tessa."

"What if we can both be satisfied?"

He trails a gentle hand along my jaw. "I get joy out of pleasing you, Tessa."

I smile up at him. "I'm glad. But can't we both please each other?"

Rafe

She can't be serious. That possessive, animalistic lust rears its head, howls inside me at the thought of what I think she's suggesting.

"What?"

"If we lay down next to each other and—"

"I'm aware of the mechanics." A disbelieving smile slowly spreads across my face. "I'm just wondering how you do."

"One, I read. Two, Katie is not exactly discreet when it comes to her and Nathan's love life."

"It's a very intimate position."

The minx closes her mouth over the tip of me, gives one long suck that has me struggling to not roll her on her back and slide inside her.

"So is this."

"All right." I lean down, tilt her chin up and kiss her hard. "You lead."

She whisks her top off, revealing a lacy bralette the color of violets. She shimmies out of her shorts. The glimpse of the matching scrap of lace barely covering her most intimate skin leaves my chest so tight I can barely suck in a breath.

"Lay back."

Her whisper is a command, one edged with an innocent shyness that rocks me. Slips beneath my skin, past my walls and straight into my heart. I lay back, wait for her to lie down next to me. I lay my palm against her hip as I feel her fingers wrap around me again. I pull the strip of lace aside and lower my mouth to her core.

Everything fades. Everything but her, me and the heat blazing between us. I can feel her getting close to the edge, her body tightening as her hips press against my mouth. She's dragging me closer to the edge, so fast I'm not sure if I'll be able to hold myself back as the wet heat of her mouth closes over me.

She comes apart beneath my mouth, moaning my name as she shudders. I release her for a fraction of a second as I sit up to grab a condom out of my pants, sheath myself before I cover her body with my own. She's still trembling as I ease inside her. Her body clamps down on me as her eyes fly open, wide with wonder and pleasure.

"Rafe," she gasps as I begin to move. "Don't let go."

Through the haze of pleasure and desire, I hear something. Something deeper in her words. A request I can't honor, a promise I can't keep. I bite back the words I want to say in the moment. Words brought on by the moment, not anything tangible that could last.

But I can give her pleasure.

I kiss her as I move, thrusting in and out of her body, driving us both to the peak. We break together as she cries out. I groan her name and barely resist from collapsing on top of her. Slowly, I lower myself next to her, then reach over and pull her into my arms. Her body is hot, her limbs limp as she chuckles. The simple happiness of it rolls through me.

Until I think about what I have tucked belowdecks. The reason why I invited Tessa out onto the yacht. After diving with her today, accepting that she had invited me to be a part of something intimate and watching as she did something less than 1 percent of people in the world got certified to do, I knew the time had come. I was falling for my wife. I needed to let her go while I still could, when both of us might be able to walk away with as little pain as possible.

Tessa curls into my body, one hand resting over my heart. It gives a hard thump, as if protesting what I'm about to do.

Tomorrow, I tell myself as I close my eyes and pull my wife closer. *Just one more night*.

CHAPTER SIXTEEN

Tessa

I WAKE UP to the gentle rocking of the boat and the heat of Rafe's arms wrapped around me. I blink, my eyes adjusting to the dim sunlight filling the room he carried me to at some point during the night.

Last night seems like a faraway dream. One where I transcended all expectations of what having a satisfying sexual relationship could be. One where I went to the edge of my boundaries and then flung myself over the edge, trusting Rafe with my body.

And my heart. I know as I lie there listening to his quiet, even breathing, that I am in love with him. I never stopped. That first bloom of love was innocent, with no context or depth. But that didn't make it any less meaningful. Over time it did what love was supposed to do; change, grow, persist.

Perhaps a part of me will always love him. Even when I leave Greece, and Rafe, behind and move on with my life.

Rafe stirs at my side. I feel him growing hard against my hip. I turn my head. Pale blue eyes look into mine. This morning there is no mask, no walls. There's only pain. Regret. A want I wish he would submit to so we didn't have to say goodbye.

Desperation fills me. I roll on top of him and wrap my hands around him. His hands move to my hips, supporting me as I lower myself onto him. I moan as he fills me, a delicious tenderness from last night's lovemaking heightening every sensation.

I start to move, then falter. My legs feel weak. My thighs tremble.

Rafe threads his fingers through mine before raising his arms off the mattress, giving me something to brace on. Tears prick my eyes as I rise up, then slowly ease back down. He remembered. He remembers so much about me, so many details about who I am. He sees me like no one ever has.

I just wish he could let himself love me the way I love him.

I ride him with a frenzied passion. He answers, thrusting his hips upward, driving so deep into me I can feel him in every cell of my body.

My peak comes so fast I don't have time to prepare, can't hold back my half scream. He reaches his pinnacle a moment later, his fingers tightening on mine as he grinds out my name. I collapse on his chest and clench my eyes shut to keep the tears from spilling onto his skin.

His hand drifts up and down my back. His lips press a soft kiss into my hair. I could lie here like this forever.

But there is no forever.

I ease myself off him and lay next to him. He's still for a moment. Then he rolls away and gets up.

I feel the severing of our connection like a physical snap.

He disappears into the shower. I wait until the lump in my throat dissipates, until I can open my eyes without letting a tear escape. I pull my wheelchair close and shift into it, grateful for the wider doors and hallways of this yacht that probably costs the same as five years of rent on my apartment.

I grew up in luxury. But not this level. Not where I could buy yachts on a whim and take lessons just to close a deal on millions, if not billions, of euros. Another way Rafe and

I are different. Even if he finds no joy in it, his purpose is to make money. To achieve goals.

Not compatible.

I repeat the mantra to myself in the shower of the guest suite. Say it again as I pull on my dress from yesterday since I hadn't anticipated us sleeping on board and move to the stairs where I left my crutches. I opt to scoot up and drag them behind me. Yesterday I would have had no problem waiting for Rafe and asking him to carry me to the top.

But now, I need to do this on my own. Need to put a stop to any kind of touching. Any kind of intimacy.

I finally make my way up to the lounge. I keep my eyes off the cushions on the floor where we made love to each other in the dark of the night, look out instead to the horizon where the sky meets the sea.

I'm still up there, watching as the sun climbs higher in the sky, when Rafe joins me. He hands me a cup of tea, taking care not to let our fingers graze. Warmth fills my hands, along with the soothing scent of lavender and honey. A sharp contrast to the coldness inside my chest.

"I told you when Gavriil came to live with us that Lucifer told me to keep his distance."

I nod.

"What I didn't tell you was that Lucifer told me if he ever caught me being kind to Gavriil, offering him any sort of friendship or comfort, he would kick Gavriil out of the house and back to the slums."

I nearly spill my tea as my head whips around.

"What?"

Rafe's face is hard, as hard as I've ever seen it. I finally see it for what it is; not a mask worn by a man incapable of emotion. But one who is holding back so much hurt because if he lets even a fraction of it loose, he might break.

"Having your eight-year-old brother look at you with hope

and wanting, needing to respond to that, and knowing that if you do you're consigning him to a horrible fate, does something to you." He speaks coldly, clinically. "The only way to survive, to do what needs to be done even when you pass by his door and hear him crying in the night, is to not feel anything."

He looks at me then. "You make me feel, Tessa. More than I ever thought possible."

He holds my gaze. Let's me see just how much he's withdrawn, how far away he is as he locks everything up.

"But I will never be able to be a good husband or a good father." His voice hardens, as if he's trying to keep his demons at bay through sheer willpower. "My actions proved that a long time ago. I want you to have everything you want, Tessa. Everything," he repeats. "I can't give you everything."

I hate it. I hate Lucifer, I hate what he did to his sons. My mind grasps for a reason, something that would explain why.

But for once, I understand what Rafe said. It doesn't matter. There is no why that will explain this away. That will make things right.

I want to push. I want to ask him to fight. To talk to me. But he's set his boundaries. He has, once again, been honest and up front with me since the beginning. He doesn't believe himself capable of being a good husband. He doesn't want children, not after the trauma he suffered with Gavriil.

I do. I want a husband who will be present, who will love me without reservation. I want children. I want Rafe, too. But I will not restructure my life around someone else. Suppress what I want until it all falls apart.

I set my tea down. Lean over and give him one last lingering kiss on the cheek.

"It's okay, Rafe."

I grab my crutches and move to the stairs, ease my way down and go to the bow of the boat. I sit on one of the benches and gaze out over the sea. A few minutes later, the motors come to life and the boat moves out of the cove.

As we fly across the water, I know I'm doing the right thing. Respecting his choices, standing up for my own.

So why does it feel so wrong to be letting him go?

CHAPTER SEVENTEEN

Tessa
Three weeks later

I SIT ON my balcony, my feet propped up on the railing as I watch night sweep over the city. Lights come on in the windows of the apartments across from me. The Eiffel Tower will be putting on its first show of the evening in just a few minutes. A glass of chardonnay sits at my elbow.

A perfect evening in Paris. A reward for an extremely long but productive day.

Too bad my chest still feels like a hollow pit.

I pick up my glass of wine. The recommendations Rafe made for Tessa's Interiors have already paid off. I hired an assistant last week who has already earned her salary and will be getting a nice bonus at the end of the summer. Her assuming the administrative tasks has left me more time for my designs. I'm sticking to my proposed prices for Juliette's house and an upcoming project for a London penthouse. But another new client, one I just signed a contract with yesterday, agreed to my new pricing.

And then there's the addendum on my website. The one where I take on a limited number of clients a year who don't have the funds or resources to afford my regular fees but need help the most. My ability to take on more clients with Veronica's help, along with my higher fees, will help absorb the cost. So, too, will the partnerships I'm starting to develop with quality suppliers.

Business life is good. My limited personal life is, too. Yesterday was Katie and Nathan's engagement party aboard a boat that cruised the Seine and gave awed guests jaw-dropping views of Paris at night.

I kept a smile pasted on my face most of the evening and offered up what I thought was an excellent toast to Nathan and Katie's future happiness. I even managed to greet my parents and then keep my distance from them the rest of the evening. It didn't stop my mother's eyes from watching me like a hawk. Nor did it wipe the glower off my father's face.

I inhale as somewhere a clock chimes. The lights of the Tower come to life, a distant sparkling gleam.

A knock sounds on my door. Too soft and tentative to be Rafe. Not that it would be him, I remind myself as I grab my crutches and get to my feet. For the first week, a foolish part of me held on to some distant hope that he might reach out. Might tell me that he wanted to change his mind.

Silence. Complete and utter silence. Which meant the next time I would hear from him would be in five months when he signed the divorce papers and officially ended our marriage.

With that cheery thought on my mind, I unlock the door without looking through the peephole.

And come face-to-face with my mother.

"Oh."

She gives me a nervous smile. "Hello, Contessa."

I wrinkle my nose at my full name. "Hi, Mom."

She looks over my shoulder. "May I…? That is…"

Have I landed in an alternative universe? One where she's asking to come in instead of just barging past me? Is this some sort of trap, or perhaps a bid to convince me to come home?

"Sure. Come in." I step back and let her enter, closing and locking the door behind her.

She moves into the middle of the room, her eyes sweeping over the living space, the kitchen, the dining nook, the balcony and the Eiffel Tower. She turns in a circle, her eyes taking in the details like the mirror over the fireplace, the vase of pale blue flowers in the corner.

Flowers I bought that morning because they reminded me of a certain set of eyes.

God, I'm pathetic.

"It's beautiful, Contessa."

I grit my teeth, waiting for the other shoe to drop. "Thank you."

She turns back to me, hands clasped in front of her. She's nearly sixty, but she could easily pass for someone fifteen years younger. Dark brown hair, the same color as Katie's. A heart-shaped face with the faintest lines by her eyes and mouth. The same brown eyes as mine.

Eyes that are now full of sorrow.

I steel myself, waiting for the guilt trip.

"I'm sorry."

I blink. "What?"

"I look around this room and I see…you." She sighs. "The woman I imagine you would have discovered a long time ago if I would have just let go."

Of all the things she could have said, this was the last thing I was expecting.

"I'm… Mom, I hope you can understand why I'm a little confused."

"I can." She takes a deep, shaky breath. "If now's not a good time, I can—"

"No." I take a moment, trying to wrap my brain around what's happening. "Let's sit down. Would you like a glass of wine?"

"Yes. But I can get it…" Her voice trails off. She blinks, then takes another deep breath. "That would be nice. Thank you."

I recognize her words for what they are. An acknowledgment of my independence, that she doesn't need to be hovering nearby, doing everything for me even as she slowly takes away my autonomy.

"I'll let you know if I need help, Mom."

She nods, her lips pressed together, and moves out to the balcony. I join her a minute later, setting her glass down as I ease into my chair and prop my crutches against the railing. My mom's eyes are trained on the Eiffel Tower, her expression awed.

"How did you ever find this place?"

"A friend of Katie's. She came here for a semester abroad, fell in love with Paris and stayed. She works for a property company that rents out places mostly to students." I glance back at my apartment, pride filling my chest as the soft glow from the lamps washes the ivory walls with a pale gold hue. "I love it here."

"I can tell." She raises her wineglass. "You look happy."

I take a sip of my own wine, trying to come up with the right words. Finally, I just blurt out what's on my mind.

"Why are you here, Mom?"

The faint wrinkles in her forehead deepen as she frowns. "I was very angry when you first left. Like all the work I'd poured into keeping you safe all these years was for nothing."

Even though I know I have nothing to feel ashamed for, my body responds to the decades-old fear of hurting my mother. My stomach pitches down to my feet as I force myself to hold her gaze.

"I'm sorry if I worried you, but—"

"I made a mistake, Tessa. A lot of them," she adds into the surprised quiet that follows her pronouncement. "Too many. Mistakes I had ample time to reflect on once I was alone in the house. But you, or rather how I treated you, is probably the biggest mistake of all."

My heart twists in my chest as anger I didn't even realize I'd been holding on to started to unknot itself. "Mom…"

"I don't know if you're going to excuse what I did, so let me be the first to say there is no excuse. I…" Her eyes glint with unshed tears. "I feel like I clipped your wings. Like there were so many times you could have been happy, and I stole that from you because I was so afraid of letting you fall again."

I reach over and cover her hand with mine. For the first time in a very long time, I feel connected to my mom.

"I'm the one who fell, Mom."

She shakes her head. "I'm your mother. I didn't lock the door that morning. I knew I was too tired, and I should have taken your aunt up on her offer to help. But I wanted to prove to your father…" She falters as a dull red stain creeps up her neck. "He was working so hard to try and earn your grandfather's approval. I told him I could handle it. You, Katie, the house. We were fighting so much. I wanted to show him I could do it, and you paid the price."

I look down at our hands stacked on top of one another, mine tan from my time in Greece, hers with the beginnings of wrinkles etching themselves into her skin. So much time has passed since that day. So much has changed. Yet the guilt we both carry lingers.

"I felt like it was all my fault for the longest time."

Mom sniffs. "Makes us quite the pair."

"I think what upset me the most was you not wanting me to use crutches. The wheelchair is easier, but I like having the choice and being able to move."

"And I should have let you. Just after that incident in Dublin, I didn't want you to be embarrassed again."

I frown. "What incident?"

She stares at me. "You don't remember."

"No."

She blinks rapidly. "I can't believe you don't remember. We

went back to Dublin for a visit when you were ten or so. You were attempting to use crutches here and there. You stumbled and fell in a store. Some other girls laughed at you." Her eyes narrow as they snap with anger. "There was a woman, too, who made a horrible comment about how I should just put you in a wheelchair instead of trying to show you off."

I gasp. The vague stirrings of a memory, of laughter as I lay on a tile floor, stir. But it's just that, a vague recollection.

"That was my final straw. After that, I just... I just wanted to keep you safe." She sniffs. "And instead I hurt you."

I want to say it's okay. But it's not. Finally, after years of suppressed hurt and frustration, my mom and I are clearing the air. Dismissing her apology would be a disservice to both of us.

"Thank you, Mom."

She looks back at my apartment. Her smile is tinged with pride. Deep inside, I feel the edges of an old wound start to come together. Far from healed. But starting down a path I never thought possible.

"Yet look at all you've accomplished. It's incredible."

"Thank you." I glance down, suddenly shy. "I actually just took on a new client. And hired an assistant."

Her smile widens. "You always did have a knack for decorating. Maybe you can give your father and me some tips."

The thought of going back to Santorini, of visiting, still makes my chest tight. But not nearly as much. And as I think of the home I grew up in, with its huge windows and colorful furniture, I smile.

"I'd like that. How is Dad?"

A shutter drops over my mother's face. "Well, I think."

"Is he not here?"

"No, he went back to Greece this morning."

The pain in her voice is faint but present.

"Are you two okay?"

She shrugs. "After we saw you at Katie's engagement party, we had…a very hard conversation."

Alarm shoots through me. "Are you two…?"

Another shrug. "I don't know. We both said a lot of things we'd been holding in for years. My anger at how he became so fixated on his career. His anger at what he saw as my lack of support and how I can become…fixated on things." Her expression turns sad. "We both knew about that. But I didn't realize the remorse he'd harbored all those years."

"Remorse?"

"I think he knew, deep down, that he threw himself too hard into his career for where we were at in life. He's carried guilt around all these years that if he hadn't gone to Dublin that day, maybe you wouldn't have fallen."

I shake my head. "It's hard to realize how much we've all been letting regret run our lives."

"Until now." My mother's smile is almost shy. "You and Katie have accomplished so much. You especially since you left."

She takes a sip of her wine. Even though it was the right thing to do, I realize that her staying back in Greece after I left, making a conscious choice not to interfere, to let me live on my own and make my own successes and mistakes, was not only a gift to me but must have been incredibly hard on her.

"Thank you, Mom. I…" I glance out over Paris, at the sights that have become so familiar to me. "I'm happy here. Happier than I've ever been."

"But you're still sad."

I think of Rafe. Nod.

"You went to Corfu with Rafe."

"How did you…?"

She gives me a look. "One, I'm your mother. Two, people talk."

"Gossip strikes again," I mutter, with no small degree of irritability.

"Are you and he getting back together?"

I shake my head, will myself not to lose my control and cry. "No. I wanted to, but he… Lucifer really did a number on him."

"On both those boys," my mother says grimly. "I had my suspicions. But every time I talked to Lucifer or them, they would either say nothing or insist everything was fine."

"He… Rafe doesn't think he can be a good husband. And he doesn't want kids."

"Oh." Her mouth tightens. "But you…"

"Yes," I say gently. "I can."

Her eyes glint as she gives me a watery smile and then looks away. We sit for a long time, watching as more lights wink on across the city and life streams by on the sidewalks below.

"Do you love him?"

I don't even hesitate as I nod.

"Have you told him?"

"What's the point?" I finish off my glass of wine and set it down harder than I intended. "He doesn't want kids."

"If he truly doesn't and you do, then no, it won't work." She frowns. "I just wonder…"

"I don't want to push him, Mom. I don't…" I try to think of a way to rephrase my next words so I won't hurt her.

"You don't want him to feel pressured into being someone he's not."

I nod, grateful she understands.

"I agree. I respect you, too, for learning a lesson I should have learned far sooner. I just wonder if he told you something and you backed off, or if you had a conversation about it. If you told him how you felt about him."

The thought of telling Rafe I love him makes my breath hitch.

"I didn't."

"Because it was the right thing to do?" my mother asks gently. "Or because you're afraid?"

The question stabs straight to my heart. I stare at her as the truth of why I held back even as I fervently wished for Rafe to put his soul on the line.

"Oh, God." I run my hands through my hair. "I'm an idiot."

"No. You're just in love." My mother surprises me by laughing and clapping her hands together as she looks up to the sky. "One of my wishes was that my daughters would always fall in love."

"Well, we know Katie's story has a happy ending. Mine may not."

My mother is the one to reach across the table this time and grab my hand. "No matter what happens, enjoy the time you've had. Don't focus exclusively on the bad. I missed out on twenty-one years because of that."

"So did I." I take a deep breath. "And maybe Rafe won't be a part of my future. But I'm not ready to give up yet."

CHAPTER EIGHTEEN

Rafe

I'M SITTING IN a plush gray chair, staring out over the sea, when James calls me.

"Your brother is here, sir."

There's a muffled growl on the other end of the line.

"Pardon, sir...*brothers*."

I arch a brow. "Michail?"

"Yes, sir."

The last thing I want is to have both my brothers here. Especially Michail, who I've seen all of two times since learning of his existence. Once at Lucifer's will reading and the other at Gavriil's wedding, where we exchanged mutual looks of extreme dislike before continuing on to opposite sides of the celebration. He believes Gavriil and I are just like the man who seduced and abandoned his mother. I know it's unfair, but when I learned my father had another son, one just a few years younger than me, I had felt betrayed. Deceived. Ridiculous, I know, but it doesn't stop the feelings.

"Send them up."

Easier to tell them to get the hell out of my house in person. And Michail strikes me as the person who would have no problem bullying my butler with his immense size and glower that matches mine in intensity.

Less than two minutes later, the door slams open. Gavriil strides in.

"There you…" His voice trails off as he takes in the room. "What the hell? I thought you were selling the place."

"I am."

Although it will be hard to let go of this room. The room Tessa decorated for me.

A week after she left, James appeared upstairs in my office, looking as close to concerned as I'd ever seen him.

"Sir, there's a group of people here who says they're under orders from Mrs. Drakos to update the master bedroom."

I'd nearly told him to dismiss them. I wanted no memory of Tessa, nothing of her in this house to haunt me.

But a deal had been a deal. So I'd simply told him to let them in, so long as they kept their activities to the master bedroom. I'd avoided that section of the hall while they were here, and five days after they left.

Until one night, when I had to go downstairs to fetch something out of the vault and passed by the gym. Glimpsed my reflection in the mirror and immediately saw Tessa lying limp and satisfied in my arms.

I couldn't shake her; the sound of her laugh, that occasional floral scent that seemed to appear out of nowhere. I thought I was going mad at times.

I walked up from the lower level and went straight for the master bedroom. If I confronted what remained of her in this house, faced it down and showed myself I could stay strong, then I could move on.

And then I'd opened the door and walked into my own private paradise.

Still the same ivory walls. Still the same vivid blue curtains. But instead of the heavy, claw-footed furniture trimmed in gold brocade, Tessa had swapped it out for soft grays that reminded me of a misty morning on the sea, and clean lines that appealed to my sense of efficiency. Plush rugs covered areas like the floor beside the bed, no longer a four-poster but a massive king with a gray headboard.

But of all the things she'd included, my favorite had been the art. Paintings of the sea, of the olive groves. Artwork, I'd realized, of the villa. Of Corfu. I'd called up the person who had left a business card behind and learned all of the paintings were done by local artists.

I hadn't slept in here yet. Hadn't been able to bring myself to. But I spent countless hours in this room, drawn to it in both calm and tumultuous moments over the past week.

Gavriil turns in a circle. "This is... Did Tessa do this?"

I nod. "She did."

Michail glances around. "Nice."

"You let her go." Gavriil refocuses on me and glares. "Again."

"I believe I recall telling you that what happens between *my* wife and me is none of your concern."

My voice is low, dangerous. I already feel like my guts have been ripped out. The void I existed in before Tessa was one of comfort. A blessed nothingness where facts and efficiency ruled.

But this...this is hell.

"It is unless I see two people I care about hurting."

I shoot up out of my chair. "You saw her? When?"

He smirks at me. I don't even care that I've shown my hand. I just want to know if she's all right.

"Two nights ago. Her sister's engagement party."

"She looked beautiful," Michail adds.

I whirl on him, this behemoth of a mountain man with his thick beard and eyes just like mine. Jealousy pounds through me as he shoots me a cocky smile.

"You were there?"

"I had business in Paris. I've done work for her sister's fiancé's company."

Gavriil's glare deepens. "She looked like she's had her heart broken."

His words gut me, just as Gavriil intended. I turn away.

"Better now than later when we were even deeper."

"Why?"

I look over my shoulder. "Why what?"

"Why are you doing this? Why are you shoving her away? And don't give me that damned speech about her deserving better than you," Gavriil adds as I start to reply. "I want the real reason."

"As I said, it's none of your concern."

Michail shakes his head. "Stubborn ass."

I narrow my eyes at him. "I've heard you're even more so."

"From who?"

"Alessandra."

Bull's-eye. Michail stiffens at the mention of our father's estate lawyer.

"When did you talk to Alessandra?" he growls.

"I didn't." I allow myself a small smirk. "But it was obvious to anyone with eyes that something is going on between you two."

"Focus," Gavriil snaps. "We'll get to your mess next. You," he says as he stabs a finger in my direction. "Tessa loves you. And I suspect you love her."

"Suspect no longer, brother. I love her. As much as I can, anyway," I add with a slight smile at the shell-shocked expression on Gavriil's face.

"Then why?"

I move over to the sideboard, also done in that misty gray wood, and pour myself a finger of bourbon. Gavriil shakes his head when I hold up the bottle, but Michail nods with more enthusiasm than I've seen for anything else.

"You told me at Paul's retirement party that I left you alone all those years ago. Had nothing to do with you."

Gavriil's hands tighten at his sides.

"That's exactly what you did."

"For a reason." I shove a glass into Michail's hand before raising my own to my lips. "Had I so much as told you things were going to be okay, Lucifer would have kicked you back out onto the streets."

Gavriil's face goes slack. "What?"

"He held that threat over my head until the day you moved out. Then it became he would take away your share of the company."

"You're saying you stayed away all these years to protect me?"

"That sums it up, yes."

I almost feel bad for my little brother as he stands there looking at me as if he's never seen me before.

Michail laughs under his breath. "I'm glad I only met the bastard once."

"You were fortunate." I take a drink, savor the rich burn of bourbon down my throat. "Withdrawing from the world was the only way to survive the hell he created."

"Rafe…" Gavriil's voice is thick with emotion. "I'm sorry."

"Don't apologize. We were both at his mercy."

"But…all the things I said…"

I shrug. "When you have a heart of ice, it doesn't matter much," I lie.

"Except Tessa does matter."

My throat tightens. "She does. Like I said at the party, the best thing I can do is let her go."

"Really? Because I'm guessing by the way she stayed by the railing all night and stared out over the city, she feels differently."

"I don't want children, Gavriil. She does."

But even as I say the words, something shifts in my chest. The certainty that I've always had toward children, or rather not having them, is no longer rock-solid. Now it's faint, interspersed with a suddenly crystal-clear image of Tessa and me on the yacht, sitting on the bow with a toddler between us, with my dark curly hair and her beautiful caramel-colored eyes.

I've never allowed myself to dwell on the possibility. To even consider it. Not when those first few years of having Gavriil living in the house, of seeing his eyes following me with mixed hatred and yearning as I ignored him, left scars etched so deeply on my heart I can never be rid of them.

I was backed into a corner by a monster. But at some point, I became one, too. The deeper I retreated into the void, the more it angered Lucifer, drove him to the brink of losing control by simply feeling nothing.

What will it be like to let go? To feel…everything?

"You're nothing like him."

Gavriil's pronouncement has my head snapping around.

"Really? I could have sworn you've been saying the opposite all these years."

"I wouldn't be working with you if I thought you were truly like him. I was angry, yes," Gavriil admits. "Hurt. The worst part was not understanding. But damn it, Rafe, you're an honorable man. You're a great leader. I've learned a lot from you."

The rare compliments fly straight as arrows into my chest.

"I'm glad I could—"

Before I can react, Gavriil crosses the room in two strides and envelopes me in a hug. I freeze, shooting Michail a look over Gavriil's shoulder.

"Don't look at me," Michail says as he takes another swig of bourbon. "I just came because he told me we were coming to kick some sense into you."

"Gavriil..."

My brother pulls back and grasps me by the shoulders.

"Thank you."

The gratitude behind his words, the unspoken acknowledgment of what Lucifer put me through in an effort to set Gavriil up to fail, hits me. I nod.

"You're welcome. You can thank me by never hugging me again."

Gavriil's smile flashes white and bright.

"What can I say? Love does crazy things to a man's head."

They leave five minutes later, Michail saying something about an important meeting he has to get to in New York. He avoids my gaze as he says this. I make a note to call Alessandra in a couple days. We're not friends. But I respect the hell out of the woman. She's the only estate lawyer who Lucifer didn't fire or scare off.

Blessed silence descends. I sit back in that gray chair, the one with the high armrests and slightly inclined back. It invites me to sit, to relax.

Just as Tessa would have.

I stand and move to the balcony. Even out here, I can see her touch. The swapping out of the ostentatious patio furniture for white lounges and dim lighting that, when it grows dark, will enhance the intimacy of the terrace.

Quiet. Privacy. Rest.

She knows me. Has known me for years. She never once said she loved me. But I saw it in her eyes, heard it in her voice as she talked to me, especially on that last day when I could feel her heart breaking. When mine broke along with hers.

I turn and glance back at the master suite. It's perfect, right down to the framed photograph on the bureau of Gavriil and me from our first press conference in California following Lucifer's death. A subtle touch, but one that matters, especially in light of Gavriil's and my conversation today.

The room is perfect. Except one thing's missing.
Tessa.

Just like that, the puzzle pieces of my relationship with Tessa fall into place. The room doesn't make sense without Tessa here. My life doesn't make sense without her.

And I let her go. Again.

Urgency grips me. I yank my phone out of my pocket, start to dial the number for my secretary in Corfu as I rush to the door. I need to get to Paris, need to tell her everything, need to ask her to cancel the petition for divorce—

A knock sounds on the door. I grit my teeth, not in the mood to deal with Gavriil's or Michail's machinations.

I grab the door handle and yank it open.

"I told you two…"

My voice trails off as I realize who's standing on the other side of the door.

Tessa.

CHAPTER NINETEEN

Tessa

I STARE AT my husband, standing framed in the doorway looking impossibly handsome as always in black pants and a black shirt.

"Tessa."

I want nothing more than to go to him, press myself against him and fling my arms around his neck. Tell him everything that's on my heart.

Slowly. I need to go slowly so as not to send him running off into the night.

"Hello, Rafe."

"What are you doing here?"

My resolve falters. Is he not happy to see me?

And then I shake my head. Maybe after I tell him everything I've come to say, he'll still stick to his resolve to have nothing to do with me. That having a family of his own is the last thing he wants.

But I can try. I can tell him everything I'm feeling, take the risk and reap the rewards or leave Rafe in my past knowing I did everything in my power to try.

"I… I forgot something."

Ah, yes. The lamest excuse I could possibly come up with.

His brows draw together. "In the master suite?"

"Well…" My voice trails off as I take in the room beyond him. "Oh! It really turned out well, didn't it?"

He glances over his shoulder. Then, at last, he opens the door wider and steps aside, gesturing for me to come in. I try to ignore the heat of his body as I pass by. I sweep a critical eye over the furnishings, the decor. It turned out even better than I anticipated.

"Do you like it?"

"Yes."

I glance at him over my shoulder. He's watching me with an intensity that unsettles me. Momentarily knocks me off my course.

"I'm glad."

"The paintings were a nice touch."

"Thank you." I hesitate. "I always saw you looking out. I thought after a long day, this might be a good place for you to come."

He takes a step toward me. My breath freezes in my chest.

"I always commended myself on my powers of observation. But you have considerable skill of your own."

"Thanks." I try to force a smile, even as it feels as though a dozen birds are madly beating their wings against the inside of my rib cage. "An important skill for an interior designer."

"You failed to notice one thing, however."

I blink, unsure of what to say. "Oh?"

"You didn't notice the most important thing that's missing in here."

My eyes roam around the room, trying and failing to think of what I missed.

"What?"

"You."

Time stops. We stare at each other, hearts thudding, pulses pounding. I swear I can hear his from across the room.

And then we're moving, crashing into each other as though

it's been years instead of a few weeks. His arms band about my waist. I release my grip on my crutches, slide my arms out of the cuffs and let them drop as I fling my arms around his neck and bury my face against his shoulder.

"Rafe."

His name comes out on a sob. His fingers tangle in my hair as he pulls back just enough to seal his lips over mine. The kiss travels through me, lightning bolts of pleasure that blend with the sensation of coming home.

"Tessa." He keeps one arm around my waist to steady me as the other comes up and cups my face. He presses a tender kiss to my forehead. "I was going to come to you. To Paris."

"Guess I beat you to it."

I cling to him. His initial reception gives me hope. But I know there's still so much to be done. So much for us to figure out.

For now, though, just for this moment, there's us. There's hope.

"I did forget something, you know," I murmur against his neck.

"What's that?"

I steel myself, summon every ounce of courage I have even as I fight against a deep-seated fear.

"I forgot to tell you I love you."

His fingers still on my back as his body tenses in my arms. My heart catapults into my throat. Have I made a mistake?

One hand grips my chin and tilts my head up. His mouth crashes down onto mine. A deep, possessive kiss that makes my soul sing.

"Tessa."

He murmurs my name, says it over and over again as he kisses my lips, my cheek, my forehead.

"I should have told you." I hold on to his neck, lean into his touch. "I didn't want to tell you and have it come across like I was using my emotions to keep you tethered to me. To influence your decision."

He pulls back and gives me that half smile that drives me crazy. "If you haven't noticed, I rarely surrender to the wishes of others."

"It wasn't worth the risk." My tone is serious, my conviction strong. "I never wanted you to feel trapped, Rafe. I already felt like I had used you when we got married. I couldn't bear to do that again. To either of us."

"I don't know if you telling me then would have made a difference. I was so entrenched in the idea that I wasn't enough for you that I was blind to everything else." He glances around the room. "It took you being gone for me to realize the kind of life I could have with you. And the kind of life I would have without."

He leans down, presses his forehead against mine. "The possibility of having a real marriage, a family, all of it seemed impossible because I had never really contemplated it. When I saw you in Paris, I wanted more. But my only basis for comparison were my experiences with Lucifer and my mother and Gavriil."

I trace a soothing hand down the side of his face. "Gavriil wasn't your fault."

"I talked with him."

"When?"

"Just before you arrived. You must have just missed him." He shakes his head. "Michail was here, too."

"The Drakos brothers all together." I laugh slightly. "I would have paid to see that."

"It was something." His smile fades as his gaze intensifies. "It was…helpful. I don't know where it will lead. But I didn't realize until Gavriil forgave me that I'd been carrying that weight around with me for so long. It impacted me more than I had realized. Once I didn't have that hanging around my neck…"

His breath rushes out. He moves one hand between our bodies. When he settles in on my stomach, I can't help it. Tears gather on my lashes. One traces a warm trail down my cheek.

"I thought about it, Tessa. I thought about it and suddenly I wanted it like nothing I've ever wanted before. Well," he says as he looks up from where his hand rests, "except you. None of it means anything without you."

"Rafe." His name is a broken sob as love swells inside me.

"I love you, Tessa. I've loved you for far longer than I ever realized. When you left…" His breath rushes out. "It nearly killed me, Tessa."

"I missed you, too. It was like a piece of me was missing. I couldn't have survived."

"You could have." His voice is strong, firm in his belief. "You are so capable, Tessa. I still have things to figure out with Drakos Development and what my future will look like. But I promise to never hold you back. Your company, scuba diving, mountain climbing…"

I laugh. "Mountain climbing?"

"I have literal billions at my disposal." He kisses me, as if he can't bear to stop touching me. "No matter what the future holds for us, you will always have the freedom to do what you want."

"Rafe, that means so much. But," I add gently as I brush a kiss along his jaw, "you're a part of this, too. That means we'll figure it out together."

He guides me over to the edge of the bed and helps me sit. He holds up a finger and disappears, giving me a moment to look around the room and take in everything from the wood ceiling fan spinning lazily overhead to the picture frame he kept on the bureau.

I thought I was happy in Paris. That was nothing compared to the complete and utter contented joy filling me to the brim.

Rafe walks back into the room, a sheaf of papers in hand. He drops down to one knee in front of me and holds them up.

"Tessa Drakos, may I have the honor of ripping up this petition for divorce?"

I can't help my laugh. "Yes."

He grabs the corners of the petition and rips it clean down the middle. He tosses the torn shreds on the floor behind him, then grabs my left hand in his. A smile spreads across his face as he sees the engagement ring made of citrines and diamonds and its matching platinum band.

"You put it back on."

"It seemed right since I was coming back here to tell you I wanted to give us a little more time."

"And now?" he asks as he gently tugs the rings off.

"Now I want forever."

A shudder passes through him.

"The last time I proposed, I asked you if a marriage would be agreeable."

I press my lips together to keep from smiling. "I remember."

"This time, though," he says as he slides the engagement ring back onto my finger, "I'm asking you to stay married because I love you. I admire you. I want to dive with you in the ocean and wake up with you in my arms every morning. I want to travel the world and, when the time comes, I want to be the father of your children."

Tears are falling down my cheeks, steady now, but I don't care.

"Yes, Rafe. Yes."

He slides the silver band onto my finger. I barely have time to look at the rings together before he eases me back onto the bed and covers my body with his. I respond in a heartbeat, every fiber of my being trembling as his firm weight settles on top of me. His breath feathers over my skin.

"I haven't slept in this bed yet."

I blink back more tears. "I'm not normally this weepy."

"So long as they're good tears." He kisses one away as it slips down my cheek. "The thought of sleeping in here without you...it felt wrong."

I kiss him. "I'm here now."

"You are," he says with another true smile that melts my heart. "And I'm never letting you go again."

EPILOGUE

Rafe
Three years later

TESSA DARTS BACK and forth just a few feet above the sea-floor, her movements confident and strong as she follows a school of fish. I smile behind my regulator. The woman is a mermaid in the water.

I glance at my dive computer. Signal to her that we're okay to surface. She nods and we slowly ascend together. We break the surface of the water, pulling our masks down as we fill our vests with air and float.

"It never gets old," she says with a laugh.

"Never will."

I reach out, grasp her hand in mine and bring it to my lips. Her eyes darken as she smiles at me, the curve of her lips promising decadent things.

A soft coo reaches my ears. I turn and smile up at my daughter.

My daughter, I marvel as Adessa smacks the railing of the yacht with a chubby hand. Her Ttheía Katie keeps one arm around her waist. Her Theíos Nathan snaps a photo.

Even after ten months, it doesn't seem real. To have a beautiful little girl who looks exactly as I pictured her: dark-haired with caramel-colored eyes and the most incredible smile.

Tessa and I had taken our first year together to just be.

Waking up in Paris on Saturday mornings and making love before going out to explore the city. Traveling back to Santorini so she could visit her father and make amends with her past while redecorating the villa where Gavriil and I had spent so many horrible years.

On our second anniversary, we'd decided to try for a family. The year that had followed had brought numerous joys, including Tessa's business expanding to include another decorator that handled some of the higher-end designs and gave Tessa more time to devote to her passion projects, including designing accessible suites for a luxury hotel along the southern coast of France.

We'd needed every one of those joys as each month the test had read negative. As we'd had long discussions about how to proceed. Her doctor had been optimistic, but even her words couldn't fully erase Tessa's fears.

Until two months after our third anniversary when she'd sent my heart pounding with a scream that filled the villa on Corfu. I ran into our suite to find her sitting on the bed, a test clasped in her hands. She'd looked at me, eyes shining, her face lit up with her smile.

We're pregnant.

The pregnancy had thankfully gone almost perfectly, aside from the usual exhaustion and morning sickness. The wait to get pregnant had brought about an unexpected blessing, too. As we'd passed the year mark trying to conceive, we'd explored other options for expanding our family. When Adessa turned two, we planned to give her a sibling through adoption.

Tessa glances over the deck.

"Where's Mom and Dad?" she calls.

Katie grimaces. "Don't ask."

Tessa makes a retching sound as I grin. It took a solid year of counseling, but Tessa's mother and father managed to work through years of guilt, anger and misunderstandings. The unfortunate side effect is that they have become notorious for slipping off to catch up on "lost time."

"You got a call, Rafe," Nathan calls down. "Another client."

I shake my head. "Great."

Tessa playfully splashes me as we paddle toward the yacht. "Hey. At least people like you."

True. Shortly after Tessa and I reunited, I sold my shares of Drakos Development to Gavriil. Michail, predictably, wanted nothing to do with them. Within months, Gavriil had a CEO lined up, one who agreed with Gavriil's vision for the direction of the company and jumped into the fray without hesitation.

Leaving me to set up my own consulting business doing what I specialize in as well as enjoy: organizing, planning, scheduling. It also gave me the freedom to join Tessa wherever she needed or wanted to be: the States, Paris, London and beyond.

Including what I've come to think of as "our cove" just a few miles away from our villa on Corfu. A place that has become a gathering for Tessa's family and mine. Once a place I loathed and now feel like I'm coming home every time I walk in the door.

"Da-da!"

My head snaps around. Adessa is grinning at me, her beautiful little face lit up with a cheeky grin.

"Did she just…?"

"Sorry," Katie says to her sister with a slight laugh. "I think she did. Baby girl's first word!"

As Katie and Tessa exchange jokes, my eyes drift between my wife and my daughter. A few years ago, I never would have imagined such happiness was possible. But now, as I reach the back of the boat and help Tessa out of her vest before she pulls herself onto the back of the boat, I can only think about how grateful I am that Tessa came back.

"What are you thinking of?"

She's sitting on the edge of the platform, her gear next to her, legs drifting in the water.

"I'm thinking that I'm the luckiest man in Corfu."

I haul myself up, set her gear aside and shrug off mine before I sit beside her.

"Just Corfu?" she teases.

I lean in, sliding one hand beneath her chin as I raise her face to mine, savor the sparks of love and desire I see in her eyes.

"In the world."

I seal my words with a kiss that shakes us both.

"Tonight?" she murmurs.

"Tonight," I whisper against her lips. "Tonight and forever."

* * * * *

Were you blown away by

Still the Greek's Wife*?*

Then you're sure to enjoy the first installment in the Brides for Greek Brothers trilogy
Deception at the Altar

And check out these other stories from Emmy Grayson!

Cinderella Hired for His Revenge
His Assistant's New York Awakening
An Heir Made in Hawaii
Prince's Forgotten Diamond
Stranded and Seduced

Available now!

MILLS & BOON®

Coming next month

ROYAL BRIDE DEMAND
LaQuette

'Reigna.' He called her name with quiet strength that let her know he was in control of this conversation. 'I am Jasiri Issa Nguvu of the royal house of Adébísí, son of King Omari Jasiri Sahel of the royal house of Adébísí, crown prince and heir apparent to the throne of Nyeusi.'

Her jaw dropped as her eyes searched for any hint that he was joking. Unfortunately, the straight set of his jaw and his level gaze didn't say, 'Girl, you know I'm just playing with you.' Nope, that was a 'No lies detected' face staring back at her.

'You're…you're a…prince?'

'Not a prince, *the* prince. As the heir to the throne, I stand above all other princes in the royal line.'

She peeled her hand away from the armrest and pointed to herself. 'And that makes me…?'

He continued smoothly as if they were having a normal everyday conversation and not one that was literally life-changing. 'As my wife, you are now Princess Reigna of the royal house of Adébísí, consort to the heir and future queen of Nyeusi.'

Continue reading

ROYAL BRIDE DEMAND
LaQuette

Available next month
millsandboon.co.uk

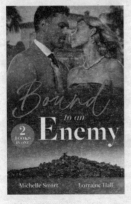
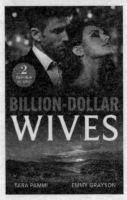

Afterglow Books is a trend-led, trope-filled list of books with diverse, authentic and relatable characters, a wide array of voices and representations, plus real world trials and tribulations. Featuring all the tropes you could possibly want (think small-town settings, fake relationships, grumpy vs sunshine, enemies to lovers) and all with a generous dose of spice in every story.

🎵 @millsandboonuk

📷 @millsandboonuk

afterglowbooks.co.uk

#AfterglowBooks

For all the latest book news, exclusive content and giveaways scan the QR code below to sign up to the Afterglow newsletter:

SCAN ME

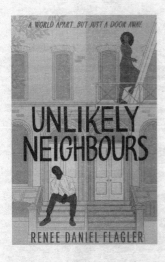
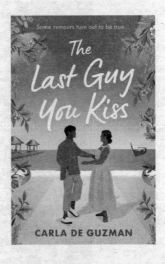

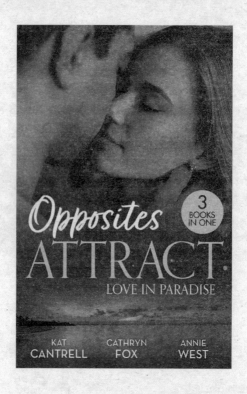

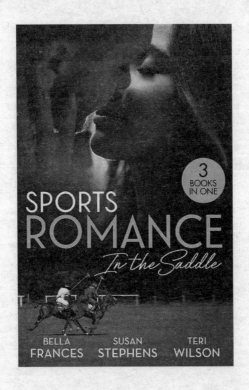

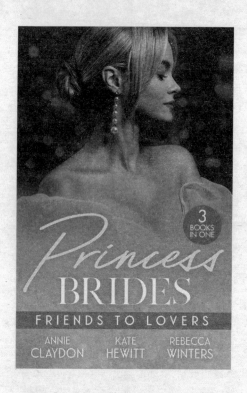